African Foreign Policy
and Diplomacy from Antiquity
to the 21st Century

African Foreign Policy and Diplomacy from Antiquity to the 21st Century

Volume 2

DANIEL DON NANJIRA

Praeger Security International

 PRAEGER

AN IMPRINT OF ABC-CLIO, LLC
Santa Barbara, California • Denver, Colorado • Oxford, England

Library of Congress Cataloging-in-Publication Data

Don Nanjira, Daniel.
    African foreign policy and diplomacy : from antiquity to the 21st century / Daniel Don
Nanjira.
        2 v. cm.
    Includes bibliographical references and index.
    ISBN 978-0-313-37982-6 (hard copy : alk. paper) — ISBN 978-0-313-
37983-3 (ebook)
    1. Africa—Foreign relations. I. Title.
    DT31.D625   2010
    327.6—dc22   2010015498

ISBN: 978-0-313-37982-6
EISBN: 978-0-313-37983-3

14 13 12   2 3 4 5

This book is also available on the World Wide Web as an eBook.
Visit www.abc-clio.com for details.

Praeger
An Imprint of ABC-CLIO, LLC

ABC-CLIO, LLC
130 Cremona Drive, P.O. Box 1911
Santa Barbara, California 93116-1911

This book is printed on acid-free paper ∞

Manufactured in the United States of America

Contents

VOLUME 2

African Geopolitics, Foreign Policy, and Diplomacy in the 19th, 20th, and 21st Centuries

CHAPTER 10

How Europeans Conquered Africa from Coast to Interior

FROM ADMIRATION OF NATURE TO EUROPEAN COMPETITION AND "PEACE" FOR AFRICA

The Industrial Revolution of the 19th century in Europe opened the way for great advances in science, technology, and medicine. Technological advancement was a great asset to European expansionism overseas. The same can be said of the medical advances that were useful to Europe, as they could cure tropical diseases, which, in the age of exploration and discovery in Africa, killed many European scientists, geographers, explorers, and missionaries.

If examined in the context of value systems, the 19th and 20th centuries were "lost centuries" for Africa, since the alien European invasions of the African continent succeeded in destroying the African spirit and identity, imposing European (i.e., Western) values at the grave expense of African values, dehumanizing and humiliating the African people, as well as at transforming Africa into a by-product of Western civilization at the expense of the rich civilizations that Africa had borne, nurtured, and preserved for millennia prior to European colonization of the African continent.

As analyzed in Volume I, the European conquest and domination of Africa happened at two levels: in ancient times, when two European nation states (Greece and Rome) and the Phoenicians imposed their colonial rule over North Africa, and in more recent times when Western Europe conquered and colonized Africa.

One wonders what would have happened if the slave trade had continued indefinitely across the Atlantic; would the Europeans have returned to dominate in the interior of Africa, or would they have limited their preserve to the African coastal areas? Would Africa as a whole have been colonized at all? This is a vital question. Nevertheless, the abolition of slavery and slave trade did facilitate the European return to Africa and the colonization of the continent's interior.

In the period preceding the European "scramble for Africa" from 1867 to 1883, European interests in Africa were revealed in four stages in the absence of slavery and the slave trade that had been legally abolished in 1807 (even though the slave trade continued until the late 1860s).

The first stage comprised the decision to return to Africa with the original three Gs and three Cs (glory/civilization, gold/commerce, and gospel/Christianity), but aimed at invasions and changes to be brought to the African interior for the benefit of Europe.

The second stage comprised the sending of missions/caravans of European agents to Africa, individually and collectively for kings, governments, government agencies, and companies, etc., in order to bring the influence of a variety of European powers to Africa. Here, the agents included volunteers, doctors/physicians, explorers, geographers, missionaries, astronomers, scientists, merchants/businessmen, journalists/writers, humanists, research institutions, agents, and others. Included among these agents of change and transformation in Africa and the world were member of parliament William Wilberforce and Dr. Samuel Johnson Ledyard in Egypt and Gambia; and Major Daniel Francis Houghton in Gambia. During this time, some agents started to sign agreements or treaties of cooperation with African rulers and kings. That was the case, for example, when an 1837 treaty was signed between African leaders and the foreign rulers of Europe through their agents. Some agreements included abolition of the slave trade, economic issues, and other bargaining points. The motivation of the agreements at the core of European imperialistic and colonial expansion was the three Gs and three Cs.

The European agents, explorers, and adventurers especially represented the newly established associations and societies in Europe such as the London Missionary Society (LMS), which employed Dr. David Livingstone (1813–1873), the explorer cum missionary; the Church Missionary Society (CMS), which commissioned many of the explorers; and the government, like that of Great Britain, which used the British colonial secretaries to send individuals such as Lord Bathurst (1762–1834), the renowned politician who led Britain in the war against Napoleon Bonaparte, to Africa. Unfortunately, almost all of these explorers and their relatives who accompanied them on their missions to explore and discover things and places in Africa perished because of diseases, notably Malaria, or faced the hostility of African warriors like the Zulus who killed the sojourners. Interestingly, most of the explorers who came to Africa during that era were Scottish like David Livingstone and many were English, as will became clear later in this chapter.

The third stage consisted of the explorations that explorers made during their travels across the continent—the natural beauty, the geography, the topography containing great lakes, rivers, mountains, and the like that had not been seen before by Europeans were called "discoveries."

The fourth stage was the arrangements that were made for "spheres of influence" from Europe and the fierce competition between and among the European powers like France and Great Britain or Belgium and France. Although the European powers showed interest in specific areas of Africa, many of their interests coincided, with the result that rivalry became tense and often nasty. The abolition of slavery and slave trade became a great concern among the French. France decided to abolish the slave trade and slavery for the first time between 1794 and 1802. The decision to abolish slavery and the slave trade in all of the French colonies came in 1848. The difficulty in France was that slavery and the slave trade had been abolished in French possessions before Napoleon became Emperor. When Nepoleon took the throne, he decided to reintroduce slavery in the French Empire.

Portugal abolished slavery at home in 1761 and in Portuguese India in 1836. In like manner, Great Britain abolished slavery in Scotland in 1776, in Wales and England in 1772, in the British colonies in 1833, and in all of the British Empire in 1807. Similarly, slavery was declared illegal in other nations as follows:

- Sweden and Finland, 1335: slaves born of Christian parents to be freed;
- United States, 1847: slaves were brought from slave states to free states;
- Demark and all Danish colonies including the Danish West Indies, 1848;
- United States: the dates differed from one state to another; but between 1777 and 1864 many slaves were freed by the enactment of the 13th Amendment;
- Puerto Rico (a colony of Spain), 1873;
- Madagascar, 1896;
- Zanzibar, 1897;
- Sudan, 1924 (officially) but slavery still is reported in this country;
- Ethiopia, 1936;
- Mauritania, 1980, although slavery was abolished in the country by France in 1905; and
- Niger, 2003, although the practice was criminalized and slave markets closed during the French colonization of Niger.

Concerted international actions by certain European nations, including in particular Britain, Portugal, Spain, and France, greatly assisted in the campaigns and actions taken against slavery and the slave trade. In France, it started with Napoleon's invasion of Egypt in 1798. The abolition efforts were made in France, for example, when René Caillié (1799–1838) campaigned at Timbuktu. In 1799 also, the Rosetta Stone for hieroglyphics was discovered. The other African nations where abolition of the trade was effected included Senegal, Sierra Leone, Djenne, Kabara, the Sahara, and Fez. In Britain, a group of abolitionists including William Wilberforce campaigned against the slave trade and convinced the lawmakers in the British parliament to pass laws to abolish the inhuman slave trade. A British Parliamentary Act abolishing the slave trade was enacted in 1807.

In East Africa

In the period 1808–1855, the various interests to acquire some territories for the mother country following the abolition of the slave trade grew. The first British trips to Africa in search of slaves were undertaken in 1550 CE. In Zanzibar, the British presence in the 19th century was enriched by the British agreement with the Sultan of Zanzibar, Sultan Seyyid Said (1797–1856). This was a very powerful sultan who engaged in politics and economics that prompted the British government to sign a treaty with him in 1822. This treaty was signed by British representative Captain Moresby, and made Zanzibar a British protectorate. The sultan ruled the coastal areas and a 10-mile-long strip of land along the Indian Ocean on the coast of Kenya. From around 1795, British East Africa became a colony, but the protected strip of land was known as a protectorate. So the two pieces of land became known as the Colony and Protectorate of Kenya. A similar agreement was signed with Kabaka, the king of Buganda, which also made it a protectorate—it was called Uganda Protectorate.

Explorers who visited East Africa and made significant discoveries include Ludwig Krapf and Johannes Rebmann, two German missionaries who arrived in Mombasa in 1844. These two men were agents of CMS in East Africa. Krapf arrived in Mombasa from Ethiopia and was joined by Rebmann. They ventured inland after hearing rumors regarding great mountains and lakes. In 1847, both started to explore the interior. In April 1848, Rebmann saw the snow-capped peak of Mount Kilimanjaro (19,321 ft.). Krapf went farther and saw Mount Kenya (17,040 ft.).

In Central and Southern Africa

David Livingstone arrived in Cape Town in 1841. He went to Victoria Falls and the Chobe River as well as to the Zambezi River in August 1851. In 1854, Livingstone started on a 3,000-mile journey from the Atlantic to the Indian Oceans. The journey took two years to accomplish. On the way from the west, Livingstone was the first white person to see the world's largest waterfall, which he named Victoria Falls, after the queen of England. In 1856, Livingstone returned to England, but in 1858, he went back to Africa with other missionaries and scientists. They went to the Zambezi to explore its potential for trade and settlement. He also worked for the abolition of the slave trade in Africa as a whole.

By 1862, most of them, including Livingstone's wife, had died of tropical disease (malaria) while in the Zambezi region of Central/South Africa. Livingstone noticed that there were still too many slaves who were being taken to inter-tribal warfare. Among the fiercest warriors were those of the Ngumi tribe, descendents of the Zule people. Also in 1962, William Baldwin and Price Helmore arrived on the scene and were conducting scientific explanations of the area including Victoria Falls. With so many casualties, the British government recalled the expedition back to England but this time Livingstone aroused British conscience in Africa. He gained the support of the British public when he reported the heavy losses of British lives. This prompted the government to action.

In West Africa

Mungo Park (1771–1806), Hugh Clapperton (1788–1827), Walter Oudney (1790–1824), Dixon Denham (1786–1828), and the two brothers Richard (1590–1675) and John Lander (1595–1692) were busy exploring places in Nigeria, Niger, Gambia, Western Sahara, Lake Chad, the Niger River, the Niger Delta, and North Africa. They were all trying to claim territory while discovering rivers and other things of value in West Africa.

Of particular interest were the German explorers Adolf Overweg, Heinrich Barth, Alfred Vogel, and Gustar Nachtigal in Timbuktu and other places. Among them were Alexander Laing and James Richardson. By 1855, West Africa and Southern Africa up to Zambezi all had been "discovered."

Central Africa

Explorers were also geographers. In 1857, Richard Burton (1821–1890) and John Speke (1827–1864), two British army officers, arrived in East Africa's Bangamoyo and traveled to Tabora. Speke later reached Lake Victoria, and later still he discovered Lake Tanganyika and the source of the Nile. In 1860, Speke, with James Grant, was sent back to Africa by the Royal Geographical Society (RGS). At Ukerewe, west of Lake Victoria, he visited the Buganda Kingdom, which was developed with wide roads and tidy villages under King Mutesa. Then they traveled to Khartoum, to the Nile, and to Cairo in two-and-a-half years. In 1863, Speke and Grant met Samuel Baker and his Hungarian wife on a journey down the Nile. Many Europeans, bushmen, and missionaries died of fever, including John Speke.

The Bakers continued on to "discover" Lake Albert, which they named after the prince consort of England. Two years later, the Bakers reached Chartien and then returned to Great Britain where, in 1869, Samuel Baker was knighted and sent back to Khartoum as governor.

Joseph Thompson was a Scottish explorer and geologist who played an important part in the scramble for Africa. He was born on February 14, 1858, at Penport, Scotland. On August 2, 1895, he was commissioned by the Royal Geographical Society. He created a route from Dar-es-Salaam to Lake Nyasa and Lake Tanganyika and covered more than 3,000 miles in 14 months.

In 1879, Joseph Thompson's expedition in East Africa traveled from the Masaai Territory to Lake Naivasha. Thompson was a Scottish geologist. He later went to Lake Malawi, the eastern side of Lake Tanganyika, then back to England. In 1882, Thompson was sent back to Africa where he traveled to Uganda via Masaai lands from Mombasa to the Kikuyu forests to Mount Kenya via the Rift Valley and discovered Lakes Nakuru, Baringo, and Elementaita. In 1883, his expedition route was from the eastern coast of Africa to the northern strip of Lake Victoria. In 1883–1884, he reached East Africa, traveling from Kenya on to Uganda. His beautifully written book, *Through Masaai Land*,[1] probably inspired the construction of Africa's railroad, which was started years later from Mombasa to Kampala, and forms the Mombasa–Uganda Railway.

Thomson Falls in Kenya, now known as Nyahururu District, and the delicate Thomson's gazelle, are named after him.

Another explorer, Henry Morton Stanley (1841–1904) was an American journalist for the *New York Herald* who, while working in Europe, befriended the king of Belgium, Leopold II. The king commissioned Stanley to explore the Congo Free State. Stanley later was commissioned and sent by the *New York Herald* to Africa. His assignment there he was to find Livingstone, who had returned to Africa for a seven-year expedition. The now-famous Livingstone had not been heard from for years, his whereabouts and condition—potentially dead, captured, or alive and well—were unknown and very newsworthy. It was at Ujiji, the lakeside town on the shores of Lake Tanganyika in present-day Burundi, that Stanley found Livingstone. Livingstone had not been seen by a white man for five years. He and Stanley spent four months together at his location, and it was Stanley who uttered the now famous exclamation, "Dr. Livingstone, I presume?" Livingstone died of malaria on May 1, 1873, after traveling 30,000 miles through Africa.

King Leopold II of Belgium was a cousin to Queen Victoria of England. Leopold, mindful of his father's dream, aimed at giving Belgium a huge commercial expansion. His eyes fell on East Africa, and he decided to go after a Belgian protectorate there. Consequently, Leopold convened a conference in Brussels that was attended by six countries including Russia, France, Germany, and Italy. He started the idea of European exploration of Africa. For this venture, an organization called the International African

Association (IAA) was created. The IAA was a Belgian organization that worked for Europe, and Leopold started expeditions to Africa for a six-year period.

Leopold commissioned Stanley to go to Africa where he spent 5 years in the Congo, obtaining signatures from chiefs to hand Congo's sovereignty over to King Leopold II. Laying the foundation of the Congo Free State, which covered almost 1 million square miles, took 450 treaties. Ruthless and bestial methods were used by Stanley for the king to subdue the Africans, and 10 million Congolese were subjected to brutality and cannibalism of the mercenaries.[2]

Soon after, Carl Peters, a 26-year-old German, created an Association for German Colonization in 1884 and went to East Africa to make treaties there like Stanley had done in the Congo. Thus, Stanley triggered a scramble for Africa that was unstoppable. Soon the French, the Portuguese, the Belgians, the Germans, and other Europeans were all in Africa.

As will be seen in the next chapter, the scramble for European influence in different parts of Africa might have saved Europe from possible wars and conflicts, similar to the ones that had been prevented by the European Treaty of Westphalia of 1648. They included the 100 Years' War, which was a series of wars from 1337–1453 CE between two royal French houses for the French throne—The House of Valois and the House of Plantagenet, also known as the House of Anjou (the House of Valois claimed the title of King of France, whereas the Plantagenets from England claimed to be Kings of France and England); the 80 Years War (1568–1648) between Spain and the Republic of the Seven United Netherlands (Dutch); and the 30 Years War (1618–1648), which was ended by the Conference of Westphalia that produced two treaties—the Treaty of Osnabruck, signed on May 15, 1648, and the Treaty of Munster, signed on October 24, 1648.[3] That Treaty not only stopped the European wars, it introduced a system of empirical statehood that marked the origin of the modern state system. But alas, the European peace over Africa did not benefit Africa. It divided the continent, and its consequences have continued to haunt Africa ever since.

THE POWER OF KNOWLEDGE AND THE INVENTION OF TECHNOLOGY AND THE ICTs

What made nations and continents great has not really been their human biology, but their continental environments. The information revolution with all of its international communication technologies (ICTs) has shrunken our planet to a global village. So, the I's have big roles to play in the information revolution: information, inspiration, incentives, indicators (in economic terms), inclusion, involvement, invention, investment, and innovation are all responsible for the Internet that exists. They represent the power of knowledge through the use of technology; and with modern technology, guns and powder, germs and steel, and inventions have been facilitated to Western powers that use these tools not only to cure and prevent diseases, but also to subdue, dominate, conquer, enslave, and even kill! And when translated into financial resources, Africa can never compare nor compete with Western Europe, for instance, in discoveries in medicine, in the use of weapons, and in the application of science and technology for the maintenance of European superiority over Africa.

THE MAJOR POWERS

Even Italy never had a long colonial grasp over Africa apart from small periods of occupation of Somaliland, Eritrea, and Ethiopia. Nonetheless, Italy is one of the economic powers of Europe. Italy was one of the participants in the struggle for power and political influence in Africa. She is hence regarded as one of the major European powers that emerged in the late 19th century. Portugal and Spain are among the relatively poor nations of Western Europe and cannot be considered as major powers of Europe even though they eventually participated in the partition of Africa for the purpose of European colonization. The issues and circumstances leading to European colonization of Africa are analyzed in the next chapter of this book.

NOTES

1. Joseph Thompson, *Through Maasai Land* (London: Sampson Law, Marston, Searle & Rivington, 1887) See. pp 144–147.

2. Joseph Conrad, *The Heart of Darkness.* (London: Penguin Books, 1995).

3. For further details, see http://www.wise.virginia.edu/history/wciv2/westphal.html.

CHAPTER 11

Motivations, Processes, Procedures, and Consequences of the "Scramble for Africa"

MOTIVES FOR COLONIZATION OF AFRICA

From the preceding chapters it is evident that the European colonization of Africa was a piecemeal process in which gradual undertakings occurred. The "seeds" of the scramble for Africa were established between 1808, the date of the formal legal abolition of slave trade in the world, and 1883, the year after which the formal process of European colonization started.[1]

Europe's interest in Africa was prompted by the dictates of the new imperialism. The Berlin Conference on the Partition of Africa (November 15, 1884–February 26, 1885) mainly was held to create international guidelines for territorial acquisitions, control, exploration, and administration. It was not for the good of the colonized Africans, but was intended to protect the interests of the home countries in Europe.

Other motivations for the European scramble for Africa included the:

- Drive and desire to dominate the world, spread European culture, and impose European values on others;
- Desire to avoid prolonged wars on territorial aggrandizements that had rocked Western Europe prior to the Treaty of Westphalia of 1648, which established empirical statehood in Europe;
- Desire of Belgian King Leopold II to fulfill his father's wish for external control of distant lands for the benefit and esteem of the tiny Belgian Kingdom;
- Acquisition of the three Gs and Cs (glory/civilization, gold/commerce, and gospel/Christianity) by the European countries to the maximum extent possible;

- Emergence of Europe from the Middle Ages ("the Dark Ages") with an "enlightened" drive to go to libraries of ancient times in order to learn, and acquire knowledge about Europe and the entire world;
- Curiosity in Europe about what lay beyond European borders, contact with the Middle East where civilization had begun within Mesopotamia ("between the Rivers Tigris and Euphrates"), and development of jealousy in Europe;
- Drive to acquire "better civilization" that is an enormous ability to adapt within this "broad-faced" tiny continent;
- Favorable European climate for intellectual stimulus to think, imagine, and be visionary; and
- Spread of evangelism in which Christianity sought to "civilize" other nations by converting them to Christianity, and also to educate them in the "correct" (i.e., non-African) ways of living and doing things.

In other words, Europe aimed at imposing their values and civilization on other races for dominance. That was why the Portuguese and Spaniards went to the Western Hemisphere, whereas the British, French, Dutch, Germans, and Belgians went into Africa, Asia, and also into the Americas, including the Caribbean. Thus, apart from the illegitimate slave trade and slavery that had dominated early commercial relations among and between continents and nations, the late 19th century for Europe meant a new kind of relationship dominated by Europe's desire "to impose" its values and systems on other races and parts of the world.

"Western" civilization was thus synonymous with "European" civilization. This expression emerged from the "Dark Ages" following the collapse of the Ancient Roman Empire and its magnificent glories in culture, law and order, architecture, etc. European expansion very much aided in European prosperity and a sense of the security of the empire. European intellectuals began to be more mindful of European common values embodied in Europe's might. The great cultural changes that emerged in European lives after the Dark Ages fostered the development of a European "superiority complex" following European "discoveries" that Europe had developed from the origins of civilization in Mesopotamia and conquests, especially those dating back to the 15th century, that nurtured a sense of dominance provided by the institution of slavery and centuries of successful slave trade.

As a discipline, Western civilization had been formed from two distinct traditions. The classical culture of Greece and Rome was a major influence. After all, we are all by-products of Greek and Roman civilizations, can we not therefore say that in terms of civilization, the ancient Greeks were our great-grandparents, and ancient Romans our grandparents?

The Christian religion, especially Western Christianity, and the Enlightenment of the modern era (i.e., following the signing of the Treaty of Westphalia in 1648 which guaranteed "peace for Europe" through empirical statehoods), were significant milestones in the development of humanity; and the period for Africa from 1800 marked the origins of modernity with liberation from slavery and the slave trade, the assertion of the African Diaspora as a force to be reckoned with for Pan-Africanism, Negritude, the total emancipation from slavery and later from colonialism, and the demand for political independence for, and in, Africa. All these complex issues are analyzed for a better understanding in the course of this study.

The era of Enlightenment in Europe consisted of the ages of the Renaissance and the past glories that had elevated European values to the dominant role of a superiority complex. The Renaissance or "rebirth" not only recalled and glorified Greek and Roman learning of ancient times, it also glorified and resurrected the classics, literature, culture, humanity, and the philosophy of intellectualism that were cognizant of the "Enlightenment" (i.e., of being anti-ignorant and anti-superstitious), and sought knowledge and truth. Thus, three big Rs (Renaissance, recollection, reinforcement) emerged in this great process of ages. The age of Renaissance recalled the glories of Ancient Rome and Ancient Greece and the reinforcement of curiosity in Europe, curiosity in diversity, exploration, discovery, and subsequently led to colonization of distant lands by the European nations. The three Rs were even bigger than the three Gs and Cs!

Thus, exerting European values as being superior to other values of the world became an important objective in which the beliefs, practices, and cultural habits of Europe became, or were made, superior to those of other peoples of the world, especially those Europe had been conquering and subduing over the centuries. Thus, to the European of the time, savage civilizations would benefit from Europeans developing their intellectual capacities and enduring many upheavals in which they rose up against the barbarism, ignorance, and darkness of the Middle Ages that replaced the glories of Rome plus the ancient world.

Western civilization came into broad use around 300 years ago, when European intellectuals saw great differences between their manners of viewing things, values, and cultures, and those of other peoples that the Europeans met. So, it was a "noble" battle of Western civilization versus the "savage ignorance" or "primitive barbarism" of the non-European world. Thus, whether one interprets "the West" in terms of people, culture, experience, knowledge, or civilization, it all came to dominate the rest of the world because Europe had

- Superior military technology;
- Better and stronger legal codes;
- The muscle of conquest;
- The power of the economy of Europe;

- Curiosity, as explained earlier, as well as expansion into conquests and aims to acquire gold and commerce;
- The drive to convert distant nations to Christianity and to civilize (i.e., to subdue and educate others to emulate European/Western values and reject native values);
- A strategic location in the Mediterranean area with excellent weather for intellectual stimulus, as well as sea and water routes that provided easy access and facilitated global commerce;
- Envy—aiming to do better than other races and to improve on what they saw and learned about others;
- Prosperity after emergence both from the "Dark Middle Ages" of poverty and potential domination that catapulted Europeans into the Age of Enlightenment and the Renaissance;
- The spread of European languages (especially English, French, Spanish, and Portuguese) to distant lands following their colonization by European motherlands—with language came culture;
- The transfer of political systems started in Europe that were installed and utilized elsewhere in the world, following the signing of the Treaty of Westphalia of 1648 that started the modern state (city) system;
- The spread of European influence (i.e., ideas, traditions/cultures, and customs) through the writings of philosophers, theologians, poets, essayists, etc. that Europe considered important, including Socrates, Aristotle, and Plato, Marcus Aurelius (Emperor of Rome), Saints Augustine, Jeremy, Francis de Sales, Cyprian, Catherine of Alexandria, Thomas Aquinas, Bonaventure, John Locke, Rousseau, Calvin, Martin Luther, and many others;
- The drive for perfectionism in domestic and global literature—productivity, networking, trade and development, as well as European technology, agricultural methods, fashions, and the advances created by business people, doctors, explorers, geographers, missionaries, etc.
- Domination in global economy and trade, military dominance—conquest and colonization and cultural diffusion; and
- Cultural traits spread from civilized centers to less urbanized areas through migration, trade, invasion, and religion.

People have pride of that which distinguishes humans from other species, and the Europeans were proud of the heights that their civilization attained. In their zeal, civilization thus became the highest cultural grouping of people and the broadest level of cultural identity.

OTTO EDUARD LEOPOLD VON BISMARCK: ARCHITECT OF EUROPEAN "PEACE" FOR AFRICA

Otto Eduard Leopold von Bismarck (1815–1898) was a prince of Bismarck, duke of Laufenberg, and count of Bismarck, Schönhausen.

A German statesman and aristocrat, von Bismarck was the minister and president of Prussia (1862–1890) who oversaw the unification of Germany. In 1867, he became chancellor of the North German Confederation and later served as emperor when the Second German Empire was created in 1871, following the defeat of France in the War of 1870. He was actually the first chancellor of the German Empire until 1890. As leader, he practiced realpolitik that gained him the nickname of "The Iron Chancellor." He became one of Germany's most influential leaders with great political clout at home and in international relations, especially in European politics during and after his time of service.

In foreign affairs, Bismarck unified his nation and aimed at promoting peace in Europe with his skills in statecraft and statesmanship. He had to confront France in her desire to avenge the loss in the Franco-Prussian War, better known as the French revanchist. Bismarck had to diplomatically isolate France while maintaining cordial relations with other states in Europe. He avoided discord with the United Kingdom, the naval power of the day. In 1872, he offered friendship to the Austro- Hungarian Empire and Russia, whose rulers had joined Wilhelm I in the League of the Three Emperors.

All along, Bismarck opposed colonial acquisitions, arguing that the burden of obtaining, maintaining, and defending such possessions would outweigh any potential benefit. However, in the late 1870s and 1880s, public opinion shifted to favor colonies, and he converted to the colonial idea. The pretext was economic. He was influenced by Hamburg merchants and traders—his neighbors at Friedrichsruh. Creation of Germany's colonial empire proceeded with minimum friction. Other European nations, in particular Britain and France, had exercised their superior powers and acquired colonies in Africa and elsewhere.

In the 1880s, Germany joined the European powers in the "scramble for Africa," as will be described in more detail later in this chapter. Germany acquired Togoland, which was part of Ghana, as well as Togo, Cameroon, German East Africa (currently Rwanda and Burundi), and Tanganyika in Tanzania. Germany further acquired German southwest Africa (now Namibia). Germany also acquired colonies in the Pacific. Bismarck weltpolitik (i.e., "world policy") earned him great respect at home for commercial purposes and abroad for peaceful coexistence. It was Pan-Germanism that prompted Bismarck to show keen intent in European affairs in Africa.

One fundamental drive in Bismarck's interest in a conference of Europe on Africa was the Treaty of Westphalia 200 years earlier. Bismarck remembered that Germany had hosted that very important treaty for European peace—after wars lasting 100, 80, 30, and 7 years. He could see that a similar confrontation was imminent between the Europeans, so he aimed at preventing war from erupting among the European powers.

After the Berlin Conference, Germany became the third largest colonial power. Credit for this status must go to Bismarck but, at the same time, Pierre Paul François Camille Savorgnan de Brazza (1852–1905), the marine officer and Frenchman, had been very aggressive in exploring the Congo Kingdom for France and worked hard in Central Africa for France. Congo, Chad, Gabon, Madagascar, and other parts of Africa were eventually partitioned to France. This will be explained in greater detail later in this chapter.

BACKGROUND TO THE PEACE TREATY OF WESTPHALIA

The Peace of Augsburg of 1555 brought a temporary truce in the religious conflict in the German States. The settlement only recognized Lutherans and Roman Catholics, but Calvinists had subsequently made gains in a number of states. The Calvinists began to demand recognition of their rights. The Thirty Years' War (1618–1648) began as a result of conflict in the Hapsburg-ruled kingdom of Bohemia. During this time, German Protestant princes fought the Holy Roman Empire under the Hapsburgs in alliance with German Catholic princes. The resolution of this war effectively ended the dominance of the Holy Roman Empire and started a modern state system.

The Bohemian Period (1618–1625)

In 1617, the Bohemian Diet elected Ferdinand of Styria king of Bohemia. Two years later, he became Holy Roman emperor (1619–1637) as Ferdinand II. He was a member of the Hapsburg family and an ardent supporter of the Catholic cause. His election alarmed Bohemian Calvinists who feared the loss of their religious rights. In May 1618, a Calvinist revolt began when the rebels threw two Catholic members of the Bohemian royal council from a window some 70 feet above the ground. Luckily, both councilors suffered only minor injuries as they fell into a pile of manure that became known as the defense strategy of Prague.

Maximilian I (1573–1651) was a Bavarian Duke/leader of Catholic league troops of the Holy Roman Empire, and Bavaria, commanded by Baron Tilly (1559–1632), invaded Bohemia. Tilly won a decisive victory over the forces of Fredrick V at the Battle of the White Mountain near Prague. The Hapsburg power of the Catholic Church alarmed Protestants everywhere. A new Protestant leader became King Gustavus Adolphus (1611–1632) of Sweden. The Swedes moved into Germany later in the year. France and Sweden signed an alliance and France entered the war against the Hapsburgs.

Thus, the Thirty Years' War was begun primarily as a German conflict over religious issues. The conflict now became a wider European war fought mainly over political issues as Catholic France and Protestant Sweden joined forces against the Catholic Hapsburgs. In November 1632, at the Battle of Lutzen, the Swedes, Protestants under King Gustavus Adolphus II (1594–1632, ruled 1611–1632) defeated the Imperialists of the Holy Roman Empire under Albrecht von Wallenstein (1583–1634), but Gustavus Adolphus was killed in the fighting. When Wallenstein entered into secret negotiations with Sweden and France, he was assassinated a few days later. The emperor's army decisively defeated the Swedes at Nordlingen in Southern Germany.

The Danish Period (1625–1629)

Danish period of conflict began when King Christian IV (1588–1648), the Lutheran ruler of Denmark, supported the Protestants in 1625 versus Ferdinand II. King Christian was also king of Holstein and a prince of the Holy Roman Empire. Ferdinand secured the help of Wallenstein. He raised an independent army of 50,000. The combined forces of Wallenstein and Tilly defeated Christian in 1626 and then occupied the duchy of Holstein. Taking control of Prague, the rebels declared Ferdinand deposed and elected a new king, Fredrick V (1596–1632), the elector of the palatinate in western Germany. He was a Calvinist. The German Protestant union that Fredrick headed provided some aid to the Bohemian rebels. The Treaty of Lubeck of 1629 restored Holstein to Christian IV, but the Danish king pledged not to intervene further in German affairs. The Danish period of the war, like the Bohemian period, also ended with a Hapsburg and Catholic victory.

The Swedish Period (1630–1635)

In the Autumn of 1634, Ferdinand II's army defeated the Swedes at the Battle of Nordlingen. In 1635, the Treaty of Prague ended the Swedish war period and enhanced the position of the Emperor compared to that of the Princes. The French Bourbons were concerned about the growth of the power of the Hapsburgs and wanted to take the Province of Alsace from Holy Roman Empire. Richelieu plotted against Spain and its Hapsburg king, Philip IV (1621–1665).

The French Period (1635–1648)

The Treaty of Prague of 1635 ended the Swedish period of the war, strengthened the Hapsburgs, and weakened the power of the German princes. This treaty was wrecked by the French decision to intervene directly in the war. Cardinal Richelieu (1585–1642), the chief minister of King Louis XIII of France, wanted Frederick exiled to Holland. Emperor Frederick II regained the Bohemian throne. Maximilian I of Bavaria acquired the palatinate. The Bohemian phase of the 30 years thus ended with a Hapsburg and

Catholic victory. The Chief Minister of King Louis XIII, Cardinal Richelieu, aimed at weakening the Hapsburg power and gaining territory.

The Treaty of Westphalia: 1648

Westphalia is a historic region and former duchy of west central Germany, east of the Rhine River. One of the most memorable and historic events of the region happened in the 17th century when expansionism and territorial aggrandizement in Europe were common events among the dukes and kings of Europe. Many of the wars lasted for long periods of time—100 years, 80 years, 30 years, 7 years, etc. Especially in Germany, those conflicts and wars ignited where Protestantism had been born and initiated by an ex-communicated Roman Catholic priest named Martin Luther. On October 31, 1517, Luther wrote 95 formal statements called theses in which he attacked the greed and indecency of the Catholic Church. He called for reforms to the point that his "protesting" ignited the Protestant Reformation, created a split in the Catholic Church, and thereby started Protestant Christianity. By 100 years later in 1618, religious wars broke out among Protestants, Catholics, and Calvinists. These sharp religious differences in Europe had caused other wars lasting for 80 years. These wars divided Europe, and included the Thirty Years' War lasting from 1618 to 1648. It was in Westphalia that a treaty called the Peace Treaties of Westphalia was negotiated and signed among the European nation states.

The Peace Treaties were the result of deliberations that started in 1644 and ended in 1648. They addressed complicated issues, collectively known as the Issues of the Treaty of Westphalia, which had considerable impact on the modern state system.[2,3]

Thus, the Peace Conference of Westphalia assembled representatives of 16 European states, 66 Imperial States of the 140 Republican Imperial States of the Holy Roman Empire, and the Holy Roman Empire itself. The parties to the Treaty of Westphalia were the Holy Roman Empire; the Kingdoms of France and Sweden; the Republic of the Seven United Netherlands, also known as the Dutch Republic, or the United Dutch Province, and their respective alliances among the princes; the Republican Imperial States of Italy and the Swiss Confederacy: Brandenburg-Prussia, Mantha, Bavaria, Tuscany, Lucca, Moderna, and Parma.

It is also noteworthy that the Thirty Years' War was fought on German soil; that a new doctrine of the "balance of power" helped end the war; and that the Peace Treaty of Westphalia also ended the Eighty Years' War fought on the basis of the sharp religious differences involving Catholicism, Calvinism, and other forms of Protestantism. The Eighty Years' War was waged between the 1500s and 1600s. For 80 years, the armies grouped in Catholic Spain and fought against the Dutch Protestants and the French Protestants.

Simmilarly, in Germany during the Thirty Years' War, Catholics fought against Protestants. Both sides lost and gained. The Hapsburg Catholics initially won against their Protestant opponents. Thus, Ferdinand III had his allies from Spain and Austria. They fought against Bohemia and the Czech Protestant princes supported by Denmark from 1625 and Sweden from 1630. That pattern of alliances and fighting wars continued in later years, for example during the Seven Years' War in Europe (1756–1763), when alliances were formed in European battlegrounds. Thus, Austria supported at that time by France, Sweden, Saxony, Russia, and Hungary waged war against Prussia, allied to Great Britain and Hanover.

The outcome of the Westphalia Peace Treaty had important historic consequences for Africa and the rest of the world. These consequences are discussed in the remainder of this section.

First, it was evident that territorial settlements and religious tolerance and freedom were at the core of the differences and wars in Europe. Many territorial changes made in Europe resulted in giving Sweden control of the Baltic Sea and the North Sea, assuring France a clear frontier west of the Rhine River in the area known today as Alsace and providing her allies with additional lands. The German princes acquired total independence from the Holy Roman Empire, and each German prince's state could and would decide on the religion to be followed in his state; independence was granted to the Swiss Confederacy and to the United Provinces of the Netherlands. These were recognized as independent states. But Germany was not united. Some new independent states emerged and were recognized as sovereign municipalities in the 17th century. Germany and France emerged as the greatest powers after the Thirty Years' War in Europe. Sweden also gained from the war, but Austria and Spain lost. The British stayed out of the war. The dominance of the Holy Roman Empire effectively ended, and a modern state system was created.

Calvinism, the most hated of the three branches of Christianity in Europe, was granted equal privileges with Lutheranism and Catholicism and, as stated, each Protestant prince decided on the religion of his state.

In terms of international law and relations, as well as of foreign policy and diplomacy, France and Sweden emerged as the triumphant powers. From the signing of the treaty onward, a new world order started. The modern system was born in which there would be tolerance and freedom of worship and faith guaranteed to all denominations; barriers to trade and commerce erected during the war were abolished; a degree of free navigation was guaranteed on the Rhine; and doctrines of equal sovereignty, territorial integrity, and non-intervention were all put in place. Prior to Westphalia, the concept of state sovereignty had not really existed. From the time of the treaty onward, no interference in the internal affairs of other sovereign political entities would be tolerated. In fact, any attack by a state, whether within or beyond the terms of the treaty, would ipso facto be considered an attack on all the states parties to the treaty.

Thus, sovereignty gave overall and ultimate control and power to the governments of the member states over the state's natural resources and assets in economic, social, political, and environmental respects. This novel statecraft established a new system of statehood called empirical statehood, which has been handed down to all the regimes of the world that are by-products of western civilization as passed on to us from Western Europe through the Greeks and Romans.

The modern state system was thus born in the systems that were established by the Treaty of Westphalia. These systems included the diplomatic political system for dispute settlement between and among nations. Although there was no talk about sovereign equality, the concept of empirical statehood introduced a system of international law in which all states have equal sovereignty. In short, there were four major principles that emerged from the Westphalia Treaty of 1648, as follows:

- Sovereignty of states and the fundamental right of political self-determination,
- Equality (legally enforced) among states,
- Internationally binding treaties between or among states, and
- Non-intervention of one state in the internal affairs of another state.

These four principles are the basics of empirical statehood. The world order of sovereign states thus started with the peace of Westphalia of 1648, which ended the Thirty Years' War. The Westphalia Peace Treaty created a new world order based on the principle of sovereign states.

BISMARCK AS ARCHITECT OF EUROPEAN PEACE FOR EUROPE: FROM WESTPHALIA TO BERLIN

From the previous section, it is safe to conclude that the convener of the 1884–1885 Berlin Conference (also called the Kongokonferenz) to discuss Europe's presence in Africa had at least two thoughts in mind. First, he must have remembered the role that Germany played in search of a durable peace in Europe after 100 years of war. Second, in the late 19th century, it must have been clear that unruly competition in Africa with modern technology—guns and other new weapons—would be more devastating that were the warfare tactics of the 17th century.

Thus, Bismarck was a visionary who foresaw calamities and grave wars in Africa between and among the Europeans if they did not strive for peaceful resolutions to their colonial scramble for the Africa. Hence, a "peace for Europe" in Africa had to be sorted that would avoid European infighting and wars.

Another aspect of Bismarck's initiative to convene the Berlin Conference to discuss the future of European involvement in Africa was his vision of commerce and trade that would benefit Europe. It was evident that Africa offered a huge market for European goods and services and Europe was also a huge market for African goods. It was clear that the conference convened in Berlin at the initiative of Bismarck aimed at establishing regulations and rules for the acquisition of African lands, especially in order to protect free trade in certain parts of the Congo Basin.

EUROPEAN IMPERIALISM IN AFRICA

In the context of this study, "imperialism" means the policy of extending a nation's authority over other nations through economic and political means. In this sense, imperialism thrives under the economy of an imperial nation and its political might. This is because, in general, hegemony helps in political and related control. Thus, European imperialism is the global expansion of the industrial economy and culture of Europe resulting in Europe's discovery and exploitation of the tropical world. Technological advancement facilitated oversees expansionism just as the Industrial Revolution facilitated industrialization in Europe using raw materials, such as cotton, rubber, hides, and skins, from Africa, among many places.

In the latter part of the 19th century, imperialism appeared in two forms. First was "informal" imperialism lasting from the 1880s to the outbreak of World War I in 1914. This form of imperialism was composed of the application of military force, influence, and economic dominance. This dominance had to include European civilization as had been the case for centuries when European domination had been demonstrated through acquisition of distant lands, slaves, and lucrative goods and services. However, when European economic might started to decline because of the long depression of 1873–1896, a new kind of imperialism emerged. This was one of "divide et impera," which means "divide and rule" in Latin, and was a form of domination using the dominated people and their endowments for the good of the European colonial power. Africa offered an excellent platform for this new form of imperialism. The European powers developed disputes among themselves triggered by imperial competition and formed alliances for attaining their objectives in Africa for trade, for markets, and their empires.

The European rivalries involved agents such as American journalist Henry Morton Stanley who, while working for the *New York Herald*, traveled to Europe to look for Dr. David Livingstone (as discussed in the previous chapter) and to work for the king of Belgium. Stanley founded the Congo Free State for King Leopold II of Belgium. With industrialization came improvements in transportation and communication—advancements included the use of steam propulsion, railroads, better navigation methods, and the telegraph.

All of these new technologies facilitated travel into the African interior in search of territory and natural resources and furthered the imposition of imperialistic influences. The man who did a lot of all that for France was a marine officer named Pierre Savorgnan de Brazza. He was responsible for acquiring many African colonial possessions for France in Africa. He went to western Congo basin and founded Brazzaville in 1881. These imperialistic initiatives in Africa had started earlier, for example when British magnate, financier, and colonizer Cecil Rhodes (1853–1902) went to southern Africa and established commercial mining with his De Beers Mining Company, which carved out "Rhodesia" for Rhodes. Leopold II later did the same thing in the Congo Free State.

Thus, before Europe agreed to meet in Berlin to partition Africa in their respective "spheres of influence," the European nations and their companies already had been competing for territory, gold, and religious conversion in Africa. This occurred from Egypt to South Africa and from Cape Verde to Somalia and was accompanied by agreements signed by local African chiefs. European influences were already in place even before the Berlin Conference was held—the British, for example, were in Egypt in 1882.

Berlin Conference of 1884–1885

The Berlin Conference was convened and organized by Otto von Bismarck upon the proposal of Portugal. The convening of a conference of European powers in Berlin from February 26, 1884 to November 15, 1885 was conducted according to the following fundamental guidelines: (1) resolution of differences among nations should be by peaceful means— including through diplomatic channels, and (2) state sovereignty is non-negotiable and must be honored as required by international law that regulates international behavior of "civilized" states; empirical statehood must be preferred over juridical statehood.

The main purpose of this conference was twofold. As follows, it was intended to:

1. Regulate European colonization and trade in Africa during the new period of imperialism, which coincided with the emergence of Germany as an imperial power in Europe under Otto von Bismarck; and

2. Partition Africa for Europeans to share Africa through peaceful means and avoid engaging in warfare similar to that which had rocked Europe before the Treaty of Westphalia of 1648.

Thus, peaceful coexistence required nations to advance and promote their interests vis-à-vis other nations with good and fair economic competition.

The General Act of Berlin, 1885

The General Act of Berlin was the ultimate result of the Berlin Conference. This act formalized the "scramble for Africa" that had been going on throughout the 19th century, heightened colonial activities in Africa, and suffocated African desires for autonomy, self-governance, and rule.

The general outcome of the conference as embodied in the General Act consisted of the following seven points:

1. The free state of the Congo became the private property of King Leopold II of Belgium.
2. Free trade must be guaranteed for the parties to the act who attended the conference. Free trade should be granted to all the parties in the Congo Basin, in the Lake Nyasa (Niassa) south of 5° N.
3. Free shipping would be allowed in the Niger and Congo Rivers.
4. International prohibition of the slave trade must be enforced.
5. The Principle of Effectivity must be applicable, that is, there should be no setting up of colonies if national flags were to fly there, unless treaties were signed with the local chiefs and the colonizing power(s) established an administration in the territory to govern it with a police force. (This was translated in post-colonial era as the doctrine of "lit possidetics uris," which in Latin means "boundaries established by law are inviolable.")
6. Any fresh act of taking possession of any portion of the African Coast would require that the power taking possession notify the parties to the act, or assure a protectorate to the other signatory powers. (This guideline was applied in several places, such as Egypt, Kenya, Togo, Cameroon, Bechuanaland, and other areas of Africa.)
7. The division or partition of Africa between the main powers of Europe.

Fourteen countries attended the Berlin Conference and signed its General Act. These were: Germany, Austria-Hungary, Belgium, Denmark, France, the United Kingdom, Italy, the Netherlands, Portugal, Russia, Sweden-Norway (united until 1905), Spain, the Ottoman Empire, and the United States. Seven of these powers emerged as the main colonial powers in Africa: Germany, Belgium, France, the United Kingdom, Italy, Portugal, and Spain.

European Colonies in Africa

Although Holland was the first European country to colonize Africa, she was not a major colonial power. In like manner, Spain was minimal as a colonial power in Africa and concentrated on the Americas. The United States had no colonial possessions in Africa since her only colony, Liberia, gained political independence in 1847. Furthermore, some African countries (Ethiopia, South Africa, Egypt, Libya, Morocco, Eritrea, and Sudan) enjoyed "colonial immunity" since they had not been colonized sensu stricto under the Berlin system of imperialism.

The General Act of the Berlin Conference partitioned Africa into European "spheres of influence," which were, in reality, geographical lines in Africa. The partition lasted as indicated here and was as follows:

- Germany became the third largest colonial power in Africa. Germany's portion included southwest Africa (present-day Namibia, Togoland, Cameroon, Tanganyika, Rwanda- Burundi) up to World War II.
- Belgium's portion included the Congo Free State, which was known as the Belgian Congo after 1908. When embarrassed by the victimization of the Congolese people by Leopold II, Belgium's Parliament passed a law annexing the Congo as a colony. The Belgian Congo became Rwanda-Burundi during World War II and is now the Democratic Republic of the Congo.
- France's portion included Congo Brazzaville, Senegal, Mali, Niger, Chad, Upper Volta, Gabon, Tunisia, Algeria, Mauritania, Seychelles, Comoros, Mayotte, Madagascar, Côte d'Ivoire, Mali, and Togo.
- Portugal's portion included Cape Verde, São Tomé and Príncipe, Guinea-Bissau, Angola, and Mozambique.
- Spain's portion included Western Sahara, Rio de Oro, Melilla, Spanish Guinea (Equatorial Guinea), Spanish Morocco, Rio Muni (now in Equatorial Guinea).
- In addition to Egypt, which was a British protectorate before the Berlin system, the United Kingdom's portion included British Somaliland, Anglo-Egyptian Sudan (now Sudan), British East Africa (Kenya, Uganda, Tanganyika), Southern Rhodesia (now Zimbabwe), Northern Rhodesia (now Zambia), Bechuanaland (now Botswana), Orange Free State (Cape Colony since 1795), British South Africa (now South Africa), Gambia, Sierra Leone, Nigeria, British Gold Coast (now Ghana), and Nyasaland (now Malawi).
- In addition to Italian North Africa (now Libya), Eritrea, and Ethiopia (briefly under Italy), all of which belonged to Italy before the Berlin Act, Italy's portion included Tripolitania, Cyrenaica, and Italian Somaliland.

The imposition of European alien rule on Africa marked the beginning of the transformation and impoverishment of Africa that has rocked and haunted the continent and its populations up to today. The nature, method, and function of this multidimensional impoverishment of Africa are explained in subsequent chapters, especially in Chapter 13.

CONCEPTUAL UNDERSTANDING: COLONIAL POLICIES AND PRACTICES AS ENGINES OF AFRICA'S TRANSFORMATION

The imposition of alien rule in Africa was piecemeal. Stages in this process were evident first following the signing of the Berlin Act that created "spheres of European influence" in Africa. The stage was set for the colonial spirit to take hold of Africa. Before the colonial administrations were established on the African Continent by European colonial departments (generally, nationals who were already in Africa, whether missionaries, settlers, or businessmen), they were "commissioned" to start preparing the ground for Africa's colonization. By 1912, the structures had been put in place. However, in most cases, within 15 years—by 1900—the preparation and migration to Africa had been done.

The second stage evident was the movement to Africa of the colonial officials who would administer the newly acquired territories for the motherland. Once in the colonial country, the new administrators had to figure out how to set up effective colonial administrations. The establishment of colonies was quite a challenging task.

The third stage occurred once the colony was established and the colonial work of subjection and exploitation of the newly colonized people of Africa was done by the colonial newcomers.

The fourth and final stage in the initiation of the colony was to start imposing alien (European) rules of governance and government in Africa. This was the ultimate duty of the colonizers: to civilize (i.e., develop/educate the colonized people and their territories in European ways, cultures, values, traditions, and civilization). It was this imposition of European values on Africans that produced clashes and the transformation of Africa into a by-product of Western civilization.

Some conceptual expressions that are relevant to the discussion of African international relations, foreign policy, and diplomacy have already been defined. Different definitions can be, and are, given to other expressions that are relevant here. Nonetheless, these concepts are often given other meanings in other contexts, which also need to be well understood. These include those terms that follow in this section, which are defined as they are used in this book.

Concept of "Colonia" in Africa

In politics and history, and for all practical purposes, a colony is a territory under the immediate political control of a state. The metropolitan sovereign state is the state that owns the colony. In ancient Greece, the city that owned a colony was called "metropolis" within its political organization. The mother country is a reference to the metropolitan state from the viewpoint of citizens who live in its colony.

Nowadays, the terms "overseas territory," "dependant territory," or just "colony," are used interchangeably. People who migrated to settle permanently at the third stage of the colonial process in Africa and elsewhere had to work for their country of origin, which controlled everything in its overseas territory. These agents were called colonists or settlers.

Usually, the local population did not enjoy full citizenship rights even if they were granted such, as was French colonial policy. In British and Portuguese colonial policy, the colonial people were subjects. In all cases, the political processes restricted the colonies and excluded any considerations of independence. It is noteworthy that the system of Apartheid ("separate development") in South Africa and the colonial policy of the Ian Smith regime in Rhodesia, as declared on November 11, 1965, did not envision independence for the colonized people of those countries until perhaps after 1,000 years!

When the Greeks talked of colonization, they actually meant the foundations of a new city or settlement. In fact, the term "colony" is derived from the Latin "colonia," meaning a place meant for agricultural activities. "Colonialism" is synonymous with "imperialism," and it is the expression of a nation's sovereignty over a territory beyond its borders by the establishment of either settler colonies or administrative dependencies in which indigenous populations are directly ruled or displaced.

Policy, Process, and Procedure

The expression "policy" is used to refer to a definite course or method of action selected to guide and determine present and future decisions. It comprises a series of actions and/or non-actions intended to attain certain results. In the case of African colonization, colonial policies and practices had the duty of imposing the will and wishes of the European powers on the African people and countries. "Process" is used to refer to a systematic course or series or method of actions and operations aimed at accomplishing results. "Procedure" means a manner or method of proceeding, of going forward, or a formula applied to doing something.

The foreign policy of any state has domestic and external factors (often referred to as endogenous and exogenous factors) in the foreign policy process by which states identify goals in the international system and act, react, pro-act, interact and "non-act" in order to achieve a set of goals. Here the decision-making process is led by policy makers of a country in their dealings with other political entities in the global system.

African foreign policy thus means those African foreign policies that address specific factors in the domestic and external environment of all kinds economic development, conflicts, diplomacy, peace and security, human rights, health, poverty, education, geopolitics, the arms race, and the like. Therefore, African foreign policy is the totality of interactions, contacts, and non-actions that sovereign African countries perform as members of the world community and as independent political entities. These policies may be made or undertaken with other sovereign states and international legal persons in order to attain a set of goals created by various decision makers of a country acting on the international stage and in pursuit of their own interests (defense, development, diplomatic, glory, protection, promotion of peace, security and stability, peaceful coexistence, etc.) as displayed in their foreign policy and diplomatic intentions. A nation promotes and protects its national interests through foreign policy.

Concept of Diplomacy

The Concise Oxford Dictionary of Current English defines diplomacy as "management, skill in managing international relations. Diplomacy is the art and practice of conducting negotiations between states."[4] Thus an art, not a science. The same applies to "politics" which is the art of government. Diplomacy is designed to facilitate negotiations and find peaceful ways of resolving differences. Thus, it is against resorting to war as a means of solving disputes. Diplomacy is the art of negotiation and, in this sense, diplomacy and foreign policy are tools for managing relations between and among nations.

Cultural Diplomacy

"Cultural diplomacy" has several meanings and is defined as specifying a form of diplomacy that carries out a set of prescriptions that are material to its effectual practice. These prescriptions include the unequivocal recognition and understanding of foreign cultural dynamics and observance of the universal tenets that govern basic dialogue; understanding; and the exchange of ideas, information, art, lifestyles, value systems, traditions, beliefs, and other aspects of cultures.

"African international relations" is an expression used to refer to the identity of all of these elements of this definition, that is, the totality of international dealings, transactions, actions, and non-actions conducted or performed between and among the sovereign states of Africa at the intra-African level.

"Political entities" means sovereign states and non-state entities possessing international legal personality like the UN system of organization. At the sovereign state level, relations are conducted between/with African states, across state borders, and with stateless international entities. Thus, although African international relations, like other international relations, are normally conducted between sovereign states/actors, such dealings also are conducted with non-state actors like non-governmental organizations (NGOs) and intergovernmental organizations (IGOs) if so authorized under the principles of international law.

National Interest

"National interest" is an expression used to signify a state's sense of survival and security in its competition and external dealings. Each nation must protect its physical, political, economic, and cultural identify, assets, etc. against encroachments by other nations. National interest is therefore the central factor in African, and any other, international relations and foreign policy with other states and continents. As a concept, national interest is a tool that identifies the goals and objectives of foreign policy. It's an all-embracing political discourse.

As with any other continent, African national interest is inscribed in every African foreign policy decision and aims at protecting its political, economic, cultural, social, material, and other interests. People of every African nation state are African nationals, both abroad and at home.

Country, Nation, and State

The African nations, like any other nation, are comprised of a population or group of people united voluntarily by a common culture, solidarity, values, standards, and allegiance to a government. Even if differences happen among this group, the bond of nationhood and statehood can never be denied. This often happens when ethnocentrism, tribalism, ideology, and other doctrines divide the people—as did colonial policies and practices that either amalgamated different nations incorrectly or separated the same people under the Berlin colonization process.

It is noteworthy that the expressions "country," "nation," and "state" are used interchangeably to refer to the sovereign states of Africa. However, it should also be noted that under normal circumstances "a nation" refers to the people of the country or state. A state is usually the people plus the borders, government, and territory or land that enjoys sovereignty. Hence, it is more than just the mere population of a country. "Country" also is often used interchangeably with "territory."

Furthermore, a distinction must be made between the use of the term "state" to refer to a nation and a state like New York state in the United States. (New York has no sovereignty; the United States has soverignty.) For example, Cuba is a sovereign state that enjoys equal sovereignty, although not sovereign equality, with the United States in international matters (e.g., passing a new international law at the UN). Thus, the United States and Cuba are states, not continents. Africa is a continent, not a state. In like manner, dependence is not synonymous with dependency. Dependence means relying on others, whereas dependency means neo-colonialism.

Transformation of Africa

From the foregoing, it is clear that the disciplines of foreign policy, diplomacy, and international relations of the African states are shaped by many endogenous and exogenous considerations. The colonization of the continent aggravated the already complex situations of the African nation-states whose international relations, foreign policy, and diplomacy fall into three periods—the pre-colonial, colonial, and post-colonial eras and their mini eras. It is also evident, that by making Africans by-products of Western civilization, great-grandchildren and grandchildren of ancient Greece and ancient Rome, the European colonial policies and practices completely transformed Africa and generally threw the African value system through the window. There could not have been a worse method of doing an injustice to the African value system. There could not have been a more arrogant display of power and might than trying to turn Africans into European robots and to turn the African value system into a European value system! The colonial powers embarked upon the impossible task of Europeanizing Africa. For this, Africa deserves compensation!

Similarities and Divergences in European Colonial Policies and Practices

Following the signing of the Berlin Act of 1885, Africa was partitioned among seven European powers—the United Kingdom, France, Germany, Portugal, Italy, Belgium, and Spain (which did not acquire many colonies in Africa but instead concentrated on the Americas)[5]—that emerged as the colonial powers in Africa.

The process of establishing colonial administration in Africa was slow but progressive, and by 1900 almost 90 percent of the African "cake" had been shared by the Europeans. By 1912, colonial rule in Africa was established not only in four stages as already explained in this chapter, but also according to four different types.

- Rule by charter,
- Direct rule,
- Indirect rule, and
- Settler rule.

For tame countries, charters were granted to economic companies which were charged with the responsibility of starting the colonization work in the newly acquired colonial territories. In the early colonial days, these private companies were created to administer the colonies. The companies were granted large territories in Africa formed by businessmen interested in exploiting the natural resources there, and they set up systems of taxation and labor recruitment. Thus, the British East Indies Company, the Dutch East Indies Company in South Africa, and the British East Africa Company were set up in 1888 to administer present-day Kenya. The British South Africa Company, and many other chartered companies, flew their homeland's national flag and served as colonial administrators for the royal families and countries.

The second type of colonial rule was the direct rule method. This kind of rule did not involve the indigenous structures. The colonial administrators controlled everything for the mother country and ran the affairs from the center of the colony. Local indigenous authorities were not involved in governance or government because it was a system of divide and rule that implemented policies intended to weaken the local authorities to subordinate status. In this way, colonialism as the occupation and control of one nation or country by another applied direct rule as a system of centralized administration in urban areas, which stressed policies of "assimilation." This meant that the colonialist wanted to civilize (i.e., educate the African societies by merely turning them into European value systems). There were no roles for indigenous populations or authorities. This direct rule system was particularly favored by the Germans, Belgians, French, and Portuguese.

The third type of rule was the indirect rule, which was applied by the British, but the Germans and other European colonial powers also applied indirect rule. This was because under this type rule, the traditional local power structure was incorporated into the colonial administrative structure. The system of indirect rule was practiced mainly by the British in their empire, especially in British India and in Nigeria where the architect of indirect rule, Lord Lugard (1858–1945), applied the policy extensively first in Nigeria and later in East Africa. The colonies at that time were known as "princely states" as in India, Malaysia, and elsewhere. However, not all of the British colonies were under indirect rule. Britain applied colonial policies of direct and indirect rule in the South Africa Company, created in 1887 under the control of Cecil Rhodes. Using force and coercion, Rhodes colonized three territories in south central Africa: Nyasaland (Malawi), northern Rhodesia (Zambia), and southern Rhodesia (Zimbabwe). This system of government assumed that all Africans were "tribes" ruled by chiefs.

Thus, indirect rule was a system of heavy reliance by the early colonial administrators upon the work of local "officials" who functioned under instructions. Indirect rule was a system of mixed administration considered a practical solution to the problems of administering colonial territories where communication was poor, European knowledge of African traditions and customs was almost zero, money was short, and the amount of European staff was low.

The fourth kind of colonial in Africa was mainly applied in Southern Africa, and it was known as settler rule. This policy of rule gave the European settlers in Africa the right to impose direct rule on their colonies, because where settler colonies existed there were significant numbers of immigrants from the empire who were neither missionaries nor

European colonial officials. This resembled the situation in the United States and Canada, where the Europeans planned to make the colonies their permanent home. Especially in South Africa, Zimbabwe, Kenya, and other places, the European settlers exercised authority over African land and population and believed that they, the settlers, would have been in charge of Africa for 1,000 years before the Africans could be ready to stand on their own feet.

British Colonial Policies and Practices

The British emphasized that education was essential to train an elite class of colonized nationals to be administrators capable of manning the institutions of self-government and modern economy. Economic developments and foreign investment were necessary to raise the living standards of the colonial people and to develop agricultural, mining, and simple industrial facilities enough to assure the colony of an income from world markets once they became independent.

There was a gradual introduction of political self-government that progressed from self-rule at village to district levels, creation of colonial legislatures with elected majorities that increased autonomy to the choice of a native cabinet from freely elected members of parliament (MPs) to political independence, and the choice of belonging to the British Commonwealth of Nations.

Spanish Colonial Policies and Practices

The Spanish had very little influence in Africa because their colonial efforts were so concentrated in the Americas. But Spanish colonial policy basically consisted of two ideas: promotion of the trading monopoly between Spain and the New World for Queen Isabella of Spain until her death in 1504, and a strong religious inclination favoring Spanish nations at the expense of the conquered and colonized American Indians.

In 1524, Charles V, who was a powerful Catholic emperor, created a council of the Indies that was a law-making body for the Spanish colonies. For 300 years, the council worked for the greater glory of Spain, but too much bureaucracy consequently dominated Spanish colonial policies in the New World. The treatment of the American Indians was inhumane, however Spanish religious organizations opposed government mistreatment of the American Indians who became slaves and perished from diseases imported into the New World from Europe.

Portuguese Colonial Policies and Practices

For the Portuguese, their African territories were overseas provinces. The policy of assimilation was applied to them so that they were equal and practically argued that Portugal had no colonies in Africa, only overseas territories. The African colonies were not adequately prepared for self-rule.

Belgian Colonial Policies and Practices

Belgium's African possessions were concentrated in the central African region of the Congo. In 1876, King Leopold II actually triggered the idea of the European "race for Africa" under the scramble for Africa process. He ordered Henry Morton Stanley, his colonial agent in the Congo, to apply the cruelest of treatment to the Congolese people. If someone stole a banana or an item using his left arm then that arm had to be cut off. This cruelty forced the Belgian legislature to pass a law depriving the king of administrative powers over the Congo (which he purchased with his own funds) and assuming colonization of the country. In this manner, the legislature saved the tiny country from the international embarrassment that the country had suffered from when the king was in personal charge of the Congo Free State.

In the Congo in subsequent years, rapid commercialization and industrial development were advocated, but no process of technical and political education for natives was provided until five years before the political independence of the Congo in 1960. In Ruanda-Urundi, later to become Rwanda and Burundi at independence in 1962, the Belgians, who had been given these two former colonial possessions of Germany to administer after World War II, introduced a policy of divide and rule that set the Hutus and Tutsis of Rwanda and Burundi against each other with a hatred that still haunts those two tiny nations. The colonial policies and practices of Belgium, like those of the Portuguese, were among the worst in Africa.

Dutch Colonial Policies and Practices

The Dutch were the first European nation to colonize in the interior of Africa. The first Dutch settlers in the Cape region of Africa from 1652 pursued policies of enslavement of Africans, possessed a superiority complex, and enforced the "color bar" (one was important in society according to the color of one's skin).

The Dutch colonial policies and practices assisted in the promotion of Dutch concepts of civilized society, as well as community flexibility and religious conversion (especially to Catholicism and Protestantism), which became important goals for the Dutch, as well as diasporanism, which meant the spread abroad of Dutch sentiments of civilization and cultural values.

Dutch colonial policies and practices promoted racism, ethnicism, and racial prejudices. In 1652, in a cape colony of South Africa, the Dutch began systems of separate development called "Apartheid" that rocked the country until the acquisition by South Africa of majority rule in 1994.

German Colonial Policies and Practices

The Germans administered direct rule with maximum harshness and cruelty—with an iron fist.

Extreme cruelty was performed by German political agents called "akidas," who were usually Swahilis and Arabs alien to the people they controlled. Akidas were subheads of sub-districts above chiefs and other native rulers.

The Germans deprived Africans of their traditional lands, which became crown lands via enactments of land laws. They then imposed forced labor on Africans who were required to work alien settler plantations. The Germans introduced a "hut tax" of three Indian rupees per year, despite the fact that the Africans had no money.

The treatment of the Africans by Dr. Karl Peters, the German colonial administrator in Tanganyika was so noteworthy that Peters was later praised by Adolf Hitler as having been a German "star" when he was colonial administrator. Peters used to take the wives of African servants and turn them into his harem. When their husbands went to him to ask for their wives back, he would castrate them and send them away from his offices.

Nations with "Colonial Immunity"

African nations that enjoyed "colonial immunity" include the following:

- Ethiopia, independent since 982 BCE;
- Liberia, independent since July 26, 1847;
- South Africa, independent since May 31, 1910;
- Egypt, independent since February 28, 1922;
- Libya, independent since December 24, 1937; and
- Morocco, independent since March 2, 1956.

The main characteristic of colonial immunity for these African nations was that they were not subject to the colonization process that ensued after the Berlin Conference of 1884–1885. Hence they were "immune" from that main African colonization process and were never part of the scramble for Africa. They were not, however, completely free from colonial policies and practices, and were still helped by the Organization of African Unity (OAU), who made important contributions and created roles that were vital to African independence movements.

Ethiopia

It is one of the oldest countries in the world. It was established as a kingdom in the 10th century BCE and ruled by the Queen of Sheba for a long time. Some of humanity's oldest bones (from "Lucy"), which were about 3.2 million years old, were found in Ethiopia, indicating that the area was part of the cradle of humanity in Africa. That significant discovery in November 1974, near Hadar, Ethiopia, was one of the earliest traces of human evolution. The dynastic history of Ethiopia began with the reign of Emperor Menelik I. Different dates have been suggested as the date of political independence of the country. According to some data, Menelik, the offspring of the Queen of Sheba, succeeded his mother around 950 BCE. Other sources state that Sheba was a very powerful queen of Ethiopia around 960 BCE. Still other sources indicate that Menelik became king in 1000 BCE, and that the year 980 BCE was the date of independence for Ethiopia. It is also stated that Ethiopia's roots date back to the Aksumites, and that the Aksumite Empire adopted the name "Ethiopia" in the 4th century BCE, but consolidated its might as a kingdom only in the 1st century CE. In this writer's estimation, the date of independence for Ethiopia must have been about 982 BCE. This means that Menelik I was about 22 years old when he assumed the kingship of Ethiopia from his mother. Ethiopia officially became Orthodox Christian in the 4th century CE.

Much later, in the inter-bellum years between World War I and World War II, Benito Mussolini (1883–1945) made every effort to colonize a number of African countries, including Somalia, Libya, Eritrea, and Ethiopia. In fact, between 1936 and 1941, Mussolini occupied Eritrea and Ethiopia and brutally treated the Ethiopian people. Ethiopia was liberated in 1941 by British troops and Ethiopian patriots. Ethiopia is now a federal parliamentary republic, with Girma Wolde-Giorgis (1924–) as president, and Meles Zenawi (1955–) as prime minister. Zenawi is one of the younger generation of African leaders. Ethiopia's population in 2006 was estimated to be 75,067,000.

Liberia

Slightly larger than the U.S. state of Ohio, Liberia's population in 2006 was estimated to be more than 3 million. Ethnic groups are as follows:

- Kpolle: 20,000;
- Bassa: 16,000;
- Gio: 8,000;
- Kru: 7,000; and
- Others: 49,000.

English is the official language, and there are 16 other native languages. Economic activities include iron mining, rubber, and harvesting an abundance of grains and pepper seeds.

Liberia means "land of the free" and was founded by freed U.S. African Americans slaves in 1820. On 6 February of that year, 86 immigrants from the United States established a settlement in Christoplis, which is now Monrovia, thus named for U.S. President James Monroe. Thousands of other freed African Americans arrived from the United States during the following years. On July 26, 1847, Liberia declared its independence from the United States and became the Republic of Liberia.

South Africa

Modern human beings have inhabited South Africa for more than 100,000 years. South Africa was the first African country to be colonized in the interior of the continent. In 1652, after the "discovery" of the Cape Sea route, a station refreshment post was created by the Dutch East Indies Company in what is now Cape Town. The Dutch ship that anchored and remained there was called *The Harlem*. In 1806, Cape Town became a British colony after the British captured the colony from the Dutch.

By the 1820s, European settlement expanded in Cape Colony as the Boers (original Dutch Boers). British settlers claimed land in the north and east of the country. Conflicts arose between Zulu and Xhosa Tribes, who were the original inhabitants of the land that was occupied by the new European settlers.

The "discovery" of diamonds triggered conflicts, resulting in a devastating Anglo-Boer War for control of South Africa's mineral wealth. The Boers were defeated, and an agreement was reached whereby limited independence was granted to the Boers as a compromise in South Africa on May 31, 1910. On that date, a union of the four colonies was consummated into the independent South Africa, comprising the Cape Colony (region), the Orange Free State, the Transvaaal, and Natal. South Africa also gained status as a British Dominion in 1910.

In 1949 Apartheid was imposed on the African people as a form of separate development of the races in South Africa. Dr. Hendrik Verwoerd was the architect of the Apartheid Doctrine, which did not actually spring full-blown from 1949. The Apartheid dogma had existed all along, but it was from 1949 that Apartheid was applied brutally and unconditionally as a system of government everywhere in the country.

In 1961, republican status was declared by Apartheid's National Party, which promulgated segregation. By 1990, President F. W. de Klerk (1936–) began to dismantle Apartheid legislation and status. In 1994, the first democratic elections were held in South Africa, and Nelson Mandela (1918–) won the elections through the ruling African National Congress (ANC).

Egypt

Like Ethiopia, Egypt is one of the most populated African countries. Population is estimated at 75,042,000. Ancient civilization included the Pyramids, the Giza complex, and the Great Sphinx. Evidence of human habitation dates back to the 10th millennium BCE and the culture of hunting and gathering.

In 8000 BCE, climate changes/overgrazing resulted in the formation of the Sahara Desert. By 6000 BCE, organized agriculture and large building construction was present in the Nile Valley. In 3150 BCE, King Menes united Upper and Lower Egypt, which gave rise to the city-state system and a series of dynasties that ruled Egypt for the next three millennia. Egyptians began to refer to their unified country as Tawny, meaning "two lands." Culture and civilization flourished.

There were two historic periods, as follows:

1. The old kingdom period lasted from 2700 to 2200 BCE and was ruled by the first two dynasties; and
2. The new kingdom from 1550 to 1070 BCE started with the 18th dynasty.

Between old and new kingdoms, there were mini eras of rulers (e.g., the first intermediate period lasted 150 years from 2200 BCE until the middle kingdom in 2040 BCE). The periods in between underwent many political upheavals.

Libya

The name "Libya" is indigenous (i.e., Berber). People living west of the Nile in ancient Greek tribes were called "libyes" and the country was called "Libya."

The Phoenicians were the first to establish trading posts in Libya when merchants of Tyre in present-day Lebanon developed commercial relations with Berber tribes and signed treaties with them to ensure their cooperation in the exploitation of raw materials. By the 5th century BCE, Carthage, which was the greatest of Phoenician colonies, extended hegemony across much of North Africa where a distinctive Punic civilization was born. Punic settlements in Libya included Oea (Tripoli), Libdah (Leptis Magna), and Sabratha. All of these were settlements were in present-day Tripoli.

The Greeks conquered eastern Libya when Greek settlers/colonialists crowded the Island of Yhera in 630 BCE. Greeks founded the city of Cyrene. Within 200 years, more important Greek cities were created. They included the following:

1. Barce (Al Marj);
2. Euhespefides (Bereruse), which is the present-day Benghazi;

3. Teuchira (later Artsinoe), which is the present-day Tukra; and

4. Apollonian (Susah) port of Cyrene.

Together with Cyrene, these cities were known as the "pentapolis," meaning "five cities."

Later, the Romans unified the three regions of Libya and, for more than 600 years, Tripolitania and Cyrenaica became prosperous Roman provinces. Tripolitania and Cyrenaica, however, retained their Greek character even after Roman colonization.

General Abdullah bin Saad conquered Libya in 7 CE during the reign of Caliph Usman. In subsequent centuries, many Muslims, Islam, and Arab language and culture have been prominent in Libya.

The Ottoman Turks conquered Libya in the mid-16th century and subordinated the three Libyan states of Tripolitania, Cyrenaica, and Fezzan to their empire.

In 1911–1912, the Italo-Turkish war gave victory to Italy and unified the three states into colonies. From 1912 to 1927, Libya was an Italian colony also referred to as Italian North Africa. From 1927 to 1934, Libya was split into two colonies: Italian Cyrenaica and Italian Tripolitania. Both were ruled by Italian governors. In 1934, Italy adopted the name of "Libya" used by Greeks to refer to all of North Africa, except Egypt, as the official name of the colony, comprising Cyrenaica, Tripolitania, and Fezzan.

King Idris I (1890–1983), Emir of Cyrenaica, led the Libyan resistance to Italian occupation between both world wars. Omar Mukhtar (1858–1931) was the leader of a Libyan uprising against Italian occupation in Libya. From 1928 to 1932, the Italian military killed half the Bedouin population via starvation in war camps. After World War II, from 1943 to 1951, Cyrenaica and Tripolitania were put under British administration. Fezzan was put under French control. Idris returned to Libya from exile in Cairo but would only go to live in Cyrenaica in 1947 after the removal of some aspects of foreign control from Cyrenaica. In the 1947 peace treaty between Italy and the Allies, Italy relinquished claims to Libya.

On November 21, 1949, the UN General Assembly passed a resolution calling for Libya's independence before January 1, 1952. Idris was Libya's representative in subsequent negotiations. On December 24, 1951, Libya declared its independence as the United Kingdom of Libya, a constitutional and hereditary monarchy under King Idris. Significant reserves of oil and petroleum found in 1959 to make Libya a "golden plate" in North Africa.

On September 1, 1969, a 27-year-old army officer named Muammar Abu Minyar al-Gaddafi lead a small group of military officers against King Idris while Idris was in Turkey for medical treatment. After the coup, his nephew Crown Prince Sayyid Hassan ar-Rida al-mahdi as Sanussi became king with less power. Gaddafi and his military officers abolished the monarchy and proclaimed the new Libyan Arab Republic. Even today Gaddafi is referred to as "brother leader and guide of the revolution" in official press and all government statements.

Today, Lybia has the third highest GDP per capita in Africa, behind Seychelles and South Africa.

Morocco

Today, the land of Morocco borders two Spanish autonomous cuiries, Ceuta and Mella, in the Straight of Gibraltar where the Atlantic Ocean separates Spain from Morocco. Morocco is the Latinized name for the medieval Latin "Moroch" which referred to the name of the former Almoravid and Almohad capital Marrakech. Marrakech is derived from the Berber word "Mur-Akush" meaning "land of God." Berbers were the original inhabitants of Morocco. Later, the Phoenicians and Romans occupied this land as alien settlers. As the Roman Empire declined, Visigoths and vandals arrived, and then the Byzantine Greeks followed. Medieval Morocco underwent Islamization from 670 CE, the year of Islamic conquest of North Africa, especially along the coastal plain. Berbers became influenced by Arabs, and Morocco became Arabized with subsequent Arab rulers and dynasties.

The Alaolite Dynasty flourished between 1666 and 1912. It secured political independence for Morocco against the Spanish and the Ottoman Empire invasions. The country became a wealthy kingdom.

In 1684, the Alaonites annexed Tangier. Morocco was the first country to recognize the fledging United States as an independent nation in 1777. Because of European hostility toward Armenian ships in Atlantic Ocean, on December 20, 1777, Morocco's Sultan Mohammed III declared that Armenian merchant ships would be under protection of the sultanate and could thus enjoy safe passage.

The Moroccan-Armenian Treaty of Friendship with the United States is the oldest non-broken U.S. friendship treaty. It was signed by John Adams and Thomas Jefferson and has been valid since 1786. President George Washington wrote a letter to Sultan Sidi Mohammed enhancing ties between the United States and Morocco. The U.S. legation consulate in Tangier is the oldest diplomatic possession of the U.S. government abroad.

Morocco remained free of European influence for centuries, but was very wealthy and hence attracted European interest. France showed strong interest in Morocco from as early as 1830. In 1904, the United Kingdom recognized France's sphere of influence in Morocco, and Germany reacted strongly against this French move. The June 1904 crisis between Germany and France was resolved through negotiation.

In 1906, Spain recognized French interest in Morocco and showed her own interest. The second Franco-German crisis followed but was resolved by the Treaty of Fez on March 30, 1912, which made Morocco a French protectorate. By the same treaty, Spain assumed the role of protecting power over the northern and southern Sahara zones on November 27, 1941. During World War II, Moroccan soldiers served in the French Army, as well as in the Spanish Nationalist Army.

SUMMARY: EUROPEAN COLONIAL POLICIES AND PRACTICES IN AFRICA AND ELSEWHERE

Similarities include the following:

1. Exploitation of the Africans; paying Africans very low pay for work done and the Europeans very high pay for similar work done. i.e., government employees;
2. Treatment of Africans on slavery terms: women in slavery and colonial;
3. Alienation of prime African lands and resettlement of Africans on poor malaria-inflicted marshes called "African reserves";
4. African laborers as salves on alienated lands;
5. Heavy taxation of Africans who produced cash crops for export to benefit the European settlers;
6. Relations between Africans and Europeans and their countries were not international relations, but relations between bosses and subordinates. The colonial state and African society were very bad relationships;
7. Indirect rule: European especially German and British;
8. Direct rule: Europeans;
9. Artificial border separating the African colonial possessions;
10. Perpetuation of dependence and dependency even after African independence. Weak states at independence forced them to rely heavily on colonial and ex-colonial masters and metropolis;
11. Weak political and economic institutions for Africans even after independence;
12. The divide-and-rule policy destroyed the African sense of identity and harmony and prevented any emergence of African international relations that would be original in African outlook;
13. A "we–they" mentality was perpetuated in Africans and intensified tribalism and regionalism in African countries that continue to haunt these countries and their populations unto today;
14. Promotion and practice of racial stratification in the colonies according to colors of the skin; and
15. For administrative purposes, the colonies were divided into smaller units: provinces, districts, divisions, locations, sublocations, and villages,

The administrators of these colonies were colonial officials, some of whom had retired from active service as policemen, military officers, or administrative governors/high commissioners who later became rulers of the colonies; and after independence the colonial systems of administration were retained in Africa.

Divergences include the following:

1. Direct versus indirect rule as favored by some colonial powers
2. For Portugal the colonies were "overseas provinces"
3. Dutch colonial policies and practices in South Africa (Apartheid or separate development) mixed ethnic discrimination and brutality with racial stratification.
4. For France "assimilation" and "association" (after 1945) with the mother-colonial country.
5. Britain, France, and to a small extent Germany, trained a small elite to emerge as the ruling class in the colonies following the value system of the colonial power.
6. Belgium, Portugal, and the other colonial powers used minimal education as a tool for perpetual control and subjugation.

NOTES

1. Vincent B. Khapoya, *The African Experience* (Upper Saddle River, NJ: Prentice Hall, 1998).

2. Konrad Ropgen, Negotiating the Peace Treaty of Westphalia. In *1648: War and Peace in Europe, 3 Vols.* Klaus Bussmann and Heinz Schilling (eds.), (Catalogue of the 26th Exhibition of the Council of Europe on the Peace of Westphalia, 1998).

3. C.V. Wedgwood, *The Thirty Years War* (London: Jonathon Cape Ltd., 1938).

4. H.W. Fowler and F.G. Fowler, eds. *The Concise Oxford Dictionary of Current English,* 5th ed., revised by E. McIntosh (London: Oxford University Press, 1964), 387.

5. D.D.C. Don Nanjira, *The Status of Aliens in East Africa. Asians and Europeans in Tanzania, Uganda and Kenya* (New York: Praeger Special Studies, 1976), 1–12; 28–51, and 76–102.

CHAPTER 12

Understanding Ottoman Diplomacy and the Influence of Leadership by African Women

EUROPEAN AND OTTOMAN DIPLOMACY AND EFFECTS ON AFRICAN LEADERS, MODES OF GOVERNANCE, TRADITIONS

The Turks under the Ottoman Empire, founded by King Osman I in the 14th century, engaged in expansionism in Africa from 1453 to 1683 in locations where the Berbers resisted alien rule for a long time. Between 1830 and 1880 CE, North Africa was brought under the influence of Turks who applied great skills and diplomatic methods to convince the Africans of North Africa to fall under Turkish feudalism better known as Turkish suzerainty. Under this kind of influence, the Turks, especially with the backing of the powerful and globally influential Ottoman Empire, applied suzerainty to the extent that the Ottoman Turks controlled the international affairs of Africans north of the Sahara, but allowed the Africans to manage their own domestic affairs and enjoy their sovereignty at home.

The globalization of Islam brought considerable influence in culture and religion to North Africa and hence, by the 1830s, the Ottoman Turks had created suzerainty over Algeria, Tunisia, Tripoli, Fama and Cyrenaica in modern Libya, as well as in Egypt. In 1891, Libya was still under the strong influence of the Ottoman Turks.

Of particular interest, however, is that the Turkish Ottoman Empire did not impose Islamic laws on non-Muslims. Thus, although they were Muslims, their goal was not to impose their religion on other nations. In fact, they permitted their conquered subjects—Christians, Jews, or those of other faiths—to practice their own religious worship.

It was during the era of Pax Ottomana that the empire's expansionism flourished toward the southwest and into North Africa. Equipped with fleets, soldiers, and arms, the Ottoman Turks entered the Indian Ocean region and supported Muslims wherever they might be in danger, like in Kenya and in Indonesia. This kind of support and Pax Ottomana became valuable when the European colonial empires started to impose their imperialistic policies and practices in Africa.

In North Africa, the emergence of the Barbary states in Tripolitania, Tunisia, and Algeria was an asset to the Ottoman Empire since the piracy of the Barbary states was useful to the Ottoman Turks in their threats and attacks in Spain and Portugal. What helped the Ottoman Turks was their naval dominance in the Mediterranean region. The great diplomatic skills of the Ottoman Turks also aided them in their efforts to conquer other lands and empires. For example, Emperor Charles V (Charles I of Spain) was defeated by the Ottoman Turks in 1536 when the Turks allied themselves with Francis I of France. Suleiman I (also called Suleiman the Magnificent) joined forces with the king of France to fight and defeat the king of Spain.

Ottoman control in North Africa produced a culture of seafaring and piracy that terrorized the seas as far as Western Europe. In Africa, the notable Ottoman conquests included Egypt in 1517 CE; Algeria in 1519 CE; and the East African Coast and the Swahili Coast at Mombasa in 1585. During the 19th century, the Ottoman influence in North Africa began to decline as the French occupied Algeria and Tunisia, the British took Egypt, and the Italians claimed Libya.

Of particular historic recognition is the Italo-Turkish War, which was fought from September 29, 1911 to October 18, 1912. This war was initiated by Italy against Turkey in Libya as part of Italy's aim to acquire a modern empire. Italy allied with France, Germany, Russia, and Austro-Hungaria against the stipulations of Italy's Congress and the provisions of the 1885 General Act of the Treaty of Berlin in which the European Powers pledged to guarantee the sovereignty and territorial integrity of the Ottoman Empire. With the support of these countries, Italy invaded Libya and defeated the Turks. One of the soldiers on the Turkish side was the future founder of modern Turkey, Mustafa Kemal Ataturk (1881–1938). Before being dismantled after World War I, the Turkish Empire was in the Sudan in Africa, as well as in East Africa. It was Suleiman I who, in 1535, introduced traditional friendship between France and Turkey against Hapsburg Austria and Spain. Nonetheless, the Ottoman Empire was founded on the principles of Islam. The Ottoman Empire had to maintain the spirit of leadership fights against infidels, and since according to the Koran one can enter heaven if killed in a Jihad (a holy war), then international terrorism, mass killings, and beheadings would be acceptable under Islam if carried out under the slogan or premise of Jihad. Here lie many of the problems that people of Judeo-Christian traditions have faced in dealing with the principles of Islam. It is not just Judeo-Christianity that has had problems with such religio-cultural beliefs and pursuits, but humanists around the globe and in Africa who would find those principles and tenets unacceptable.

In African countries where the Ottoman Empire became influential because of Islamic tenets were the so-called Barbary states of North Africa. African leaders have had to implement modes of governance and government that have been found to be wanting in human rights observance. The present Arab-led regime in the Sudan, with its support of terrorism and murder against Africans in Darfur, is a good example. In cases where fundamentalism dominates in Islam, many violations of legal procedure and international and national laws have been made. Codes such as those of Hammurabi advocating "an eye for an eye and a tooth for a tooth" have had a lasting impact on Islamic practices and traditions. Sharia law has been applied by some Islamic leaders in Africa. For example, in Somalia and among the Muslims of Nigeria, Sharia law calls for the stoning of women for whatever reason; in Saudi Arabia Muslims are prohibited from marrying, or even dating, Christians. These have been considered grave violations of human rights and inappropriate behavior for "civilized" nations.

When the Ottoman Empire declined, and the weakness of the empire was made obvious by Italy's conquest of Libya, the great European powers were faced with the difficult diplomatic question of deciding how to carve out the Ottoman Empire and distribute the territory among themselves in such a way as to not upset the balance of power.

Ottoman Traditions

The Ottoman Empire left behind a legacy worthy of emulation. This is especially true for the following reasons:

- The empire introduced a system of succession of leadership that seems to have kept the Turks from competing. From Osman I there was a familiar line of succession from him through his descendant rulers from the start to finish of the Ottoman Empire.

- The empire adopted and enacted a legal system that was respected throughout the empire period. The Ottoman Empire was founded on the principles of Islam and the Koran. It also was founded on clear laws defending the nation of Islam and freedom of religion and worship.

- The early Ottomans were raiders, plunderers, and supporters of conquest, especially against "infidels" who must be sought out and brought to justice. The leadership of the Ottomans was a war-loving population who believed in conquest. The Pax Ottomana thus sought to introduce policies and practices that were consequently emulated by later-century leaders wherever they might be, including in Africa.

- Ottoman doctrines and practices still have strong effects on African leaders in the Islamic countries, and this is important because it is the leaders who enact and implement such laws and traditions. Ottoman diplomacy succeeded in cases where they could permit subjects to practice their faiths, keep their cultural values, and strike deals and alliances with Christian monarchs (for example, in order to subdue enemies of perpetuated Pax Ottomana around the world where Ottomanism had come, seen, and conquered).

ROLES OF INFLUENTIAL WOMEN LEADERS OF AFRICA IN HISTORICAL PERSPECTIVE: SOME CASE STUDIES SHOWING THEIR PAST AND PRESENT CONTRIBUTIONS TO AFRICAN CAUSES

Issues in African leadership form a vital part of the African Condition as a subsystem of the global system. Leadership is a huge paradox in Africa, and one keeps on returning to this problem because so many other issues of prosperity, poverty, and "backwardness" in Africa stem from the kinds of leadership that exist in African countries. The other primary determinants of the African Condition include rightful education of Africa and self-reliance. One area of leadership not elaborately discussed so far in this study, relates to the issue of women and their leadership in the African context. As used here, "women in power" only means those women who exercise, or have exercised, political authority and other official positions.

The status of women in traditional African society can cover a broad area of research. The social, economic, political, and housewife status of women in African society, as determined by custom and tradition, have been parts of African values that have not been well presented in history.

The phrase "female leadership in Africa" as used in this chapter refers to the political and other contributions to African causes, and to the leadership roles that African women have played over the centuries, and even millennia, and will no doubt continue to play in their respective nations, and in Africa as a subsystem of the international system.

Traditionally, the African woman and man have played fundamental roles in African society. These roles have been clearly defined by custom and tradition. Unfortunately, many of the magnificent—and even historically significant—roles played by women in Africa have, ironically, either been ignored, taken lightly, or even regarded as unimportant. These roles have not been given the kind of appropriate attention and analysis that they deserve.

From time immemorial, there was a clear division of labor between men and women in African societies. The woman, whether as wife, mother, or consort, was the main provider of the daily necessities of life for the children and the entire household. Her duties and responsibilities included preparing meals for the family; collecting firewood, fetching water for cooking and drinking from rivers and dug holes or springs of water; the untiling of land and planting of food crops, especially those for the subsistence of the family; protecting and feeding young children; and the like.

The main roles of the man as husband and father was to be the protector of the family, keeping his family from physical harm as well as from natural and human disasters and enemies; hunting and tilling the land, especially for what came to be known as "the cash crops" (sugarcane, coffee, cocoa, and sisal), which usually take much longer to mature than do subsistence crops; and looking after the herds, or providing fodder for their herds of cattle, sheep, goats, and the like. This life order in African society was instilled quite early in the human evolutionary process in Africa, and dates back to time immemorial. It evolved during the early nomadic years of Africans, when they moved from one African place to another in small groups, exploring, looking for green pastures, and developing in their various stages of evolution, from the *Homo genus* stage to the *Homo sapiens* stage of the hominids, as explained in Volume I of this study. This mode of living in Africa prevailed until, and through, the era of permanent settlements following the appearance of the Sahara Desert.

The necessity to observe that division of labor and roles in African society between women and men became imperative, especially after the new Saharan order led to permanent settlements in Sub-Saharan Africa and north of the Sahara. Then came the Europeans, who imposed new ways of living on the African people that, in effect, destroyed the clear division of labor between men and women that had reigned in African society from the earliest times. As the colonial masters took African husbands and men from the rural areas to work as servants ("boys") for the new imperialists in the urbanized areas of Africa, women were left alone with their children in the villages. This forced women to abandon their traditional duties of growing subsistence crops, etc., to grow cash crops. That new development not only destroyed the African social order as had been dictated and practiced all along by custom and tradition in Africa, but it also forced the African women to ignore their traditional roles in society, and to take over the roles that their men had been playing by custom and tradition.

The ultimate result of the new colonial order in Africa was that African women became overwhelmed by the newly imposed burdens on them and had to be subordinate to the men at the expense and abandoning of their traditional roles. That led to the impoverishment of Africa in many respects. For example, Africans were forced to concentrate on growing cash crops that were taken to Europe for eating, drinking, enjoying, and using—tea, cocoa, coffee, gold, diamonds, salt, manganese, and sisal for the European industries created by 19th century Industrial Revolution and its prosperity.

Some of these colonial policies and practices have been responsible, as explained in earlier chapters, for the continued impoverishment of Africa and for Africa currently being poorer now than she was 25 years ago or even longer. This was compounded by the slave trade and slavery of captured Africans, protectionism, reverse resource flows from Africa to the north, and the many other reasons stated in this book for the continued impoverishment of Africa.

Women Leaders' Opposition to Unjust Colonial Practices in Africa

Obviously, Africa and the African people had to rise up against European exploitation, humiliation, and dehumanization. These African sentiments became widely known and applied until decolonization and Africanization had to occur to replace imperialism, colonialism, and colonization in Africa. Some of the greatest opposition to the alien occupation and exploitation in Africa came from Africa's women leaders—whose roles and contributions to African causes and to decolonization improved the image, prestige, and development of their countries and all of Africa. Because of their gender, these powerful leaders have not, as stressed before, been as adequately recognized and applauded as they should be. The following section, therefore, highlights of some of the fundamental tasks that African women leaders—queens and empresses, political leaders and others—have accomplished for the betterment of Africa's humanity and prosperity.

Governance and Leadership of Africa by Women

African women rulers of African nations, especially the ones who showed great power and might, became rulers with considerable romantic sentiments. These were some of the qualities that many successful queens and empresses of Africa displayed—those women leaders became involved in lots of romance. In fact, many of the African women rulers of antiquity, especially the queens and empresses, actually became legendary for their charms, natural beauty, exercises of power, and love affairs. These included the queens, queen mothers, and pharaohs of Ancient Egypt (which, in ancient and classical times, was better known as Kemet or KMT), as well as those of ancient Ethiopia. In the entire classical world, Egypt emerged as the factory and superpower par excellence of the world. Egypt had been the proud recipient of ancient civilization almost at the dawn of the appearance of civilization on Earth, as practiced in Mesopotamia and in Africa. Egypt's proximity to the Mesopotamian region that produced civilization and some of the greatest and earliest inventions (stone and iron tools and weapons; writing, architecture, pyramids, astronomy, etc.), had to become "primus inter pares" (first among peers) for a very long time, and so Egypt became the center of great learning and reference for the whole world.

Kemet was followed by Ethiopia, which in ancient times was known by more than one name (Abyssinia, Sheba, Saba, Axum, Kush or Cush, Meroe, etc.), and that was partly because of the reign of some of the women rulers of these countries who are still remembered today, for their charms and even romantic lifestyles. This includes the following legendary women described in the remainder of this section.

Queen EyLeuka of Ethiopia (4530–3240 BCE)

This legendary queen, who was quite powerful, was also known as Dalukaha. She ruled Ethiopia for 45 years.

Pharaoh Meritneith of Egypt, alias Meryet-Nit (ca. 2952–2939 BCE)

This powerful pharaoh came to power after it had been decided that women in Egypt could become queens and inherit reigns. She succeeded Pharaoh Zir, and became the third ruler of the First Dynasty of Egypt. First, she acted as regent to her son, Den, and then later became ruler herself.

Regent Dowager Queen Ni-Maat-Hepi of Egypt (ca. 2720 BCE)

As queen of Egypt, she acted as regent for her son, Djuser of the Third Dynasty.

Queen Nehasset Nais of Ethiopia (ca. 2585–2145 BCE)

This queen ruled Ethiopia for 30 years, and that was more than 2,500 years before the legendary Queen Bathsheba ascended to the throne!

Queen Hatshepsut of Kemet (1503–1482 BCE)

As a young girl, Empress Hatshepsut was quite efficient. Her father, Pharoah Thothmes I noticed that quality in her early on, and was highly impressed. Consequently, he groomed her to become ruler of his kingdom. He married his daughter to her half-brother, Thothmes II, who ruled only for 13 years before she succeeded her husband. Queen Hatshepsut actually started to reign in the name of her son, Thotmes II, as regent, but proclaimed herself as pharaoh and ruled Egypt for 21 years.

Pharaoh Hatshepsut was one of the brightest rulers in Egyptian history, and one of greatest and most romantic queens that Kemet ever produced. She proved that a woman could, and can, be a very strong and effective ruler. Hatshepsut is the first great woman in history of whom we are informed!

This warrior queen was aggressive, disciplined, and overpowering, but a great and skilled diplomat at the same time, and made peace, for example, with Kush/Nubia. She sent diplomatic missions to East African nations and to Asia. She was a conqueror, and great promoter of commerce and commercial ventures between Kemet and other political units of the neighboring regions. Kemet conquered distant lands and their kings, and subjected them to Kemetic power and authority. Simultaneously, the queen was a true Africanist: she promoted and continued trade between her empire and other kingdoms and empires; promoted international diplomatic relations; perfected Kemet's national defense and influence; constructed public buildings, etc. Romantically, Hatshepsut is reported to have commanded men to do what she wanted them to do, including ordering those she willed to act as her husband, and they are all reported to have obeyed her orders to the letter. She ruled Kemet for 21 years in the county's second Golden Age. During her reign, Egypt enjoyed great stability, as she was a skilled diplomat who visited other nations, such as Puntland which was know in those days as "God's Land."

She was known as King of the North and South of Kemet; Son of the Suni; the Heru of God; Bestowerer of Years; Goddess of Risings, Lady of Both Lands, Vivifier of Years, Chief Spouse of Amen, and the Mighty One. The queen died suddenly and mysteriously; it is believed that her son, Pharaoh Thothmes III, murdered her.

Queen Cleopatra VII of Kemet (69–30 BCE)

Queen Cleopatra is believed to have ruled Kemet from 69–30 BCE. She was the most popular of Ancient Egypt's seven queens. She was a great linguist and skilled diplomat who made Egypt into the top superpower of the times. She was known to have had extravagant romantic relations with some of Rome's emperors and leaders, including Julius Caesar and Marc Antony.

Nubian Queen Tiye of Kemet (1415–1340 BCE)

The beautiful Nubian Queen Tiye is recorded to have been one of the most influential queens of Kemet. She had been affectionately known as the Charming Princess Nuhu, and became the "Great Wife" of the ruler of Egypt, King Amanhotep III. She succeeded Amanhotep at his death, acting as queen mother and regent before her sons could become kings of Kemet. The first son became King Amenhotep IV, and was also known as Akhenaton, S. Menkhare, and the second son became King

Tutankhamun. The queen mother supervised both until they became monarchs of Kemet.

Queen Ahmose-Nefertari of Kemet (1292–1225 BCE)

This great queen was the wife of the Rameses II of Lower Egypt. The marriage between Nefertari and Rameses ended 100 years of war between Upper and Lower Egypt.

Royal Queen Nefertitti of Kemet (1372–1350 BCE)

Queen Nefertitti (Nefertiti), also known as Nefertitto of Kemet, was an active queen who reshaped civilization using the power of her husband, the king. She wanted to be remembered and regarded as the wife of King Akhenaten, who was equal to a divine partner, and she was to be after her husband the god of the capital city of Kemet called Akhenaten. She was very supportive of her husband's efforts to do well for this. She became his chief consort and held many titles. She was revered as one of the most beautiful women of ancient times.

Queen Makeda of Ethiopia, alias Queen or Empress Sheba of Ethiopia (960 BCE)

Queen Makeda is also known as Empress Sheba. She is one of the most legendary women rulers of all time in Africa, because of her great wealth and romance with King Solomon of Israel that started the imperial might of Ethiopia in Africa.

Queen Sheba became a symbol of beauty. She was originally known as Makeda (which is what her subjects preferred to call her) or Maqueda, and many other of her names. She is also known as the Queen of Ethiopia. She had the qualities of being an exceptional monarch. Basheba was an empress of Ethiopia whose father came from Sheba (Abyssinia) in Yemen. In Islamic tradition she is known as Balgiis or Balkis. She probably came from an Arab city in Sheba (present-day Yemen) or Arabia. The Roman historian Felix Josephus called her Nicaule. Sheba's exact year of birth is not known; but she is believed to have been born on January 10, in the 10th century BCE. Many of these details can be found in the Kebra Nagast (The Book of the Glory of the Kings).

Empress Basheba came to know about King Solomon of Israel from Tamrin, an Ethiopian businessman who visited Israel for business and became very impressed by the wealth and might of the king. When Tamrin returned to Ethiopia he told Queen Sheba the story of his visit.

After hearing so much about the wisdom of this legendary Israeli king, Basheba became very interested in meeting him. So she sent word to him and it was arranged for her to visit him officially. She journeyed to Israel in an entourage and caravan of camels that took her to Jerusalem where she met and exchanged gifts with the wise King Solomon. She brought him 120 talents of gold, precious stones, and magnificent spices. She became a precious head of state visitor for him, and she accompanied him on his errands in his kingdom. After six months of visiting King Solomon, some romantic trickery developed on the side of the king, which resulted in Basheba bearing him a baby boy whom he named after his father, King David. This son became King Menelik I of Ethiopia, thereby marking the beginning of the Ethiopian dynasties of emperors as explained above.

Empress Candace of Ethiopia (332 BCE)

Empress Candace of Ethiopia was one of the queens of Meroe and one of the most revered women rulers of ancient Africa. It is recorded that Empress Candace was blind in one eye, but that she was one of the greatest military tacticians and commanders ever known in the ancient world. In 332 BCE, when preparing to attack and conquer Ethiopia, Alexander the Great had to withdraw his troops from the borders of Ethiopia when warned of the mastery of Empress Candace whose forces were going to humiliate him and his troops. Empress Candace was also a great patriot and Africanist. Kandake was a heroic title meaning "Queen" or the "Mother of the Crown Prince."

Kahina "Queen of Berbers" (7th century CE, died ca. 705 CE)

Her real name was Dihya, or Damiya, and she is believed to have been of Jewish extraction. She was born in the early 7th century CE and is reported to have probably lived and died in present-day Algeria. Kahina is also believed to have been the queen of Mauritania. She died around 700 CE, although some historical data show her death in 705 CE. Queen Kahina was a great patriot, nationalist, Africanist, and military tactician and leader who drove an Arab army northward into Tripolitania. She remained faithful to Berber worship and refused to be converted to Christianity or Islam. History remembers her as the greatest opponent against Islam who aimed at saving Africa for the Africans. She prevented the spread of Islam southward into Western Sudan. After her death, the North African countries and Sudan were Islamized. The Berbers are an ancient, indigenous people of North Africa, west of Egypt. These people comprise tribes that have maintained a closely knit culture, Hemitic languages, and a strong military power. They defeated the Vandals when they attacked North Africa. One of Queen Kahina's tasks was to drive the Arabs out of their territory in the 7th century. The Arabs swept across North Africa in the 680s CE. The Arab "jihad" is derived form the Arab term meaning "struggle or offensive war," by Muslims against all non-Muslims. The jihad is a holy war that is waged in order to convert the infidels to Islam. The prophet Muhamed who started Islam was born in Mecca, Saudi Arabia, in 570 CE, and by 620 CE, the Jihad had been installed at Mecca. Later, Islam spread to other parts of the world. Islam reached North Africa between 640 and 711 CE, when Islam consumed Algeria, Tunisia, and Morocco. These conquests followed the death of Islam's greatest enemy and conqueror in North Africa, Queen Kahina of the Berbers.

Queen Anna Nzinga of Angola (ca. 1581–1663 CE)

Queen Anna Nzingha of Ndongo and Matamba was one of the great rulers of Africa. She also held several titles: Queen of Angola and Kongo and Queen of Matamba, West Africa, or Southwest Africa. She succeeded her father and is defined as the greatest military strategist that ever confronted the armed forces of Portugal. First, she so acted in defense of her brother's army and kingdom. Then she formed her own army against the Portuguese and waged war against them for almost 30 years, during which time the central duty of her reign was to fight against the slave trade of the Portuguese who captured Africans from her empire. She entered into alliances with neighboring kingdoms to fight to expel the Portuguese and their slave trade form Africa. She allied her nation with the Dutch, thereby making the first ever African-European alliance against a European oppressor.

Queen Nzingha was immensely popular and influential among her people. She is ranked very high among the great rulers of Africa. She was an astute diplomat, tactful politician, an excellent and visionary military leader, and skilled negotiator. She successfully resisted Portuguese invasions and slave raids of her country, and negotiated peace with the Portuguese and other enemies of Angola.

When controversial developments between her and those loyal to her brother arose, friction ensued, and Queen Nzingha was forced into exile. Nonetheless, because of her quest for peace and freedom through diplomacy, she remains a great inspiration among the leaders of Africa.

Amina, Queen of Zaria (1588–1589 CE)

The Kingdom of Zaria existed where present-day Hausaland in Nigeria exists. Queen Amina was the daughter of King Bakwa Turunku who founded the Zazzau Kingdom in 1536 CE. Amina became queen between 1588 and 1589. She was a born military leader. A brilliant and forceful military strategist, she fought and won many wars and thereby expanded her kingdom after which she built the great Zaria Wall. She forced local rulers to accept vassal states and allow Hausa traders safe passage. Her legacy is that of Amina, daughter of Nikatau, a woman as capable as a man.

Queen Nandi of Zululand (AD 1778–1826 CE)

Nandi was the queen mother of King Shaka Zulu (b. 1786) the great military strategist of Zululand. She was a highly esteemed queen and mother who endowed her son with bravery, loyalty, and other strong leadership qualities. She nurtured a future king who would unite his subjects and fight to defend them from their enemies, including the European invaders who came to Zululand.

Empress and Queen Mother Yaa Asantewa (1863–1923 CE)

This queen was actually an empress of the Ashanti (Asante) people in the Kumasi Region of Ghana's northern territories, which became vassal states. Also known as Asantawa, Queen Yaa was brave and strong in character, but humble. She was Queen Mother of Ejisu of the Ashanti Empire. She was vexed by the cowardice of the chiefs and kings of the empire who would not fight against the British in 1896 when they took her husband, King and Emperor Nana Prempeh I (1870–1931) into exile. At first, the king and all his family—his parents, brother, and two sons who were heirs to the throne and war chiefs—were arrested by the British and sent to the Cape Coast Castle, then to Elmina Castle, and thereafter to Sierra Leone.

On January 1, 1997, the king/emperor and his family, except for his wife, were exiled to the Seychelles Islands. He left the Empire of Asante in the care of his wife, Her Majesty the Queen Mother and Empress Asantewa. While reigning before his arrest and exile, the emperor had refused to fight against the British because he did not want to cause the bloodshed of his subjects. Consequently, whatever the British Governor and other intruders did and demanded, Emperor Prempeh accepted to avoid bloodshed. He, however, refused British protection of his empire, and left it under the reign and protection of his wife, Her Majesty the Queen Mother and Empress of Asante. Under her rule, Asante became an example of a nation in Africa that, at all costs, engaged in resistance wars and battles against the British.

Between 1811 and 1874, the Ashanti people fought against the British seven times. Even when the vassal states of the north broke away or the emperor was under pressure from the British, the emperor patiently waited for opportunities until later when he was able to reunite the empire. But, only three years later, the scramble for Africa erupted in 1884, and the Berlin General Act of 1885 gave Ghana and the Asante Empire to the British. In fact, Asante was annexed as a British Territory in 1902. In 1824, the British had sent an expedition to Kumasi, which the Ashanti army defeated. But in 1826, the British returned and invaded Asante and overpowered the Ashanti people. The resistance of the Asante Empire continued until they were ultimately defeated by the British in 1874.

As empress, Queen Mother Asantewa took great care of her subjects. She attended meetings of the chiefs, and while attending one such meeting, scolded them for being so timid. That challenge emboldened them, and so they decided to join her when she took up arms in 1901, declared war against the British, and led the Ashanti army against the British as Commander of the Army. It was one of the bloodiest of the ten Anglo-Ashanti wars. The British troops invaded the Ashanti Empire because they wanted its gold. The queen's forces, comprising the chiefs, fought bravely against the British in Kumasi. At first, the empire's forces under the leadership of the Empress Asantawa defeated the British and won the battle; but when the British army retreated and reinforced, they returned to Ashanti with 1,400 soldiers. The Queen Mother Asantawa and her chiefs were defeated and captured, and she was sent into exile in Seychelles, where she joined her exiled husband and family. There, she remained until her death in 1923. Her husband, the emperor, lived in the Seychelles until his death in 1931.

The Queen Mother Asantewa is fondly remembered because the war and resistance that she led against the alien British invaders of her empire in Africa marked the last time ever that a major war was led by a woman in Africa.

Female Leadership in Post-Colonial Africa

Many other queens and empresses of Ancient Africa also played vital roles in promoting the welfare of their nations and peoples, or fought against foreigners for the sake of their countries. Modern women rulers of Africa include the following, which is by no means an exhaustive list:

- Premier Elizabeth Domitien (1925–2005), who was vice president of the Central African Republic from 1974 to 1976. She was a cousin to Emperor Jean-Begel Bokassa, who made her vice president of the Ruling Social Evolution Movement of Black Africa from 1975 to 1979 and deputy head of state. But he sacked her and had her imprisoned and tried in 1980. When he himself fell out of power in 1979, she was freed the following year and became a very successful and influential businesswoman.

- Paramount Chief Mantsebo Amelia Mantsaba Sempe (1941–1960) of Lesotho.

- Queen Mother and Indlovukazi Dzeliwe Shongwe of Swaziland (b. 1927), Queen from 1982 to 1983; wife of King Sobhuaz II and joint head of state and queen mother after the king's death on August 21, 1982. She consequently assumed regency for their son and appointed 15 Members of the Ligogo (a traditional advisory body or supreme council). She lost the title of Queen Mother in 1985.

- President Ellen Johnson-Sirleaf (1938–) of Liberia, elected in 2006.

- Premier and Acting Head of State of Burundi, Sylvie Kenigi (1952–), who was acting president from October 27, 1993 to February 5, 1994. She resigned the presidency and joined the Central Bank of Burundi. At the time of this writing, she works at the UN.

- Premier Agathe Uwilingiyimana (1953–1994) of Rwanda, assassinated while in office.
- Premier Maria das Neves (1958) of São Tomé and Príncipe from 2002 to 2004.
- Premier Maria do Carmo (1960) of São Tomé and Príncipe from 2005 to present.

Common Observations on Women Leaders in Africa

In discussing the leadership of prominent women in Africa in historical perspective dating from remote antiquity to the present, the following observations are noteworthy.

It has been argued in general, but with considerable accuracy, that women are more patient and more reconciliatory than men; that women are less corrupt, less ethnocentist, and less egoistical than men; more humanistic than men; more inclined to obey the law and follow the rules than men; and more insistent on accuracy than men. But it has also been argued that women can, in certain cases, be more destructive than men; more inflexible than men; and more emotional and hence more erratic than men. The expression "the weaker sex" has also been used. Be all of the above as they may, there is no justification for gender inequality in society; no justification for religious segregation (e.g., in terms of Christianity or Islam); no justification for discrimination against women and girls in matters of inheritance (e.g., of land rights and ownership).

On the question of female leadership or rule in Africa, it is best to examine this issue in historical perspective and to look back to remotest antiquity and see how women leaders in Africa used to govern, or assist in the governance of, African societies and kingdoms. The two forms of governance that existed in traditional African societies were based on patrilineal and matrilineal inheritance and the heritage of reign in Africa.

Many women across Africa have led modern liberation movements. They have fought for the liberation of their countries from external invasions, as were the cases with Ghana's Ejisu and Ethiopia's Empress Candace under her very masculine and blind-in-one-eye leadership whose reputation as a brilliant military field commander made Alexander the Great halt his army at the boundaries of Ethiopia. African freedom fighters and liberation women leaders have also worked hard to eradicate tyranny and human rights violations, as did the women of Liberia who in the 1990s, forced the then dictatorial president Charles Taylor (1948–) to go to Accra to negotiate peace and a cease-fire with the rebel warlords—leaders—of Liberia who wanted to topple Taylor. This president was later indicted and arrested by the International Criminal Court (ICC), which at the time of this writing is still considering the case against former President Taylor of Liberia.

The queens and empresses of Africa cited in this book were either wives of kings or empresses of emperors in Africa who for thousands of years have been revered, respected, honored, adored, worshipped, or idolized by their subjects, individuals, families, and foreign leaders and nations alike. Some of these women were not active and just remained spouses of rulers. Others became active as wives of kings or emperors, and desirous and able to play some roles to help their spouse rulers and kings. Some queens and empresses were rulers themselves through matrilineal ways of inheritance, or on selection by their husbands, fathers, fathers-in-law, or through regency. Queens or empresses who were fighters or female resistance leaders filled the roles of diplomats and military tacticians. These brave women were often competent negotiators and powerful and authoritative queens and empresses who decided to perform active roles in Africa.

In ancient times in Africa, Egypt, and Ethiopia were the only independent countries with statehood that produced women rulers. Egypt was first, and Ethiopia was second in the world. The term "queen" has been used interchangeably with "empress" throughout history. Most of these women were active prior to the colonization of Africa, dating back to remote antiquity. During the colonial period, however, the masters were the colonial administrators who succeeded in transforming Africa. After colonization, not all spouses became active because of the specific constitutional and democratic dictates of modern government structures.

Unfortunately, in Africa, the valuable roles that African women have played in society have not been adequately and loudly appreciated. Women's roles played in African societies from remotest antiquity, especially by women who were political leaders, have been recorded as possessing considerable "sentimental touches." The women who were rulers in ancient pre-colonial Africa and, in particular, in classical times, were strong in character, powerful, efficient, competent, effective, and quite influential queens and empresses. However, they were also distinctly romantic, and some were even often in romantic expositions.

The post-colonial period deals with cases of "mixed heritage." Thus, the subordination of women in Africa that destroyed the clear division of duties in African society was a mere introduction in Africa of the European practices in which men had always been accorded a higher status in society than women. Men were superior to women in European society, and women had to be subservient to men. In the post-colonial era of Africa then, there cannot be any about-turn. The mixed heritages of African, Arab, colonial European, and mixed influences of different religions (Christianity and Islam) are in Africa to stay. Their dictates are reinforced by modernism and modernization in Africa, as well as education and other values of the Western system that inevitably find themselves on a collision course with the dictates of African custom and tradition. The outcomes of all of these forces generally have been unfavorable to women as members of African society, despite the vital multidimensional roles that African women play in African society.

Thus, problems of gender inequality continue to rock African societies with most of the positions of leadership being allocated to men. Land ownership is still denied to women in most African societies, and the colonial remnants of men at the top and women at the lowest strata of society also are still present. However, payments of dowry are dying out in most places in Africa. The demands for democratization, democracy, and good governance, accountability, the observance of human rights, and the like, are all dictates that must be addressed and changed to promote the leadership of women in Africa.

Similarly, education for women and a New Girl Order (NGO) are demanded in Africa, as are the calls for equity, justice, eradication of corruption and ethnocentrism, and for the installation of rational uses and management of resources in Africa; free access to global markets, resource nationalism, etc. The new trends are toward empowering women and girls in African societies so that women and girls can compete and participate in business, economics, and other spheres of African life as equal partners.

As the number of African women grows in leadership positions and roles, there are bound to be changes. Thus, President Ellen Johnson-Sirleaf of Liberia cannot be the only female president in Africa for a very long time. Professor Wangari Maathai of Kenya cannot continue to be the only African woman for a very long time to get a Nobel Peace Prize in Africa; the African man cannot continue for a very long time in the future to dominate things in political, economic, and other spheres of African life at the exclusion, or minimal inclusion, of women. With the ever-growing demands for democratization in Africa, and for the empowering of increased numbers of women to vote in Africa, there must, and shall, be progress toward gender equality.

In like manner, the UN must achieve the 50 percent target of women employment in the UN system.

In short, then, neither the status quo ante, nor the status quo hodie can be sustained in Africa—or elsewhere for that matter. Increased attention must be given to increased recognition, appreciation, and promotion of the roles of women in leadership positions in Africa. This is not a question of time, but is needed *now*.

GOALS AND CHALLENGES OF LEADERSHIP IN AFRICA

The general observation that raises considerable curiosity in anyone who analyzes the issue of leadership in Africa is that, whether they be men or women, African leaders should and will ultimately be judged by at least by 14 criteria of goals and challenges, on the basis of their performance and attainment of concrete and practical results in the following areas:

1. The goal and challenge of Pan-Africanism is the oldest of all of the challenges confronting African leaders in the post-colonial era. Pan-Africanism, however, is still far from being attained as a goal.

2. Liberation is also far from being attained, as conflicts and civil wars have been raging in some African nations for years, dating back to their attainment of political independence almost half a century ago. Tribalism, nepotism, ethnocentrism, neo-dependency, cronyism, corruption, looting, exploitation, as well as incompetence and subsequent impoverishment in some African nations, are continuing challenges.

3. Reconciliation is a surprisingly hard goal to attain. In some cases, political differences have turned into personal vendettas and hatred. Differences in African societies based on ethnicity, and the lack of durable resolutions to these differences, still cause grave multidimensional impediments to progress in African countries.

4. Democratization is still a huge challenge in Africa, as are education—illiteracy—and disease.

5. Globalization is still a double-edged sword and an enormous challenge to Africa.

6. Global Africanization is a challenge and goal requiring that Africans and all peoples of African descent collaborate from wherever they may be, for the good and development of Africa.

7. Education; empowerment; equality/equity; employment; environment; engagement; enticement/endearment; and eradication of poverty and the poverty syndrome in Africa are huge challenges to every African leader.

8. Good governance and democratization are still huge challenges in Africa, requiring the promotion and protection of justice, fairness, equality, human rights, ethical and moral values, the rule of law, and rational use of human and natural resources; combating disasters, climate change, and global warming; and eradicating poverty and global public bads (GPBs), etc.

9. Development and sustainable development are challenges of multidimensionalism versus deficiency, cultism, personal glory, and survival; as well as of social, environmental, political, and economic stability and progress.

10. Nationalism and patriotism.

11. Ownership of Africa by Africa.

12. Competitiveness and self-reliance in education, political unity, and human security.

13. Business for African profit and development.

14. Resource mobilization and change of mental attitudes for self-sufficiency in Africa.

Qualities and Conditions for Effective Leadership

Again, and whether men or women lead, they must possess certain qualities and meet certain conditions if they are to be effective and efficient in their leadership positions. The conditions and qualities of effective and competent leadership include the following, among many others.

- Strength of character:

  - Fairness, a sense of duty and responsibility to the nation and the governed—patriotism;
  - Integrity, tolerance, entrepreneurship, good judgment, common sense, wisdom, consistency, decisiveness, patience, and the ability to listen and be rational before deciding on any actions;
  - Adherence to the rule of law; and
  - Adherence to the principles of participatory democracy.

- Enhancement of democracy, equality of gender, and opportunity and education for all:

  - Ability to accept failure and to adapt, including to scrap traditions, practices, policies, and development initiatives that have either failed or that are untenable;
  - Retention of loyalty to the constitution; no suspension of it, and no dismantling of democratic structures.

- Institution of human and institutional capacities for national development:

  - Ability to overcome deep-rooted challenges and temptations of bad governance, mismanagement, squandering of public wealth, etc.;
  - Avoidance of unnecessary ideological divisions and external influences;
  - Adherence to Pan-Africanism, African Socialism, and Negritude.

CHAPTER 13

Peripheralization of Africa in European and World Markets

AFRICA'S ECONOMY IN HISTORICAL PERSPECTIVE: NO IMPOVERISHMENT IN PRE-COLONIAL TIMES

Africa has a long history of trade and development in East Africa and other regions of the continent referred to in Volume I as Africa's five economic zones. As a system of human activities relating to the production, distribution, exchange, and consumption of goods and services of a nation or nations, the economy is something that the African people have been engaged in from time immemorial.

For more than 5 million years, humankind, starting in the cradle of humanity in Africa, evolved and developed cultures and civilizations embodying the African practices of nomadism, family, and permanent settlement, and adopted the following, among other of norms of the economy:

- Supporting families and social groups;
- Developing agriculture;
- Domesticating plants and animals for food and human survival;
- Expanding alliances with other social groups for coexistence through diplomatic codes, intermarriages; and
- Sharing common values like land, waters, services, and goods to feed the people, to protect each other from want, enemies, and nature, and to defend societies for the common good of humankind.

Thus, by the time kings, empires, and city-states flourished throughout Africa in ancient and pre-colonial times, the economy was a system of human activities developed through the production, distribution, exchange, and consumption of goods within Africa and with outside nations. Already at that time, primary commodities became important for consumption and trade, and these included palm oil, groundnuts, cola nuts, beans, peas, coffee, cocoa, sugar, cotton, sisal, and rubber, as well as commodities for barter such as cowries, shells, gold, diamonds, copper, silver, zinc, tin, ivory, animals, and human slaves in times of peace and war.

Until such trade, impoverishment did not really exist in the vocabulary of the pre-colonial Africans even though trade was not organized internationally as it came to be in colonial and post-colonial times (during which time trade only benefit the invaders of Africa from Europe).

ECONOMIC AND BUSINESS RELATIONS IN COLONIAL AFRICA: 1885–1960

The African economic tables were overturned following the signing of the Berlin Act of 1885, which started the subjection of Africa to European colonial rule and dominance. This transformed Africa into a Western-value-oriented continent dependent wholly on European imperialism and its economic system of capitalist exploitation. This also reduced the African to an object, rather than a subject, in international economic relations between the colonizer and colonized. Thus, the colonizer and colonized were not equals, but held the roles of superior–inferior and master–servant.

Conceptual Understanding

The phrase "colonial Africa" means the condition of Africa when the continent was under foreign domination.

When discussing alien rule in this context, it should be noted that Africa had been under colonial alien rule three times, as follows:

- Before Christ, when North Africa was colonized by the Phoenicians (between 1200 and 800 BCE);
- By the Romans (from 146 BCE to 476 CE) when the Romans conquered Carthage and North Africa, making this territory part of the Roman Empire and eventually the Western Province of the Roman Empire; and
- By the Europeans from 1885 following the Conference of Berlin.

The colony was not allowed to deal with any countries other than the mother country. So, an African businessperson or population could export their primary commodities only to the metropole in return for (purchased) manufacturing goods. Furthermore, the exporter from the colony had to rely heavily on a small number of commodity exports (e.g., oil products of the colonies and the trade in all the goods and services in agriculture-based, or mineral-based commodities and raw materials, which benefited only the North and never Africa or the African people).

The introduction of the cash crop system and single and low-value agricultural commodities never benefited the colonies (e.g., coffee from

Kenya, Burundi, and Ethiopia; pyrethrum from Kenya; cocoa from Ghana, Côte d'Ivoire, and São Tomé and Príncipe; sisal from Tanganyika; cotton from Mali and Uganda; and oil products from Nigeria, Angola, Algeria, Libya, Gabon, the Sudan, and Congo Leopoldville, etc. These items were sent to industries and countries of the North, and this practice resulted in the following:

- Century-long plundering of Africa, depriving her of her sons and daughters who were forced to become slaves;
- Expatriating Africa's natural resources and primary commodities;
- Introducing unfair taxation like the hut tax;
- Perpetuating reverse resource transfers;
- Avoiding capacity-building to empower the African people;
- Making world prices for Africa's primary commodities very vulnerable (a situation that exists today); and
- Other colonial policies and practices that aimed at preventing Africa's economic growth.

All of these European policies impoverished Africa and made her dependent on the metropoles in Europe. With such vulnerability of Africa to global capitalism and exploitation, Africa's dependence on limited commodity exports in exchange for manufactured goods was aggravated by price fluctuations, corruption, and lack of control and management by Africans of their country's valuable raw materials and minerals like uranium, platinum, gold, diamonds, copper, tin, and other resources. There was a lack of resource nationalism that would require the materials and goods to be used for the benefit of Africa and the Africans, and thereby prevent the external exploitation, plundering, corruption, and other similar practices that all "peripheralized" Africa in European and world markets. That reality deeply impoverished the continent. The negative effects of this peripheralization and impoverishment of Africa are still felt in post-colonial Africa, and are among the major reasons why Africa is poorer now than she was even at independence almost half a century ago.

A combination of debt and debt servicing results from protectionism, economic isolation, unjust international economic relations, and the lack of competitiveness and the capacity to undertake competent negotiations. The existing global negotiations system greatly handicaps Africa in her efforts to do business with the goal of sustainable development of the countries of Africa.

In summary, peripheralization of Africa started before 1884–1885 and intensified after the Berlin Conference of 1885. The negative effects of African peripheralization are still felt today, perhaps even more than they were in colonial time.

The year 1885 is thus referred to as the Annus Horribilis, the "horrible year" for Africa. On the other hand, the year 1960 is referred to as the Annus Mirabilis, "the wonderful year," because it officially marked the end of colonization and the beginning of political independence in Africa. In 1960, many of the former colonies of European nations, especially those of France, gained political independence en masse.

Political Independence but Continued African Impoverishment

Although 1960 marked the beginning of decolonization and political independence for Africa, a few countries gained independence before 1960. These were Ethiopia, Liberia, South Africa, Egypt, Libya, Tunisia, Morocco, Ghana, and Guinea. In 1960, from Britain came Somalia and Nigeria. In 1960, from France came Togo, Mauritania, Upper Volta (Burkina Faso), Dahomey (Benin), Cameroon, Gabon, Central African Republic, Congo Brazzaville (Republic of the Congo), Congo Leopoldville (Democratic Republic of the Congo), Chad, and Niger.

The colonial policies and practices that were imposed on Africans had repercussions whose effects are still felt today in Africa. They transformed Africa practically in all fields of Africa's way of life including in the political, economic, and business sectors. The economy of Africa suffered during colonization because relations and dealings were established as if between bosses and subjects/subordinates. The colonies could not create any business contacts or relations to sell or buy goods and services with/from third parties, without the permission of the colonial power.

The boss–subject relationship was created following the imposition of alien rule, which removed the successful economic and trade relations that had existed in Africa prior to colonization. Barter as a system of trade was replaced by a cash economy when the colonial powers introduced foreign currencies in Africa, notably the French franc and the British pound.

European policies and practices impoverished Africa by introducing an economic system that ignored the need for Africans to grow subsistence crops used for millennia and replaced these crops that usually take a short period of time to mature, with cash crops that require longer periods of time before they can be harvested. These commodities were sold to European markets for European consumption. Moreover, the division of labor that had existed in traditional Africa with clear roles for women and men was broken when the Europeans took the men—fathers, sons, and husbands—from the rural areas and made them servants of European households in the urban areas.

The women who had been left in the rural areas were forced to abandon their traditional roles of child-rearing, water and fire collection, etc. and had to start farming the cash crops left behind by their husbands. In this way, the division of labor between men and women was destroyed, the cash system led to the introduction of hut and other taxes that Africans had to pay to the colonial masters. The result of all this was increased impoverishment of Africans; exploitation, slavery, and slave trade; the forced neglect of the traditional roles of women in the rural areas; and the downgrading of the roles of women in African society to be what they had been for European women whose status in society was always lower than that of men.

The economy and business in colonial Africa only favored the colonial masters. African entrepreneurs could not sell anything to anyone out of the colony without the express consent of the colonial administrators. This boss-subject relationship extended to all walks of life in Africa.

Thus, post-colonial Africa still suffers from the colonial economic system that served best for the European colonial powers, but worst for Africa and her nations and people. In talking, therefore, about poverty and impoverishment of Africans, a calculated account must be taken of what European colonialism did to Africans by taking them into slavery and the slave trade; by dehumanizing the Africans and reducing them to objects like commodities; by denying Africans their rights of access to global markets and to development as a human right, to freedom of enterprise and business, to traditional ways of business practices (i.e., barter system of trade); and by introducing policies and practices that erased the African spirit, Negritude, the African soul, Africanness; and instilling a value system that was aimed at turning Africans into Europeans.

CHAPTER 14

Africans during World War I and the Interwar Period

Generally speaking, World War I erupted when most of the African men who became the founding fathers of African political independence were old enough to remember it, and some even served as soldiers in the armies of the colonial powers at the time. African founding fathers such as Kwame Nkrumah of Ghana, Jomo Kenyatta of Kenya, Gamal Abdel Nasser of Egypt, Ahmed Sékou-Touré of Guinea, and Nnamdi Azikiwe of Nigeria were already big enough to remember such a war. Although it was a European war, World War I opened the eyes of Africa to political independence. There were developments on two fronts. First, the Back to Africa Movement had become very strong through Pan-African meetings and congresses convened in Europe in order to forge out a course for political independence for Africa. Secondly, many Africans fought in the war on the side of their colonial powers, and also lost many lives. They further listened to the statements of U.S. President Woodrow Wilson of whose Fourteen Points contained point five, which in effect suggested the granting of self-rule to colonial countries and peoples irrespective of their size or level of preparedness and development. By the time of the end of the war, the Africans who had served in it emerged as advocates of self-government and liberation from the colonial yoke.

CAUSES OF WORLD WAR I

World War I was a European war that started on July 28, 1914 and ended on November 11, 1918 when the Armistice Treaty was signed. The war had a number of causes, all of which pointed to one major problem: a power struggle among the European powers.

The causes were of two types: the immediate cause and other causes. The immediate cause of the war was the assassination of the archduke of the Austro-Hungarian Empire, Franz Ferdinand, in the streets of Sarajevo on June 28, 1914. He and his wife were shot by a Serb radical student named Gavrilo Princip as their motorcade was heading to the hospital carrying the archduke who had escaped a bomb attack by another Serbian nationalist extremist. The archduke was accompanied by his wife and the mayor of Sarajevo. They were going to visit the victims of the bomb blast when they were cornered by a Serbian nationalist. The people of Bosnia resented the fact that they were ruled by the non-Serbian regime of Austria-Hungary instead of being governed by Serbians since Bosnians, like Serbes, were a Slavic people.

The other reasons were a history of 50 years of rivalry and power struggle between and among the European powers. The power struggles prompted the formation of two kinds of understandings. Alliances: a treaty of alliance required the Allied Powers to fight together against a common enemy. The other kind of agreement or understanding was the entente, which was a friendly understanding between two or more powers. Normally, there were groups of three forming an entente or an alliance. The competing powers were Germany, France, Great Britain, Italy, Russia, and Austria-Hungary. The fierce competition among these powers led to serious conflicts and divisions as follows:

- 1879: Otto von Bismarck, chancellor of united Germany, seeks to isolate France by signing a dual alliance treaty with Austria-Hungary.
- 1882: Bismarck signs a triple alliance with Italy and Austria-Hungary.
- 1887–1888: Bismarck also signs a treaty of alliance with Russia, which isolates France even more. On June 15, 1888, Kaiser Wilhelm II, king of Germany and emperor of Prussia, was crowned and reigned until November 9, 1918.
- 1890: Kaiser Wilhelm II forces Bismarck to resign and lets the treaty with Russia lapse. Russia moves fast to ally with France.
- 1894: Russia and France sign an alliance treaty.
- 1890s: Kaiser Wilhelm, the tough grandson of England's Queen Victoria, turns against the British and starts to build an empire and naval force to compete with Great Britain. A naval arms race between Germany and Great Britain starts, and Great Britain fears that Germany might be dangerous. So, Great Britain ends her isolation and signs ententes with France in 1904, and with France and Russia in 1907.

These events produced two groupings in the European power struggle: one triple alliance comprising Germany, Austria-Hungary, and Italy, and a triple entente consisting of Great Britain, France, and Russia.

The result of the power struggle in Europe was an explosive situation on the Balkan Peninsula. For almost 100 years, the Balkan entities had been trying to free themselves from the Ottoman Empire. Their freedom arrived in the 1900s when the power of the Ottomans declined, and new nations were born in the Balkans: Albania, Greece, Bulgaria, Montenegro, Romania, and Serbia. When Marshal Josip Broz Tito (1892–1980) came to power, he united most of these entities into the Republic of Yugoslavia. Nationalism was a strong force among those nations, and it found support in Yugoslavia. The problem of the Balkans was aggravated by the rule of Austria-Hungary over Bosnia and the other Balkan nations. This alien rule was strongly resented by the Slavic nations after Austria-Hungary extended its empire to include former possessions of the Ottoman Empire.

Russia, being Slavic, supported the nationalism of the Slavic countries of the Balkans. Russia encouraged them to fight for political independence from Austria-Hungary. This would cement a friendship between Russia and the Slavic nations and thereby guarantee Russia's access to the Mediterranean coast.

Consequently, in 1908, Austria annexed Bosnia and Herzegovina. The vexed Austria sought and received support to declare war on the Balkans. The crisis of the European power struggle continued until Austria-Hungary, seeking to revenge the assassination of Archduke Ferdinand in Sarajevo, gave an ultimatum to Bosnia. With Germany's support, Austria-Hungary declared war on Serbia. Russia stepped in for Serbia and mobilized against Germany's border.

Between 1908 and 1909, developments occurred in the Balkans that were unstoppable until the eruption of World War I. Germany declared war on Russia. Soon after, the alliance entente arrangements were employed.

On August 2, 1914 Germany declared war on France. France rose in support of Russia, so Germany soon realized it was fighting a war on both its western and eastern borders. On August 4, Germany ignored Belgium's neutrality declared in 1839, and marched through Belgium to fight against France. This was too close to Great Britain, so an outraged Great Britain declared war on Germany. By mid-1914, the battle lines were clearly drawn. It has been estimated that more than 2 million Africans participated in the war. African Americans could have held leadership positions during the war, but Africans from Africa could not possibly have held senior or leadership positions then because their status in the eyes of the colonial powers was that of subjects, and even objects.[1]

For Africa then, World War I was a forum for gathering information on how to be liberated and forge ahead demanding freedom and self-rule from the colonial powers. This was also a time when the Pan-African congresses and meetings to map out strategies for African unity were being mobilized, especially in England. It was U.S. president Woodrow Wilson who raised very high hopes for the people of Africa and the other developing regions of the world. In his list of points for ending the war, he said the following:

> The program of the world's peace, therefore is our program, and that program is the only possible program as we see it:
>   . . . Point V.: A free, open-minded, and absolutely impartial adjustment of all colonial claims, based upon a strict observance of the principle that in determining all such questions of sovereignty the interests of the populations concerned must have equal weight with the equitable claims of whose title is to be determined . . .[2]

It was during the interwar period (1919–1939), between the end of World War I and the beginning of World War II, that African politicians increased their demands for liberation and organized to launch tougher demands against colonialism and colonization. They mobilized support from leaders like Haile Selassie of Ethiopia who addressed the League of Nations and demanded African independence as soon as possible. At the first Pan-African Conference in London in 1919, W.E.B. DuBois quoted from his *Souls of Black Folk*, "the problem of the Twentieth Century is the problem of the color line."[3] The second Pan-African Conference, also in 1919, was held in Paris. Here it was Marcus Garvey who spoke loudest for independence. It is believed that the 19th century was a great divide between the pre-modern and modern eras of African thought. It is argued that 1919 marked the beginning of the "modern period" in Africa. This argument is, however, debatable, as can be seen from the following analysis.

DEBATE OVER MODERNIZATION IN AFRICA

The question of modernization versus African traditional values was bound to emerge strongly as the transformation of Africa had been prompted by the colonial policies and practices that had been introduced in colonial Africa. Scholars and politicians alike, and especially historians, wanted to know how to classify Africa as a "modern continent." What was "modern" Africa? What was meant by "modernization" in Africa?

No conclusion has been drawn as to the meaning of the expression "modernization of Africa," or when its use began. For all practical purposes, however, the talk about "modernization of Africa" has to start to accept that modernity—meaning consideration of Europe and its impacts and changes in Africa—has to start with the first contacts of Europeans with Africa in the post-Christian era. If this argument is "reasonable," and it has to be, since no alien influence really impacted African lives as much as Europeanism did from the beginning of the 15th century, then the year 1415 marked the beginning of the early "modern period" of both of Europe and Africa. In 1415, the first European contact was established in the enclave of Ceuta in Morocco when the Portuguese became the first Europeans to come and fight and win the battle against Moroccans and establish a colonial presence in Africa. The period 1500–1750 CE has been accepted as the early modern period in Europe. The period from 1900 to the present also is regarded as the "modern period." It should be noted that in 1876, King Leopold II of Belgium created the first step in the "modern" partition of Africa as explained earlier in this study.

However, going by the guidance of European influence in Africa means considering that the first settlement of Europeans in the interior of Africa started much earlier than 1876, when European nations began to publicly declare their interest in colonization. In 1652, the Dutch established a colony in South Africa and thus became the earliest European promoters of "modern Africa history" in the European context. By 1800, Africa was well known to European, American, and Asian explorers (i.e., Marco Polo and others that came after him) as part of their voyages to coastal Asian trading centers.

Whatever the arguments over the problems of modernization and its impact on Africa and global economy and politics in which Africa is involved, the facts of this process of modernization relating to Africa can be summarized as: the modern world political system started with the Treaty of Westphalia of 1648, which marked the beginning of an important era of "European peace for Europe" and of the city-state system on which the modern state system of government was patterned.

AFRICA BETWEEN THE WORLD WARS

For Africa, the modern system of government was heavily influenced by European colonization. Nonetheless, it started when among Africans the thought of self-rule and freedom from alien rule began to emerge following the slave trade era and the struggles against slavery and the slave trade that was crowned with the abolition of slave trade in 1807–1808. It can hence be argued that modern Africa (i.e., the hunger and drive for African liberation) gained strength from Pan-Africanism's Back to Africa Movement of the 1800s in the United States among the freed African slaves, elites, intellectuals, thinkers, and writers.

Commissions were established to be used for commercial communications and common services and purposes for the people who lived along the European rivers. Among the services to be first established were those relating to posts and harbors, railways and, later, airlines. It was then that a number of international organizations were established, like the Universal Postal Union (UPU), the International Telecommunications Union (ITU), and others.

When the League of Nations was established after World War I, these international public organizations were absorbed into the League system and subsequently became organizations first of the League system. As a dependent continent, Africa and Africans could not participate fully in the newly created League of Nations. Such participation required sovereignty, and by then only three African countries claimed political independence (Ethiopia, Liberia, and South Africa). Of particular importance for Africa in the interwar period were the Pan-African congresses and meetings convened in the early 1900s. Momentum for independence grew through growing education among the Africans in the colonial period, increased opposition to imperialism and colonialism following the establishment of the League of Nations, and increased demands for international humanitarianism to aid the poor and neglected of the world. These pressures to grant political independence to the colonial territories and peoples grew international support. As Africans living abroad, especially in Europe and the United States, became persistent in the fight against colonialism, together with the support of African-American activists, intellectuals, writers, and liberation associations, the interwar period became an era of important preparation for Africa's decolonization. Most of the Africans who called for political independence of their continent later became Africa's founding fathers.

NOTES

1. D.C. Heath, *World History Perspectives on the Past* (Lexington, MA: D.C. Heath and Company, 1992), 620.

2. See "Fourteen Points," *Wikipedia: The Free Encyclopedia.* http://en.wikipedia.org/wiki/Fourteen_Points.

3. See W. E. B. Du Bois, *The Souls of Black Folk* (Cambridge University Press, 1907) p, vii.

CHAPTER 15

From Pan-Africanism to African Unity

CAUSES OF WORLD WAR II

A number of causes have been given for the start of World War II. These include the invasion of Poland by Germany on September 1, 1939 and the invasion of the Republic of China by the empire of Japan. These were the main, immediate reasons that sparked off the war. Germany and Japan and to provocative extent, Italy, adopted military aggressions and expansionist attitudes initiated by the authoritarian ruling elites led by Adolph Hitler in Germany, Benito Mussolini in Italy, and an empire-building spirit in Japan, which was determined to acquire control over China and the rest of Asia. These aggressive actions were met with an official declaration of war, or armed resistance, by the invaded territories, which had external support from allies (e.g., Great Britain allied with Poland). The long-term causes of World War II were many and varied and, unlike the causes of World War I, which had been basically European-oriented and evolving around the struggle for power within the European theater of dominance, the causes of World War II had global characteristics that included the following:

- Anti–communism—Following the October 1917 birth of communism in Russia that had been led by Lenin and his followers, many leaders in Western Europe feared that communism and Sovietism might spread all across the European continent and beyond, against their imperialistic and colonial aspirations and possessions.

- Expansionism (imperialism/colonialism)—As the doctrine of expanding the territorial base, or economic influence of a nation, expansionism, normally by means of military aggression, became most palatable in the interwar period following World War I. At the time of World War II, a number of influential European powers including Great Britain, France, and Russia (the Soviet Union since

1917) had through imperialism and colonialism acquired large foreign lands. Unfortunately, Germany and Italy had failed to do the same because they had been defeated in World War I and even before, following the historical events that had preceded the outbreak of World War I. Therefore, Germany and Italy felt "wronged" by recent developments that seemed to deny the past glories of Italy as a "grandson" of the Roman Empire, as Mussolini believed, and of Germany as the "grandson" of the Prussian empire, which had swallowed Poland and the surrounding territories. Consequently, Mussolini thought it essential to invade the former provinces of the Roman Empire around the Mediterranean. He invaded Albania in 1939, just as he had invaded Ethiopia in 1935. He was bitter that after fighting so hard in World War I, the 1919 Treaty of Versailles (ending World War I and promising gains for Italy from parts of Austria, Albania, and Asia Minor) were not honored. In like manner, Germany had lost land to Poland, France, Lithuania, and Denmark. Those German rights included the Polish Corridor in present day Gdansk in Poland; the Memel Territory, which went to Lithuania; the Province of Posen, which was given to France; and the Province of Alsace–Lorraine, which also was given to France. Similarly, the economic hub of Upper Silesia went to Poland, and the economically rich regions of Scarland and the Rhineland were put under the authority of France. Such territorial losses were too much for Germany, and for Hitler personally, since he had been a German soldier in World War I. To Hitler, the concept of greater Italy must include parts of western Poland, Czechoslovakia. Likewise, for Germany he would have envisioned the restoration of the German statehood of 1871, following the defeat of France in the Prussian War of 1870, and including the rights of Germany to the past alliances that produced friendships with Austro-Hungarian Europe before World War I. In the eyes of the Soviet Union, she must receive back the large parts of the Russian Empire that were ceded to Poland, Finland, Estonia, Latvia, Lithuania, and Romania in World War I. Hungary, an ally of Russia, must regain her former territorial lands. Thus, in Europe following World War I, there were a lot of discussions and demands for irredentism emanating from strong feelings of revolution as they talked about greater Germany, greater Poland, greater Hungary, greater Romania, greater Bulgaria, the greater Balkans, and greater Russia, including Siberia. All these needed to be addressed or war was inevitable.

- Fascism—As a philosophy of government marked by stringent social and economic control and a strong centralized government led by a dictator, Fascism emerged in Italy under Benito Mussolini and developed into a crazy and belligerent nationalism. Fascism spread in a number of European nations and was a strong ideology by World War II. As Mussolini had declared in his book, "Fascism does not, generally speaking believe in the possibility or utility of perpetual peace."[1]

- Isolationism—A dominant foreign policy of the United States as initiated under the Monroe Doctrine of 1823, and as advanced in Great Britain and France by their population following the unnecessary losses of World War I. Neville Chamberlain of Great Britain advocated it very strongly ". . . as a man of peace from the depth of my soul."[2]

- Militarism—This was a doctrine strongly advocated by the leaders of Germany, Japan, and Italy, who had been allies in World War I.

- Nationalism—This doctrine supports the concept that groups of people are bound together by territorial, cultural, and ethnic links. So nationalism, both in Europe and in Africa in subsequent years, was used by leaders to generate public support in Germany, in Italy where Mussolini wanted the Roman Empire practices restored, and in Japan where nationalism must entail a sense of duty and honor that had prevailed over the centuries under the above circumstances. A new world war had to happen for there was no way compromises could be found in Europe to accommodate all of the above detailed demands of the various unsatisfied nations in Europe and Asia. Numerous studies support this premise.[3–5]

IMPACTS OF WORLD WAR II ON AFRICAN LEADERS

When World War I broke out, most of the Africans who later became the "founding fathers of African unity" had been born, but they were still too young or too suppressed to initiate any actions to change things against the European imperialism and colonialism that had been imposed on Africa officially and legally since 1885. That was less than 40 years earlier.

However, by the end of World War I and World War II, most of these founding fathers were active in national and African politics. They remembered the dictates that led to these world wars; they understood the value and necessity of self-rule and political independence from capitalist exploitation and subjugation. They were participating in the Pan-Africanist congresses and meetings that had been initiated in the United States and called for the total liberation of Africa from the yokes of colonialism and imperialism.

For African leaders, therefore, the two world wars were but important milestones on the path to political independence. The wars were sources of inspiration for political determination and martyrdom for freedom, self-governance, and independence for their continent and fellow Africans who had to be led from the colonial and imperial domination of the alien Europeans and their injustices that they imposed on Africa and Africans. For the African spirit of freedom and independence to be better understood and appreciated, we must examine the origins, development, and maturation of the decolonization process.

Decolonization started among African Americans in the United States and the Caribbean, which, in the 1800s, propounded the ideology of Pan-Africanism, meaning "all-Africanism." They were scholars of African descent, ex-slave descendants who personally, and in the mobilization of black churches, preached against slavery and slave trade, as well as against colonialism, oppression, and exploitation.

These scholars included founding fathers and leaders of the Back to Africa Movement such as W.E.B DuBois, Marcus Garvey from Jamaica who moved to settle in Harlem, Wilmot Blyden, George Padmore, Aimé

Cesairé (1913–2008), and many others. These scholars conveyed the following message of Pan-Africanism and were great Pan-Africanists:

- Africans and people of African descent shared common interests, experience, and history.
- They should, therefore, unite in a common struggle for liberation wherever the black man lived.
- Pan-Africanism was the forerunner of an African unity organization intended to unite Africans and their nations in Africa, as well as the African Diaspora living outside of Africa, for mutual progress.

NEGRITUDE AS AN AFRICAN IDEOLOGY

Along with Pan-Africanism was the doctrine of Negritude. It was propounded by Aimé Cesairé of Martinique. Negritude as a philosophy was later advanced by Leopold Senghor, poet and president of Senegal. In essence, Negritude was French for blackness and was very similar to Pan-Africanism. They both carried the same message and basically supported the significance and pride of Africanness and the Back to Africa movement for freed slaves from the New World. The two doctrines also stressed the need to save Africa from European imperialism.

Thus, Pan-Africanism and Negritude promoted the African arts, especially against imitations of European styles, traditions, and values often imposed on Africa during colonial times. Colonialism had ignored, dispersed, and underrated African cultural values and expressions as "uncivilized" and primitive.

Both Pan-Africanism and Negritude as cultural tools comprise three constituent elements or requirements: Blackness/Africanness; liberation of the African from all bonds of subjugation and exploitation; and self-rule, self-ownership, and self-governance.[6]

AFRICA AND THE IDEOLOGY, IDEAS, IDEALS, AND SPIRIT OF PAN-AFRIANISM

Defining Ideology

An ideology is any system of ideas that acts to support or subvert accepted modes of thought and behavior. It is a system of ideas and ideals that manifests in different forms—political, economic, ecological, "Greek," etc. African ideology has its roots in Pan-Africanism. All ideologies have their historical contexts, changing in response to changing conditions and circumstances. Ideologies are born of crises and fed on conflict. Ideologies are authored or conceived by thinkers.

Ideologies comprise constituent elements of ideology, as in the following examples:

- Political events need to be explained for proper understanding and ideology does this job through the constructs of Marxism, communism, capitalism, socialism, conservatism, liberalism, etc.
- Economic and social doctrines rivaling private and public ownership of the means of production and distribution of goods and services.

Sources and Kinds of Ideology in Africa

From African heritage emerged forms of ideology that matured into systems supporting and promoting the African value system. For example, African Socialism is based on the principle of African values that supports decision-making by consensus, village parenthood, respect for age and wisdom, and extended family codes. From such thoughts and practices have emerged the African based ideologies of communalism. Colonial heritage is the totality of the remnants of colonialism and colonization, which not only seek to perpetuate the European/Western value system in Africa but also to retain the ability to exploit and impoverish, as well as to promote and impose European values in Africa. Thus, not only should the reasons be explained for colonization and expansionism of European cultures, civilization, and their global dominance, but also their long-term impacts on Africa.

The emergence of Europe from the Dark Ages and the impact of the Renaissance, starting from Venice in Italy and spreading to the rest of Europe, revived learning and innovative thinking, as well as intellectual curiosity that aimed at systematic and consistent globalization. The globalization of Europeanism led to the Europeanization of the world in a broad and dominant way, as reflected in the three Gs of glory, gold, and gospel and the three Cs of civilization, commerce, and Christianity. If one conceives of the European colonial ideology as having been based upon European Renaissance ideals, European expansionism for the three Gs, and European domination and imposition of its ideas and ideals on Africa and her people, then historical eras and issues emerge in European contacts and eventual presence in Africa, which can be highlighted as follows:

The first modern era of contact in Africa dates back to 1415 and lasted until 1798. In 1415, the Portuguese launched a war against Morocco and captured Morocco's enclave called Ceuta. From that date onward, a new era of European presence in Africa was launched. The legitimate trade that had existed between Africa and other races, notably the Phoenicians and Arabs, was supplanted by a new but more lucrative trade in humans—in captured African slaves. The years from 1415 to 1798 were a period of vast trade in natural and human goods as African slaves were regarded as objects for sale, exploitation, subjugation, and enslavement.

The years from 1798 to 1808 marked the age of exploration in African history. During this period, an aggressive and vigorous campaign was launched by European individuals and institutions that was supported by their governments. The point of this campaign was to find out what lay inside that "dark continent." This campaign was triggered particularly by the anti-slavery humanistic movements in Europe supported by humanists like William Wilberforce and his colleagues and co-activists. Wilberforce worked for the abolition of slavery and the slave trade. Abolition finally happened in effect on January 1, 1808—the legal abolition. But, in practice, the lucrative trade in captured Africans continued until the latter second part of the 19th century. This formal abolition of the slave trade was accompanied by heavy penalties against ships and individuals caught doing the business; those concerned Europeans abandoned the trade and turned to the study of African nature instead. That was why these years became known as the "age of exploration," curiosity, discovery, documentation, and reporting of the discovered topographical and geographical objects like rivers, mountains, lakes, and related natural order facts. The religious dimensions Christianity and Islam also led to many conversions of Africans at this time.

In 1804, a revolt occurred in Haiti by a French colony of African American slaves. This led to the Haitian revolution. Haiti thus became the first black nation in the Western hemisphere and in the world populated by the African Diaspora to gain political independence. For its recognition by its ex-colonial power, France, the newly independent nation of Haiti had to pay compensation equal to $21 billion in today's dollars to the French,[7] who argued that Haitian independence deprived them of profits from their slave ownership.

ABOLITION OF SLAVERY AND SLAVE TRADE

The movements against slavery and the slave trade emerged among humanists and, ironically, they started in Great Britain, which had been one of the greatest proponents of slavery and the slave trade. The British trade in slavery began in 1562 during the reign of Queen Elizabeth I. In that year, John Hawkins led the first slaving expedition. The alliance of what became known as "the saints," rose against the slave trade in the United Kingdom and was led by William Wilberforce, a British humanist and a member of Parliament. The "saints" became staunch anti-slave campaigners. The Slave Trade Act was passed by the British parliament on March 25, 1807. This act, while abolishing the slave trade in the British Empire, did not abolish slavery itself, which remained legal until the British Slavery Act of 1883.

It is noteworthy that in the United States the slave trade was abolished on March 2, 1807, when Thomas Jefferson, the third U.S. president (1801–1809) in that country's short history, signed a bill abolishing the slave trade effective on January 1, 1808. Slavery and the slave trade were thorny political, moral, and economic national policy issues. As a concept, slavery is an ideology born of a superiority complex and subjugation of the majority poor and under privileged by the minority rich, or even domineering, class.

THE PARADOX OF AFRICA'S IMPOVERISHMENT AS A PRECURSOR OF NEW FORMS OF IDEOLOGY

A paradox is a contradiction. In this context, this is more than a simple paradox. It is many paradoxes. From the paradox of Africa's "darkness" emerged the paradoxes of enslavement and the trans-Atlantic slave trade. Then followed the paradox of the administration of Africa's nature and the natural beauty by the Europeans who described the era in Africa following the abolished slave business as the "age of exploration" in Africa. Then came the colonial period following the Berlin Conference of 1884–1885.

This relatively short period of history produced at least five paradoxes in Africa. As follows, they are the:

1. Paradox of Africa's darkness where humankind not only started but enjoys the longest amount of daylight in the world;
2. Paradox of humiliation through enslavement and dehumanization;
3. Paradox of natural beauty where innocence and generosity make Africa the most burdened and wronged continent on Earth;
4. Paradox of poverty where vast resources, rich cultures, diverse civilizations, and fundamental human values are regarded as primitive and ignored, then destroyed and replaced by European (Western) values; and
5. This is also a paradox of impoverishment triggered by the various colonial policies and practices that were imposed on the African people.

From such paradoxes emerged new forms of fundamental issues and challenges already in colonial Africa. These include:

• Acculturation of Africa—another serious paradox confronting Africa as a transformed continent;
• Invasions of Africa by European ways of living and acting (behaving);
• European civilization, education, religion, money, and ways of thinking and acting in political, economic, social, religious, cultural, legal, environmental, and other ways—thus, racial stratification and dependency start out as good examples of the civilizational remnants of Europe's presence in Africa;

- The scramble for Africa in the late 19th century and the division of the continent into European (British, French, Portuguese, Italian, Spanish, German, Belgian, and Dutch) spheres of influence;
- Clashes of African and European alien cultures produce a loss of African identity (Negritude), corruption, tribalism and ethnocentrism, nepotism and majimboism (regionalism), parochialism as opposed to patriotism, etc.;
- Increase in African elites, some of whom were groomed by the colonial masters in order to advance colonial interested by training and using Africans to advance European colonial causes and policies;
- Growth of anti-alien sentiments in Africa as instigations of ideology in Africa, such as anti slavery, slave trade, imperialism, neo-colonialism, colonization, exploitation, and humiliation of the Africans;
- Creation and spread of African ideologies such as nationalism, pan-nationalism, African nationalism, and Pan-Africanism, from which emerged latter-day postcolonial ideologies (afro-pessimism, afro-socialism, afro-capitalism, afro-communism, and afro-liberalism) in Africa that had been prompted by the East-West ideological divide;
- Struggles for political freedom and independence, as well as for economic and social development (welfare) equity and equality were strongly backed by ideological beliefs of African leaders;
- East-West ideological confrontation in Africa's post-colonial period, which led to increased invasions of Africa by foreign ideologies, mainly of European origin; and
- Proliferation and growth of African ideologies in independent Africa that posed problems of governance and government as well as problems of ideology and its negative impacts on African development.

The following three ideologies have dominated the African ideological stage:

1. Nationalism,
2. African nationalism, and
3. Pan-Africanism.

Nationalism

Nationalism is the assertion of a group to constitute an autonomous community whether or not the group coincides with a recognized state.

African Nationalism

As opposed to tribalism, parochialism, and ethnocentrism, African nationalism calls for the creation of a nation (in Africa) within defined territorial borders and with a government run by indigenous Africans. Patriotism must replace ethnocentrism. African nationalism is thus the welding together of people speaking different languages and having different traditional cultures into one nation state. African nationalism stresses the primacy of a nation territory and state.

Pan-Africanism

This ideology was fostered by the Back to Africa Movement, which was propounded by African American and Caribbean scholars, especially, W.E.B. DuBois and Marcus Garvey, who preached against slavery, slave trade, colonialism, oppression, and exploitation of the people of Africa and those of African descent. These founding fathers of Pan-Africanism and African nationalism shared common interests, experience, and history. They should therefore unite, they believed, in a common struggle for liberation wherever the black man lived. Thus, in Pan-Africanism was born the unity of African nations in Africa, which was fought for, and won, by the founding fathers of the Organization of African Unity (OAU) in May 1963, and was preceded by a difficult period of decolonization. Decolonization intensified after the attainment of independence for the first time in sub-Saharan Africa by Ghana, with Kwame Nkrumah as the first president.

Thus, in the African context, ideology can be defined as system of ideas owing its roots in Pan-Africanism and Negritude, which aimed at setting African sentimentalism against every alien influence or domination in Africa.[8]

TWO PERIODS OF DECOLONIZATION

From the 1800s to 1945 and from 1945 to 1980, there were two distinct periods of decolonization. It should however be noted that Namibia, Eritrea, and South Africa gained political independence in 1990, 1993, and 1994 respectively.

An influence during the decolonization period from the 1800s to 1945 was the Back to Africa Movement. It should also be noted that the Back to Africa Movement in America actually started in 1776, following America's gaining her independence from the British. However, it was from 1816 that the movement gained greater momentum, following the abolition of the slave trade in 1808 and the increased encouragement of African Americans to settle in Africa. That was how Liberia was born and served as the impetus for the Pan-African meetings of 1900 and 1911.

KINDS OF INDEPENDENCE

There were the following three ways of gaining independence after colonization:

1. By fighting for it,
2. By surrender of the colonial power, and

3. By negotiation in cases of mandated and trust territories snatched from the vanquished of World War I and World War II.

In the case of the mandated territories taken from Germany and Italy (Tanganyika, Cameroon, Togo, Ruanda-Urundi, and South West Africa) after World War I, the League of Nations was authorized to administer over these parts of Africa. The trust territories after World War II were given to the UN to administer over, and negotiations led to the granting of independence.

AFRICAN NATIONALIST RESPONSE TO ALIEN RULE IN AFRICA

The factory where Pan-Africanism, African nationalism, African ideology, African foreign policy and diplomacy, and African international relations originated was the Diaspora. The Diaspora originated from the Greek word "diasporeia," meaning "dispersing of people," and referring first to the Jews who were taken to Babylonia as slaves. But in modern times, the African Diaspora consists of people of African descent wherever they may be: in Africa, the United States and the Americas, Europe (especially Western Europe), the Mediterranean, north of the Sahara, the Middle East, Arabia, and Asia.

As a unifier of people of African descent, the African Diaspora began to fight against racism and imperialism and colonial rule. All the Pan-African meetings were great sponsors of African unity and togetherness. But it was the Pan-African Congress of 1945 that marked the turning point in the fight against colonialism. That Congress, for the first time, enunciated a Pan-African deal and adopted two historic documents—the Declaration to the Colonial Peoples, demanding freedom for all colonized people from imperialist control and demanding to elect their own governments without restrictions, and the Declaration to the Colonial Powers, demanding a speedy end by force lest Africans would be required "to appeal to force as a last resort in the effort to achieve freedom." From those demands and the resolutions of the Accra Conference of 1958, it was clear that it was just a question of time before political independence would happen in Africa. So, the African leaders interpreted the African dreams as necessitating the establishment and consolidation of African unity in an organization that would serve as the pillar of African unity.

Of particular interest to Africa was the 1945 Conference in Berlin that discussed the issue of decolonization and administration of the former League of Nation's mandated territories and the future UN trust territories in Africa and elsewhere.

PAN-AFRICANISM AND THE NEW STATES OF AFRICA

The Africans were very unhappy with European colonial policies and practices, which they resisted and rejected everywhere throughout Africa.

They were unhappy because despite the losses and involvement in World War I and World War II and the more than 2 million Africans who fought and served in both wars, the Europeans were not grateful. All that African nationalism thus emerged as an ideology that had to be nurtured and used. The "panist" movements continued to be influential politically, and Negritude, Garveyism, anti-slavery and anti-colonial reaction to alien colonial rule mounted. Pan-Africanism thus took its roots from slave trade, colonialism, oppression, and exploitation. The founding fathers of Pan-Africanism were from the West Indies and North America. They and their ideologies made a big impact on African nationalists who organized mass nationalism embracing common interests of separation from, and rejection of, the colonies. Demands grew for political independence. The African Diaspora politics were revived after World War II. Independence movements emerged. UN Resolutions on self-rule also grew in number, beginning with the UN Resolution of December 1960 on the Granting of Independence to Colonial Peoples and Territories.

At independence, the Africans had a lot to digest: dependency and neo-colonialism, unity and cooperation for development, phonism created by the European colonization of Africa, development and gender inequality, membership of Africa in the global system, degradation of the environment, climate change and global warming, rational use of natural resources, and global public goods, etc. As a political bloc on the international scene, the African states had to recall the role that U.S. president Woodrow Wilson had played with his 14 Points for Peace after World War I. In his fifth point, the president addressed the importance of self-rule for political entities of the developing world. This point stressed that political independence should not be denied by anyone, irrespective of the size, status, or wealth that the country and its people may possess.

ORIGINS OF INSTITUTIONALIZED CONTINENTAL AFRICAN UNITY

After the Pan-African Congress of 1945, the process of decolonization of Africa accelerated. Strong winds started to blow in the opposite direction, and the granting of political independence to Ghana in 1957 marked the beginning of creating new nations en masse during the decolonization era. Subsequently, the following six periods in the decolonization process of Africa emerged *sensu largo:*

1. 1958–1963
2. 1963–1965
3. 1965–1975
4. 1975–1985

5. 1985–1990
6. 1991–1995

Sensu stricto, however, one can talk of three major periods of post-colonial African political events. The first period (1958–1963) fostered the development of the Pan-African doctrines on continental African unity (political).

The second period (1964–1990) was a time during which African political leadership underwent numerous trials and challenges. In 1964, the OAU doctrine of "uti possidetis juris" (i.e., borders fixed by law are inviolable) was pronounced and there was an emergence and flourishing of politico-economic ideologies of afro-liberalism. There were many impacts of the Cold War on Africa as ideology from the East-West ideological divide coming from Cold War politics affected African politics. These also were years in which one partyism (uni-partyism) and autocratic/dictatorial rule persisted in Africa.

The third period (1991–present) coincided with the collapse of the Soviet Bloc and of Cold War politics. The Cold War led to Cold Peace and its dictates, while in Africa multipartyism returned. There was a shift from OAU to African Union (AU) (1963–2002).

Thus, African continental unity had to be based on a marriage of convenience among three schools of thought, each of which preferred its own ways of retaining post-independence goals for Africa. So they chose to pursue the goals in three different approaches, as follows:

1. The Radical School of Thought, through which the Casablanca Group advocated total independence of Africa.
2. The Minimalist School of Thought, which was promulgated by the Brazzaville Group of former French colonies; and
3. The Moderate School of Thought, advocated by the Monrovia Group.

These groups met in separate venues between 1958 and 1963 when they agreed on the persuasion of Ethiopia to form the OAU when they signed the OAU charter on May 25, 1963.

Kwame Nkrumah convened the first conference of independent African states at Accra on April 15, 1958. This meeting was attended by African leaders, academics, writers, and political activists from Africa and North America, heads of state, and government representatives from Ghana, Ethiopia, Libya, Egypt, Sudan, Morocco, Tunisia, and Guinea. South Africa was not invited to the conference because of Apartheid policies and practices. At that time, the United Arab Republic was a federation of Egypt and Syria. Nonetheless, there were 10 independent countries in Africa by the time of the meeting of the African leaders in 1958.

The Accra Conference had a dual purpose:

1. Consolidation of African nationalism, pan-Africanism, liberty and political independence, freedom, and unity; and
2. Discussion by African leaders of the establishment of the kind of political organization that should be created in order to foster African unity.

It should be noted that nationalism is a strong force for measuring tensions and inflaming hatreds as well as augmenting the sovereign ideal of an independent (African) nation state. The Accra conference was thus a historically important conference on independent African soil representing the collective expression of the African people's disgust and hatred of the colonial and imperialistic systems of Europe.

The year 1960 is often referred to as the "Annus Mirabilis" because that year marked the beginning of the attainment of legal and political independence en masse in Africa. In fact, in that year alone, 16 former African colonies gained independence (Somalia and Nigeria, Niger, the Central African Republic [CAR], the Democratic Republic of the Congo [DRC], Congo Republic, Cameroon, Chad, Mauritania, Madagascar, Dahomey [Benin], Senegal, Upper Volta [Burkina Faso], Togo, Côte d'Ivoire, and Mali). These 16 African countries that had gained independence joined the original 10 (Ethiopia, Liberia, Egypt, Libya, Tunisia, Morocco, Sudan, Guinea, Ghana, and South Africa), bringing the number of independent African countries to a total of 26 in 1960, truly a miraculous feat in this miracle year.

DOCTRINES ON AFRICAN UNITY

Origins of Institutionalized Continental African Unity

1. Kwame Nkrumah was the first president of Ghana, and Ghana was the first African country to gain independence south of the Sahara. Educated at Lincoln College (now Lincoln University in Pennsylvania), Nkrumah was a bright and visionary leader who advocated a united states of Africa concept patterned on the U.S. system. He, with his close friends, Ahmed Sékou-Touré of Guinea and Modibo Geita of Mali, convened a conference of the independent states of Africa in Accra in April 1958 and urged the assembled leaders of Africa to seek their political kingdom. Participants were eight heads of state and government of Africa and other leaders, academicians, writers and political activists. The heads of state were from Ghana, Egypt, Guinea, Nigeria, Liberia, Libya, Morocco, Tunisia, and Sudan.

A big split happened on the attainment of the African unity goals at the conference from which three schools of thought emerged: the Casablanca Group, led by Kwame Nkrumah (1909–1972); the Monrovia Group led by William Tubman (1895–1971) of Liberia, Nigerian president Nnamdi Azikiwe (1904–1996), and Nigerian prime minister Tafewa Balewa (1912–1966); and the Brazzaville Group comprising Francophone member states.

These groups held separate meetings until persuaded to unite by Emperor Haille Sellassie of Ethiopia on the architecture and advice of Ethiopian foreign minister Ketema Yufru (1929–1994). The outcome of their deliberations in Addis Ababa, Ethiopia in 1963, was to consolidate by forming the OAU. The trends in the thinking of the African leaders were nonetheless revealed in their doctrines as enunciated by the three groups, which are highlighted next. The concept of African unity that eventually emerged was actually a compromise.[9–19]

Casablanca Group

Leaders were Kwame Nkrumah, Gamal Abdel Nasser, Ahmed Sékou-Touré, and Modibo Keita. Their doctrine was maximalist: "being a small fish in a big ocean." These were socialist-oriented states run by radicals. They boycotted all meetings of the Monrovia and Brazzaville Groups. They adopted an African charter creating a Pan-African advisory assembly and Pan-African political and cultural committees. They advocated total independence. African unity should be based upon renouncing sovereignty by individual states to the development and political benefit of a Pan-African intergovernmental political institution like in the United States.

The architects of the Casablanca Group included Ghana, Guinea, and Mali. These countries invited many African states and Asian states to attend. But only eight states attended: Ghana, Guinea, Tunisia, Ethiopia, Egypt, Liberia, Morocco, and Libya. Important dates include the following:

1. January 7, 1961: First meeting in Casablanca, Morocco. Egypt, Guinea, Mali, Tunisia, Libya, Algeria, and Ghana attened. Moderates of this group were Morocco and Libya.
2. January 7, 1961: Algiers, Algeria. They met there to decide on collective measures dealing with the Congo crisis that would lead to the assassination of P. E. Lumumba in February 1961.
3. June 1962: Second meeting in Cairo, Egypt, where the group adopted resolutions stressing anti-colonialism. They opposed the rather soft positions taken by African states in the other two groups.

The Casablanca Group also advocated revolution in Africa, and discussed questions of African unity and socioeconomic and cultural cooperation. In addition to adopting an African charter, they agreed to work for liberation of African territories, to get assistance to discourage the creation of foreign troops and bases in Africa, and to liberate Africa from economic pressure and political intervention. They took an extremist stand on African problems with the aim of attracting other African states to the Casablanca Group, which called for new progressive and revolutionary measures to attain political independence. They seriously discussed problems of Congo, Algeria, Mauritania, and Palestine. They determined that Africa's independence and security must be protected.

Note that the union of Ghana and Guinea occurred on December 23, 1958 and was modeled after United States. Mali joined the Union in 1960.

Endorsements included the following:

1. Radical approach as advanced by Nkrumah;
2. Africa must unite: Nkrumah said, "seek ye first the political kingdom; prosperity will follow";[20]
3. There must be political union of all independent African countries for Pan-Africanism to succeed in Africa and for African development and security to be possible; and
4. Patterned African independence on the U.S. model.

In addition to the group's host, King Hassan II of Morroco, who ruled from 1961 to 1999, Casablanca Group leaders, their independent countries, and years in power include the following:

- Ahmed Sékou-Touré, Guinea, 1958–1984;
- Ben Bella, Algeria, 1962–1965 (interim government);
- Colonel Gamal Abdel Nasser, Egypt, 1954–1970;
- Kwame Nkrumah, Ghana (the first country south of the Sahara to gain political independence), 1957–1966;
- Modibo Keita and Colonel Moussa Traore, Mali, 1960;
- King Mohamed V, Morocco, 1961;
- Julius Nyerere, Tanzania, 1961–1999; and
- Haile Selassie (Regent: 1916–1930; Emperor: 1930–1974) and his MFA, Ketema Yufru, Ethiopia.

Brazzaville Group

The Brazzaville Group included heads of state and governments of 12 states that had founded the African and Malagasy Union in 1960 at a meeting from December 15–18. They met at Brazzaville and adopted resolutions on North African cooperation for all French-speaking states of Africa that founded UAM (Union of Africa and Malagasy). At this meeting they also adopted a resolution convening a Pan-African conference at Yaounde in 1961.

Their second meeting held in 1961 at Yaounde took the stand that no binding rules were laid down at Brazzaville in 1960. The principle was that their foreign policy would firmly and directly aim toward the search for peace and that there would be concerted diplomacy to achieve this. They sought to avoid total dictatorship. In international conflicts their stated stand was as follows: not to take sides, but to mediate between the parties.

They did not propose any compromises, but invited the parties to a dialogue from which alone can come a solution that constitutes positive progress toward peace and international cooperation. They wanted to just consolidate national economic policies in standard diplomatic practices and maintain close association and collaboration with the former colonial power. They followed international norms for independence, and UN and international law. They found no need for continent-wide institutions.

These mainly Francophone nationalists and leaders initially were from 12 African countries (former French colonies, except Guinea and Mali). Leaders, their independent countries, and years in power include the following:

- Ahmadou Ahidjo, Cameroon, 1960–1982;
- Foulbert Youlou, Congo-Brazzavile, 1959–1963;
- Felix Houphouet–Boigny, Côte d'Ivoire, 1959–1993;
- Hubert Maga, Dahomey (Benin), 1960–1963;
- Leon M'ba, Gabon, 1961–1967;
- Maurice Yameogo, Upper Volta (Burkina Faso), 1960–1966;
- Philibert Didier Tsiranana, Madagascar, 1960–1972;
- Hamani Diori, Niger, 1960–1974;
- David Dacko, Central African Republic, 1960–1965;
- Leopold Seghor, Senegal, 1960–1981;
- François Ngarta (Tombalbaye), Chad, 1960–1975; and
- Moktar Ould Daddah, Mauritania, 1960–1978.

Monrovia Group

This group held their first meeting in May 1960 in Brazzaville and founded the Union of Africa and Malagasy (UAM).

For their second meeting they convened the first summit of the Monrovia Group on May 8-12, 1961 in Monrovia, on the initiative of the 12

Brazzaville Group states but not with the Casablanca Group, which boy-cotted that summit. This Pan-African conference (summit) of heads of state and government of Africa also was attended by Ethiopia, Liberia, Libya, Nigeria, Sierra Leone, Somalia, Togo, and Tunisia.

The group was comprised of mostly moderate pro-Western Francophone African states. They adopted five principles and resolutions rejecting the Casablanca approach and affirming sovereign inviolability of borders. Their third meeting was a summit at Monrovia. They made resolutions leading to OAU charter in May 1963 at Addis Ababa. The OAU was the product of a compromise between Africa statesmen, who wanted political union of all independent African states, and those who preferred functional cooperation as a building block toward the construction of an African socio-psychological community.

Leaders, their independent countries, and years in power include the following:

- Emperor Haile Selassie, Ethiopia, 1930–1974; Foreign Minister Ketema Yifru, Ethiopia;
- William Tubman, Liberia, 1944–1971;
- Sir Alhaji Abubakar; Tafawa Balewa, Prime Minister, Nigeria, 1960–1966;
- Sir Milton Margai, Prime Minister, Sierra Leone, 1963–1966;
- Aden Abdulla Osman, Somalia, 1960–1967;
- Sylvanus Olympio, Togo, 1960–1963, assassinated;
- Prime Minister Patrice Emery Lumumba, Congo: Leopoldville (DRC), June–September 1960, assassinated; Prime Minister Tshombe, 1960–1965, and President Kazavubu 1960–1965; and
- Habib Bourguiba, Tunisia, 1956–1987.

The Monrovia Group included the following:

- Twenty member states of the Conseil del 'Entente, a French West African organization established in 1959 in order to promote economic development;
- Three countries that achieved their independence in 1960 (Côte d'Ivoire, Niger, Upper Volta, and Dahomey [Benin], which achieved independence in 1959 but was endorsed in 1960); and
- Twelve states (Cameroon, Congo-Brazzaville, Côte d'Ivoire, Dahomey [Benin], Gabon, Upper Volta [Burkina Faso], Madagascar [Malagasy Republic], Niger, Central African Republic, Chad, Mauritania, and Senegal) that were members of the African and Malagasy Union (UAM).

Other countries of the Monrovia Group included Sudan under various leaders since 1956, including Prime Minister Lieutenant General Ibrahim Abboud, Majlem Muhammad Siad Barre, and General Jaafar Al Nemeiry.

The Monrovia Group's doctrine was "being a big fish in a small pool." They did not advocate being a united states of Africa but desired maximum cooperation of African countries in a loose state organization and no political union of Africa. They stressed sovereignty and social, financial, economic, and legislative cooperation similar to the East African Community (EAC) in East Africa. The Monrovia Group boycotted the Casablanca conferences and would not endorse the Casablanca formula for a political union of Africa that was fostered by Nkrumah and Nasser. They sought territorial integrity of African nations with a great degree of cooperation in a loose organization that acted like a "club" or association, but had no enforcement authority over African states. They also sought not to be too loose/extreme.

They upheld international norms stipulated under the UN charter. This proposed loose association of African states was stronger than that proposed by the Brazzaville Group. They promoted and guarded African independence and cooperation in all spheres—political, economic, legal, social, etc., sought to avoid total dictatorship, and aimed to harmonize, oversee, and enhance African policies.

OAU Charter Stipulations

The OAU charter was the product of a compromise between Africans who wanted a political union of all independent African states and those who wanted a loose union or association of sovereign states. The charter was based on natural law and the UN charter. It promoted the liberation of Africa, no neo-colonialism, and no neo-imperialism. African independence was to be characterized through no conflicts and no military or armed interventions to resolve disputes; nonaggression was a fundamental concept, as was the promotion and protection of human rights and the right to independence. The OAU charter envisioned an Africa that performed collective tackling and searching for solutions to African economic, social, and other problems, and aimed for self-sufficiency through capacity building, education, training, economic development, peace, security, and happiness. It promoted respect for sovereignty and the territorial integrity of member states as well as the member states' inalienable right to independence in their international conduct.

There were sovereign equality of the OAU member states and stipulations that OAU would not interfere in the internal affairs of member states and would not engage in subversive international activities against member states. The charter provided full condemnation of political assassination and upheld economic development, social welfare, human rights, education, and cultural values. It encouraged increased resistance to European and American intimidation, active participation in African affairs to shape the world of Africa, and defense of African national interests while promoting an increased partnership for political, economic, military, security, social, and other aspects of African development based on power theory, survival, and struggle for the good of Africa using millennium politics and millennium development goals (MDGs) of the UN.

Settling Differences Leads to the Birth of the OAU

The three groups reconciled thanks to the mediation of a young foreign minister from Ethiopia, Ketema Yifru, who convinced the respected Emperor Haile Selassie to convene an all-Africa summit at Addis Ababa to iron out the groups' differences and reach a compromise. All three groups agreed and met at the invitation of Emperor Selassie in May 1963. Yifru, a visionary young Ethiopian minister of foreign affairs, saw no willingness to compromise, especially from the Casablanca Group, but saw that the majority supported the Monrovia approaches, especially after the Monrovia Group and the Brazzaville Group merged. Via the persuasion of President Sékou-Touré, the Casablanca Group attended the Ethiopian summit.

The resulting summit in Addis Ababa produced an OAU charter adopted by all assembled on May 25, 1963, and the Monrovia approach prevailed thanks to Ethiopia's persuasion and the diplomatic skills of Minister Yufru. In OAU, Monrovia sought to create a continent-wide overseer and to enhance the policy harmonization of Africa states. The OAU endorsed Monrovia's vision of African international relations and became the first pan-intergovernmental organization (IGO) with a clear structure (chair, secretary general, secretariat) and charter principles based on national law and the UN charter. Founding principles were security, territorial integrity, sovereign equality, and nonaggression.

The visionary concept of Kwame Nkrumah was realized. He had made the following proposals:

- Formation of an OAU Executives Council as the executive arm of the African Assembly of Heads of Government,
- Selection of Executive Council's chairperson by the heads of state or government (this group would make policy recommendations and initiatives to OAU heads of state or government), and
- Creation of a general OAU secretariat.

The Monrovia conference held May 8–12, 1961 defined African unity as unity in aspirations and actions from the standpoint of social and political togetherness in Africa but not (just) political integration of the sovereign African states. Thus, African unity is equal to a community of ideas and aspirations that people are trying to externalize by concerted action. The Monrovia group prevailed, and the OAU was formed as an association for cooperative self-help, thanks in great part to the efforts of Ethiopia's young foreign minister, Ketema Yufru.

Thus, the OAU was formed to

1. Promote the unity and solidarity of the African states;
2. Coordinate and intensify the cooperation and efforts of African states to attain a better life for the African people;
3. Defend the sovereignty, territorial integrity, and independence of African states;
4. Eradicate all forms of colonialism from Africa; and
5. Promote cooperation with due regard to the 1945 UN charter and 1948 universal declaration of human rights.

The charter embodied all those principles of sovereignty and was signed by 31 states excluding South Africa. Thus, by May 25, 1963, when the OAU charter was signed, 32 states in Africa had gained independence. The 1964 OAU Summit re-endorsed borders and adopted a new OAU policy of uti possidetis juris. The 1965 OAU Summit adopted a Declaration on the Problem of Subversion, as follows:

• To condemn all forms of international subversion among members of the organization of African unity or any subversive activity from outside Africa,
• To refrain from conducting media campaigns against one another and from creating dissension across borders by fomenting or aggravating ethnic antagonism,
• To maintain regional peace order, and
• To advance the African ideology of anti-colonialism and anti-Apartheid.

In 1975, the Portuguese colonies gained their independence, and the process of anti-colonialism and anti-Apartheid intensified in South Africa, which had gained its independence in 1910. Although independent, South Africa did not attend the Addis Ababa conference because of the country's Apartheid policies and racial minority rule. African majority rule and the end of Apartheid came to South Africa in 1994 when Nelson Mandela became the first African majority president of the country. South Africa signed the OAU charter at this time.

The OAU has not been without controversy. The Sahrawi Arab Democratic Republic (SADR) was recognized by OAU in August 1982. Morocco, which claims this territory and calls it Western Sahara, objected to that recognition and walked out of the OAU. Morocco has not attended OAU/AU meetings since then, and continues to regard Western Sahara as part of Morocco even to the time of this writing (2010). Other challenges have included conflicts, wars, coups, corruption, civil strife, refugees and displaced persons, development challenges, education and leadership, global trade and business development partnerships, and Africa's paradoxes.

Long negotiations from 1999 to 2002 brought changes to OAU. In 2002, OAU became that African Union (AU) at a Durban, South Africa OAU/AU summit. Colonel Gadafi of Libya was the architect of the process. The AU has 54 member states and is the largest group of states in one region of the world.

AFRICAN UNION

On July 11, 2000, 49 heads of state and government of OAU adopted a constitutive Act of the AU, which replaced the OAU and its charter. The adoption of the AU Act was officially performed on September 9, 1999, but was formally transferred in 2002. It has repeatedly been argued and stated that most of the leaders in Africa after her political independence have failed the exams of democracy and leadership of the West in which Africa must fit in the present-day world.

Democracy and Leadership in Africa in the Post-Independence Era

Since the 1950s, via the granting of independence to Africa, the fight for political liberation of Africa from the colonial yoke was led by a number of Africans from within Africa and Africans from outside Africa. The African Diaspora in the Americas produced the Back to Africa Movement of the 1800s, which prompted the 1900s Pan-Africanism and African nationalism and lead to the Pan-Africanism movements of 1963. Soon after the world agreed upon political independence for Africa, the concept of African unity took hold in the formation of the following independent states by year of their independence:

- Period I, Until 1963

  - 1847: Liberia
  - 982 BCE (1930): Ethiopia (under Emperor Menelik I)
  - 1910 (1931, 1961): South Africa
  - 1922: Egypt
  - 1951: Libya
  - 1956: Sudan, Morocco, Tunisia
  - 1957: Ghana
  - 1958: Guinea
  - 1959: Dahomey (Benin), endorsed in 1960
  - 1960: Annus Mirabilis countries
  - 1960: French Cameroon joined by British Southern Cameroons (in 1961, renamed the Federal Republic of Cameroon)
  - 1961: Tanganyika, Sierra Leone
  - 1962: Algeria, Burundi, Rwanda, Uganda

Table 15.1
Post-Colonial Phonist System in Africa

Anglophone	Francophone	Lusophone	Spanish	Arabphone
Ethiopia	Algeria	Angola	None	Egypt
Ghana	Benin	Mozambique		Libya
Liberia	Burkina Faso	Guinea Bissau		Morocco
Nigeria	Burundi	São Tomé and Príncipe		Tunisia
Sierra Leone	Cameroon	Cape Verde		Western Sahara or the Sahrawi Arab Democratic Republic (SADR)
Somalia	Central African Republic			
Tanganyika	Chad			
United Republic of Tanzania (Union of Tanganyika and Zanzibar as of 26 April 26, 1964)				
Uganda	Congo, Brazzaville			
	Congo, Leopoldville			
	Côte d'Ivoire			
	Madagascar			
	Mali			
	Mauritania			
	Niger			
	Rwanda			
	Senegal			
	Togo			
	Guinea			

- Period II, 1963–1965

  - 1963: Kenya, Zanzibar
  - 1964: Malawi, Zambia
  - 1965: Gambia

- Period III, 1965–1975

  - 1966: Botswana, Lesotho
  - 1967: Gabon
  - 1968: Mauritius, Swaziland, Equatorial Guinea
  - 1972: United Cameroon Republic
  - 1974: Guinea-Bissau
  - 1975: Angola, Cape Verde, Mozambique, São Tomé and Príncipe

- Period IV, 1975–1985

  - 1976: Seychelles
  - 1977: Djibouti
  - 1980: Zimbabwe
  - 1982: Sahrawi Arab Democratic Republic (SADR) = Western Sahara

- Period V, 1985–1995

  - 1990: South West Africa (Namibia)
  - 1993: Eritrea is re-born from Ethiopia
  - 1994: South Africa

Independence Totals

As stated, by 1958, 10 African countries were independent, and two years later that number climbed to 26. By 1963, there were 32 independent countries in Africa.

ISSUES AND CHALLENGES IN AFRICAN LEADERSHIP

Conceptual Understanding
What is leadership?
Kinds of leadership include in-born, natural, learning/application. Leadership qualities include the following, for example:

- Nationalism/patriotism versus ethnocentrism/parochialism, genial versus hierarchical;
- Decisive/smart versus indecisive/hesitant/vague;

Table 15.2
Independent African Countries as of May 25, 1963 Signing of Charter of OAU

	Member States	Leaders
1.	Algeria	President Bella
2.	Benin	President Maga
3.	Burkina Faso (Upper Volta)	President Yameogo
4.	Burundi	President Ndumwe
5.	Cameroon	President Ahidjo
6.	Central Africa Republic	President Dacko
7.	Chad	President Tomalbaye
8.	Congo Leopoldville	President Kasavubu
9.	Congo Brazzaville	President Massamba-Debat
10.	Côte d'Ivoire	President Homphouet-Bolgny
11.	Egypt	President Nasser
12.	Ethiopia	Emperor Selassie
13.	Gabon	President M' Ba
14.	Ghana	President Nkuruma
15.	Liberia	President Tubman
16.	Libya	King Idris
17.	Madagascar	President Tsiranana
18.	Mali	President Kaita
19.	Mauritania	President Ould Daddah
20.	Morocco	King Hassan II
21.	Niger	President Diori
22.	Nigeria	President Azikiwe Premier Tafawa Balewa
23.	Rwanda	President Kayibanda
24.	Senegal	President Senghor
25.	Sierra Leone	Prime Minister Margai
26.	Somalia	President Osman
27.	Sudan	Prime Minister Lt. Gen. Abbona
28.	Tanzania	President Nyerere
29.	Togo	President Olympio
30.	Tunisia	President Bourguiba
31.	Uganda	President Obote

Note: South Africa did not sign the OAU charter.

- Docility/patience versus egoism/impatient: ability to listen and be a good learner;
- Wisdom/fairness/justice versus error, injustice;
- Decency/correctness/good behavior/character versus greed, corruption/ indecency/morality;

- Courage/boldness/determination *versus* fear/cowardice;
- Virtue/good example/diligence *versus* arrogance/deceitfulness/laziness cunning/exploiting;
- Good organization/properness/correctness *versus* disorganization;
- Vision/imagination/broad thinking/asking right questions *versus* disorder/narrow outlook/limited thinking;
- Constructive criticism/maturity of thought and understanding/tolerance/reasoning;
- Practical ideas/high motivation/intellectual capacity to think, create and conclude versus closed thinking/no innovation;
- Willingness to take responsibility/no procrastination/decision making;
- Delegation of responsibilities/trust in own and other's right judgment;
- Mental toughness/tenacity/discipline *versus* too lax/intimidation;
- Peer respect/character/personality *versus* dullness/inconsistency;
- Family respect for authority and rights *versus* disorderly behavior/dictatorship; and
- Justice/equality of treatment *versus* bias/unfairness/discrimination of treatment.

LEADERS OF POST-COLONIAL AFRICA

The first leaders of independent African countries often were African male politicians who became political leaders of their respective countries in the years leading to, and in, the beginning of their countries' political independence (first-generation leaders of Africa). From them came the first prime ministers and presidents.

The first-generation leaders of Africa became the first rulers of their respective independent countries either after formation of competing political parties in which they won in general elections or when they were supported by the outgoing colonial rulers who had pursued policies of "divide and rule" and prepared only a very small African elite to tow the lines of former colonial administrators. In this way, colonial heritage, colonial legacy, and colonial remnants were retained in the former colonies. The impact of these policies is still felt today, many years after political independence in Africa.

Later leaders were a mix of civilian, military, hereditary monarchies, and others. There was a marked increase in cultism and ethnocentrism, encouraged coups, and corruption, which have left a very negative mark on African leadership and promoted leadership deficiencies throughout post-colonial Africa.

Current leaders are still a mix of military, hereditary, and civilian, but there are fewer military coups. Instead, cultism and autocracy still haunt many political leaders in Africa. There has been a clear trend toward democratization and decisions by ballot instead of unchecked dictatorships of the ruling class. There also has been a clear trend toward generational changes from old to young rulers and a general trend toward less dogmatism in African politics. There are fewer ideological current leaders than the first-generation leaders, but tendencies to stay in power as long as possible (power perpetuation) are still strong in Africa.

LEADERSHIP AS A QUALITY OF GOVERNANCE IN AFRICA

The essence of leadership must be multidimensional development. Therefore, to lead is to govern, and to govern is to protect, defend, adapt, promote, and provide for the interests of the people, state, and government under the rule of law as exercised by those who govern. National interests include the people, assets, dignity, image, and prosperity of the nation. Anyone who does the above is a leader who promotes overall development. Therefore, to lead is the same as to provide guidance and assure accountability, transparency, and governance. Hence, to lead is to work for development.

In this context, good leadership means effective leadership. In Africa, leaders should go beyond the concept of democracy and embrace multidimensionalism in development of Africa. It must also be noted that African democracy is quite different from Western democracy. Therefore, African leaders should not be judged merely on the basis of votes (i.e., majority rule). After all, failure of African leaders is a failure of Western civilization because the African leaders are by-products of Western education and values. Therefore, failure of democracy and leadership in Africa is also, de facto, a failure of Western civilization in Africa. Cultism must be considered as a major influence on African leadership. African leaders are cultists (i.e., they have assumed godlike qualities of prestige, superiority, and unquestioned authority).

Political leaders in Africa since independence can be clustered into the following six groups:

1. Styles of rule (leadership and goals),
2. Generations of leaders,
3. The character and qualities of African leaders,
4. Kinds of ideology, and
5. Challenges to African leadership now and in the future.

Table 15.3
Capitals, Dates of Independence, Status, and Leaders of African Countries at Independence and Now (2009)

Country	Capital	Date of Independence	Status	Leaders/Dates of Rule
Algeria	Algiers	July 5, 1962	Republic	Pres. Ahmed Ben Bella: 1962–1965; Pres. Abdelaziz Bouteflika: 1999–
Angola	Luanda 1979	November 11, 1975	Republic	Pres. Antonio Agostino Neto: 1975–1979; Pres. Jose Eduardo Dos Santos: 1979–
Dahomey (renamed Benin in 1975)	Porto Novo	August 1, 1960	Republic	Pres. Coutoucou Hubert Maga: 1960–1963; Pres. Yayi Boni: 2006–
Botswana	Gabarone 1966–1980; 1998–	September 30, 1966	Republic	Pres. Sir Seretse Khaman: 1966–1980; Pres. Festus Mogae: 1998–2008; Pres. Lt. Gen Seretse Khama Ian Khama: 2008–
Upper Volta (renamed Burkina Faso in August 1984)	Ouagadougou	August 5, 1960	Republic	Pres. Maurice Yame'ogo: 1959–1966; Pres. Blaise Compaoré: 1987–
Burundi	Bujumbura	July 1, 1962	Republic	King Mwami Mwambutsa II: 1962–1963; Pres. Pierre Nkurunzinza: 2005–
Cameroon	Yaounde'	January 1, 1960	Republic	Pres. Ahmadou Ahidjo: 1960–1982; Pres. Paul Biya: 1982

Cape Verde (in federation with Guinea Bissau)	Praia	July 1975–January 1981	Republic	PM Pedro Pires: 1975–1981; Pres. Antonio Mascarenhas Monteiro: 1991–2001; Pres. Pedro Pires: 2001–
Central African Republic	Bangui	August 13, 1960	Republic	Pres. David Dacko: 1960–1965; Jean-Bedel Bokassa: 1966–1979; converted to Islam in October, 1976 and became known as Eddine Ahmed; gave himself several titles: Field Marshal and Head of State (1966); President for Life (March, 1972); Emperor Bokassa I (1976–1979); overthrown by Pres. David Dacko (September, 1979), Pres. Francois Bozizé Yangouvonda: 2003–
Chad	N' Djamena	August 11, 1960	Republic	PM Francois Ngarta, or Francois Tombalbaye: 1960–1962, President, 1962–1975 (assassinated); Pres. Lt. General Idriss Deby: 1991–

(Continued)

267

Table 15.3 (Continued)

Country	Capital	Date of Independence	Status	Leaders/Dates of Rule
Comoros	Moroni	July 6, 1975	Republic	Pres. Ahmed Abdallah Abderemane: July–August 1975; Pres. Ali Soilih Mtsashiwa: Jan. 1, 1976–October, 1977; Pres. Ahmed Abdallah Mohamed "Ayatollah" Sambi: 2006–
Congo Democratic Republic, former Congo Leopoldville	Kinshasa	June 30, 1960	Republic	PM Patrice Lumumba: June–September 1960, (assassinated); secessionist Moise Kapenda Tshombe Pres. of Katanga Province became PM of Congo Dem. Rep. in 1964–1965; Pres. Joseph Kasavubu: 1960–1965; Military Ruler Col. Joseph Desire' Mobutu: 1965–1997, became pres. (Sese Seko after January 10, 1972) and changed name of country to Zaire on October 27, 1971. Used until his overthrow on May 17, 1997 by Laurent D. Kabila; Pres. Laurent D. Kabila: 1997–2001 (assassinated); his son, Pres. Joseph Kabila: 2001–

Congo	Brazzaville	August 15, 1960	Republic	Fulbert Youlou: 1960–1963; Pres. Denis Sassou Ngueso: served four times as president: 1979–1992, 1997–2002
Côte d'Ivoire	Yamoussoukro	August 7, 1960	Republic	Félix Houphouët-Boigny: May 1959–December 1993; Laurent Gbagbo: 2000–2005; PM Charles Banny: 2005–2007; PM Guillaume Soro, 2007–
Djibouti	Djibouti	June 27, 1977	Republic	Pres. Hassan Gouled Aptidon: 1977–1999; Pres. Ismail Omar Guelleh: May 1999–
Egypt	Cairo	February 28, 1922	Kingdom Republic	King Farouk I: 1922–1952; Gamal Abdel Nasser: 1952–1970; Pres. Anwar el-Sadat: 1970–1981; Pres. Muhammad Mubarak 1981–
Equatorial Guinea	Molabo	October 12, 1968	Republic	Francisco Macias Nguema: October 1968–July 1972; Francisco Macias Nguema Biyogo: July 1972–September 1975; Teodoro Obiang: 1979– ; PM Ricardo Mangure: 2006–
Eritrea	Asmara	May 24, 1993	Republic[1]	Issaias Afwerki: May 1991, power sharing; June 8, 1993 elected president

(Continued)

Table 15.3 (Continued)

Country	Capital	Date of Independence	Status	Leaders/Dates of Rule
Ethiopia	Addis Ababa	982 BCE	Empire	Succession of emperors and empresses between 1000 and 982 BCE Empress (Queen) Sheba: ca. 960 BCE Menelik I, son of Queen Sheba and King Solomon of Israel: ca. 982 BCE Other emperors Emperor Haille Sellassie: 1930–1974 Haile Mengistu, military junta ruler
			Socialist state	Pres. Girma Wolde-Giorgis: 2001–
			Republic	PM Meles Zenawi Asres: 1985–
Gabon	Libreville	February 17, 1967	Republic	PM Gabriel Leon M'Ba: 1959–1961, pres., 1961–1967; Omar Bongo 1967–June 2009; PM Jean Eyeghe: 2006–; Ali Bongo Odinmba: June 2009–
Gambia	Banjul	February 18, 1965	Sovereign state	PM Sir Dawda Jawara: 1962–1970; Pres. 1970–1994
			Republic	Pres. Yahya Jammeh: 1996–

Ghana	Accra	March 6, 1957	Republic	PM Kwame Nkurumah: 1957–1960, Pres. 1960–1966; Pres. John Kufuor: 2001–2009; John Evans Atta-Mills: January 7, 2009–
Guinea	Conakry	October 2, 1958	Republic	Ahmed Sekou: 1958–1984; Lansana Conté: 1984–; PM Eugene Camara: 2007–; PM Lansana Kouyate: 2007–
Guinea-Bissau	Bissau	September 10, 1974	Republic	Pres. Luiz De Almeida Cabral: September 24, 1973–November 14, 1980 (assassinated); Pres. Joao Bernado Vieira: 2005–; PM Aristidies Gomes: 2005–2007; PM Marinho Ndafa: 2007–; Pres. Malam Bacai Sanha': September 8, 2009–
Kenya	Nairobi	December 12, 1963	Republic	PM Jomo Kenyatta: 1963–1964, 1964–1978; Pres. Daniel Moi 1978–2002; Mwai Kibaki: 2002–; PM Raila Odinga: April 8, 2008–
Lesotho	Maseru	October 4, 1966	Kingdom	King Motoltlehi: 1966–1970; Chief Lebua: (civilian coup) 1970–1986; King Letsie II: 1966–; PM Pakalitha Mosisii: 1998–

(Continued)

Table 15.3 (Continued)

Country	Capital	Date of Independence	Status	Leaders/Dates of Rule
Liberia	Monrovia	July 6, 1847	Republic	Pres. Joseph Jerkins Roberts: January 3, 1856 (served seven times as president, 7th time was from March 1, 1872–January 3, 1876) William Vacanarat Shadrack: 1944–1971; Pres. Ellen Sirleaf-Johnson: 2006– (first woman president in Africa)
Libya	Tripoli	December 24, 1951	Kingdom	King Idris: 1951–1959
			Socialist state	PM Col. Muammar Qaddafi: September 1969–1972, the Guide of the Revolution: 1972–[2]
			Socialist people's Libyan Arab Jahamiriya	
Madagascar	Antananarivo	June 26, 1960	Republic	Philibert Tsiranana: May 1, 1959–October 11, 1972; Pres. Marc Ravalomanan: 2002–2009; PM Jacques Sdylla: 2002–2007; PM Charles Rabemananjara: 2007–; Pres. Audry Rajoelina: March 2009–
Malawi	Lilongwe	July 6, 1964	Republic	PM Dr. Hastings K. Banda: 1966–1994; Dr. Bingu wa Mutharika: 2004–

Mali	Bamako	September 22, 1960	Republic	Modibo Keta: 1960–1968; Amadou Touré: 2002–; PM Ousmane Maiga: 2004–
Mauritania (Islamic Republic of Mauritania)	Nouakchott	November 28, 1960	Republic	Pres. Mokhtar Ould: 1961–1978; Pres. Ely Ould Mohamed Vaìl, military chair, 2005–2007; PM Sidi M.O. Boubacar: 2005–2007; PM Zeine Ould Zidane: 2007–; Pres. Sidi Ould Cheikh Abdalla: 2007–
Mauritius	Port Loius	March 12, 1968	Sovereign state Republic	PM Sir Seewoosagur Ramgoolam: 1968–1982; Pres. Anerood Jugnauth: 2003–; PM Navin Ramgoolam: 2005–;
Morocco	Rabat	March 2, 1956	Kingdom	King Mohammed V: 1961; King Hassan II: March 1961–July 1999; PM Driss Jettou: 2002–2007; PM Abbas El Fassi: 2007–
Mozambique	Maputo	June 25, 1975	Republic	Samora Moises Machel 1975–1986; Joaquim Chissano: 1986–2005; Armando Guebuza: 2005–; PM Luisa Diogo: 2004–
Namibia	Windhoek	March 21, 1990	Republic	Sam Nujoma: 1990–2005; Hifikepunye Pohomba: 2005–; PM Nahas Angula: 2005–

(Continued)

Table 15.3 (Continued)

Country	Capital	Date of Independence	Status	Leaders/Dates of Rule
Niger	Niamey	August 3, 1960	Republic	Haman Diori: 1960–1974; Pres. Mamadou Tanja: 1999–2010; PM Hama Amadou: 2001–07; PM Seyni Oumarou: 2007–
Nigeria	Abuja	October 10, 1960	Sovereign state	PM Alhaji Abubakar Tafawa Balewa: 1960–1966 (assassinated); Dr. Nnamdi Azikiwe: 1963–1966; first President Gen. Olesegun Obasanjo: 1999–2007; Umaru Yar' Adua: 2007–
Rwanda	Kigali	July 1, 1962	Republic	Dominique Mbonyumetwa: January 28–October 26, 1961; Gregoire Kayibanda: 1961–1973; Juvenal Habyarimana: 1973–1994 (plane crash/sabotage); Paul Kagame: 2000–; PM Bernard Makuza: 2000–

Sahrawi Arab Democratic Republic (SADR)	Recognized by OAU at the Nairobi OAU Summit of February 1982, but claimed by Morocco and not recognized by international community which together with Morocco, still regards it as Western Sahara; a former Spanish colony that has no capital since it is only a Non–Self Governing Territory. However, its largest city has been regarded as the capital of SADR since February 1982 when OAU at its summit in Nairobi recognized the SADR as an independent republic and admitted SADR to OAU. SADR Ayoun, El-Ayoun, and El-Aaiun are not, however,	Disputed: Republic	El-Ouali Mustapha Sayed: 1975–1976; Leader of Liberation (Ruling) Movement, National Father of the Nation, assassinated. Pres. Mohamed Abdelaziz: August 30, 1967–

(Continued)

Table 15.3 (Continued)

Country	Capital	Date of Independence	Status	Leaders/Dates of Rule
		recognized by Morocco, which walked out OAU summit of 1982 and has never since then attended any of AU/OAU meetings. Not recognized by the UN. Morocco continues to claim sovereignty over SADR or Western Sahara; still regarded as part of Morocco.		
Senegal	Dakar	August 20, 1960	Republic	Leopold Sedar Senghor: 1960–1981; Diof: 1981–2000; Abdoulaye Wade: 2000–; PM Marcky Sall: PM, 2004–2007; PM Cheikh Hadjibou Soumaré: 2007–
Seychelles	Victoria	June 29, 1976	Republic	James Mancham: 1976–1977; James Michel: 2004–
Sierra Leone	Freetown	April 27, 1961	Sovereign State Republic	PM Sir Milton Margai: 1961–1964; Ahmad Tejan Kabbah: 1909–2007; Ernest Bai Koroma: 2007–
Somalia	Mogadishu	July 1, 1960	Republic	Aden Abdulla Osman: 1960–1967; Said Barre: 1967–1991; Pres. Abdullahi

Country	Capital	Date	Government Type	Leaders
				Yusuf Ahmed: 2004–; PM Ali Mohammed Ghedi: 2004–
South Africa	Pretoria	May 31, 1910	Union Republic	PM Dr. Hendrik Verwoerd, 1958–1966 (assassinated); several Apartheid presidents: 1966–1994
		May 31, 1961	Apartheid Regime	Pres. Nelson Mandela: 1994–1999
			Republic, first African majority rule	Thambo Mbeki, 1999–
Sudan	Khartoum	January 1, 1956	Republic	PM Ismael al Azhari: 1956; PM Lt. Gen. Ibrahim Abboud: 1958–1964; Omar al-Bashir: 1989– ; Salva Kiir Mayard (succeeded Pres. of S. Sudan, Dr. Garang who died in a suspicious plane crash)
Swaziland	Mbabane	September 6, 1968	Kingdom\Monarchy	King Soubhuza II: 1922–1982; King Mswati II: 1986–; PM Themba Dlamini: 2003–

(Continued)

Table 15.3 (Continued)

Country	Capital	Date of Independence	Status	Leaders/Dates of Rule
Tanzania	Dar-es-Salaam	September 9, 1961 December 10, 1963 April 26, 1964	Sovereign State (Tanganyika) Republic of Zanzibar Union Republic	PM Dr. Mwalimu Julius Nyerere: 1961–1962; Pres. J.K. Nyerere: 1964–1985; VP K. Jumbé: 1963–1964; Mkapa: 1985–2005; Pres. Jakaya Kikwete: 2005–; PM Edward Lowossa: 2005–
Togo	Lome	April 27, 1960	Republic	Pres. Sylvanus Olympio: 1960–1963 (assassinated in military coup January 1963 by Sgt. later pres. Etienne Eyadema); Pres. Gen. Nicholas Gmnitzky: January 1963–January 1967; Pres. Faure Yowori Gnassingbe: 2005–; PM Agboyibo: 2005–
Tunisia	Tunis	March 20, 1956	Republic	PM Habib Bourguiba: 1956–1957; Pres: 1957–1987; Abidene Ben Ali: 1987–;PM Mohamed Ghannouchi: 1999–
Uganda	Kampala	October 9, 1962	Republic	PM Apollo M. Obote: 1962–1966, Pres: 1966–1971; General Marshal Idi Amin (coup on Jan. 25, 1971): 1971–1979; 1979–1986; Pres.

				Museveni: 1986–; PM Nsibambi: 1999–
Zambia	Lusaka	Republic	October 24, 1964	Kenneth Kaunda: 1964–1991; Mwanawasa: 2002–2008 (died of heart attack while in a Paris conference)
Zimbabwe	Harare	Republic	April 18, 1980	Pres. and Head of State Canaan Banana: 1980–1987; PM Robert Mugabe: 1980–1987, Pres: 1987–

[1] Eritrea is a small Republic, strategically located in the Horn of Africa on the southern side of the Red Sea. The country became an Italian colony on January 1, 1890, and a province of Italian East Africa in 1936 together with Ethiopia, and Italian Somaliland. During World War II, Ethiopian and British forces expelled Italians from Eritrea and Ethiopia, and in 1951, Eritrea was made a UN Trust Territory by Resolution 390 A of the United Nations. Eritrea's goal of becoming a separate state from Ethiopia was obtained in 1993, when Eritreans voted in a referendum to become an independent state.

[2] "Guide of the Revolution" is the title given to the ruler of Libya, Col. Muammar Qaddafi. In 1972, Qaddafi relinquished the title of Prime Minister and started to refer to himself as "The Guide of the First of September Great Revolution of the Socialist People's Libyan Arab Jamahiriya", or "Brotherly Leader and Guide of the Revolution."

Styles of African Leadership

Leadership styles and those Africans or African events best noted for their use are as follows:

- Traditional warrior style was borrowed from pre-colonial times and used, for example in the Mau Mau uprising in Kenya, as well as in guerrilla warfare in Angola, Cape Verde, and Algeria;
- Ujamaa leadership style of Julius K. Nyerere in Tanzania;
- Mobilization style of Patrice Lumumba in the Democratic Republic of Congo, Gamal Abdel Nasser in Egypt, Nyerere in Tanzania, to mobilize people to oppose subjugation;
- Charismatic style (used by Kenyatta of Kenya, Nasser of Egypt, Nyerere of Tanzania, Nkrumah of Ghana, Azikiwe of Nigeria, and Sir Alhaji Abubakar Tafawa Balewa prime minister of Nigeria) served to inspire the masses and others to support their goals;
- Housekeeping style in which government exists without leading verbosity, without leadership maintenance, without movement (not at presidential level but at other government levels) and was used in Kenya in 1980s;
- Disciplinarian style popularized by General Murtala Muhammad of Nigeria, who was assassinated, and by Muhammad Buhari of Nigeria;
- Patriarchal or kingly style used by Kenyatta of Kenya who was known as "mzee," meaning old man or elder; by Felix Houmphonet Borginy, Côte d'Ivoire's first president, who was in office from 1960 to 1993; and by Nelson Mandela, first majority president of South Africa, who was in jail from 1964 to 1990 for his opposition to Apartheid;
- Personalistic political style, similar to the monarchical style of Kamuza Banda of Malawi and General Jean-Bedel Bokassa of Central African Republic;
- Technocratic style used by Museveni of Uganda, Mbeki of South Africa, Kibaki of Kenya, all of whom were academics turned politicians;
- Liberation style of Sékou-Touré of Guinea, Samora Machel of Mozambique, Nkrumah of Ghana, and Mugabe of Zimbabwe;
- Reconciliation style of Olesegun Obasanjo of Nigeria; and
- Autocratic/dictatorial style of many African leaders, including General Abacha of Nigeria, Colonel Mobutu Sese Seko of the Democratic Republic of Congo, Field Marshall Idi Amin Dada of Uganda.

Generations of Leaders

There is no strict rule that "generations" of African leaders have to be over-lapping. Thus, the first generation of African leaders were Pan-Africanist civilians who had been heroes and champions of African freedom from colonial rule as triggered and promoted by distinguished African Americans (basically in the United States and the Caribbean), W.E.B. DuBois, Marcus Garvey, G. Padmore, Aimé Cesairé) who initiated the talk of freedom of the people of Africa and those of African descent from slavery and colonialism.

First generation African leaders include Kenyatta of Kenya, Azikiwe and Balewa of Nigeria, Nkrumah of Ghana, Sékou-Touré of Guinea, Leopold Sedar Senghor of Senegal, Julius Nyerere of Tanganyika, Ben Bella of Algeria, Habib Bourguba of Tunisia, Nasser of Egypt, Ahmadou Ahidjo of Cameroon, Lumbumba of Congo Leopoldville, Dr. Hastings Banda of Malawi, Kenneth Kaunda of Zambia, Boigny of Côte d'Ivoire, Macias Ngyema Biyogo of Equatorial Guinea, Sylvanus Olympio and Etienne Eyadema of Togo, David Dacko of Central Africa Republic, Sellassie of Ethiopia, Maurice Yameogo of Burkina Faso (Upper Volta), and Obote of Uganda.

You can call them "the old guard" of African independence or "the guns" of African independence, most of whom attended or signed the OAU charter in 1963. It helps to describe this parcel of African leadership as stretching from 1951 to 1977, the last year of colonization of Africa when Djibouti gained political independence from France. By December 1976, all the Portuguese African colonies had gained political independence.

Generally elected by popular vote, however most cases had been hand-picked by the colonial powers as statesmen acceptable to London or Paris, Brussels, Lisbon, or Rome.

The second generation of African leaders stretched from 1976 to 1990—in my classification—and included a mixed leadership of civilian and military rulers in Africa. These leaders were younger and less dogmatic than their predecessors, but held on to power like the "old guard." Some rulers date back to first decade of political independence in Africa: 1960–1970. The leaders included: Antonio Agostinho Neto of Angola, Emperor Jean Bedel Bokasa of Central African Republic, Idi Amin of Uganda, Hassan Gouled of Djibouti, Mobutu of Zaire-Congo, Democratic Republic, Luiz de Almeida Cabral of Guinea-Bissau, Dr. Mamel Pinto da Costa of São Tomé and Príncipe, James Mancham of Seychelles, Robert Mugabe of Zimbabwe, Samora Machel of Mozambique, Sam Nujoma of Namibia, and Daniel Arap Moi of Kenya.

The third generation of African leaders—again, in my classification— can be found in the period from 1991 to 2009 (present). They are a mix of civilian and military leaders. Thus, Yoweri Museveni of Uganda, Paul Kagame of Rwanda, Prime Minister Zelewi of Ethiopia, Kibaki of Kenya, and Mbeki of South Africa. Although they are heirs of the old guard generation, they are younger, less dogmatic, less nationalistic, and less ideological but also hold on to power like the earlier generations of leaders.

Characteristics and Qualities of African Leaders

In Africa, according to custom and tradition, a leader, whether chief tribal king, or another political leader, is a very important person in society. Generally, a leader will stay in office until death or assassination, silence all opposition or democratic voices against them, and avoid grooming successors to lessen the possibility of a coup. This results in a power vacuum into which unqualified leaders take charge with a power base but without popular support.

The third generation is concerned with shaping, reshaping, and generation of power and tends to select young persons as their ministers and implementers of policy. They tend not to pursue policies or experiments that would diminish their own power. Thus, leaders who have run Africa have done so with the primary objective of fulfilling self-interest with a few exceptions like Nyerere, Kenyatta, and Mandela. Cultism, psychology, and style of the ruler are highly most important.

African leaders and their lifestyles have a tremendous influence on their countries, foreign and domestic policies, and international relations. Thus, national interest and its defense depend on the perception of the political leader, but many leaders have tended to behave like demi-gods. What a country *is* often depends solely on who the president *is*. A foreign policy of an African country is basically the policy of the ruling leader and reflects the leader's character, lifestyle, cultism, etc. These leadership traits determine the destiny and foreign policy of that government. So among African leaders since independence there have been various types of personality character and leadership. These have ranged from true nationalists, statesmen, and intellectuals to military despots and murderers or autocrats. Corruption and nepotism is common among many of them, and sharing booties with the military and elites is a common ploy of leaders trying to stay in power for a long time.

Some African leaders have done very little to help end extreme poverty, having instead amassed wealth at home and abroad for themselves and their cronies and families. Here, external tolerance is also to blame. Others, although relatively few, have been genuine leaders of their nations and put loyalty to the nation first (e.g., Nkrumah of Ghana, Nyerere of Tanzania, Mandela of South Africa).

Ideology and Cultism in Africa

All rulers/presidents are cult figures, and most African leaders have been cultists. Cultism is promoted as an art: leaders have bestowed godlike qualities upon themselves and given themselves the unquestioned authority of the most powerful chieftain. Most are not leaders in the true sense. They are images—the creations of a sort of African-style public relations campaign.

There is value to the central authority appealing to the masses—if not exploitative, but enjoyable by the people, this is acceptable. Cultist African rulers include Mobutu of DRC, Kenyatta of Kenya, Nyerere of Tanzania, Félix Houphouët-Boigny of Côte d'Ivoire, Macias Nguema Biyongo of Equatorial Guinea, Daniel Moi of Kenya, Kenneth Kaunda, and Jean Bakassa of Central African Republic. Some of these leaders and their leadership ideologies/slogans are described as follows:

- Mobutu Sese Seko's "nkuku ngwebendu wa zabanga," which means, "the all-powerful warrior who, by his endurance and will to win, goes from contest to contest leaving footsteps in his wake";
- Nyerere, "Mwalimu," the teacher;
- Kenyatta, "Mzee," wiseman, proponent of Harambee, which means "let's all pull together";
- Dr. Banda, "the chief," "the chief of chiefs," "the chief of the village";
- Félix Houphouët-Boigny, "the peasant," "the No. 1 Farmer";
- Maccas Biyongo, "the National Miracle";
- Daniel Moi, "Nyayo" meaning "footsteps, following what has come before";
- Idi Amin Dada, no other person in Uganda can be addressed as president; and
- Kenneth Kaunda, "Mr. Humanism," the "Humanist."

These slogans, if progressive, are fine.

Challenges to African Leadership

Since 1991, there has been a new world order with only one super-power in the world and multipartyism in Africa. There have been increased voices for African democracy. Africa must have political systems that are in-bred and inborn, not imported from outside. The elementary democracy and leadership in Africa must be based on, and inherent in, the African character of socialism and capitalism.

Is this achievable? Yes. It was achieved by Mandela and Nyerere—both have shown that it can be done. African leaders must follow the ideologies that will benefit the African people. Cultism, godlike qualities, and the unquestionable authority of the most powerful chieftains are untenable and obstructive to African peace, security, stability, and development. So, African cultural values must be restored.

Students of African studies and future leaders should learn from the past lessons of African democracy and leadership and reshape the continent on a different, and more appropriate, path for the 21st century. In this regard, African leaders need to get rid of cultism in Africa.

Furthermore, it must continue to be accepted that things and events change, and Africa must change with them. Thus, female leadership must, and will, be accepted (e.g., Ellen Johnson-Sirleaf in Liberia and Wangari Maathai in Kenya). Africa's leaders need to tackle statehood issues for the common good of their nations and promote political dialogue, multidimensional development, national and regional economic development, and integration. They must protect national interests and avoid alien communism, capitalism, socialism, or populism that is un-African; instead stress African socialism. Africa's leaders need to put Pan-Africanism into nonalignment, nonalignism and eradicate all undue influences of colonial heritage/remnants/legacies. They must create trust in the people and strive to use diplomacy and peaceful means for resolving differences and disputes. Africa's leaders need to re-examine the AU doctrine of uti possidetis juris, and put it on the African agenda as a standing item. They must also concentrate on development and ownership of African initiatives by Africans.

AFRICA TRANSFORMED

Before 1885, Europeans went to Africa as explorers, scientists, geographers, business people, astronomers, missionaries, etc. Colonialism and imperialism were European colonial policies in Africa that were marked by ruthless exploitation, acculturation, humiliation, fragmentation, marginalization, and impoverishment with a total rejection of African civilizations. Colonialism and imperialism are concepts that describe the state of relations between Africa and Europe from their first period of contact to the end of World War II. Imperialism is the exercise of power by a state beyond its borders. The imperial power dominates the subjugated country in economic, political, cultural, and other aspects. In this sense, Africa's transformation by Europeanism has been complex, and it continues to haunt Africa to the present. Whether and how this transformation can or will be changed is a huge question. For Africa, hope, if any, can exist in hoping for change in the arenas of foreign policy, diplomacy, and international relations. How these managers of Africa's presence on the global stage will change the equation to reclaim Africa's identity and ownership of Africa at home and abroad remains to be seen.

In the periods between 1985 to 2009, Africa underwent major changes including the dismantling of the unitary system of government and the adoption of the multiparty system. This happened especially following the collapse of the communist socialist system of Russia and her East European neighbors. In this period also, Ethiopia spilt and Eritrea emerged as an independent state in 1993. In 1990, Namibia gained political independence whereas South Africa's Apartheid system collapsed in 1994 when the first majority rule in South Africa was installed with Nelson Mandela as the first South African president of a racial majority democratic South Africa.

NOTES

1. Benito Mussolini, *The Doctrine of Fascism* (Rome, Ardita, 1932).

2. Neville Chamberlain, *In Search of Peace* (Whitefish, MT, Kessinger, 2005) p. 393.

3. Andreas Hillgruber, trans. Anthony C. Kirby, *Germany and the Two World Wars* (Cambridge, MA, Harvard University Press, 1981).

4. Donald Cameron Watt, *How War Came: The Immediate Origin of the Second World War, 1938–1939* (New York, Pantheon, 1989).

5. Robert Young, *France and the Origins of the Second World War* (New York, St. Martin's Press, 1996).

6. Aimé Césaire, *Cahier d'un retour au pays natal* (Paris, Volontés, 1939).

7. For an interesting analysis, consult Anthony Phillips and Brian Concannon, Jr., "Economic Justice in Haiti Requires Debt Restitution," September 7, 2006, available at http://americas.irc-online.org/pdf/commentary/0609Haiti's Debt.pdf.

8. Randy Zormelo, "Pan-Africanism: The Forerunner of the OAU," *Sunday Nation*, Nairobi, May 15, 1988, p 6.

9. Randy Zormelo, "Pan-Africanism: The Forerunner of the OAU," *Sunday Nation*, Nairobi, May 15, 1988, p 6.
Godfrey P. Okoth, ed., *Africa at the Beginning of the 21st Century*, Nairobi University Press, 2000.
James Shikwati, ed., *Reclaiming Africa*, Inter Regional Economic Network IREN (Kenya), Nairobi, 2004.

10. Aloo Ojuka and William Ochieng, eds., *Politics and Leadership in Africa*, East African Literature Bureau, Kampala, Nairobi, Dar Es Salaam, 1975.

11. John Hatch, *Africa Today and Tomorrow: An Outline of Basic Facts and Major Problems*, Dennis Dobson Books, London, 1959.

12. Macharia Munene, J.D. Olewe Nyunya, and Korwa Adar, eds., *The United States and Africa: From Independence to the End of the Cold War*, East African Educational Publishers Ltd, Nairobi, 1995.

13. Kwadwo Konadu-Agyemang and Kwamina Panford, eds., *Africa's Development in the Twenty-First Century: Pertinent Socio-Economic and Development Issues*, Ashgate Puiblishing Company, Burlington, VT, 2006. See Part IV on Development Issues.

14. Fantu Cheru, *African Renaissance: Roadmaps to the Challenge of Globalization*, Zed Books, New York, 2002.

15. Arthur Gerstenfeld and Raphael J. Njoroge, *Africa: The Next Decade*, Business Books International, New Canaan, CT, 2005.

16. David S. Fick: *Entrepreneurship in Africa:A Study of Successes*, Quorum Books, Westport, CT, 2002.

17. *Les de Villiers: Africa 2009* (annual updates and editions), Corporate Council on Africa & Business Books International.

18. Godfrey P. Okoth, ed., *Africa at the Beginning of the 21st Century*, Nairobi University Press, 2000.

19. James Shikwati, ed., *Reclaiming Africa,* Inter Regional Economic Network IREN (Kenya), Nairobi, 2004.

20. Kwame Nkrumah, First Conference of Independent African States, Accra, Ghana, April, 15–22, 1958.

CHAPTER 16

African Development and Security in Theory and Reality

DEFINING "DEVELOPMENT" AND "SECURITY" IN AN AFRICAN CONTEXT

In whatever way Africa is discussed and analyzed in terms of development and security, it must be remembered that this continent hosts the largest number of the least developed countries in the world. Africa is the only continent that is poorer today than she was some 50 and even 25 years ago! This is a huge paradox—why and how could a continent like Africa that is endowed with such vast resources, both natural and human, be so poor? Why is South Africa considered a developing country in Africa when South Africa is in reality richer than Portugal and even Spain, both of which are defined as "developed countries" in Europe? What is development? What is security? These and related questions of definition present difficulties in determining the question of development as applied to Africa. This chapter makes an attempt to explain the meaning of development as the instrument through which human needs are satisfied and the quality of life and human well-being are improved. The following discussion will also analyze the complexities of Africa's paradox of poverty in plenty and present the measures that must be taken in concrete and practical terms for the attainment of genuine development and security in Africa.

Of particular importance will be a discussion of peace and the role of development as tools for opportunity and perfecting African foreign policy, diplomacy, and international relations as agents for the advancement of Africa's image, goals, and objectives. Also affected are the continental and national interests of Africa as a subsystem of the global system.

CONCEPTUAL UNDERSTANDING: DEVELOPMENT AND ITS PREVAILING PARADIGMS

The discussion of development and development paradigms as presented in this study refers to Africa, but it is applicable to any other developing region of the world. It is not easy to determine which of the conceptual expressions relating to development is most appropriate to Africa; where development theory ends and development practicum starts, why some among the poor countries of the world are described as "least developed," like many in Africa; how a developing country can be simultaneously described as "least developed," and what then does "least developed country" (LDC) mean if the country so developed is still developing? All these contradictions present challenges to Africa and the world as a whole. All must be clarified.

Nonetheless, this neither minimizes nor eradicates the fact that development is the overarching issue for the countries of the developing regions of Africa, Asia, Latin America, and the Caribbean.

African Development[1-3]

The concept of "development" is applicable to Africa as it is applicable to any other developing area. The term "developing" is used in this study to refer to the countries of Africa, Asia, Latin America, and the Caribbean. The expression "developed" states refers to the countries of Europe, North America, New Zealand, and Australia.

Development is a complex, multidimensional process encompassing more that the mere traditional measures of economic welfare as well as the material and financial sides of people's lives. In the African context, the process of development should embrace profound changes and possess the following characteristics:

- Improvements in national incomes, productive capacity, and in real national outputs, normally measured at national levels overall and per capita, GNP growth at annual rates of about 5 percent or more;
- Radical changes in institutional structures, as well as in mental, popular, and national attitudes and even behavior, quality and character, customs, thoughts, and beliefs;
- Reorientation and reorganization of entire economic and social systems;
- Acceleration of economic growth;
- Reduction of inequality in the nation;
- Eradication of absolute poverty; and
- Satisfaction, within an entire social system, of diverse basic needs and desires of individuals and social groups so as to assure or provide them with a situation or condition of a better life.

Thus, African development is about improving the quality of life of the African people and expanding their ability to improve their own futures. Progress in welfare is not, and cannot be, assured by GNP alone. Other values and qualities that add up to the African character must also be assured to Africans for their attainment of full development.

African Security

African security is likewise multidimensional in nature. It is more than the mere military or policy measures required to maintain law and order. It also needs to be durable for the good of Africa and the African people.

African security, like the sustainable security of any other region or people, has to be considered together with African development because both serve the same overall goals and purposes. As a process, development must go beyond mere ideology and theory to embrace concrete and practical "progress" and effective "performance" in real terms. The process of development must remove poverty, ignorance, and disease from the lives of the African people and replace these with peace, stability, happiness, and a better quality of life for the African people who require the satisfaction of basic human needs to live appropriately.

African security is actually the absence of wars, civil strife, conflicts, and instability, as well as protection against inequality or injustice, famine, armed conflicts, and calamities. African security further entails the following seven fundamental requirements, among others:

1. Intellectual soundness and independence,
2. Sound and adequate education,
3. Gender equality,
4. Security of ownership of land, trees, forests,
5. Incentives for long-term investment in the land,
6. Guarantee of legal rights and duties of individual farmers on reuse of land, trees, and water, and
7. Self-reliance in development.

Developmental Purposes of African Security

Four elements of security to assure sustainable development are particularly noteworthy. Security is essential in order to attain food, which requires environmental sustainability and sustainability science; mitigate material and organizational vulnerabilities in various social contexts, in groups, communities, states, and regions; build capacities and institutions for protection from enemies and obstacles; and ensure that economies thrive. Whereas development is a process, economics is a science.

The expression "economics" comes from an ancient Greek term meaning "the management of a household." Economics can be defined as the practical science of the production and distribution of wealth. Economist Adam Smith discussed economics in his book titled *An Enquiry into the Nature and Causes of the Wealth of Nations*.[4] In this book, Adam Smith generally advocates a free market economy as being more productive and more beneficial to society. Economics is thus a social science that is concerned with money, prices, the cost of living, savings, and employment. Economics is about "economizing in the midst of scarcity and hence the need to make choices" in dealing with ends and scarce means to meet those ends; humankind is concerned with acquisition and the use of income for human welfare. Therefore, the study of wealth and the study of humankind are for the welfare of mankind.

The topic of economics is quite relevant to this study because African development and growth are vital to African welfare. African foreign policy, diplomacy, and international relations cannot succeed unless they work for the promotion, projection, protection, and defense of African interests to strengthen Africa's economy and further the development of African countries. Economics also is an essential study area because economic development is the fundamental requirement for the durable development of Africa.

Criteria for African Development

In order to sustain African development, at least the following criteria have to be met:

- Sustained growth entails increases and improvements in income and outputs;
- Equality of distribution of wealth, property, power, reduction of inequality, and the like;
- Human dignity, which helps in efforts to gain self-reliance, security, and confidence, and to promote changes in mental attitude for "competence performance" and "uninjured pride" which are good human qualities;
- Autonomy and self-reliance are the sine qua non-requirement for ownership of one's development destiny, independent thinking, and action;
- Popular participation from the bottom up, which requires engagement and involvement of the people in the decision-making process on issues affecting their daily lives and also can be described as "vox populi, vox dei" (the voice of the people is the voice of God);

- Expansion of state capacity to ensure that the state works toward the development of the African people through government measures taken in order to end economic and development hardships imposed on Africans and to improve their living standards;
- Education, which is the passport to African development because without an efficient system of education, self-reliance is denied, and without self-sufficiency, competent performance and effective and just leadership, no durable development can be assured—education provides information and knowledge and these are power, and power is development if employed in the right way;
- Multidimensionalism is essential to sustainable development; and
- Bilateralism and multilateralism promote sustainable development if applied in equitable and just economic and other relations embracing partnerships for development, investment, technical, material, and financial collaboration, promotion of tourism and exchange programs for research and development studies (attracting students as well as bilateral and multilateral negotiations for trade and business, foreign aid, disarmament for development, disaster management for development, capacity-building, and the like).

Requirements and Determinants of Durable Development

Several factors determining sustainable development in Africa feature quite prominently among others because they can, if applied competently and persistently, improve the well-being and quality of human life in Africa. Of great importance is the people's level of education because more equitable education translates into job opportunities. Rational, non-exploitative, and enjoyable use of Africa's natural resources also breed happiness and wealth at national and continental African levels. Security in many forms—security of thinking, acting, in basic needs like water, food, and general freedom from anxieties, conflicts, wars, ignorance, debt, and other "enemies" of development—is a critical element of sustainable development, as are the peace and stability guaranteed by security. Sustainable development takes all of the population—not just select segments—and that means that greater equality empowering women, girls, youth, the handicapped, and other members of the most vulnerable strata of African society is needed. There is a need for increased per capita income at the lowest levels of African society so that basic needs can be met. Sick or malnourished people cannot be productive members of society, so the state of people's health, improved health, and good nutrition are essential elements in building a strong workforce and ensuring prosperity. A cleaner, more sustainable natural environment also promotes good health. A richer cultural life, cultural development, and diversity promote pride and happiness, which reinforce well-being. The existence, promotion, and maintenance of vibrant communities, a spirit of enterprise, engagement, participation, and involvement in sustainable development efforts and initiatives will make the goal of sustainable development attainable. Broad civil and political freedoms that embrace a vibrant urbanism, with basic amenities such as health care, education, infrastructure, and efficient social services, as well as an impartial juridical legal system also are key elements in sustainable development.

DEVELOPMENT PARADIGMS AND THEIR APPLICATION TO THE THEORY AND PRACTICE OF DEVELOPMENT IN AFRICA

Described in simple terms, a paradigm is something that serves as a pattern or model. A development paradigm is thus a development concept that advances analytical arguments on how best to overcome the many challenges in the area of development, as well as conceptualization of the ways and means of addressing development issues and problems that go deep to the core values of Africa (or any continent) as a study area.

For the purpose of this study, development paradigms applicable to Africa can be clustered into two categories. The first refers to development paradigms dating back to early post–World War II, which ushered in a pattern of development that had to address the needs of the developing areas of Africa, Asia, Latin America, and the Caribbean. These Third World nations and peoples had been colonized by European countries since the late 19th century, and the period 1945–1990 marked numerous development efforts by the world community. These efforts, in particular, followed the creation of the United Nations in 1945. Between 1945 and 1960 many African and other Third World nations gained political independence and joined the UN. A condition of their UN membership was the demand of these newly independent nations that their development be prominently on the UN agenda.

Therefore, in terms of "contemporary" development paradigms, the period 1945–1990 marked a new era, referred to in this study as the "old development paradigm." It is "old" because it was the first development model pushed by the newly independent countries that sought not only practical independence but other forms of independence, competence, and self-sufficiency.

As a new subsystem of the international system, Africa paid particular attention to new ideas that were being introduced on the world stage to address economic development and other aspects of development that would come to be referred to as "sustainable development." Thus the "old" concepts of development comprised an "old" development paradigm that lasted until about 1990. The year 1990 was an important year in geopolitics since just a year earlier, in November 1989, the old system of Russian sovietism, as imposed predominately on Russia and her neighboring countries of Eastern Europe, collapsed. A new world order emerged with one superpower—the United States dominating political, economic, and other affairs.

The East-West ideological divide collapsed and thus economic and development ideologies prevailing since 1947 based on global capitalism and global communism inevitably had likewise to collapse. From 1991 to the present, a new kind of development paradigms was born—especially following the convening of the UN Conference on Environment and Development (UNCED) in 1992. Thus, since 1945, two development paradigms have been applied globally and to Africa. In this author's view, the "old" development stretched from 1945 to 1990 and the "new" development paradigm starting sensu stricto from 1992 to the present. The salient features of each of the two are examined in the following sections.

AFRICA AND THE "OLD" DEVELOPMENT PARADIGMS

The new world order was instituted following the collapse of the Soviet Union in 1989, which forced the old developments to start collapsing in the 1990s, when new ideas and development concepts started to be applied to Africa, among other developing areas of the world. New strategies, tactics, and adjustments led to the formulation of new development models to replace the old models. But which were the "old" development models that needed to be developed? Which models had failed?

As established in previous chapters, a brief historical analysis of the pre-1990 development models reveals that in pre-colonial times Africa had had vibrant economic, social, and political systems in which trade and business flourished. Even in ancient times, especially following the "permanent" settlements of the African people in the post-Saharan appearance period, this is a noted fact. Nomadism was replaced by agricultural production and productivity in accordance with the African value system. Then came the second colonization of Africa by Europe in the 19th century—a period of massive impoverishment of Africans by Europeans. The colonial and imperialistic transformation of Africa included the lavish trade in Africans in which people were reduced to mere objects with neither economic nor development identity or rights. The economic business and development relations introduced in colonial Africa created a boss–subject cum servant relationship in which all of Africa's goods and services, wealth and economy, had to (and did) benefit, not Africa and her people, but Europe and Europeans. Under such a socioeconomic, business, and development scenario in Africa, talk of a development paradigm for Africa was unthinkable. However, with the rise of an African nationalist response to the economic, political, and other domination of Africa by alien values, independence movements started in the 1800s for Africa culminated in the eventual political liberation of Africa and demands for economic justice and equity.

The year 1945 was important for Africa because so many historically significant events happened in that year. First the Pan-African Congress held in Manchester, England, adopted an agenda for Africa's self-determination in a multidimensional fashion that marked a landmark about-turn for

African self-rule and development. Then came other events helpful to Africa, which included the 1945 establishment of the UN, to which a good number of Third World countries were admitted, including four from Africa (Ethiopia, Liberia, South Africa, and Egypt). Thereafter, political independence and development became overarching songs and demands for Africa. As a process, development would henceforth undergo many interpretations and phases of definition. Between 1945 and 1958, 10 African countries gained independence and joined the UN.

In 1960, the Annus Mirabilis in Africa, many African countries became politically independent. In 1960, the UN General Assembly adopted Resolution 1514 on the Granting of Independence to Colonial Counties and Peoples. The years between 1960 and 1970 brought the granting of political independence to former colonial territories of Africa and the other developing regions of Asia, Latin America, and the Caribbean. The topic of development gained greater prominence at the UN since the developing nations needed development more than anything else that the UN could potentially provide.

A system of international development strategies (IDS) was introduced through which 10-year UN development decades started to be adopted. That system has prevailed until today. Thus, since the first UN development decade was launched in 1962 (1962–1970), subsequent UN development decades (UNDDS) were launched. At the time of this writing, the 5th development decade is underway.

During the 1970s and 1980s, following the 1973 global energy and economic crisis triggered by the Organization of the Petroleum Exporting Countries (OPEC) energy cartel, Africa was one of the hardest hit continents by those crises prior to 1973 expressions of partnership for development, human development, and international cooperation for development. The slogan, "development and international economic cooperation" (DIEC), was coined at the UN. At this time, the UN made efforts to start a new international economic order (NIEO) to return the economic and social sectors to the UN system. Little progress was made by the advent of the 1980s. This was known as the "lost decade" because despite the launching of global negotiations within the UN system starting from 1979, and the ongoing General Agreement on Tariffs and Trade (GATT) mutual trade negotiations, not much was achieved.

The old development paradigms failed because of a number of reasons, which included the following, among many others:

- Political obstacles: There was as extended lack of political will to follow up and implement the decisions made in the global forum. There were too many conditionalities and no enforcement mechanisms because the UN is not a government power. Voluntarism has paralyzed the UN in the absence of political commitment by member states.

- Economic obstacles: As the global economy worsened, African countries experienced their worst poverty in history. This poverty syndrome continues today and dates back to the early 1970s. A series of domestic conflicts, civil wars, and coups, also aggravated African poverty. At global levels, the developed countries adopted conditionalities of neo-colonialism, structural adjustment strategies (SAPs), protectionism, capitalism exploitation, and other negative measures. There were problems with a lack of UN Official Development Assistance (ODA) flows to the south and reverse resource flows from the south to the north. Combinations of natural and human disasters, debt and debt servicing burdens, refugees and displaced persons who fled civil wars, conflicts, and natural disaster, took their effects on the African populations, and combined with ever-deteriorating international aid flows and a lack of bottom-up development initiatives. With the advent of modernization, urbanism and urbanization spread throughout Africa, bringing with it a lack of social and equality mobilization. Failures of agricultural economics in Africa led to famine, hunger, and poverty growth. A lack of social and political empowerment and capacity-building was accompanied by population explosions that led to crises in human habitats and many other economic hardships and difficulties.

- Moral obstacles: There was a considerable, and aggravating, lack of moral and ethical imperatives essential for social equity and development.

- Scientific and technological impediments: The colonial education system in Africa failed to introduce scientific and technological capabilities in Africa. This is catastrophic because science and technology are the engines of durable development.

- Social impediments: In the first three decades of Africa's political independence, social problems of health, poverty, poor education, inequality, and social discrimination against women and other members of the most vulnerable strata of society greatly suppressed African efforts for development. Genuine economic development is not possible without social development and equity for justice, as well as the attainment of a sound environment and its protection.

THE "NEW" DEVELOPMENT PARADIGMS

From the foregoing analysis it is evident that the old concepts of development prior to 1990 were not implemented adequately. Unfortunately, the development challenges of Africa are much more grave today than they were 20 years ago partly because of new and emerging developing challenges such as HIV/AIDS and other pandemics, refugees and displaced persons, globalization and globalism, urbanism and urbanization, high maternal and child mortality, and other development challenges analyzed in the UN millennium development goals (MDG) agenda, known as Agenda 21. These are coupled with the challenges of modernization, economic and agricultural reforms, infrastructural development (ICTs including the Internet and other elements of the

Information Revolution). Only a few of the elements of the Agenda 21 platform have been successful. All of these, and other evils of the new development paradigm, will continue to haunt Africa for a long time.

The expression "new development paradigm" is a pluralitantum expression, because development involves multiple criteria in nature and, as an equation, development takes many forms. This is thus the totality of contemporary paradigms which, if compartmentalized, can be grouped into 14 clusters closely related to one another. These paradigms, some of which we have touched upon already, are as follows:

1. Sustainability;
2. Sustainable development;
3. Environmental sustainability;
4. Sustainability science;
5. Globalization;
6. Global public good (GPG) versus global public bad (GPB);
7. New and emerging issues in development agenda;
8. Bilateralism in international negotiations;
9. Multilateralism in global negotiations;
10. Millennium development goals (MDGs);
11. Disaster and development preparedness, prevention, reduction, mitigation, and management;
12. Criteria for least developed countries' (LDCs) and the highly indebted poor countries' (HIPCs) categorization for development; and
13. Multilateral global negotiations, the UN conference system known as the GATT/WTO system.

SUSTAINABILITY

The term "sustainability" was coined and used for the first time in a 1712 book, titled *Sylvicultura Oceanomica* by Hans Carl von Carlowitz, a German mining scientist, forester, and tax collector. In his book, Carlowitz described the issues and problems of sustainability (in German, this is "Nachhaltgkeit"). This concept was later adopted by French and English scientists with reference to the planting of trees, and they used the expression "sustained yield forestry" in the 1970s following the adoption of a platform on the human environment at the UN conference held at Stockholm in 1972. Environmental issues that became serious in the 1970s gained attention in view of the disequilibrium that existed with the basic ecological support system.

In modern times, sustainability aims at attaining continuity of economic, cultural, social, institutional, and human society, as well as the non-human environment. This concept of sustainability also entails the following four other elements:

1. Being an instrument or means of configuring civilization and human activity to society and its members;
2. Instituting national economies aiming at meeting the needs of human beings in their communities and expressing their greatest potential in the present while preserving biodiversity and natural ecosystems and planning and acting for the ability to maintain these ideas for a very long time;
3. Affecting every level of organization from local neighborhoods to the entire planet; and
4. Endeavoring to provide the best outcomes for the human and national environments both now and into the indefinite future.

Types of Sustainability

Sustainable development involves the concept of continuity or the ability to maintain balance in process, functions, development, biodiversity, productivity, and the like. This is applicable to many situations and areas of development. These areas include sustainability in human welfare and development, growth development, equity and social development, environment, urbanism, economics, education, empowerment, energy for development, science, agriculture, ownership, involvement (popular), investment, initiative, indicators development, information, incentives, innovations, inspirations, inputs, invention, industrialization, and tourism. The following types of sustainability are needed for development:

- Institutional sustainability: enhanced institutional structures to deliver technical cooperation;
- Economic and financial sustainability: technical cooperation results in economic benefits;
- Ecological sustainability: benefits generated by technical cooperation lead to protection of the physical environment, production, well-being of groups and society;
- Sustainable development: continuation of benefits after major aid from the donor; and
- Brain trust sustainability: knowledge base to prevent collapse of the project.

Factors Influencing Sustainable Development

Several factors are important in sustainable development. Participation and ownership mean having stakeholders to genuinely participate in design and implementation and build on their initiatives and demands. Capacity-building and training of stakeholders to take over from the start of any project and continue throughout require that people be motivated and that a transfer of skills occur. How well aligned development projects are with local government policies can have a great degree of influence on the potential success of the project. Training in local fundraising, identifying and linking with the private sector, and encouraging policy reforms can increase chances of financial success. Management and organization should integrate activities with local structures. New ideas, technologies, and skills with gender division and cultural preferences should be mindful of social, gender, and cultural aspects. Technology should be able to adapt in order to be culturally acceptable. The poor should be involved in the management of the environment and urban committees that manage waste disposal and pollution risks.

KEY SUSTAINABILITY SECTORS

It is evident that agriculture is the mainstay of Africa's economy. Nonetheless, commercial production and the sale of goods manufacturing (meaning industrialization and industries) are vital for Africa's continued development as well. Africa's broad economic and development sectors are the public, private, and informal sectors. The development that appears in all of them in Africa, whether relating to the environment, technology, labor, education, child welfare, or mental attitudes, can become beneficial to the African people for a long time only if this process is durable in its efforts to improve the living conditions of the African people. As determined above, this is possible only if other improvements happen in the other areas of the African condition (i.e., in the areas of competent leadership, education, and a sound natural resource base—which is essential for meeting our basic needs without compromising the ability of the future generations to met their own needs).

In addition to the need for agriculture and industry, development also depends on tourism, energy, water and sanitation, infrastructure, the economy and trade, education and competent leadership, as well as the other priorities for African development such as peace, security, stability, and democracy (democratization), poverty reduction, debt relief and cancellation, trade/business and market access, mitigation of HIV/AIDS and other pandemics, capacity-building, good governance and observance of human rights, and resource mobilization by African governments from domestic and external forces. This implies the need for resource nationalism in Africa, cultural protection, and development ODA flows for African development as well as the information and telecommunication technologies (ICTs) required for sustainable African development.

INTERACTION OF CONSTITUENT ELEMENTS OF SUSTAINABLE DEVELOPMENT

Sustainable development is a process consisting of economic developments and economic growth as well as protection and preservation of the environment. These are the essential elements of sustainable development. Their interactions are sine qua non conditions for genuine sustainable development. In real terms, growth and development in African economies are closely related, but each has its own area of emphasis. Whereas in growth there is an increase in productive capacity, in development there is an increase in real incomes and outputs.

Economic development of Africa is a process in which an economy of an African country experiences an increase in real incomes and outputs per capita, and undergoes major structural changes—notably infrastructure developments and a reallocation of resources to the agricultural, industrial, and service sectors. This process of economic development in Africa will succeed only if appropriate and practical actions are taken at the following three stages:

1. At the agricultural stage, when most of the populations of African countries have jobs in farming;
2. At the manufacturing stage, when most of the African population has jobs in industry; and
3. At the service sector stage, when African workers move from the agricultural and industrial stages into the service sector and have jobs in the food sector, Internet (telecommunications networking) repair, telephone and transport services, etc.

The results of economic *development* of an African country include eradication of poverty, provision of employment for African populations, and the attainment of equity to eradicate inequality within society. Economic *growth* of Africa, on the other hand, is the production of more and better goods and services for a higher standard of living in the African country concerned. In this regard, the country's productive capacity is increased in real national income as measured in gross national product (GNP) per capita. The rise or increase in national incomes is sustained and can be identified over a period of years or over time. For economic growth to happen in Africa, there at least must be growth of the total amount of common and preferred stock available, labor force, and labor sector.

In addition to these three constituent elements, technological progress has to occur since technical skills are essential for boosting economic growth.

Ecological/Environmental Sustainability

Technical skills and cooperation are essential for the protection and conservation of the environment in Africa. Empowerment of Africa to attain this goal requires the capacity to prevent degradation and destruction of the environment in Africa through the process of environmental or ecological sustainability. This is the ability of African and other countries to rationally and competently use their natural resources and to protect the environment in a sustained fashion indefinitely.

As a process, environmental sustainability has been in operation for many years. In modern times, however, this concept dates back to the post–World War II period, when the utopian view of technology-driven economic growth was replaced by a new perception that linked the quality of the environment to economic development. Thus, a sustainable environment as a development paradigm gained popularity during the environmental movement of the 1960s, which raised considerable awareness on the need to use the environment rationally and protect it from degradation.

A Stockholm conference on the human environment addressed this issue seriously, and in 1973 in the Club of Rome, a group of European economists and scientists, was created to address these environment-related issues. Then, in 1974, commissioned by the Club of Rome, Donnella Meadows, Dennis Meadows, and Jorgen Randers published *The Limits of Growth*, predicting dire consequences if Earth's resources continued to be exploited and utilized by nations and people around the globe.[5]

This book adopted as a credible solution to the problem the abandonment of economic development. In subsequent years, other authors raised even more frightening alarms that rapid population growth in Africa and elsewhere in the world was using up Earth's resources. There was a rallying cry that something concrete must be done to prevent major catastrophe form happening over the issue of environmental degradation.

Those concerns forced the creation of the United Nations Environment Programme (UNEP) in 1973, which currently operates form Nairobi, Kenya, and is the only seat or headquarters of a UN body in the Third World. The discussions on the environment continued into the 1980s, culminating in the establishment of the Brandt Commission, which produced the so-called *Brandt Report* that defined sustainable development as "the ability to meet the needs of the present generation without compromising the ability of future generations to meet their own needs."[6]

That definition of sustainable development was coined in the context of the environment and development. Thus "without compromising" actually means "without jeopardizing." In particular, environmental sustainability calls for meeting human needs while preserving biodiversity and natural ecosystems and planning and acting to maintain these ideals persistently.

The environment is thus one of the fundamental determinants of African foreign policy, diplomacy, and international relations. It requires efficient and responsible use of all of the human societies resources—natural, human, and economic—rationally and productively for the benefit of humankind.[7]

Sustainable (Sustainability) Science

Sustainability science is a new development paradigm. Sustainability science means a new area of knowledge and concerns for the human condition. Although discussed in a few academic circles in Europe at the close of the 20th century, this development paradigm is actually a new 21st century academic discipline whose birth statement was made at the World Congress on Challenges of a Changing Earth. Organized in Amsterdam by the International Council for Science (ICSU) the Geosphere-Biosphere Programme (GBP), the International Human Dimensions Programme on Global Environmental Change (HDP), and the World Climate Research Programme (WCRP), this new discipline (paradigm) assembles scholarship and practice, global and local perspectives from the north and south, and disciplines across the natural sciences, social sciences, engineering, and medicine. Sustainability science thus is derived from concepts in environmental science.

As a discipline, sustainability science is the cultivation, integration, and application of knowledge about earth systems gained especially from holistic and historical sciences (e.g., geology, ecology, climatology, and oceanography). The discipline concerns knowledge about human inter-relationships gained from the social sciences and humanities in order to evaluate, mitigate, and minimize the consequences regionally and globally of human impacts on planetary systems and on societies across the globe into the future (knowing the Earth using science and technology in interaction with the social sciences and ecosystems for sustainable development).

Although sustainability science is a new discipline, its precepts are not new. For example, the Iroquois's seventh-generation philosophy believed that chiefs must always consider the effects of their actions on their descendants through the seventh generation into the future. As a development paradigm, sustainability science advances the following prerequisites:

- Knowledge and know-how are sought to help feed, nurture, house, educate, and employ the world's growing human population while preserving the world's basic life support systems and biodiversity.
- Concerted efforts are made to bridge and integrate the natural, social, and engineering sciences with environmental and development communities'

multiple sectors of human activity, geographic, and temporal scales. This is achieved with a view to using the knowledge acquired form such integration and activities for protection of the environment and promotion of human development.

- Enhanced sustainability of positive human and natural interactions is promoted for obtaining benefits to humankind and parts of the environment.
- The unity of nature and societal systems is addressed with a view to expanding on human nature interactions that can be mobilized further and shaped for better development and benefits via the application of knowledge and know-how.

Thus, in short, science and technology should be harnessed to support sustainability, and efforts must be made to advance scientific knowledge and know-how for the benefit of sustainable development for humankind. This development paradigm of sustainability science presents the following four fundamental conditions:

1. Meeting the needs of society must not lead to depletion or degradation or even undermining of Earth's essential life-support systems (water, land, air, atmosphere, natural resources).
2. Population growth and the environment must be planned for human benefit, but they must be prevented from destroying the environment, our global ecosystem.
3. Interaction between human society and the environment must not endanger the life-support systems of Earth.
4. The natural, social, and other sciences should participate actively in the search for, and means of, enabling human society to prosper without depleting the environment.

How about Africa and Sustainability Science?

Africa cannot, and does not, benefit a lot from sustainability science because she already suffers greatly from environmental degradation and its consequences. Since the 1960s, Africa has experienced severe droughts and desertification, diseases, floods, famine, food insecurity, water shortages, malnutrition, etc. (e.g., in the Sahel region) and has no capacity to deal with these difficult and complex issues. Unless human and institutional capacity is enhanced in Africa to enable her to conquer some of these problems (e.g., to use existing technologies to improve efficiency and produce clean, new, renewable energies for African development), actions must be taken to provide Africa with the necessities and measures for water resources, reduction/prevention/management of natural disasters, adaptation to climate change, adequate and competent tackling of biodiversity problems confronting Africa and concerted efforts to reduce and prevent negative impacts of natural disasters on Africa. The required actions must be taken at global, regional, sub-regional, and national levels from within and from outside of Africa.

NOTES

1. C. Young, *Ideology and Development in Africa* (New Haven, CT: Yale University Press, 1982).

2. Walter Rodney, *How Europe Underdeveloped Africa* (Washington, DC, Howard University Press, 1982), 3–29, 31–71, 149–211, 283–288.

3. Paul and Jan Willen Gunning, "Why Has Africa Grown Slowly?" *Journal of Economic Perspectives 13* (Summer 1999): 3.

4. Adam Smith, *An Enquiry into the Nature and Causes of the Wealth of Nations* (Oxford Paperbacks, 1776).

5. Donella H. Meadows, Dennis L. Meadows, and Jorgen Randers, *The Limits of Growth* (The Chelsea Green Publishing Company & Earthscan, 1972).

6. UN General Assembly Resolution 42/187, *Brundt Report* (United Nations, 1987).

7. UN General Assembly Report A/42/427, *Report of the World Commission on Environment and Development* (United Nations, 1987).

CHAPTER 17

Understanding the Determinants of African Foreign Policy: Case Studies on Some African States and Their Modes of Foreign Policy

INTRODUCTION[1-6]

This chapter briefly examines the major determinants of the foreign policies of South Africa, Cape Verde, Egypt, Gabon, Nigeria, Kenya and the Democratic Republic of Congo.

As described in Volume I, African "foreign policy" is a pluralitantum expression meaning "foreign policies" of the African states that, in effect, are the domestic polices of these states elevated to the international scene for the purpose of promoting, protecting, projecting, and defending the national interests and image of the African states. The diversity in the nature, ideology, and function, as well as the level of development and development situation of each of the African countries, need to be borne in mind when analyzing the foreign policies of the African states.

In the case of South Africa, Egypt, Gabon, Nigeria, Kenya, Cape Verde, and the Democratic Republic of the Congo (DRC), their foreign policies have both diverse and similar characteristics that are highlighted in this chapter. In this chapter, these countries are compared, contrasted, and examined in the context of the diplomatic practices of these nations and of their relationships with other sovereign countries. A comparative analysis of the foreign policies, diplomacy, and international relations of these nations is made in the areas of their colonization, decolonization, system of government leadership, foreign policy-making and execution, membership in international organizations, national interests, and the issues of foreign policy implications facing them in the new millennium. The end of this chapter will describe the similarities and divergences that are noteworthy in the foreign policies of these seven African countries.

PURPOSES OF AFRICAN FOREIGN POLICY

For the African states, including the seven states mentioned in this chapter, the following goals and objectives are fundamental in their foreign policies:

- To protect, promote, project, and defend the image and national interests of the country, and to propose ways and means of improving the country's relations endogenously in Africa and exogenously on the global scene;
- To contribute to knowledge and to the causes of humankind as advanced and protected by international law and as announced, promulgated, and practiced by international and universal norms and principles of international law and the charters of the UN and AU;
- To participate in, and contribute to, international and global debates and negotiations as advanced in global, international, and African international relations and diplomacy for the advancement of peaceful coexistence and cooperation for development, disarmament, and social welfare for the benefit of humankind and of the populations of the concerned African states;
- To aim at attaining national, international, and global peace and security through the protection of the global environment and containment of the effects of climate change and global warming; and
- To promote cooperation for the eradication of poverty, disease (including pandemics like HIV/AIDS), and ignorance (illiteracy).

CONCEPTUAL DEFINITIONS

Thucydides (ca. 460–395 BCE) has proposed that identity of interest is the surest of bonds, whether between states or individuals. This identity of interest is a very important goal for foreign policy protection. It is the central factor in African foreign policy in which African states deal with other states. National interest is the sense of survival of a state in its competition and external relations. Each nation must protect its physical, political, and cultural identity against encroachments by other nations. It is the tool identifying the goals and objectives of foreign policy and is an all-embracing concept of political discourse. National interest is the absolute standard for political action by every nation.

On the essence of foreign policy and diplomacy, policies can be defined as plans or specific courses of action calculated (i.e., national purpose). Policies are calculated to achieve broadly conceived and defined goals.

Hence, foreign policies are political concepts of national interest. They are the means of a nation's effort to promote and maintain its interests vis-à-vis other nations. They are the overall course of action a country proposes to follow in its foreign relations, backed by supporting programs.

"Power theory" is one of the international relations theories that is applicable to Africa. The other international relations theories applicable to Africa include the natural law theory, the state-building theory, and others as explained in Chapter 18 of this book.

National security is a complex and sensitive issue that, like foreign policy, embraces a broad spectrum of aspects of a country's overall policy, including its political, diplomatic, economic, and military aspects. However, other factors frequently come into play, and these include ideological, moral, cultural, and psychological factors of a nation's general policy. All of these forces are normally grouped together under one political umbrella.

Although foreign policy begins where domestic policy ends, there is no distinct borderline between them because foreign policy is part and parcel of domestic policy. Both exist in the same compartments and are related fruits of the same leadership. Also, foreign and domestic policies originate in the same basic, national purposes.

As an element in the foreign policies of Egypt, Gabon, Cape Verde, Kenya, Nigeria, South Africa, and the DRC, the power theory requires these African countries to be engaged in a systematic and constructive fashion in the international politics and relations of this group of seven African countries.

Similarities

Similarities of these seven nations include the following characteristics:

- A similar colonial past, even though under different colonial policies and practices;
- Attainment of political independence by fighting for it;
- Foreign policy, education, economic, and political systems that are based on those of their former colonial powers;
- The maintenance of special relationships with their former colonial masters;
- Membership in the UN and its system of regional, political, and socioeconomic groupings; and
- Similar determinants of their foreign policies in most respects, and many similar features to the processes and procedures of foreign policy in these countries.

These, as we have seen, include the essence of African policy and diplomacy, question of African national interest and ideology, goals and systematic objectives, and African goals and diplomatic strategies in the UN system. Also included are the causes, consequences, and cures of conflicts, civil strife, coups, and corruption in Africa, as well as the determinants of foreign policy, such as political, security, economy, historic, social (e.g., African socialism), and value systems (heritage).

Shared African challenges, whether common to Africa or particular to certain countries include the following for the countries studied in this chapter:

- Colonial legacy: colonial remnants;
- Subalternism, or weakness: juridical statehood;
- The doctrines of uti possidetis juris; and
- Secessionism, confederacy, communism, governance issues, the environment and ownership of Africa's development process by the African countries.

DIVERGENCES

The divergences in the foreign policies of the African countries under study include the following, among others:

- Colonial immunity: South Africa and Egypt, like Ethiopia, Liberia, Libya, and Morocco, enjoyed colonial immunity in the sense that they were not subjected to the colonial process initiated at the Berlin Conference of 1884 to 1885 on the partition of Africa. Thus, even though these six African states suffered from the colonial yoke of the late 19th century, their colonization was one of a suis generis type. In effect, it has been argued that Ethiopia and Liberia were the only African countries that were not colonized by Europe. That conclusion is inaccurate. Even though their colonization was relatively short, these two countries were once colonies of the United States (Liberia) and Italy (Ethiopia).

- Colonial legacy: Since 1652, South Africa was a victim of Lutheran and Calvinist influence and dogma that permeated South Africa for centuries until 1994. That dogmatic conservatism produced a system of "separate development" better known as Apartheid, which not only enforced racial stratification in the country but regarded Africans as sub-humans unworthy of equal treatment with the white race. Obviously, colonization also introduced racial stratification and, for some time, Africans were regarded as objects to be sold into slavery and were believed to be without souls! Even the Roman Catholic Church beginning in the 15th century adopted this bestial, hypocritical, and shameful stand while preaching brotherhood, equality of humanity, and salvation.

- Colonial policy: Belgium's colonial policy ignored basic human rights principles and exerted maximum cruelty, mistreatment, and denial of basic education upon the people of the Congo.

- Politico-cultural belonging: Egypt belongs to African and Arab-Middle-Eastern cultures, but in terms of political belonging, Egypt has ties to AU, the

Arab League, and to their regional organizations. Kenya became a big melting pot for English, Swahili, Arab, and African cultures. Nigeria's melting-pot situation was even more extreme because it was a huge colonial assembly of different nations placed in one pot called Nigeria.

- Ethnic "Fusion": All seven African nations underwent difficult ethnic fusions and amalgamations. Many nations with different cultures, civilizations, customs, and traditions were put together under the Berlin Act when the resulting geographical expressions were drawn on the African map with complete disregard of indigenous ethnic orientations and values. Ethnic fusion is one of the grave remnants of colonial domination of Africa by Europeans.

- Ethnic "Fission": This resulted from the separations of people—ethnic groupings and their cultures and civilizations, who, in reality, belonged to one nation. Somalia is a good case in point. This has resulted in the doctrine of irredentism that Somalia has constantly sought to secure and has claimed parts of Kenya (northeastern) and Ethiopia (southern). These colonial remnants continue to pose serious foreign and domestic policy challenges for the interactions of these countries with other political entities around the globe.

Each of the seven African states had to adopt the Western value system of the former colonial power: for Nigeria and Kenya, it was the British value system; for Gabon, it was the French value system; for DRC, it was the Belgian value system; and for Egypt it was the British and Arab value systems.

SOUTH AFRICA'S FOREIGN POLICY

The essence of the foreign policy of South Africa is to promote South Africa's national interests. New foreign policy of South Africa prompted by the popular April 1994 elections and presidential inauguration of May 10, 1994 ushered in a new foreign policy that replaced the long, unpopular Apartheid policy. The end of Apartheid and the East-West ideological divide transformed South African foreign policy in a novel way, since the new government no longer had to worry about embargoes, isolation, and sanctions launched by the international community as a reaction to Apartheid policies.

As the economic superpower of Africa, South Africa is expected to play leadership roles at the national, sub-regional, African continental, and global levels in the areas of international peace, security, environment, and development. In particular, the North-South and South-South relationships require South Africa to take leadership roles in global negotiations and in the various kinds of development paradigms that will dominate international discussions of the new millennium.

To shake off the shackles of Apartheid, there is an imperative need for the new foreign policy formulation and implementation machinery to revamp and restructure those branches of the South African government that are responsible for the country's foreign policy matters. Thus, beginning with foreign affairs, reforms would be essential in the departments/ministries of home affairs, defense, finance and national planning, law and order, and others. Academic and other private sectors of the nation should contribute ideas to enable South Africa to lead in world affairs as Africa's superpower. South Africa's national ideal, "there shall be peace and friendship" should be at the core of foreign policymaking and execution in South Africa as a nonaligned developing African state that respects the principles of international law and the UN charter. South African policies focuses on respecting human dignity, human rights, and the goals of democracy, as well as national and international peace, security, and economic rights and duties of South Africans and other peoples of the world.

The new foreign policy of South Africa stresses at least seven principles:

- Full observance, recognition, respect and promotion of human rights, goals and ideals;
- A belief in democracy and democratization in all forms of government;
- All relations between and among nations should be guided by international law and justices;
- Differences and disputes between and among all nations should be resolved through negotiation and agreement, but not through the use of force;
- The foreign policy of South Africa should defend and promote Africa's interests;
- South Africa's economic development should help promote regional integration and international economic co-operation;
- South African international relations should help advance and cement democracy at national levels and global economic interdependence.

The other issues in South Africa's foreign policy include the UN ideals, collaboration on issues of global economic development, environment, climate change, global negotiations and global warming, and the Montreal Protocol on the Depletion of the Ozone Layer.

South Africa now maintains diplomatic relations with the Middle East, Asia/Oceania, Western Europe, Central and Eastern Europe, North America, Latin America and the Caribbean. International economic relations aim at participating actively in the international trading system and include relations with the UN, multilateralism, South-South cooperation, the Antarctic region, refugees, security, and disarmament. South Africa maintains membership in the British Commonwealth, Non-Alignment Movement, "The Group of 77," and the Diplomatic and Foreign Service.

Cape Verde's Foreign Policy

The determinants of the foreign policy of Cape Verde, both domestic and external, can best be understood if examined in historical perspective. Cape Verde is an African island in the Atlantic Ocean which, together with Sao Tome and Principe and Guinea-Bissau, became colonial possessions of Portugal in the Atlantic Ocean. Portugal became the first European power to establish modern contacts with Africa when, in 1415 CE, Portugal attacked Morocco and captured and occupied Ceuta, which was a Moroccan enclave in Gibraltar.

Following the capture of Ceuta in 1415 CE, Portugal expanded its interest in trade with Africa, both in legitimate trade in gold and other natural resources as well as in illegitimate trade in captured Africans. The African slaves were taken by Portugal from the forest kingdoms of West and Central Africa and brought to the three islands in the Atlantic and settled there on plantations before being eventually shipped to the Americas.

The Lusophone (Portuguese) colonial policies toward the Portuguese colonies, including the islands, described them as overseas provinces of Portugal. There was little or no education of the people until the process of decolonization that swept across Africa. The decolonization struggles produced political independence in Africa and the determination of trends in foreign policy and diplomacy that prevail in Cape Verde today. This policy is characterized by maintaining close relations with the ex-colonial power while being a member of the African Union, the UN System, and of the regional arrangements in Africa such as the Economic Community of the West African State (ECOWAS). Cape Verde is one of the small states of Africa that gained political independence in 1975 and was classified as a least developed country (LDC) under the UN categorization until 2007, when the island graduated from the LDC category. Principles guiding Cape Verde's foreign policy have included the following among others:

1. Principles of Public International as enshrined in the charters of the UN and the OAU/AU:

    (a) Non-interference in the internal affairs of states
    (b) Territorial integrity and respect for sovereignty of states
    (c) Peaceful settlement of disputes among states
    (d) Peaceful co-existence with other states
    (e) Good neighborliness
    (f) Promotion of collaboration, democracy, and observance of human rights.

2. Equity, equality, employment, and environmental protection for sustainable development of Cape Verdians and of all Africans.

3. Membership in the non-aligned movement, and in other international organizations.
4. In general, the foreign policy approaches of Africa, as demonstrated in the arrangements of the AU and of the regional African organizations to which Cape Verde is a member, which determined to a large extent the formulation and execution of Cape Verde's foreign policy.

The island's economy has greatly been helped by the discovery of oil in 2007. Cape Verde became the second small island state/LDC to be graduated from the LDC category. The first country to attain that graduation was Botswana in 1994. Currently, Africa is a host to 33 LDCs. As an island, Cape Verde is also a member of the Association of Small Island States (AOSIS), which includes six SIDS of Africa. They are Cape Verde, Guinea-Bissau, Sao Tome and Principe, Mauritius, Comoros, and Seychelles, three of which are in the Atlantic and others are in the Indian Ocean. The priorities of AOSIS and SIDS are important to Cape Verde and include disaster prevention, preparedness, and management.

As regional markets for African goods and services the SIDS of Africa and AOSIS are emphasized. The use of Portuguese and national African languages that are used for communication especially among Africans speaking different languages are Arabic, Spanish, Portuguese, French, English, and Kiswahili.

As a former colony of Portugal, Cape Verde adopted the foreign policy of multilateralism and multilingualism. These have served Cape Verde well both in bilateral and multilateral relations. Another issue determining Cape Verde's foreign policies include religion, especially Christianity and Islam. The Island became a melting pot for various kinds of European influence.

In recent years, the island has shown peace and stability that are prerequisites for sustainable development. In the coming decade and beyond, Cape Verde will be confronted by new and emerging challenges of the 21st century. These include disease—pandemics such as HIV/AIDS and Ebola—environmental degradation, climate change and global warming, and related challenges. Resolutions to these problems will require concerted international and African efforts to which cape Verde will be expected to contribute commensurably.

The Democaratc Republic of Congo's Foregn Policy

The Democratic Republic of Congo (DRC) was a Belgian colony acquired through the personal efforts and resources of King Leopold II of Belgium. The King had bought the territory, then known as Congo Free State, already by the time of the partition of Africa at the Berlin Conference of 1884–1885.

Belgian colonial policies and practices were among the worst, and by the time of independence in 1960, no efficient and adequate preparation had been made for political independence. Consequently, conflicts, corruption, and civil war have rocked the country since 1960. This country is an LDC despite its vast wealth of mineral resources, oil, and agriculture-based cash crops. The Congo is also a strategically placed country.

As a determinant of the foreign policy of the DRC, the natural resource base has placed the country in a vulnerable place, attracting Cold War politics and dividing Africa on the kinds of measures needed in order to resolve Congo's problems.

The country has changed names a few times. Prior to 1885, it was known as the Congo Free State then it became known as Belgian Congo and underwent horrible colonial policies, which disallowed appropriate preparation for political independence.

Prime Minister Patrice Lumumba was assassinated on January 17, 1961, which was soon after his assumption of that position on September 30, 1960. Lumumba's son is still looking for an explanation as to why and how his father was murdered. Was it with the connivance of the former colonial power? Was it as a result of the Cold War between the superpowers of the day? Or was it a result of ethnic rivalries stirred by the leaders of the day including President Joseph Kasavubu, Prime Minister Moise Tshombe, and Col. Joseph Mobutu, who eventually overthrew the government of the day in 1965 and ruled the country for 32 years until his ousting on May 17, 1997?

Any nation experiencing such a political history is bound to adopt a foreign policy that depends on the person who stages the coup d'état and governs the country. This leader will decide to pursue a foreign policy that suits his or her governance preferences. Under President Mobutu, the country's name was changed to Zaire in 1971, but when Laurent Desire Kabila overthrew President Mobutu in May 1997, he changed the name back to the Democratic Republic of Congo. After the assassination of President Kabila in 2002, his son Joseph Kabila retained this name.

The foreign policy of the Congo has experienced changes in orientations and prioritization since 1960. First, the Lumumba foreign policy approach stressed a strong independence from external, European forces and an alignment with the goals and principles of the African Unity Organization, with also a strong inclination toward socialism. This caused worry in the West, who in Cold War politics aimed at preventing the Soviet Union's influence in the Congo. Under President Mobutu, there was a clear leaning toward the West, supported by Belgium and the U.S. government, which became distant controllers of political, military, and other developments in Zaire. President Mobutu assumed a plutocratic style of governance that impoverished the country and sustained the exploitation of Congo's resources by Western governments and companies.

Such foreign policy was not useful nor helpful in the promotion and protection of Zaire's national interests. The president's personal interests, and those of some Western powers such as Belgium and the United States, were protected and advanced at the expense of national interests. The ill conceived policies and the ill advised processes and procedures resulted in escalation of domestic conflicts and war that still haunt the country in 2010. A regime facing civil war and struggling to survive has no time to spend on development efforts and initiatives. The country's foreign policy and diplomacy will continue to be handicapped so long as domestic strife, conflicts, and civil war continue. This is a basic requirement for the people of the Democratic Republic of Congo.

Gabon's Foreign Policy

Like the Democratic Republic of Congo, Gabon is located in Central Africa. It was a French colony that gained political independence in 1960.

In Africa, the foreign policy, image, prestige, and national and international performance of a country depend on the character, personality, and lifestyle of its leader. In Africa also, the fewer the leaders that govern a country, the fewer the fluctuations and distortions in the foreign policy positions of the country are in question.

In the case of Gabon, two main factors can be mentioned that have greatly helped in shaping Gabon as a reasonably stable country: First, the ethnic composition of Gabon lacks the many features that characterize the tribal rivalries existing in many other African States. Secondly, the long rule of President Omar Ondimba Bongo provided a huge measure of stability for Gabon.

Omar Bongo became president in 1967 and remained the sole ruler of the country and head of government until his death in 2009. The French colonial policies and practices in Gabon followed the same pattern as in other French African colonies. Colonial remnants have not disturbed the peace and stability that Gabon enjoys in international affairs. Issues of political stability, development, tourism, etc. have been admired by the rest of the world, and Gabon has continued to enjoy healthy respect in France and elsewhere overseas as well as in Africa.

Political stability and the call for investments, tourism, and good commercial relations with other nations have augured well for Gabon.

President Omar Bongo Ondimba forged a progressive foreign policy that advanced regional collaboration and integration for economic performance of Gabon in the African Union and in the Economic Community of the Central African States (ECCAS) as well as in the Economic and Monetary Community of Central Africa (CEMAC,) the Bank of Central African States (BEAC), the Central African Development Bank, and many other institutions.

The achievements of Gabon under the leadership of President Omar Bongo Ondimba are visible, and the country is now ruled by his son Ali Bongo Ondimba. The integrity, decency, and respect that Omar Bongo enjoyed as president of Gabon is unquestionable. Under his rule, Gabon became an important producer of oil and joined OPEC until Angola replaced Gabon in Africa's membership of OPEC. Gabon is expected to continue playing an important role at regional levels and has shown great maturity at home. It remains to be seen, however, whether President Ali Bong Ondimba will show the kinds of international mediation skills that his father showed as he was guided by the charters of the United Nations and the Organization of African Unity/African Union. His father was successful in promoting economic and business relations within the African, Caribbean, and Pacific/European Union, the Lome Convention, and the Group of 77 developing countries of the United Nations and the French Commonwealth better known as Francophone. Continued success would call for maintaining Omar Bongo's visionary approach to resolving African economic and political problems.

Nigeria's Foreign Policy

Nigeria also gained political and independence from the British in 1960, but the gravest errors of the Europeans at their Berlin Conference in 1884–1885 was probably their decision to amalgamate nations such as Nigeria that should have been kept separate or to separate nations like Somalia that should have been held together. The outcomes of those colonial policies and practices have been conflicts in the various African states that have had to deal with negative impacts of colonialism and colonization in their formulation and implementation of foreign policies and diplomacy.

In the case of Nigeria, a number of foreign policy determinants can be outlined as follows:

First, the interest of the military in national politics has had a profound negative impact on Nigeria's foreign policy. The era of military rule began in Africa in the late 1960s and spread throughout the continent in the 1970s; but it was in Nigeria that military coups assumed a systematic pattern as they were staged one after another and were mainly bloody military topplings of governments. It was not until General Olusegun Obasanjo (1937–) became president of Nigeria that the bloodbath pattern of rule was interrupted. He ruled from February 13, 1976 to October 1, 1979 when he handed the power peacefully to his successor. He came back into power in 1999 until 2007.

Secondly, ethic diversity has dominated Nigeria's domestic politics and led to deep parochialism in Nigeria and to the secession of Iqboland from the main country in 1967 under the leadership of Col. Chief Odumegwu

Ojukwu who became president of Biafra in 1967 to 1970 and was recognized by a few nations, including Tanzania and China. However, Biafra could not be sustained as a sovereign country for too long in the midst of the strong opposition and efforts of the Nigerian federal government to end the secession.

When the military hunger for political power subsided and civilian rule was restored, a new perception of democracy emerged. That was a major step toward long-term democratization of the country, as Nigeria had been repeatedly accused by the international donor community of being deficient in civil governance and rule.

Nigeria's first civilian prime minister, Sir Alhaji Abubakar Tafawa Balewa (1912–1966), was actually assassinated in the first military coup in independent Nigeria in January, 1966.

In the 1990s, following the restoration of civilian rule in Nigeria, foreign policy initiatives shifted from concentrating on African issues to the global scale. The concentration on Africa prior to 1990 was prompted inter alia by the strong external criticism that Nigeria received from developed non-African countries. That criticism seemed to have prompted Nigeria's political leaders to deal more with their African peers who minimized their criticisms against the military coups in Nigeria.

Thirdly, with just one superpower, the United States, left in the world and a Cold Peace era having replaced Cold War politics, the issues facing nations in Africa and elsewhere have assumed a different nature and are global in character as opposed to the predominantly domestic issues and challenges that faced Nigeria and Africa from the 1960s to 1990.

Consequently, Nigeria's foreign policy was expected to stress global issues such as democracy, globalization, human rights, etc. Nigeria is the largest African nation population-wise, with close to 150 million people as of May 2010.

Nigeria has vast natural resources, including oil, and was thus expected to play a leadership role in Africa in economic and socio-political issues in terms of the world stage. Military rule was accused of excessive corruption and parochialism, and it is evident that the global expectations for Nigeria to play leadership roles for Africa have not been met satisfactorily.

As the African nation with the largest population, speaking at least 250 different languages, Nigeria is also expected to use cultural diplomacy to promote ethnic diversity at home and cooperation among the various races and people living in Africa.

Thus, the various foreign policy advisors in Nigeria have the formidable task of elaborating on foreign policy initiatives inter alia through promotion of:

- Cultural cooperation and developments
- Economic development
- Technical and economic cooperation among developing countries

- UN reforms, e.g., to get agreement to enlarge membership in the UN Security of which Nigeria and Southern Africa would be beneficiaries
- Reform and reviews of Africa's policies and internal relations in the coming decade and beyond

As a nation with the largest population and ethnic groups in Africa, Nigeria should strive to play an increased role as promoter of African culture and cultural diplomacy, peaceful settlement of conflicts, and defender of African national interest, both in and out of Africa.

In this case, Nigeria's foreign policy approaches would benefit Africa as a whole if the political, economic, scientific, cultural, and environmental interests of Nigeria would be elevated to the level needed in Africa and the African Diaspora, who aim at promoting tourism investment and collaboration between the various phonist systems in Africa, e.g., from within the Economic Community of the West African States that assemble countries of the Anglophone, Lusophone, and Francophone into one regional grouping.

Promoting of the economic and technical cooperation among African countries and leading Africa at the UN for reforms could enhance the common cause of Africa. This role could be played well by Nigeria.

Egypt's Foreign Policy

Egypt has a large population. As a country, Egypt is unique in several ways. For example, it was one of the first countries to be civilized on Earth, with its history of Mesopotamia where civilization is believed to have been developed. Egypt was also the first country to create a city-state in 3100 BCE when the Kingdom of Upper Egypt was united with the Kingdom of Lower Egypt under the first king known as Pharaoh Narmer, or Nemes I.

Egypt's foreign policy has also been shaped by other factors such as its strategic geographical location, which includes its proximity to the Middle East and the OPEC oil producing and exporting countries (which include Angola, Algeria, Libya, and Nigeria), and to the Mediterranean regions as well as to Europe. Expectations from the world community are for Egypt to be a mediator between the Palestinians and Israelis and to be a power broker in that region. This augurs well for as the largest military unit in the Middle East.

In like manner, Egypt's strategic location in the Middle East and Africa has prompted the government of Egypt to develop special relationships with other governments around the world. Egypt enjoys such relationships with:

- The United States of America, primarily because of Israel and the Israel-Palestinian questions, the oil routes to the Middle East, and the United States' strategic and national interests in the Greater Horn of Africa and the Middle East

- Muslim countries globally: with the Organization of the Islamic Conference (OIC) and other regional organizations such as the Non-Aligned Movement

- The Arab League and the African Union: like the other countries of Northern Africa (Algeria, Tunisia, Morocco, the Sahrawi Arab Democratic Republic, and Libya), Egypt belongs to the Arab League in the Middle East and to Africa. This is why it is necessary to talk of special relationships of Egypt with other countries. Egypt often plays extraordinary roles in affairs relating to Africa. The first African Secretary-General of the United Nations, Dr. Boutros Boutros-Ghali, was an Egyptian, and when the discussions among the African leaders started on the formation of a New Partnership for African Development (NEPAD), the founding fathers of this organization were the presidents of Egypt, Mohammed Hosni Mubarak; the president of Algeria, Abdelaziz Bouteflika; the president of South Africa, Thabo Mbeki; and the president of Senegal, Abdoulaye Wade.

- The Mediterranean countries such as Cyprus, Malta, and the African countries of North Africa as well as Italy, Portugal and Spain, Israel, Turkey, Lebanon, Syria and the Palestinian Authority. Most of these nations are Islamic states.

- The European Union

- Other donor community countries such as New Zealand, Australia, and Canada

- The East European nations including Russia and Poland

- The global community

- The UN Systems and others

Kenya's Foreign Policy

Kenya's population growth has decreased in recent years, but it used to be one of the highest in Africa.

At independence in 1963, then Prime Minister Jomo Kenyatta, (1894–1978) inherited a British system of government with the British Commonwealth as an important forum for foreign policy. That applied to all ex-British African and other colonies. In 1964 when Kenya assumed a Republican status, Kenyatta (affectionately known as Mzee for a man of respect) became the first president of Kenya, but as a Pan-Africanist and one of the founding fathers of African Nationalism and African Unity, Kenyatta's main interest in foreign policy lay in Pan-Africanism and the liberation of Africa from all forms of colonial domination and exploitation. Consequently, Kenya's foreign policy continues to lay stress on non-alignment, Pan-Africanism, and on the African political doctrines and ideologies as well as on the principles of public international law and diplomacy. The foundations of Kenya's foreign policy also include:

The charters of the UN and of the African Union as well as the UN Universal Declaration of Human Rights of 1948. The principles of good neighborliness, African solidarity, socialism, and peaceful co-existence are also applicable to the other African states as fundamental tenets of foreign policy and diplomacy.

In recent years, stressors have been balanced, so as to include sustainable development, cultural diplomacy, environmental protection, and equity, stressing empowerment of the marginalized strata of society. Thus, while retaining the original political, military, economic, and national security interests in the political area, foreign policy options for Kenya now aim at satisfying the needs of the Kenyan people in a multidimensional way. A combination of bilateralism and multilateralism in Kenyan diplomacy and foreign policy now serve the nation more effectively, with special relations being pursued with the former colonial power, Great Britain and other valuable donor countries such as the United States, Canada, Germany, France, and Italy, besides the UN System and other international organizations.

In economic and business terms, the European Union is still the largest market for Kenya. But the diplomacy of culture and development and business and trade as well as globalization and global finance for development still offer serious challenges to the country, as do the vulnerability to natural disasters, diseases and pandemics such as HIV/AIDS and Ebola, as well as education, the global environment climate, and self-reliance in development initiatives. These new and emerging issues pose daunting challenges to Kenya in the area of foreign policy and diplomacy of the new millennium. Time changes, and issues and dictates change with it. This calls for constant review and updates in foreign policy and diplomacy initiatives of countries in their relations with each other.

The strategic geographical position of Kenya and the relatively secure interests of Kenya with other nations present a huge potential for business, tourism, trade, and mediation between and among the nations and institutions of the world. It is thus essential that the Kenyan government map out an aggressive foreign policy posture that will boost Kenya's image and prestige on the global stage at sub-regional, regional, African continental, as well as global levels.

In the new millennium, the foreign policy and diplomacy of Kenya will continue to be guided by the principles, goals, and objectives that have characterized Kenya's external relations since independence. However, it is evident that the new and emerging issues in regional and global contexts, given the inevitable dictates, shall shape the foreign policies and diplomacy of nations, new and old.[7]

NOTES

1. G.M. Khadiagala and Terrence Lyons, eds, *African Foreign Policies: Power & Process* (Boulder, CO: Lynne Rienner, 2001).

2. C. Clapham, *Africa and the International System: The Politics of State Survival* (Cambridge: Cambridge University Press, 1996).

3. J.W. Harbeson and D. Rothchild, eds, *Africa in World Politics: Reforming Political Order*, 4th ed. (Boulder, CO: Westview Press, 2009).

4. R. Gardner, J.M. Anstee, and C.L.O. Patterson, eds, *Africa & the World* (Addis Ababa: Oxford University Press, 1970).

5. Ali Mazrui and Michael Tidy, *Nationalism and New States in Africa: From 1935 to the Present* (Portsmouth, NH: Heinemann, 1986).

6. W. Tardoff, *Government and Politics in Africa,* (Basingstoke, UK: Palgrave and Macmillan, 2002).

7. For an interesting account of issues in Kenya's Foreign Policy and Diplomacy, see *Government Guide,* (Washington DC, International Business Publications, 2006) pp. 128–157.

CHAPTER 18

African International Relations in Theory and Reality

THEORETICAL ASPECTS OF THE "THEORY" OF AFRICAN INTERNATIONAL RELATIONS

One wonders what the meaning of "theory" might be in the study of African—and indeed any other—international relations! Just like "foreign policy" and "diplomacy," the term "theory" has to be utilized in the plural since there are so many aspects of international relations theory. These conceptual definitions are basically issues of an academic nature. However, in real life, states—African states in particular—have no time to spend theorizing or hypothesizing on interrelated propositions, which is what theories are all about. The leader of a nation where the people struggle to survive on a daily basis cannot waste time on theoretical discussions!

Therefore, this chapter makes an attempt to define and analyze the standing of Africa in the discussion of international relations theory, and to highlight those theories, if any, of international relations that are applicable to Africa as a member of the international community. Furthermore, the chapter will address the issues, problems, and challenges that confront Africa in practical terms—in reality—as an international actor and how African countries behave and relate in their endogenous and exogenous dealings and relations. The chapter will conclude with a note on the future of African international relations in theory and reality.

WHAT IS "THEORY" IN AFRICAN INTERNATIONAL RELATIONS?

What does any theory in international law, relations, and diplomacy mean? As indicated above, this is an academic issue that has not had, so far at least, any analytical discussion in deep African context, and one dares say, in the Third World context as well. The theorizing of international relations has appeared mainly in the West; but even there, one is still hard-pressed to see deep and constructive debates as to what the value of theory is in international relations.

Nonetheless, "theory" is an expression that is often used in academic circles to refer to three constituent elements of a proposition or hypothesis relating to knowledge, whether juridical or empirical, that is required for an understanding or resolution of a problem. Those elements are as follows:

1. A set or group of propositions and hypotheses that are put together for analysis because of their interrelated nature.
2. The group of hypotheses and propositions are analyzed in a systematic and logical fashion, with a view to getting concrete results, as well as knowledge and research for scholarly purposes.
3. The results of the research are to be used as guidelines for further empirical and normative research on the same study area for practical purposes. Therefore, theories of whatever kind are ideas or concepts or sets of hypotheses, propositions, preferences, and conclusions that have no real meaning unless they can construct and address reality. This can be done by determining the real issues, challenges, and problems that must be tackled and resolved in the process of international affairs and politics, of which international relations are a part. Africa has to be engaged in such affairs as a member of the international system.

Ways, however, still are to be found on how the theories of international relations will benefit Africa's subsystem of the global system. When ideas and concepts are provided for systematic discussion, with a view to reaching conclusions on the attainment of specific and general goals and objectives resulting from research on given issues, or arising from the behavior of certain actors (i.e. sovereign states), these theories will be helpful and useful only if they prompt actions or lead to further enquiry into research ahead of international relations law or diplomacy. Theories can be useful only if they can be applied to get, produce, trigger, or accumulate knowledge, the doing or guiding of research, and the development of concepts for application to various fields of international relations in academic terms, be they legal, social, political, or economic fields for the benefit of nations like those of Africa. Thus, as it will become clearer in the course of this chapter, international relations theory stands very little chance of finding wide and popular application in African international relations except in a few cases that may be applicable to African conditions.

Examples of International Theories

Among the theories of international relations, the following stand out prominently as theories, traditions, and knowledge, often referred to collectively as international relations theory:

- Subsystem of the international system,
- State theory,
- State and law theory,
- Statehood: empirical and juridical,
- International law theory,
- International relations theory,
- International diplomacy
- International/global system,
- Sub-altruism,
- Subalternism,
- Subaltern state,
- Irredentism,
- Uti posidetis juris doctrine,
- Majimboism,
- Multipartyism,
- Unipartyism,
- Anarchy,
- Rational choice,
- Alliances,
- General systems,
- Power struggle,
- Politics,
- National interest, and
- Others.[1-4]

Examples of development paradigms are as follows:

- Sustainable development in science, environment, education, agriculture, empowerment, employment, etc.;
- Sovereignty;
- Realism (classical), neorealism, liberalism, neoliberalism;
- Scientific theory;
- International society/community;

- Equilibrium;
- State sovereignty and state authority;
- State system;
- International (state) system;
- Natural law;
- State-building theory;
- Dependence;
- Democracy; and
- Independence.

A brief examination of these international relations theories reveals that most of the theories are applicable in Western democracies (i.e., in the United States and Western Europe). The Third World nations have different priorities in their relations with other states and among themselves. Also, empiricism in statehood—the "state" theory—is a Western concept. The modern state system, as determined herein, was born in 1648 at the Treaty of Westphalia among the European powers. That treaty introduced the idea and practice of trilateral branches of government: the executive, legislative, and judiciary branches, with a system of "checks and balances," to promote accountability. The concept of Western "democratic" institutions basically called for creating states with constitutions, political institutions, and territorial borders that were inviolate, and sovereignty to give the ruler of a state control and a monopoly of the government over the use of force within those borders. The people or population assembled within those borders did so voluntarily, and had to acknowledge the authority of the state and government. The people owed allegiance to the flag of the country.

This Western concept of statehood was imposed on Africa and the other developing areas. Complications arose when European colonization of Africa drew geographical lines on the African map and called these territories "African countries." Those actions and decisions, forced upon Africa without Africa's participation in 1885, started the state and border problems that still haunt many African countries today. These geographical lines either amalgamated nations that should have been separate but have been recognized as one state (like Nigeria), or divided nations and their peoples who should have been kept together (like Somalia).

The state and law theory is, likewise, a European concept that is not very applicable to Africa. One authority on state and legal theory was Professor Stanislaw Ehrlich (1907–1997) at the University of Warsaw, Poland (this writer was the proud and lucky student of Professor Ehrlich and benefited considerably form the his authoritative mastery of issues of state and legal theory).[5]

The statehood theory is also a by-product of Western democratic institutions initiated by the peace process of Westphalia. Whereas the Treaty of Westphalia introduced the concept of empirical statehood, the 1885 General Act of Berlin on the Partition of Africa introduced the concept of juridical statehood. The difference between the two theories was/is remarkable, for whereas empirical statehood leaves no room for any "cracks" in the territorial, military, economic, and political integrity of a state, juridical statehood introduced to Africa made the African state weak and vulnerable to external interference, invasions, and even encouragements of secession within African states. The problems of this colonial legacy continue to haunt Africa in the Sudan, the DRC, Somalia, and other African states that continue to be shaken by civil wars and anarchy.

Other parts of international relations theory, although not applicable to Africa, are nonetheless highlighted in the next section of this chapter, which specifically applies to Africa.[6]

Africa and International Relations Theory

As shown, international relations theory has many divergent approaches.[7-13]

As a subsystem of the global system, however, Africa's international relations system can be outlined as a study area or discipline addressing/meaning the totality of actions, non-actions, contacts, interactions, approaches, proactions, dealings, transactions, and relations and relationships that are conducted or performed between and among entities or actors dealing with each other or one another as political units or groups, whether sovereign—i.e., with state-based and across-borders relations of countries or stateless relations—or even with international legal persons.

Such dealings become inter- or intra-national relations when conducted between/among sovereign states or nations. In this regard, African international relations bear the following features:

- National.
- Across borders of sovereign entities, and
- Internal, or within Africa.

Historically, Africa's international relations fall into three categories or time periods:

- From ancient times to 1884, in pre-colonial times, relations were either nomadic, stateless, or between/among empires and city-states.

- From 1885 to 1960, in colonial times, relations were not sovereign nor among equal sovereign entities, but they were between bosses (i.e., the colonial powers and their metropolises) and their subjects (i.e., the colonized peoples of Africa).
- From 1960 to the present, in the post-colonial era, sovereignty is the common denominator in African international relations that are intra-national (within) Africa and international (between Africa and the rest of the world). These are inter-state and across-border relations that recognize and stress sovereign equality.

Relations in Africa developed as follows from remotest antiquity: family relations became extended family relations, which became community relations, which became village relations, which became sub-clan relations, which became clan relations, which became sub-tribe relations, which became tribal relations, which became tribal kingdom relations, which became empire relations, which became nation relations, which became state relations, which became super-state relations, which became super-nation relations.

Thus, in this way, African peoples evolved from the relations of nomadic and stateless systems. Then, especially after city-state formation and the formation of permanent settlements, their relations grew into across-border relations.

Defining the Discipline of International Relations

Although, as previously identified, international relations is used to identify all (i.e., the totality of all) interactions, dealings, transactions, actions, and non-actions conducted or performed between and among sovereign states and other entities possessing international legal personality (like the UN system organizations), for Africa, stress in such relations is put on the following features:

- International relations are usually/normally between and among state-based actors and across state borders. In this sense, international relations is both a process and a multidisciplinary area of study or discipline, like international politics, although international relations is broader than international politics. A discipline is a branch of knowledge aimed at the systematic understanding of a subject.
- In international relations, dealings can be and often are conducted between sovereign states/entities and non-sovereign entities (e.g., an NGO that violates international rules or law).

Thus, African international relations and foreign policies address the same issues and operate in domestic and external environments. This is because foreign policy elevates the domestic agenda to the international arena. The difference between African international relations and African foreign policy is that the former is broader than the latter. Hence, African foreign policy, as explained earlier, "manages" African international relations, just as African diplomacy executes or implements foreign policy decisions in the African international relations arena.

This also is why African international relations embrace the totality of interactions, dealings contacts, actions, non-actions, proactions, and approaches that sovereign African states and other actors in international relations maintain between and among themselves. International relations is therefore the discipline of the study of relations between and among states and other international legal persons. As a study area and a science concerned with observation and analysis, international relations engages in theory and theorizing to examine and explain processes of interactions of states, as well as between such states and other states.

In this regard, African international relations is connected to international relations theory and should predict outcomes of analyses of processes which states agree to pursue between and among themselves as members of the global system.

Therefore, what international relations should do is use the knowledge acquired from theoretical traditions, hypotheses, and propositions in a systematic fashion for the advancement of cooperation and improvement of the relationships that emerge from across-national-border transactions that exist in inter-state relations. When interpreted more carefully, international relations are part of international politics, international affairs, and political science. In this connection, African international relations, which are a part of international relations, are a discipline for the study of human behavior, and international relations theory is part of political theory or thought.

AFRICAN INTERNATIONAL RELATIONS IN REALITY

The study of African international relations in the context of the international relations theory reveals that there is no theoretical framework for the study of African international relations. There is no debate on it. This is because the majority of the theories of international relations and systems do not fit African international relations since they are basically Western concepts that serve the interests of the developed world—the West in particular. Of the international relations theories applicable to African conditions, the following are noteworthy: statehood, democracy, diplomacy, subalternism, irredentism, majimboism, unipartyism, multipartyism, uti possidetis juris, subaltern state, state and international state system, national interest, development paradigms, anarchy, dependence, dependency, and independence. Strictly speaking, however, the only fundamental international relations theories applicable to the African situation are the nation-state building theory, natural law theory, and "power (balance/ struggle)" theory. Other automatically invoked theories (expressions) and features of the international system include the following:

- State and state sovereignty (state sovereignty is a state's characteristic of being politically independent of all other states—every state under the Westphalian order is sovereign);
- State as a political unit; and
- The application of a system (i.e., a network of structures and channels using organized methods and procedures in a harmonized fashion).

The state system exercises relations between politically organized human groupings occupying distinctive territories and enjoying and exercising a measure of independence from each other. The basic values of a state system include security, freedom, order, justice, and equality of opportunity, welfare, and territory (i.e., a political unit). Thus, a state is a political unit or organization with the following features:

- An effective government;
- Inviolate geographical borders;
- Monopoly over the use of force within those borders;
- An absolute authority (i.e., a sovereign power with one sovereign ruler);
- A demarcated territory; and
- A population that is voluntarily assembled, belongs together, and is subject to one sovereign, and owing allegiance to the flag of its nation.

Among the theories of International Relations, the following issues should be noted:

- Modern state authority (i.e., an arrangement of centralized political authority);
- Anarchy, which occurs when there is no central rule in the international system, no power or central rule (government) to curb the aggressive ambitions of others;
- National choice theory (i.e., a chosen behavior that normally optimizes material self-interest);
- Sovereignty (i.e., state control with no external control, which was legitimized since the 1648 Treaty of Westphalia);
- Alliances theory (i.e., changing alignments are a response to changing power configurations and circumstances in the international system—bloc politics and alliances such as NATO); and
- Subaltern states are those that are weak and of inferior rank (the Westphalia system versus the African state system that followed the 1885 Berlin process).

The Scientific Theory

International relations is a science and should be treated as such. Therefore, there is no such thing as the "power" or "realistic" theory in international relations.

African National Interest

An analytical tool identifying the goals or objectives of foreign policy of Africa, and as an all embracing concept of political discourse used by African states as sovereign entities precisely in order to justify particular African policy preferences. It implies Africa's basic determinants that guide African state policy vis-à-vis the external environment.

Sustainable Development

Includes internal development, international development, and economic growth.

The Equilibrium Theory

Under this theory, states undertake to secure the best attainable position of equilibrium in their relations and interactions. Unfortunately, this is a tricky theory, since what exists in the international system is sovereign equality but not equal sovereignty. So it is difficult to see how equilibrium can be guaranteed in African international relations, or even in international relations!

The "Power Struggle" Theory, Also Known as the "Realistic" Theory

This theory is based on realism. International relations are about the power struggle. They are about international politics—and the fact is that competition in the international arena leads to struggles about survival, domination, subjugation, and power politics. If anything, it is this power theory that fits the African international relations best because Africa is all the time engaged in the struggle for survival. African nations must preserve sovereignty, territorial integrity, and independence. They must struggle to provide the basic necessities of their populations. They must struggle to acquire economic and political power as crucial national goals and as a means of acquiring military power for national defense and increasing the might and prestige of the African state and influence in international relations.

This theory of the "balance of power" is actually a doctrine and an arrangement whereby the power (i.e., authority and influence) of one state, or a group of states, is checked by the countervailing power of other states. This dominance of power politics dominates African international relations. These African countries had to struggle and even shed blood in order to gain political independence. It is an on-going struggle. This theory therefore manifests itself very clearly wherever we examine the African affairs dealing with the problems of democracy, ideology, and leadership in contemporary African international relations.

International System

The international system is a collection of political entities, or units, especially sovereign states as the basic or main actors, which maintain regular patterns of across-border interactions (reactions, proactions, non-actions, relationships, etc.) with one another. The regular boundary-crossing interactions are independent and interdependent and are usually dominated by completion and decentralization.

Other actors, like the UN and other international and civil society organizations, also participate in the international system because they each possess an international (legal) personality. In the international system, there are both independence and interdependence, the struggle for survival, etc., in which events in one area affect other areas.

Africa is a subsystem of the international or global system, and the UN is likewise a subsystem of the global system.

An international system consists of the following five basic criteria:

1. Boundaries;
2. The nature of political units (i.e., sovereign states, international organizations, or an individual state actor like a president, premier, foreign minister, or envoy/ambassador);
3. The structure of power and influence (i.e., sovereign equality but not equal sovereignty, competition and the struggle for survival, dominance and subordination, etc., and power or authority or the ability of an actor to prevail in an encounter—each state has its own power);
4. A pattern of interactions; and
5. Rules underlying the system.

Thus, an international system is really a sovereign state system that divides the modern (post–World War II) world into the following two parts:

- Zones of peace, affluence, wealth, and democracy (i.e., the North) and
- Zones of turmoil, poverty, war, and un-development (i.e., the South, which is the Third World).

Therefore, the main features of an international system are:

- Anarchy, the supernatural government or authority;
- No central rule or authority to regulate activities and arbitrate between interests of nation-states that constitute the main units operating within it (the International System);
- A regular pattern of interactions; and
- Rules governing these interactions.

FOREIGN POLICY AND AFRICAN FOREIGN POLICY

African foreign policy, like any other foreign policy, is the process by which African states identify goals in the international system. An international global system, as explained in this study, is a collection of sovereign political units called states that maintain contacts and/or purposeful inaction between/among themselves. African foreign policy refers to a series of actions, non-actions, pro-actions, etc., that constitute the totality of interactions and contacts among African and other sovereign political entities and legal persons designed to attain a set or sets of goals created by various decision makers of an African country or other country in various sections of an African or other government section of that country/ state in its relations with other entities or states, likewise acting on the international stage, in pursuit of their own interests (projection, promotion, defense, and protection of their national interests).

AFRICA IN THE "NEW" INTERNATIONAL ORDER

Concept of "World Order"

Throughout this study the expressions "international order" and "world order" are used interchangeably. "World order" is a world arrangement of political and other sequences and eras determined or shaped and occasioned by certain events or circumstances that lead to, or necessitate, a change or changes in courses of action on a global scale.

The idea of a world order did not spring full-blown from 18th century France after the French Revolution, that, admittedly, became the main reference point for future world orders. World order had existed from remotest antiquity. In fact, world orders already existed in ancient Greece and ancient Rome. Alexander the Great of Macedonia for example, established a Greek world order with his overseas conquests. The Romans did likewise. Ancient Rome's imperial quest to bring all of the known world under one Roman political control is an example of the making of a world order.

In like manner, Emperor Napoleon of France introduced his own world order, which was the prototype of world orders created after World Wars I and II, and today. World orders as we know them today started in France because of the division of French society into three classes of society known in French as the "etats" meaning "estates" or "orders" as follows:

- The "premier" etat (estate) was the ruling class (aristocracy) that possessed absolute power and exploited the lower classes.
- The "duxieme" etat (upper) was the Middle Class (feudal lords) that had land but were the ordinary exploited silent majority that had to pay tithes of one-tenth of whatever they produced on the land that they lived on and tilled.
- The "tiers" etat (lower) was the hoi polloi—the masses who were exploited and worked under slavery conditions for the premier and duxieme classes.

The French Revolution aimed at abolishing this division of society into three orders or classes. Napoleon championed the cause of the ordinary French people and thus became very popular and was able to command absolute support of the ordinary people against the two privileged classes in French society. In this way, Napoleon established a new world order.

Adolf Hitler also tried to introduce a new world order, and the fall of the Third Reich can be seen as its failure. A world order can also be defined as the totality of events that arise, dominate, prevail, and shape the world within a specific timeframe, but that is overtaken by other events that become predominant criteria for a world order.

Thus, a world, international, or even global order, is actually an international system except that a world order is marked by the following criteria or characteristics:

- Existence of an extraordinary nature or feature,
- An arrangement of political and other sequences and eras of events and circumstances leading to a change or changes in courses of action on a global scale,
- Conformity to certain, regular patterns of behavior, and
- Specificity of timeframe and limited timeframes—things go on until overtaken by other events that originate a new world order.

PROTOTYPES OF THE MODERN GLOBAL SYSTEM AND ORDERS

The prototype of the modern international system that exists today was the Treaty of Westphalia dated October 24, 1648. This treaty marked the birth of the city-state system, as explained before. Thus, the prototype of the *modern* world/international order was the French

Revolution of 1789–1815, which started a period of modern world orders.

Periods of New World Orders

From 1648 to 1885, 17th and 18th century Europe saw a rise in new world orders. In 1648, empirical statehood began. The 17th century was a period of power balance in Europe. It introduced euro-centrism in the 18th century during which came the Industrial Revolution and Napoleonic Wars. Most important in this period was the French Revolution of 1789 to 1815. The French Revolution was inspired by the American Revolution of 1776.

The 19th century hosted the Congress of Vienna in 1815. The Congress of Vienna was a conference of ambassadors from European states. It was chaired by the great German-Austrian politician, distinguished diplomat and statesman, Prince Klemens Wenzel von Metternich (1773–1859), who was an Austrian Minister of State and key negotiator in the Negotiations of the Vienna Congress held in Vienna from September 1884 to June 1815. The main object of that Congress was to redraw the European continent's political map and settle many other issues arising from the French Revolutionary War, the Napoleonic Wars, and the dissolution of the Holy Roman Empire. France was defeated by Germany and surrendered in 1870, which ended 25 years of almost continuous war.

In 1884–1885, the struggles among the European powers produced the Berlin Conference, from which emerged the future colonial powers (Germany-Prussia, Great Britain, France, Italy, Belgium, Portugal, and Spain) of Africa.

Each major or "extraordinary" event noted above marked new world orders.

Classification of World Orders

World orders can be classified into two types:

1. Those before the French Revolution of 1789. Between 1792 and 1802, hierarchical orders put rulers on top of their internal societies in Europe. However, the Treaty of Westphalia of 1648 was a sui generis event.
2. Those that occurred after the French Revolution and began to be known as "new world" or "international orders." The new world orders started the concept of equality of all people.

Thus, after the birth of the state system in Europe, the 1648 Treaty of Westphalia marked the beginning of the modern state system in the world—the empirical state system or "New World Order"—because they have occurred ever since after a number of events and time-frames. Thus, each major or extraordinary event marked a new world order.

There are different kinds of world orders, as follows:

1. International world order,
2. Economic world order,
3. Political world order,
4. Social world order,
5. Legal world order, etc.

The concept of world order as we know it today, however, arose historically from peace groups, governments, philosophers, religious thinkers like Saint Thomas Aquinas, zealots, imperialists, and nationalists. They can be referred to as 'modern' world orders. Most of these orders have appeared after World War I and World War II.

Africa and the New World Order during the Cold War: 1945–1991

The period in the contemporary world prior to the creation of the UN in 1945 was marked by two historic world orders, namely the League of Nations (LON) world order from 1919 to 1939, which was actually an ante-bellum world order, and the World War II order from 1934 to 1945. Hitler assumed the power of leadership over Germany in 1933.

The world orders that appeared after World War I and World War II marked interesting landmarks in Africa's political history. This period contained several noteworthy highlights as follows:

1. Africa's place in global politics between her colonization from 1885 to her attainment of political independence (generally placed at having started from 1960—the Annus Mirabilis of African political history) must be recognized.
2. Within a period of 106 years (1885–1991), Africa experienced at least three world orders: 1885–1900, 1901–1960, and 1960–1991. A transition period from Cold War to Cold Peace politics was from 1989 to 1991.
3. From 1991, Africa has been experiencing a fourth world order since her colonization in 1885.
4. The year 1945 marked an important milestone on Africa's path to recognition as a member and actor within the international system or new world order.

In 1945, several events helped determine Africa's position as a member of the world community. The fifth Pan-African Congress was held at Manchester, England in 1945, at which the future of Africa as a subject—and not an object—was decided. Africa's liberation from the colonial yoke, enslavement, impoverishment, and exploitation seemed to be just around the corner. The LON system initiated in 1919 was replaced by a new UN system created in 1945 in San Francisco, California, in the United States. This new world political organization would be different from LON, since it, the UN, created mechanisms that would keep the (world) peace and promote (world) welfare in a much more concrete manner than had been possible with the LON. Moreover, UN members would predominantly be new nations from the developing areas of the world that had been colonized by Europe, including, of course, Africa.

Stress in world orders/the international system would shift from politics to development as demanded by the majority of the world community—the countries of Africa, Asia, Latin America, and the Caribbean.

The birth of the UN in 1945 not only marked the end of the old order, but also the beginning of a new world order with new kinds of rivalry and competition and international relations theories as explained earlier in this chapter. The creation of the Soviet Union in Russia starting in 1917, challenged the otherwise sole existence of exploitative capitalism as advanced by the developed countries and powers of the West. A new world political order would be born with socialism and Soviet communism as the archenemies of capitalism. That challenge came to fruition in 1947, when Sir Winston Churchill, the well-respected wartime leader of Great Britain during World War II, referred to Soviet communism as the Iron Curtain.

That marked the beginning of the schism between the West and the East—Eastern Europe led by Soviet Russia versus Western Europe and North America (the United States and Canada) led by the United States. The division between the East and West was based on ideology (i.e., on a system of ideas that acts to support or subvert accepted modes of thought and behavior).

A new era of East–West relations began, whose basis would be ideological confrontation, rivalry, competition, and power struggle. Thus, the power theory (also known as the balance of power theory, and the realistic theory), had to be put into full practice. The leaders of the West were as human as those of the East. They would entertain universal assumptions as human beings. That was the beginning of Cold War politics on a global scale.

The new East–West ideological divide not only had experienced two world wars in the 20th century, but it also had produced two world orders, two Europes (Eastern and Western), two military alliances (NATO and the Warsaw Pact), two economic systems (capitalism and communism), and two superpowers (the Soviet Union and the United States). It was inevitable that a Third World would emerge in the midst of the first (Europe) and second (United States and non-European developed states) worlds.

Africa in the New Global Power Structure

Where is Africa in all of these world orders and the new 20th and 21st century power structures? To better understand Africa's fate in the new world orders of the Cold War and Cold War politics, one needs to look briefly at Africa's political-diplomatic condition since the beginning of the colonial era and even before in Africa.

As shown earlier in this study, Africa survived the two kinds of the city-state systems (i.e., from BCE times of Phoenicia, Greece, and Rome, and from 1648 to 1885). Thus, for Africa, important events shaping the globe with definite kinds of impact on Africa can be outlined as follows:

- The rise of city-state systems occurs from ancient times to 700 CE.

- From 700 to 1600 brings the flourishing of kingdoms, empires, and super empires with African kinds of politico-economic orders.

- From 700 to 1884 marks the transition from city-states to the imposition of alien rule on Africa.

- From 1514 to 1632, European contacts with Africa lead to slavery and slave trade in Africa and to impoverishment of Africa in early stages of European exploitation and deprivation of Africans of their value systems.

- In 1652, the Dutch are the first Europeans to settle in Africa, and they start Cape Colony in South Africa in the interior of Africa.

- July 1847 sees Liberia born as an African country of freed African slaves from the United States.

- From 1884 to 1885, the Berlin Conference of European powers results in the partitioning of African into European spheres of influence.

- From 1885 to 1900, colonial settlement begins in Africa while there is an awakening in North America and the West Indies that liberation and freedom of the African Diaspora are human rights.

- From 1900 to 1914, there is a gathering storm in Europe that sets the stage for World War I.

- From 1900 to 1916, European colonization of Africa and other continents occurs and Eurocentrism (fierce competition and wars between and among Europeans in Europe) rages.

- From 1900 to 1945, the Pan-African congresses and meetings bring attention to the need for African political liberation and independence.

- From 1914 to 1918, World War I is fought, and Africa participates as part of the colonized world. Woodrow Wilson's 14 Points including Point No. 5 on the absolute right of colonial peoples and territories to self-rule and self-determination: Africa was alerted. These 14 Points became the foundation of the League of Nations. Wilson was the architect of LON.

- From 1919 to 1939. In the years between World War I and World War II, ideological doctrines are born that would eventually be felt in Africa (nationalism, fascism, and Nazism.) Benito Mussolini invades Ethiopia in 1935 and occupies it until 1941 when he was kicked out of Ethiopia with support from United Kingdom and other powers. By then, four African countries had gained independence (Ethiopia in 982 BCE, Liberia in 1847, South Africa in 1910, and Egypt in 1922).

- In 1945, the UN is created, and Africa is a member with sovereign African states.
- In 1947, the East–West ideological confrontation begins.
- In 1949, the NATO alliance is formed.
- In 1955, the Warsaw Pact military alliance is signed.
- In 1958 to 1963, many African states are created as decolonization increases. Their main concern is to establish a political platform to serve as the pillar of African unity. First, they want to gain political freedom; then create a mechanism on an African continental front; then forge a unity front that will guarantee African development on a multidimensional fashion. The Annus Mirabilis arrives in 1960 as the African leaders are still struggling to find their way out of the colonial pressures and divisions that colonialism fabricated and which will haunt Africa persistently following their political liberation.

However, the fact still remains that Africa was absent from the global scene, and absent on the international scene, until 1885 when she appeared as an object, not a subject, of international relations of European centrism. That colonization of Africa resulted in her transformation.

A world order is created either by war or by peace. The following four patterns of identity are created in people's attitudes by the process of world order:

- Regional origin,
- Language,
- Common descent, and
- Religion or ideology.

Africa's real participation as a party in world orders began after the attainment of political independence—mostly after the Annus Mirabilis in 1960.

By 1945, only a few countries had gained political independence in Africa, as explained earlier. These were Ethiopia, Liberia, South Africa, and Egypt. They signed the charter of the UN as founding/original members on May 25, 1963. By 1991, all African states were politically independent except Eritrea and South Africa. Eritrea became independent in 1993 following a referendum by Eritreans who decided to break away from Ethiopia. Majority rule in South Africa, which was attained in 1994 following the South African free general elections that dismantled the Apartheid system of government, installed Nelson Mandela as the first African president of South Africa.

During the Cold War, the African countries were caught up in the East–West ideological divide. Africa was courted publicly and split up into three camps as a result of the Cold War politics of the superpowers. The emergent ideologies in Africa were Afro-capitalism, Afro-communism, and Afro-liberalism. Most African countries simultaneously claimed to be "non-aligned" while belonging to the Non-Alignment Movement (NAM).

This condition presented a series of difficult challenges to the newly independent nations of Africa as manifested in the period between 1957 and 1963, when three schools of thought/doctrines emerged as the first generation African leaders tried to figure out how to forge a new course in African continental politics in the post-independence era when, actually, phonism (countries using the various languages of their former colonial masters for official communication) arose from the European colonization of the African continent. Phonism would require the new African states not only to protect their special relationships with former colonial powers (Anglophone, Francophone, and Lusophone), but also with their cultural, economic, and "ideological allies."

An example of "culturalism" in African international relations is the Arabphone group of states in North Africa that have also maintained strong economic ties (e.g., with the OPEC countries of Arabia). An ideological alliance would be, for example, when an African country, led by a leader who believes in socialism, expands that country's relations with the socialist bloc countries of Eastern Europe (at the time) and Cuba. The fundamental point then to be stressed here is that the situation, direction, interest, and performance in an African country's foreign and domestic policies depended then, and still depend today, on the type of leaders the country has. Thus, character, style, interest, and ability of an African leader determine that African country's posture and performance on the global and international stage.

From 1957 to 1977 was a period of active decolonization and formation of ideologies in Africa. Thus, paradoxically, in Africa, application of the balance of power (struggle) theory helped, as among the competing European colonial powers, especially the United Kingdom, a sense of realism emerge among such leaders as Prime Minister Harold Macmillan (1894–1986) who, beginning in the second half of 1950s into the 1960s, acknowledged in a famous speech to the Joint Parliament on South Africa on February 3, 1960 that the "Winds of Change" had started blowing in the opposite directions, meaning that with the costly colonization of foreign lands, the mounting pressures—economic, political, and others—at home and abroad, especially from within the UN system, efforts to retain colonies and colonial rule in Africa were not tenable.

It also became clear that the trials and tribulations of Cold War politics accelerated the abandonment of colonial rule and the granting of independence to the colonial peoples and countries of Africa and other

Table 18.1
Years of Political Independence of Sub-Saharan African Countries

	Name of Country	Year of Independence
1	Ghana	1957
2	Guinea	1958
3	Dahomey (1959, endorsed in 1960) (Benin since 1975)	1960
4	(at least 16 countries, mostly Francophone)	1960
5	Tanganyika, Sierra Leone	1961
6	Uganda, Burundi, Algeria, Rwanda	1962
7	Kenya, Zanzibar	1963
8	Malawi, Zambia, Gambia	1964
9		1965
10	Botswana, Lesotho	1966
11		1967
12	Swaziland, Equatorial Guinea, Mauritius	1968
13		1969
14	Gambia	1970
15		1971
16		1972
17		1973
18	Guinea Bissau	1974
19	Angola, Mozambique, Seychelles	1975
20	São Tomé and Príncipe	1976
21	Djibouti	1977

developing areas of the world. It thus became evident that, with the granting of political independence to Ghana—the first to attain that status in sub-Saharan Africa—a Pandora's box of independence demands had been opened in Africa and, consequently, a series of independence claims were granted practically every year from 1957 to 1977 and are summarized in Table 18.1.

Thus, the world's "new order," introduced by Cold War politics, often destabilized the countries of the developing world, especially after these countries adopted the ideologies of one of the developed world ideologies.

In Africa, the Cold War produced three babies that matured into three systems of ideology in the East–West Divide. These are as follows:

1. The populist-socialism system of government was pursued by Algeria under President Ahmed Ben Bella and by Tanzania under President Julius Nyerere. The latter introduced a system of Ujamaa—communalism—based upon the

Chinese model. This system was experimented with for 10 years (1967–1977), but had to be discontinued because it did not work for Tanzania. President Nyerere was honest and bold enough to acknowledge that Ujamaa doctrine had failed to produce the required results in the country. It was speculated that the Ujamaa of Julius Nyerere had failed in Tanzania because the elite—the senior civil servants who were supposed to implement the system—did not believe in it. So, they sabotaged it. The efforts to amalgamate Marxism, Christian socialism, humanism of Kenneth Kaunda of Zambia, Negritude and the humanitarianism of Aimé Cesairé of Martinique and Léopold Sédar Senghor of Senegal, the scientific socialism of Marien N'Gouabi (31 Dec. 1938–18 March, 1977) of Congo Brazzaville, Harambeeism of Jomo Kenyatta of Kenya, Nyayo-ism of Daniel Toroitich Arap Moi of Kenya, Arab Islamism of Muammar Qaddafi of Libya, 'Nkrumaism' (Consciencism) of Kwame Nkrumah of Ghana, and "Mobutuism" of Mobutu Sese Seko of Zaire all became the ideal concepts of the populist-socialism system of African governments led by these African leaders, among others.

2. Afro-Marxism was based on Marxism and Leninism and favored by the president of Mozambique, Machel Samora, and the chairman of the Revolutionary Council of Ethiopia, Haille Mengistu, who replaced Emperor Haille Sellassie in a military coup.

3. Afro-capitalism was practiced by Presidents Nnamdi Azikiwe of Nigeria, Jomo Kenyatta of Kenya, Félix Houphouët-Boigny of Côte d'Ivoire, and Gabriel Leon M'Ba of Gabon, among others.

The ways of attracting ideologies to the African countries, the Cold War politics and practices, deliberately tolerated and even encouraged destabilizing forces in national and African continental environments. In that way, settlement of disputes and conflicts was not easily attained in Africa, and the UN and other international organizations established after World War II were deliberately rendered ineffective in the settlement of disputes like the Security Council of the UN that failed to end the civil war in the DRC in 1960 that culminated in the assassination of the country's first premier, Patrick Emery Lumumba. This visionary, charismatic young leader of Africa lived almost half a century, or even more, ahead of his time.

In like manner, the Cold War did not help attain the development goals set for Africa and the Third World because of the conflicting politics of international economics and the economics of international politics that were advanced by the Cold War. Thus for Africa, the Cold War introduced a second scramble for Africa.

The Post–Cold War Order: 1990

The political events of November 1989 and in subsequent months, marked the collapse of the Berlin Wall and the start of a new world order of "Cold Peace." In this era of one superpower (the United States), the Western capitalist ideology, as well as multipartyism and popular democracy, were revived. They had not characterized the Cold War Era. During this period also, the other forms of world orders were revived, especially the world orders relating to the global economy, environment, law, and the social agenda.

Unipartyism had for a long time encouraged the practice and monopoly of single parties and political leaders governing with autocracy and even dictatorship in Africa for decades. Obviously, Africa is still confronted by many challenges of democracy, governance and accountability, development, empowerment, and genuine nonalignment. Nonetheless, the African leaders and their countries have entered the new millennium fully aware that the ultimate overall development of Africa in all spheres rests with the governments, peoples, and institutions of Africa. It therefore, remains to be seen how Africa will perform in the coming decade and beyond.

Issues for Africa in the Cold Peace (New World) Order

The issues for Africa from 1991 to the time of this writing have included the following:

- State survival and struggle;
- Problems of peace versus conflict, equality *versus* inequality in Africa and overseas (marginalization versus modernization/globalization);
- Fraternity, cooperation, partnerships, justice, law and order, and freedom (in human rights, good governance, decency, fairness versus corruption, and efficiency);
- Dependency and neocolonialism;
- Unfair trade, and structural adjustments of the IMF and World Bank to reduce fiscal imbalances;
- Poverty eradication *versus* disease (pandemics such as HIV/AIDS);
- Racism, tribalism, nepotism, and discrimination;
- Patriotism, nationalism, and ownership of one's actions and destiny in Africa;
- For women, gender equality;
- Environmental protection;
- Good education; and
- Demanding fair treatment in the new world order.

The new political world order in which Africa has to fit in the post–Cold War ("peace order") period, started in 1989 to 1990, following the fall of the Berlin Wall on November 9, 1989. On December 25, 1991, President Mikhail Gorbachev (1931–) of the Soviet Union resigned and was succeeded by President Boris Yeltsin (1931–2007) of the Russian Federation—which marked the official collapse and replacement of the Soviet Union and Communism in Eastern Europe.

The new world order after the collapse of the Soviet Union has the following features:

1. No superpower rivalry (ideological divide) as there is only one remaining superpower.
2. From 1991 to the time of this writing there have been no Cold War politics (as existed from 1947 to 1989). This now means "Cold Peace" politics, which exclude the spheres of influence of the former colonial powers in Africa.
3. Africa must struggle to recover and survive in three worlds: West, East, and Third World, and in the aforementioned "twos" (i.e., the two Europes, wars, military organizations, economy, politics, powers, and ideologies).

SUMMARY: *AFRICA IN THE CONTEMPORARY INTERNATIONAL SYSTEM*

As explained in this chapter, there are too many international relations theories, almost all of which are European or American concepts of Western State systems. Nonetheless, as a subsystem of the international system, Africa has roles to play, including participating adequately in international affairs.

A brief glance at Africa's presence in the global system reveals three periods of Africa's presence as stated earlier: in pre-colonial, colonial, and post-colonial periods. Since, however, the 1648 peace of Westphalia marked the beginning of the modern state system, it is useful to divide Africa's eras in international relations into three broad clusters: before 1648, from 1648 to 1900, and from 1900 to the present.

From ancient times to 1648 when Africa was an object, rather than a subject, of international relations. These were various world orders, systems, and subsystems ranging from ancient Greece, Assyria, and Persia to ancient Rome, the Middle Ages, and the collapse of the Roman Empire. In this period, Egypt emerged in 3100 BCE as the first place in the world to host a city-state. Then came the African empires, kingdoms, and city-states that maintained international relations with foreign sovereigns, sovereign states, the Barbary states, and others.

The period from 1648 to 1900 welcomed the birth of the elaborate city-state system with empirical and juridical kinds of statehood. Africa was allocated juridical statehood, which was the worst of the two types. Systems and subsystems of international orders flourished during this era. Africa's colonization denied Africa the status of an active, sovereign entity in international relations. Of particular importance for Africa during this period was the abolition of the slave trade in captured Africans, as well as the birth of "people's power politics" in

Europe and the United States. The American Revolution of 1776 and the French Revolution of 1889 would be studied as milestones in global politics, democracy, and diplomacy. The alliances and wars of superiority and conquest in Europe in the 18th and 19th centuries served as huge eye-openers that African struggles for self-rule would inevitably occur. It was just a question of time. After the Renaissance and the Industrial Revolution, Africa would have to catch up.

The period from 1900 to the present is that of the contemporary international system. On the global level, 1900–1918 was an important period with sub-periods. In 1900–1914 Africa was just "waking up" with the start of the Pan-African Conferences of the 1900s. For Europe, however, a storm was brewing that would erupt in 1914, causing the first "global" war but that, in effect, was a European war that went on for four years until 1918. Within this period, a political doctrine was born, based on the theories of German thinkers of the 1800s, Karl Marx and Friedrich Engels whose thinking inspired a young, brilliant, and passionate Russian revolutionary Vladimir Lenin (1870–1924) who, in 1917, created a Soviet system that would last almost three-quarters of a century until its collapse in 1990.

Africa would be affected by that new political ideology called communism/socialism and by subsequent, European-based political doctrines such as fascism, Nazism, and others. The defeated axis powers—Germany and Italy in World War I—were responsible for the birth of fascism and Nazism that were consolidated in the antebellum years until 1939. Meanwhile, the LON system was mobilized (1919–1939) with the 14 points of U.S. President Woodrow Wilson—the architect of the LON peace process.

The birth of the first global organizations had been initiated in the late 19th century when river commissions were created along major European rivers like the Rhine and thereby started a process of public international organization and administration. Thus, the LON system was replaced by the UN, whose system incorporated the LON organizations (ITU, UPU, etc.), and thereby enhanced the role of international relations in the promotion of peace, development, and social welfare to all nations. Thus, the period from 1917 to 1945 witnessed the birth of public international organizations that would become crucial for the development of Africa and the recognition of Africa as a significant member of the global system, given Africa's resource base and geographical and strategic location. The transition from colonial to post-colonial Africa between 1945 to 1960 witnessed the birth of new African nations that, after 1960, forced the end of African colonization.

New issues and paradigms of development emerged and have started to be tested in the development of Africa. In this regard, climate change and global warming and the traditional paradoxes facing Kenya and Africa in the 21st century will continue to present grave challenges of political, economic, sociocultural, and other outcries for resolution for the benefit of Africa and Africans in the new millennium.

NOTES

1. E.H. Carr, *Twenty Years' Crisis 1919–1939.*

2. S.G. Neuman, *International Relations Theory and the Third World: An Oxymoron?*

3. Hans Morgenthau, *"Politics Among Nations" (1948).*

4. R.H. Jackson and C. Rosberg, *Why Weak States Persist.*

5. For a more detailed analysis of this question, see Stanislaw Ehrlich, *Wladza i Interesy: Studium Struktury Polityczney Kapitalizmu* [Power and Interest: A Study of the Political Structure of Capitalism] (Warsaw, Poland: Warsaw University 1967).

6. S. Ehrlick, *Teoria Panstwa i Prawa,* (Warsaw, Poland: Warsaw University, 1970).

7. C. Clapham, *Africa and the International System: The Politics of State Survival* (Cambridge, England: Cambridge University Press, 1996).

8. Joshua S. Goldstein, *International Relations,* 6th ed. (New Delhi: Dorling Kindersley, 2007).

9. Peter A. Toma and Andrew Gyorgy, eds, *Basic Issues in International Relations* (Boston: Allyn and Bacon, Inc., 1969).

10. S. D. Krasner, ed, *International Regimes* (Ithaca, NY: Cornell University Press, 1989).

11. Daniel Clard, *Les relations internationales de 1945 a nos jours,* 5th ed. (Paris: Masson, 1993).

12. J.W. Harbeson and D. Rothchild, eds, *Africa in World Politics: Reforming Political Order,* 4th ed. (Westview Press, 2009).

13. H.M. Levine, *World Politics Debated,* 4th ed. (McGraw-Hill, 1992).

CHAPTER 19

Africa and Public International Organization, Administration, and Development

THE BIRTH OF MODERN PUBLIC INTERNATIONAL ORGANIZATIONS

The previous chapters of this study, and especially Chapter 18, have attempted to define the concept of development and the development theories and paradigms that accompany that concept. This chapter will look at the meaning and origins of public international organization and administration and the international dictates that paved the way for the creation of international organizations in 19th century Europe, which witnessed many new happenings that were revolutionary in character. A new imperialism was born during the Industrial Revolution, beginning in England in 1760 and maturing in 1860, that would change Europe and the world forever. Under its second phase between 1860 and 1954, capitalist exploitation and expansionism, engineered by Europe, spread across the world and lead to fierce competition, colonization, and the birth of a new diplomacy that would lead to alliances among European and other nations. This was especially true following the Napoleonic Wars that forced Europe to form organizations for political, economic, and social collaboration to assure international peace and development. Like at the time of the birth of civilization about 5000 years ago, such cooperative services had to be initiated along and between rivers because river courses were excellent for transportation and communication, commerce and development, and other common services and utilities similar to those that had been in demand between the Tigris and Euphrates Rivers in the great valley where civilization was born.

In the 19th century, especially in the second half of the century, a number of European rivers began to be used for similar purposes. The Danube and the Rhine are good examples. The countries of Europe neighboring these rivers began to use them for commercial, transportation, and communication purposes, and to provide common services. So, initiative was taken, especially for the common use of the Danube and the Rhine, among others.

The Danube River lies in Southwest Germany and flows about 1,770 miles (about 2,848 km) southeast through Austria, Hungary, and Serbia. The Rhine rises in Western Europe at the confluence of two tributaries in Eastern Switzerland and flows about 820 miles (about 1,319 km) north and northwest through Germany and the Netherlands to the North Sea. It was along these two major European rivers that river commissions were formed. Because the commissions served public interests, their administration and management of services was also public. The Danube and Rhine River Commissions thus became the prototypes of the public international organizations that emerged in the second half of the 19th century. The neighboring states met and signed agreements or treaties to govern their conduct in using such public services, and they had to engage public civil servants or staff from among the countries' nationals, who could get together in international secretariats, with rules and regulations to govern their behavior, salaries, and administrative requirements. Thus, by the time the International Telecommunications Union (ITU) was founded at a conference held in Paris in 1865 on the initiative of the French government, international secretariats had already been set up within the European river commissions. Even earlier than 1865, a universal postal union had been set up in 1863. On October 9, 1874, a general postal union was set up by a treaty signed at Berne, Switzerland, on that day. In 1878, the name of the organization was changed to the universal postal union (UPU). Currently the UPU has 189 member states.

As years passed, more public international organizations were set up with diverse purposes and during the LON years were absorbed under the LON system. Many of the bodies created under LON were absorbed into the UN system after 1945. Public international organization and administration in this study means an institution or mechanism formed by the will of sovereign states under an agreement signed among or between them to establish relations of various types for the common benefit of the people and parties. The administration of such an organization—be it political like the League of Nations, health-focused like the World Health Organization, or telecommunications- and transportation-related like the ITU and UPU—is laid down in secretariat arrangements.

AFRICAN PUBLIC INTERNATIONAL ORGANIZATIONS AND ADMINISTRATIONS BEFORE 1945

As seen in earlier chapters, Africa did not benefit a lot from international organizations created before the United Nations. The colonization of Africa made Africa an object, rather than a subject, of international relations and, as such, the years before, during, and even World War I and World War II were times of struggle for Africa's liberation from the colonial yoke. The African Condition at those times has been discussed in Chapter 14 of this volume.

Africa's presence in major international organizations starting with the LON, and in the UN after 1954, started to have some meaning and benefits only after the attainment of independence following the decolonization of the continent. It was then that some real benefits started to accrue in Africa. The storm-gathering years of the beginning of the 20th century, with the birth of public international organizations, was cemented by the call for Pan-Africanism. The path for Africa in international organization remained unknown (if not just mythical) since the Wilsonian doctrine in Point No. 5 of his 14 points could only enhance demands for African politico-development initiatives. But when the UN was born, these demands became a reality, and Africa's presence in the international system had to be recognized.

AFRICA IN THE UN SYSTEM

This section highlights areas where Africa can, and does, benefit considerably in multidimensional basics,[1,2] since the issues addressed by the following groups affect all Africans in their daily lives:

- United Nations (UN),
- World Health Organization (WHO),
- International Monetary Fund (IMF),
- World Bank Group,
- World Trade Organization (WTO), and
- Various NGOs.

The overarching area relates to sustainable development. There, Africa stands to benefit most in her international relations if she pays increased attention to, and participates more broadly and competently in, negotiations and other international activities relating to development. As long as Africa remains an international actor, she will always relate to the affairs of public and private international organization, administration, and development. This fact is stressed in the next chapter.

The African countries are members of the UN, World Bank Group, WTO, WHO, and IMF. Africa also maintains working relationships with NGOs. The benefits and contributions of Africa in, and to, these international organizations range from political to economic, business, financial, and social issues.[3]

The United Nations

The UN is a political institution that addresses all sorts of issues of interest and benefit to Africa. "UN" is, however, an expression that has several meanings. The UN is an umbrella organization and it can mean all of the organizations based in New York with its six organs including the Trusteeship Council, Security Council (SC), General Assembly (GA), Economic and Social Council (ECOSOC), the International Court of Justice (ICJ) based the Hague in Holland, and the Secretariat. All of these serve under the direction of the secretary-general (UNSG).

Additionally, there are the UN bodies such as the United Nations Environment Programme (UNEP), United Nations Human Settlements Programme (UN-HABITAT), World Food Programme (WFP), and others that enjoy autonomy but whose chief executives are appointed by the UNSG in consultation with the member states. There also are the so-called specialized agencies of the UN, which are in effect different international organizations with different mandates and chief executives, separately elected by member states. These agencies deal with special issues such as health, development, weather, and climate (the World Meteorological Organization [WMO]), food and agriculture (Food and Agriculture Organization [FAO]), labor (International Labour Organization [ILO]), as well as education, science, and culture (United Nations Educational, Scientific and Cultural Organization [UNESCO]), maritime issues (International Maritime Organization [IMO]), and civil aviation (International Civil Aviation Agency [ICAO]). Because these specialized institutions serve the same government of the UN, the agencies have signed memoranda of understanding (MOUs) with the UN, and this arrangement has provided the UN system. Thus, the UN can mean the UN, a UN organization (UNO), or the UN system.

Africa is a member of all of these system organizations, and of particular interest to Africa are the issues relating not just to political security and global peace, but also those that concern development, the environment, social issues (like human rights), refugees, and health issues (including pandemics such as HIV/AIDS, Ebola, tuberculosis [TB], and malaria). In general, efforts have succeeded more in the areas of social welfare and development rather than as a keeper of global peace.

New and emerging issues on the UN agenda continue to grow and include global warming. Particularly Africa needs the UN because of

Africa's juridical statehood. Socially, economically, and in terms of development, Africa needs the UN system the most.

The World Health Organization

The WHO is another extremely important UN system organization for Africa. In recent years, with the occurrence of pandemics that are devastating, and even incurable such as HIV/AIDS, WHO has become extremely important to Africa. This is an international institution—a UN specialized agency created on April 7, 1948, and based in Geneva as the coordinating authority for UN public health issues and initiatives. At its birth, 26 states ratified its charter. The WHO succeeded the LON international health organization following the International Health Conference held in 1946. With regional offices around the globe, WHO's the regional office for Africa addresses health issues and problems confronting the African continent. Every African state has a health ministry, and the minister for health usually leads his or her country's delegations at WHO conferences and meetings.

The International Monetary Fund

Another UN specialized agency, IMF was created in July 1944 at a UN monetary and financial conference, held at the Mount Washington Hotel in Bretton Woods, New Hampshire, USA. The IMF currently has 168 member states, oversees the global financial system by following the macroeconomic policies that fit member states, especially those states like the United States and Western European states that have influential power over the exchange rates and the balance of payments. The IMF has not really done too much good for African economics because some of the IMF-initiated policies implemented in Africa, like the structural adjustment programmes (SAPs) that are described in Chapter 20, have done more harm than good to Africa and other developing areas of the world.

The World Bank Group

The World Bank is a group of the following five international institutions:

1. The International Bank for Reconstruction and Development (IBRD)
2. The International Development Association (IDA)
3. The International Finance Corporation (IFC)
4. The Multilateral Investment Guarantee Agency (MIGA) and
5. The International Centre for Settlement of Investment Disputes (ICSID)

The World Bank Group is also of vital importance to Africa since the World Bank has the main purpose of helping African and other developing nations and their peoples attain sustainable development and reduce poverty. As an international institution, the World Bank also provides leveraged loans to the poorest nations of Africa and others for capital programs with the goal of reducing poverty. Thus, IBRD gives investment loans for social-economic development, and IDA gives development policy loans and financial support to needy countries and also stresses the need for institutional reforms. Of particular interest to Africa are grants to alleviate debt burdens, improve sanitation and water supply, provide support to civil society in the African counties, combat HIV/AIDS, reduce greenhouse gases, and other services. The World Bank, IBRD, and IMF were the brainchildren of the UN, and were created in 1944 at the Bretton Woods Conference. This is why they are referred to as the Bretton Woods institutions. Engaged in capacity building, research and development, and similar activities in Africa and elsewhere, they have helped in areas relating to corruption but in many areas the bank and the IMF have led to graver impoverishment of Africa. Throughout the bank's history from 1945 to the present, the bank's activities have received mixed reports, especially if these activities are clustered into the following four eras:

- 1945–1968,
- 1968–1980,
- 1980–1989, and
- 1989–the time of this writing.

The World Bank and IMF were initiated under the leadership of U.S. Secretary of State George Marshall, architect of the Marshall Plan, which was intended to help reconstruct Western Europe after World War II. Thereafter, the two institutions remained as specialized UN agencies to attend to the financial and development needs of the countries of the developing world, including Africa. The concept of the Marshall Plan is explained later in Chapter 20.

The World Trade Organization

The WTO is an international institution specializing in trade and development issues. It is based in Geneva, Switzerland. The WTO was born out of the UN system in 1947 as the General Agreement on Tariffs and Trade (GATT), an international organization promoting global business and development through international trade. The nature and function of the WTO is discussed in Chapter 20, which will address Africa and the international development practicum.

Various Non-Governmental Organizations

These groups are better known as CSOs (civil society organizations) and NGOs. In the past 20 years, they have increased their value as international non-governmental entities in Africa. During the Cold War many were suspicious of NGOs, which they believed to have been working as "spy agents" for the West. After the collapse of the Soviet system in 1989, NGOs have assumed considerable significance in international relations in the UN system, and this benefits Africa a as subsystem of the global system.

NGOs have, for example, been used as agents to supply aid to vulnerable groups in Africa where regimes are criticized for various reasons, including human rights violations. Thus NGOs like Medecins Sans Frontieres (Doctors without Borders), women's progress organizations, and other NGOs dealing with development, human settlements, education, refugees, youth, etc., have been used to promote sustainable development. Africa has been a beneficiary of NGO work in many fields, such as in area partnerships for development. Also, many NGOs operating in Africa have acquired a consultative status with the UN's ECOSOC and do quite well in helping Africa. As go-betweens for African states and the international community, especially the donor community like the UN system and the donor countries, NGOs have applied pressure on national governments in Africa and elsewhere, leading democratization, good governance, and other reforms in these countries. The areas of women's empowerment and eradication of poverty and inequality in African societies have been particularly well targeted.

OVERVIEW OF THE UN SYSTEM

The UN charter stipulates the purposes and principles of the UN, outlines the functions and relationships of the UNOs with the system organizations that are affected via MOUs between the UN and each of the system agencies, and mandates levels of autonomy and independence of the system organizations and bodies, including regional arrangements.

The nature and functions of the organizations in the UN system are as follows:

• They are completely independent from the UN but serve the same UN member states, and

• Are much older than the UN—some (e.g., UPU) were created even before the birth of the LON, and others established during the LON period.

The purposes of the UN as stipulated in the UN charter can be clustered into two broad categories (dual purpose) as the keeper of the peace, performing international peacekeeping and security tasks and as the promoter of international welfare, addressing sustainable development.

The principles of the UN charter are to sustain and pursue the natural law theory of international relations (i.e., equal sovereignty of all member states, territorial integrity, peaceful coexistence, and settlement of international disputes through peaceful means). Chapter VII of the charter deals with actions with respect to threats to the peace, breaches of the peace, and acts of aggression. It is here that the rule of enforcement mentions self-defense. Article 51 of the UN charter makes it clear that an attack on one member state is equal to an attack on all the member states who may act individually or collectively against the aggressor.

Common Characteristics among Parts of the UN System

Each organ, organization, and body of the UN system has a structure that is established by the constitution (charter) of each UN agency. Each UN system organization and body has its own mechanism for dealing with various aspects of its mandate (e.g., humanitarian issues, emergencies and natural calamities, disarmament issues, development, environment and gender issues, natural resources issues, trade and globalization issues, reforms, funding, capacity building issues, global public goods issues, and diplomacy, general debates, negotiations, etc.).

AFRICA IN THE INTERNATIONAL POLITICS AND ECONOMICS OF THE UN SYSTEM

The international relations of Africa and the UN are both subsystems of the international global system. As members of the UN system, the African states (53 of them) participate in both areas of the dual purpose of the UN—in the politics of international peace and security, and in the broad area better known as today as the field of sustainable development (i.e., in the politics of international economics and in the politics of international humanitarianism). All of these three areas (international peace and security, international economics, and international humanitarianism) constitute the international agendas of the UN conference system as follow:

• The politics of international peace and security

  • UN Charter provisions;
  • Conflict prevention, reduction, management, and resolution; root causes and proposals for resolution; and
  • International terrorism.

- The politics of international humanitarianism (social, gender issues, human rights, equality, emergencies, health, and diseases)

  - Results of conflicts; emergencies of refugees and displaced persons;
  - Rehabilitation, reconstruction, relief, and development;
  - Human rights issues; UN education decade for human rights 1995–2005;
  - Diseases, pandemics, and development;
  - Gender issues including empowerment of women;
  - Implementation appraisals of the international summits and conferences (Copenhagen, March 1995; Bejing, September 1995; Cairo, 1994; etc.);
  - Human settlements (habitat); and
  - Drugs and drug abuse.

- The politics of international economic relations

  - Politics and economics cannot be divorced from each other in the study of International Relations. The problems of international political economy emerge.
  - International economics and international politics are part and parcel of the relations that exist between and among states. Politics among nations are much affected by economic reality.
  - Political factors affect economic outcomes in three basic ways: (1) the political system shapes the economic system because the structure and operation of the international economic system is often determined by the structure and operation of the international political system; (2) political concerns often shape economic policy because economic policies are frequently dictated by overriding political interests; and (3) international economic relations themselves are political relations because international economic interaction, like international political interaction, is a process by which state and non-state actors manage or fail to manage their conflicts and by which they operate, cooperate, or fail to cooperate to achieve common goals.

Global Issues on the International Agenda

The first decade following the end of the World War II and the establishment of the UN in 1945 was a decade of transition, organization, and ideological struggle between the West and the East. With the realization that decolonization would not only result in legal and political independence of the former colonies of Europe in the Third World, there was an effort to try to provide national economic aid that would help the newly independent states seek ways and means of adopting self-reliant economic and political destinies. With this in mind, the UN began to formulate international strategies and plans for development of Africa and other developing areas. The first developing strategy was launched at the beginning of the 1960s. The UN development strategies, especially those starting from the 1970s, were supplemented by UN conferences, summits, and special sessions of the UN General Assembly and the bodies and organizations of the UN system, which were crucial for Africa's development. That was the beginning of the UN conference system, which can be outlined in the two periods from 1945 to 1990 and from 1991 to the time of this writing.

In addition to the aforementioned struggles between East–West political ideology and ideological confrontation in economical, political, and social concepts and practices, the years from 1945 to 1990 witnessed the following developments:

- Granting of independence to colonial countries and peoples (Africa: since 1960);
- Adoption of UN development strategies or development decade every 10 years;
- Adoption of two important resolutions by UN General Assembly in 1970— (1) resolution on the granting of colonial people and countries, and (2) resolution in which the UN decided on a process of Official Development Assistance (ODA) of 0.7% of OECD Development Assistance Committee (DAC) countries;
- The sixth special session of UN General Assembly on economic issues was held in 1974;
- The seventh special session of UN General Assembly on economic issues was held in 1975; and
- In 1976, Habitat I was the First UN Conference on Human Settlements held at Vancouver, Canada. In 1977, a UN Conference on Desertification was held in Nairobi. In 1978, the Group of 77 Developing Countries held a summit in Argentina. In 1979 a UN Conference on Science and Technology was held at Vienna, Austria, and the Third UN Conference on Industrialization was held at New Delhi, India, in 1980.

By these actions, a new international order was launched. Throughout the period of the 1970s to the 1980s, global negotiations on trade issues (global rounds of multilateral negotiations) occurred and were maintained until 1992 when a UN conference on the environment and development was held in June in Rio de Janeiro. The Rio conference launched a new era of international negotiations on global issues on three aspects:

(1) Global human security whereby the major branches of the UN agenda were amalgamated:

- Disarmament and international peace and security and
- Development and related issues of a legal, cultural, social, economic, and environmental nature, including weather and climate-related issues;

(2) New and emerging issues requiring a different approach; globalization, HIV/AIDS, and other pandemics

(3) Global public good and global public bad; and

(4) New paradigms in development initiatives triggered by the outcomes of the Rio conference and Agenda 21, the platform for sustainable development adopted at the UN Summit held at Rio de Janeiro, Brazil in June 1992.

After the Rio Conference 1992–2005

On November 8, 1989, the Berlin Wall was demolished. This marked the beginning of a new political order. Conferences and summits of the UN system convened to discuss development issues from 1990 included the following, among others:

- 1990: LDC conference in Paris;
- 1991: conference in Dublin on water;
- 1992: UNCED, RIO;
- 1993: Human Rights Conference in Vienna;
- 1994: Cairo conference on development and reproduction, conference in Barbados on Small Island Developing States (SIDS), Yokohama Conference on Natural Disaster Reduction;
- 1995: Social development conference in Copenhagen; Beijing conference on women, 50th anniversary of the UN at UN Headquarters in New York;
- 1996: Habitat II, Istanbul;
- 1997: Kyoto Protocol;
- 2000: Millennium Summit and millennium development goals (MDGs);
- 2001: LDC conference in Brussels, WTO in Doha Round, Qatar;
- 2002: UN conference on financing for development in Monterrey, Mexico; World Summit on Sustainable Development in Johannesburg in August and in Rio in September; and
- 2005: SIDS at the UN Headquarters in New York; Kobe Conference on disaster reduction.

Impediments to Development

In the field of international economic relations, outcomes of interactions, and negotiations among states of the UN system, there is a lack of political will. Consequently, most of the commitments and results of negotiations remain on paper and head for the UN archives. Those that are implemented are full of conditionalities. The lack of political management of government decisions at the UN and in its system is a major impediment.

ISSUES AND CHALLENGES IN HISTORICAL PERSPECTIVE AND ANALYSIS

Throughout this study, emphasis has been placed on the meaning and vital role of sustainable development as a multidimensional process, the attainment of which is crucial for the prosperity of every nation and inhabitant of Africa. Thus, the absence of development results in poverty. The poverty syndrome in Africa is, therefore, the mother of all of the enemies of African development and security.

In the remainder of this chapter, a deliberate attempt is made to explain the following issues, events, and challenges, whose proper understanding and tackling can, and will, help find ways and means of overcoming the problems in Africa:

- Reasons for Africa's persistent poverty;
- The plight of the Third World;
- Debt as the primus inter pares of Africa's gravest development burdens;
- Africa and international development: relations with the association of Southeast Asia nations and China;
- Africa and international development: Africa's economy in historical perspective;
- Impact of Agenda 21 on the African development process;
- Can the MDG process meet Africa's development goals?;
- Defining globalization;
- Global negotiations: issues, challenges, and opportunities for business and development in Africa; and
- Climate change and African politics.

REASONS FOR AFRICA'S PERSISTENT POVERTY

This writer offers the following three propositions on the African Condition:

- Africa has vast resources and endowments, both human and natural. She should not, therefore, be poor.
- Africa is poorer now than she was 40 years ago. In fact, Africa is the only continent that is poorer now than she was 25 years ago.
- That Africa should be so poor when she is so rich in resources is a huge paradox.

Conceptual Understandings

What is Africa? Africa is not a country; Africa is a continent.

What is poverty? Poverty is a condition of lacking the means to procure the basic necessities of life.

What is the poverty syndrome? The poverty syndrome is the state of events or conditions presenting, inviting, or lending to the lack or want of the means to procure/necessitate, or *secure* the basic needs of life. Poverty is a condition of insecurity and of a lack of development. The opposite of poverty is security and development in a sustained fashion.

What is Security? Security is freedom from:

- Want;
- Fear;
- Famine and hunger;
- Poverty syndrome;
- Violence or persecution;
- Murders, killings;
- Death, disease (pandemics like HIV/AIDS, Malaria; TB; Ebola, etc.), disasters (human and natural hazards such as floods, drought), and desertification, desert locusts, etc.;
- Leadership deficiency, corruption, nepotism, cultism, incompetence, ineffectiveness of leaders;
- Attacks, invasions, conflicts, coups, wars;
- Subalternism, state weakness and collapse, violations of sovereign and territorial integrity;
- Population and demographic pressures;
- Population displacements and refugees;
- Slums, and other urban health/sanitation hazards;
- Ecological life systems disasters such as pollution of air, water, atmosphere, land, and environmental degradation;
- Destruction of the global public goods (GPGs) at national, regional, and global levels;
- Destruction and irrational use of natural resources (minerals, energy, water, assets, property) and agriculture-based products such as wheat, coffee, maize, tea, sugar, cocoa, coconut, rubber, sisal, etc.;
- Economic decline and malaise; and
- Fraud, deceit, and injustice in business ventures and practices and so on.

What is development? Development is a multidimensional process encompassing more than the mere material and financial sides of people's lives, and in which the following characteristics prevail:

- Improvements in incomes and outputs, normally measured at national levels, in overall and per capita GNP growth;
- Radical changes in institutional, social (e.g., educational, political, and administrative structures), and popular attitudes, and even customs, thoughts, and beliefs;

- Reorientation and reorganization of entire economic and social systems;
- Acceleration of economic growth;
- Reduction of inequality;
- Eradication of absolute poverty; and
- Satisfaction, within an entire social system, of diverse basic needs and desires of individuals and social groups, so as to assure or provide them with a situation or condition of better life.

In short, development is the sustained elevation of an entire society and social system toward a better or "more human" life. Development implies changes or "progress" in economic and social conditions, institutions, attitudes, customs, thoughts, and even in beliefs, and represents more than economics and the quantitative measurements of incomes, unemployment, and inequality.

For the process of development to be durable, or sustainable, it has to consist of seven basic and sustained criteria:

- Growth—increase;
- Equality of distribution (of wealth, prosperity, property, and power);
- Autonomy and self-reliance;
- Human dignity;
- Popular participation ("bottom-up" involvement);
- Expansion of state capacity; and
- Education (i.e., knowledge and information).

What are the priorities for successful realization of development efforts? For concrete and practical results to be attained from the above, there is only one priority: implementation of the measures that are, or may be, proposed.

What is a paradox? A paradox is a contradiction.

Africa: The Huge Paradox

Why is Africa such a huge paradox? Because Africa should not be poor; but she is poor in plenty. Africa is very poor, while simultaneously very rich in human and natural resources and endowments (water, energy, and natural resources such as gold, copper, diamonds, zinc, tin, soda ash, aluminum, platinum, uranium, lead, nickel, antimony, asbestos, chromium, bauxite, cobalt, iron ore, manganese, phosphates, silver, oil, natural gas, coal, as well as in agriculture-based products like coffee, tea, cocoa, cotton, rubber, sisal, etc.

What are Africa's major paradoxes? Africa's poverty syndrome is triggered and sustained by a number of paradoxes, especially the following, which were previously described in Volume I, Chapter 2:

- The paradox of habitation,
- The paradox of location,
- The paradox of acculturation,
- The paradox of fragmentation,
- The paradox of humiliation,
- The paradox of education,
- The paradox of leadership,
- The paradox of statehood,
- The paradox of perpetual conflicts, coups, and corruption,
- The paradox of natural beauty,
- The paradox of categorization, and
- The paradox of poverty par excellence.

Why is Africa poorer now than she was 25 to 50 years ago? Why is Africa the only continent on Earth that is poorer now than it was 25 years ago? The answers to this question lie in the dictates that have, over the centuries, rocked and shaped Africa and landed this mighty continent in a poverty syndrome and persistent lack of development that make Africa the poorest continent in the world. These dictates and events can be clustered into five broad categories: (1) nature and the environment, (2) history, (3) economics, (4) politics, and (5) socio-cultural set–up.

Nature and the Environment

Africa is a vast continent, as the following facts reveal:

- From Ras ben Sakka in Tunisia, the most northerly point, to Cape Agulhas, the most southerly point in South Africa, is a distance of approximately 5,000 miles (8,000 km);
- From Cape Verde, the westernmost point, to Ras Hafun in Somalia, the most easterly projection, is a distance of approximately 4,600 miles (7,400 km);
- The length of Africa's coastline is 16,100 miles (26,000 km);
- Africa covers 6 percent of the Earth's total surface, and 20.4 percent of the Earth's total land;
- After Asia, Africa is the world's second largest continent with 11,725,385 square miles (30,368,609 square km), including adjacent islands (states);

- Africa is the most populous continent, with a 2008 population estimate of 940 million, which is 14 percent of the world's human population; and
- Africa has the world's fastest growing population.

Impoverishment of Africa has been caused by a combination of natural and human actions and non-actions. Africa suffers a lot from major natural disasters such as drought and desertification, floods, desert locusts, bushfires, hail stones, etc. These and other natural hazards have a negative impact on the development of Africa. Other disaster agents with devastating effects in Africa include the following:

- Climate change and global warming as it affects Africa's food production, health conditions, loss of biodiversity, etc.;
- Environmental degradation;
- Depletion of the ozone layer because of unwise production and consumption patterns;
- Population and demographic pressures;
- Ill-advised agricultural and other policies of African governments;
- Deforestation as part of the African poverty syndrome, resulting from rapid desertification—destruction of forests for the construction industry and for firewood for cooking, which results in rapid desertification of Africa, overgrazing, etc.;
- Man-made "friends of poverty" and "enemies of development," poverty, ignorance (illiteracy), and disease (pandemics, menengitis, and others mentioned above);
- Irrational use of natural resources, and so on.

History

The three periods of African history are the pre-colonial, colonial, and post-colonial. Impoverishment of Africa has been accentuated for many centuries primarily by the European legacies of:

- Slavery and the slave trade;
- European expansionism, imperialism, and colonialism;
- Colonization of Africa after the Berlin Conference on the partitioning of Africa (November 15, 1884–February 26, 1885);
- Colonial plundering of Africa;
- Transformation of Africa by European colonial policies and practices;
- Deprivation of Africa's Africanness, African spirit, and identity; and
- Replacement of the African value system, formerly based upon custom and tradition, by the European (Western) value system, based mainly on education, money, human liberties, and freedoms.

Economics

Origins of the impoverishment of Africa must be traced to the imposition of alien, European rule on the African continent. Impoverishment of Africa was accentuated for centuries primarily by the European legacies of:

- Taxation, slave labor, and illegitimate trade—the slave trade;
- Exploitation through reverse transfers of resources, cheap labor, and raw materials;
- Destruction of the African traditional structures and institutions for conducting and managing the African economies and business activities in pre-colonial times, and replacement of these by European structures in Africa; and
- Introduction of the cash crop system at the expense of the traditional African system of subsistence farming.

The cash crop system of the colonial era introduced trade practices that did not benefit Africans, but were meant to satisfy the economic and business needs of the North—Europe. The rich supply of minerals enumerated above, and the agricultural products known as the cash crops were not meant for African consumption, but for the businesses, northern factories, and consumers in Europe.

Moreover, the relations created in colonial times between the colonies/colonized peoples and the colonial powers were not of equals, but of "subjects" (subordinates, the colonized) with "bosses" (the colonizers). Thus, the colonies and their peoples could not trade with any other peoples and/or countries, but only with the mother country at non-competitive rates. Those colonial policies and practices not only prevailed even after the attainment of independence by the colonies, but they established a neo-colonial dependency syndrome that continues to haunt the African nations in this post-colonial era of the new millennium.

The legacy of colonial heritage retains many colonial remnants of the draining of Africa's resources (reverse resource transfers) and never applying the use of these resources in Africa; of economic mismanagement, non-accountability, and bad governance; of non-creation of incentives to stop the brain-drain and the rapid urbanism and urbanization; of graft and selfishness; of ethnocentrism versus patriotism, of ideological influences on African development efforts (Afro-capitalism versus Afro-communism; Afro-communism versus Afro-liberalism, Afro-socialism, etc.). All these are by-products of colonialism and colonization that have been inherited by the European-trained African leaders.

External forces impacting African development efforts include the:

- Cold War and Cold Peace politics;
- Workings of the international economic system;

- Indebtedness and debt servicing;
- Structural Adjustment Programs of the World Bank and IMF;
- Protectionism in the developed country markets and pricing of commodities versus African commodities and services (may be one or two strings attached);
- Deteriorating terms of trade: impoverishment of Africa can, and does, follow the trade collapse for African nations, which lose foreign-exchange earnings because of the fall in prices for their primary commodities (e.g., cocoa, coffee, tea, sugar, and pyrethrum) on global markets;
- Oil crises (energy costs);
- Globalization (a double-edged sword for Africa);
- The combination of the denial of access of African goods and services to global/developed country markets and the debt and debt-servicing burdens are among the greatest promoters of poverty in Africa, as well as of unfair trade and lack of symmetry in economics and trade;
- Efforts to remove inefficient, or lack of systematic, empowerment of women in development and business in Africa;
- Global recessions;
- Rising real interests, including security, gender equality, and education;
- Leadership inefficiency/deficiency in Africa because of brutal corruption, cronyism, cultism, nepotism, and greed;
- Negative impacts of climate change and global warming on African economies;
- Inadequacies of Africa's presence in global business and development negotiations;
- The uncertainty that the MDGs and the WTO global negotiations can deliver on the promises to Africa; and
- Lack of adequate popular participation in decision-making processes on issues affecting the daily lives of the African people, and the need for a bottom-up grassroots development approach.

Politics

African poverty arising from politics and political doctrines dates back to the Berlin Conference.

- European peace for Africa (1885) versus the European peace for Europe (1648);
  - juridical statehood versus empirical statehood—deliberate lack of preparation for self-reliance by Africans;
- Colonial heritage in Africa;
- "Divide et impera," and other European colonial policies and practices;
- Seven of the fourteen countries attending became colonial powers in Africa: Portugal, Spain, England, Germany, France, Italy, and Belgium. The other Powers

that attended the Berlin Conference of 1884 to 1885 were: the United States, the Netherlands, Denmark, Sweden-Norway (Union until 1905), Ottoman Empire, Russia, and Austria-Hungary;

- Conflicts, coups, corruption, consequences, and cures in Africa;
- The paradox of leadership: ethnocentrism versus patriotism and national identity;
- Problems of empowerment and ownership of development and business initiatives in Africa;
- Lack of systematic empowerment of women and other marginalized strata of society through formal education;
- Challenges of the new girl order (NGO) in Africa;
- Grave isolation by the paradoxes of habitation, location/isolation/marginalization and leadership deficiency; and
- Lack of the right mental attitude of African leaders, elites, and people to foster multidimensional development. Multidimensional development is a process that requires many changes to be made. These include an to end leadership deficiency and the need for African leaders to adopt different ways of governance

The Sociocultural Setup

The social agenda:
especially on new and emerging issues and challenges: pandemics, disasters, and development; science and technology for development;

- Africa and the challenge of globalization;
- reverse resource flows; women in business and development in Africa;
- education for all: roles of the African university in the education sector; and
- ownership of African development initiatives by Africans.

Ending the Poverty Syndrome in Africa in the 21st Century: What, When, and by Whom?

Measures need to be taken now, in the short-, medium-, and long-terms, and in the coming decades of the 21st century. Actions to eradicate poverty should be taken in the following areas, among many others, by African governments, institutions, and peoples, as well as by international organizations both public and private, and external governments, their institutions, and peoples. Africa must accept the fact that the primary responsibility for the development of Africa lies with African governments, institutions, and peoples. All of these together must initiate, develop, own, run, and manage development initiatives in order to reduce or end/eradicate poverty in Africa.

To end the poverty syndrome, Africa must perform a balancing act between modernization and the traditional/cultural/value system ways of living in Africa. She must also master a balancing act specifically between Western and African values. Can Africa reclaim her civilizations in the 21st century while modernizing to fit in to the present, predominantly Western–dictated, value system? Which of Africa's traditions, customs, and cultures (land, habits, agriculture, worship, dress, food, religion, family, and extended family codes, village parenthood, traditional rituals, etc.) should be recovered fully, and which should be dropped, and why?

Ending/reducing the enemies of progress/development in Africa (i.e., poverty, disease/pandemics, and illiteracy/ignorance) will require tackling and settling Africa's paradoxes. Africa must own Africa's development and destiny. Africa must recognize Africans as a vital resource and put brain trust ahead of brain-drain (create incentives such as assuring jobs to their nationals after they complete studies abroad). Particular attention must be given to the following:

- Environment, natural resources, and the GPGs (i.e., ecosystem, life-support systems, protection of environment, and rational use of natural resources in Africa);
- Cohabitation of Africans with nature, wildlife, and different ethnic/tribal groupings; and
- Durable or sustainable development.

Africans must Africanize Africa in the 21st century by investing, developing, and giving attractive incentives from within Africa to Africa. Africa must recover good and progressive African traditions and cultures that are fully reflective of Africanness. To end the poverty syndrome, Africa also must do the following:

- Make rational use of resource mobilization, skills, and human knowledge;
- Acquire and maintain discipline, law and order, in every African nation; Pursue development initiatives and get the development priorities right (agriculture, industry, infrastructure development, irrigation, political process of democratization, good governance, competence, imperative human and institutional capacity-building and empowerment of all including women, girls, and the marginalized strata of society via long-term strategies and financial resource mobilization.
- Provide water and other common services.
- Accomplish economic reforms.
- Create an enabling political environment to replace one of corruption, and make transparency in governance and accountability realities.
- Respect human rights, justice, representation, dignity, freedom, etc. (these are the principles to be used against neo-colonialism and corrupt practices, and they are the same principles that were so widely applied by the founding fathers of African Unity and Pan-Africanism in Africa.
- Empower women and girls against gender inequality.

- Mitigate climate change and global warming.
- Use Africanism in African solutions to African problems (i.e., conflicts, coups, wars, civil strife, corruption).
- Employ foreign policy and diplomacy as tools for conflict resolution and management.
- Use information revolution and technology transfer to Africa as strong common and aggressive public information and education programs for multifaceted development (e.g., training trainers, journalistic serialization, etc.).
- Empower current generation for competent leadership.
- Use energy for African development, especially new and renewable sources of energy (like solar, biomass/biofuels, geothermal, animal draught, hydro power, wind power, peat, tar sands, ocean energy, nuclear energy using fission and fusion).
- Return to patriotism, nationalism, and Pan-Africanism.
- Respect Africa and Africans—African pride in Africa and Africans to be earned.
- Apply science and technology to sustainable development, environmental sustainability, and sustainability science.
- Advance the reculturation of Africa instead of acculturation through the use of a common language for Africa (an African Esperanto) and other common languages (e.g., Swahili, Hausa, Lingala), as well as common cultural centers of excellence highlighting music, arts, poetry, etc.
- Increase efforts of African governments and institutions to provide fair, equitable, and balanced coverage of Africa by the mass media.
- Perform disaster preparedness, reduction, prevention, and management in Africa.
- Create African universities/institutions of higher learning, to be centers of excellence and empowerment for the common African good (like NEPAD and the regional economic integrations institutions in Africa, military, etc.).
- Employ mechanisms of AU for empowerment of Africans, security, law and order, and development in peace and political stability.
- Create a "Uniting for Peace" mechanism for Africa.
- Tackle and find solutions to major challenges facing Africa in the new millennium including diseases (such as HIV/AIDS, Ebola, TB, malaria, etc.), globalization, climate change and global warming, Global Public Bads (GPBs), inadequate education, inefficient leadership, and lack of African development.
- Work with African-based development institutions such as East Africa Community (EAC), Intergovernmental Authority on Development (IGAD), NEPAD, Southern African Development Community (SADC), Economic Community of the West African States (ECOWAS), Economic Community of the Central African States (ECCAS), Union of Maghreb Arabs, North Africa (UMA), Preferential Trade Area of Eastern and Southern Africa (PTA), the UN's Economic Commission for Africa (ECA), East African Customs Union (EACU), and OAU/AU.
- Supplement and combine Africa-initiated and -developed measures with the efforts of the global community (e.g., by the Group of 8, Group of 77 and China,

Non-Aligned Movement (NAM), and bilateral foreign aid packages such as USAID, SIDA, CIDA, NORAD, DANIDA, etc., the Global Coalition for Africa (GCA), UN system efforts such as ECA, etc.

What Roles for the World Economic Powers in African Recovery and Development?

In today's globalized world, the United States, EU, Japan, Canada, India, and China, to name but a few global economic powers, have major roles to play in the renaissance of Africa as she struggles to become a truly modernized continent. All have agreed to this premise. The test, however, lies in the types and extent of roles, both collective and individual, that these economic superpowers will be playing in Africa in the coming decade and beyond.

This is an important topic which justifies a separate discussion to be addressed in the future. Each of these countries has its own priorities in Africa. Of particular interest, however, is going to be what China comes up with as her priorities in Africa. Of late, China has become very aggressive on the African scene, and China's future relationship with Africa needs to be more closely analyzed. What is China up to in Africa? Could China become a "commercial tsunami" in Africa? We have to wait and see.

Priorities in Africa for the U.S. Government

For all practical purposes, and given the opportunities and the potential for U.S. business and development cooperation with Africa, the following objectives are noteworthy as priority areas for the United States in Africa now and in the coming years:

- Bolster fragile states in Africa.
- Enhance regional and subregional organizations in Africa.
- Enhance strategic partnerships.
- Enhance regional security capacity.
- Enhance Africa's counter-terrorism cooperation and capacity.
- Focus on humanitarian and development assistance programs.
- Stimulate Africa's economic development and growth.
- Consolidate democratic transitions, and implement U.S. presidential initiatives, such as Bill Clinton's initiative under the African Growth Opportunities Act (AGOA) and George W. Bush's initiative on HIV/AIDS.
- Encourage the search for investment and other opportunities for joint ventures, partnerships, etc., in Africa.
- Explore ways and means of enhancing the African–American relationship for business and related ventures, cooperation, and promotion.

The Way Forward, and the Great Challenges to Africa

This analysis of the African poverty condition supports a number of conclusions, particularly, that neither the status quo ante, nor the existing situation of Africa as the poorest continent on Earth, is tenable. Additionally, the primary responsibility for the development of Africa rests with the governments, people, and institutions of Africa and, hence, there is a need for Africa to take charge of her own development destiny and own it. Efforts to adopt partnerships for African development and security, such as NEPAD, should be strengthened and applied Africa-wide, since most of the past development efforts for Africa have failed. It is obvious that Africa-initiated, Africa-developed, Africa-run and Africa-managed development initiatives are the only ones that stand a reasonable chance of success.

The Global Village nature of our world now requires that all nations collaborate for development. This means that the extension of assistance to a needy country or continent has become more than a mere moral imperative for everybody and every nation. Africa is poorer now than she was 40 years ago, and even 25 years ago, because of endogenous and exogenous forces, whose resolution requires the concerted measures of African nations and peoples, with the support of the international community.

In this connection, the following reasons should be borne in mind, and call for coordinated actions at national, African continental, and global levels. Leadership deficiencies and failures in Africa can be explained by the fact that the European colonial policies and practices did not prepare Africans competently and adequately to take over as competent administrators after independence. Since colonial economic policies stressed cash crops for the European markets, there was no development of African economies. This was partly because the imperialists levied taxes, including hut taxes, to be paid in cash, which forced Africans to abandon their systematic cultivation of the African traditional crops for subsistence like cassava, millet, and sorghum, and to grow cash crops such as cotton, coffee, cocoa, and sugar cane, and to mine minerals like gold, diamonds, and copper that benefited Europe. African colonies were forced to consume goods from their ex-colonial masters, and when colonies gained independence, they started up industries that relied heavily on imports of essential components from the West. That kept money flowing northward. As these cash crops—primarily commodities—determined the foreign exchange earning of the ex-colonial African countries, any price fluctuation for these crops, or crop failures in Africa, resulted in economic decline and malaise, which were strong prescriptions for poverty in Africa.

No industrial growth could happen in the African nations because these nations had to borrow heavily from Western banks and governments in order to repay the loans that the African countries had borrowed under the so-called SAPs of the IMF/World Bank Group, following the collapse of the prices of the African primary commodities and the skyrocketing of oil prices during the energy crises of 1970s and 1980s (Mexican debt burden and its subsequent negative impacts, especially on the developing nations, as described later in this chapter).

All of the above forces hit the African countries the hardest, however. In fact, Africa never recovered, and that led to Africa's economic decline and malaise that have been experienced up to the time of this writing. Subsequent economic problems led to enhanced Afro-pessimism, and each subsequent crisis has increased poverty in Africa. Faced with those, and subsequent negative dictates that have continued to shape Africa since then, such as civil wars and conflicts, Africa still remains the poorest region on Earth, and this is why she is the only continent to be poorer today than she was 25 years ago. This African condition most certainly will continue to haunt Africans and their leaders in the coming decade and beyond.

THE PLIGHT OF THE THIRD WORLD

For all practical purposes, the developing nations of the Third World need the UN more than do the developed countries of Europe and North America plus Australia and New Zealand. Whereas Chapter 18 presented information on the structure of the UN, another large part of the international assistance equation is how states are categorized, a factor that is important in any attempt to maintain equity and justice in international economic relations.

Categorization of States at the UN

In the early 1970s, the UN called upon its Development Policy Planning Committee and the Committee on Contributions to examine the development conditions and poverty syndrome of the developing countries of the Third World, whose economic and other situations were aggravated by inflation, recession, and injustice in international economic relations dominating in the 1970s and triggered by the energy (oil) crisis of 1973 that led to the OPEC oil cartel.

To deal with the economic problems of that time, the UN adopted several measurers, including the Second UN Development Decade (UNDD) Strategy for International Development and the convening of the seventh Special Session of the UN General Assembly (UNGA). These measures led to the establishment of a New International Economic Order (NIEO), which aimed at introducing equity and justice in international economic relations. The developing countries of Africa, Asia, Latin America, and the Caribbean were hit the hardest by those economic hardships and global problems of the 1970s. There followed other problems, such as high costs of industrial products, rising food import bills, low prices for Africa's exports (mainly raw materials and processed goods), and the loss of Africa's progress and economic gains of the 1960s, which vanished in the 1970s and 1980s.

In the 1980s, a serious debt crisis arose, originating in Mexico in August 1982, when the government of Mexico failed to service its debt. The debt problems then spread fast to Latin America, Africa, and elsewhere in the developing world.

With the above problems in mind, the UN committees cited above discussed and adopted criteria for classifying the developing nations into various clusters, better known as categories. Those criteria were adopted by the member states of the UN in order to establish milestone proposals for measures to address the economic crises of the time.

Major Categories of Third World Nations

Whereas states of the UN system are divided into developed and developing countries, within the developing world, there are differentiations based upon levels of development and development situations. The UN clustered countries into four categories during the 1970s and 1980s, and the SIDS category emerged in the 1990s. The UN categories of Third World nations are as follows:

- The most seriously affected states (MSAs) such as Kenya, Egypt, Cameroon, Côte d'Ivoire, Ghana, and others, whose problems would be contained earlier than those of other categories;
- Landlocked developing countries (LLDCs);
- Small island developing states (SIDS), whose category was actually created in 1996 on their own initiative, and
- The least developed countries (LDCs), which are the most vulnerable of them all and the poorest nations on Earth, on the basis of the established criteria.

The first UN conference on LDCs was held in Paris in 1981. The established criteria for LDCs include the following, among many others:

- Possession of the characteristics of poverty (lack of power) or underdevelopment/undevelopment (i.e., a poor developing country);
- Low income as measured by GDP per capita: self sufficiency–low living levels and self-esteem;
- The predominance of agriculture with low per capita food and agriculture output;
- Dependence on agriculture exports, often just a few, with a minimal industrial base;

- Limited freedom;
- Weak human assets (resources) as measured by a composite index of life-quality based on indicators of life expectancy (at birth per capita), insufficient (low) calorie intake, and primary and secondary education enrollment and adult literacy (i.e., school attendance is limited to very low standards);
- Low level of economic diversification by index, based upon the share of manufacturing, labor force in industry, and annual per capita commercial energy consumption;
- A poverty condition characterized by a low per capita income of less than US$905 per year, and by a low per capita of productivity level of technology and development;
- A life expectancy of only about one-half of the people of the highly developed states;
- A high economic vulnerability;
- A very high degree of vulnerability to diseases (e.g., malaria, Tuberculosis [TB], HIV/AIDS dysentery, Yellow Fever, Highland Fever, Ebola, Dengue, etc.);
- A low growth in per capita GNP of less than 3.5 percent or at about 2.5 percent per annum and a low level of foreign exchange reserves;
- Food supply in low calories is about one-third less than that of the developed countries;
- Poor in supplies of basic needs such as clothing, shelter, food, and education (school attendance); and
- A population of less than 75 million per country (by 2006, the world's 50 LDCs had more than 600 million people).

In 2007, during the review exercise of membership in the LDC category, it was determined that Cape Verde had progressed well economically, thereby prompting a graduation of that country from the LDC category. That decision reduced the number of LDCs by one to 49 globally and to 33 LDCs in Africa.

Africa has the largest and the most vulnerable number of LDCs. Thirty-three of the world's 49 LDCs are hosted by Africa. The African LDCs are Angola, Benin, Burkina Faso, Burundi, Central African Republic, Chad, DRC, Gambia, Comoros, Djibouti, Guinea, Guinea-Bissau, Equatorial Guinea, Eritrea, Ethiopia, Lesotho, Liberia, Madagascar, Malawi, Mali, Mauritania, Mozambique, Niger, Rwanda, São Tomé and Príncipe, Senegal, Sierra Leone, Somalia, Sudan, Tanzania, Togo, Uganda, and Zambia. In Latin America and the Caribbean there is one LDC (Haiti), and the remaining 15 LDCs are in Asia and the Pacific. They are Afghanistan, Bangladesh, Bhutan, Cambodia, East Timor, Laos, Maldives, Myanmar, Nepal, Yemen, Kiribati, Samoa, Solomon Islands, Tuvalu, and Vanuatu.

Most of the LLDCs are LDCs. Their landlocked nature also prompted the UN to adopt special measures for the LLDCs requesting the developed countries to commit 0.15 percent to 0.20 percent of their GNP to the LLDCs. These measures were reiterated at the UN conferences on LDCs held in 1990 in Paris, France, and in 2001 in Brussels, Belgium. In Africa there are 15 LLDCs (Botswana, Burkina Faso, Burundi, Central African Republic, Chad, Ethiopia, Lesotho, Malawi, Mali, Niger, Rwanda, Swaziland, Uganda, Zambia, and Zimbabwe). There are 11 LLDCs in Asia, and 2 in Latin America (Bolivia and Paraguay).

Africa hosts 6 SIDS (Cape Verde, Comoros, Guinea-Bissau, Mauritius, São Tomé and Príncipe, and Seychelles). Note that Madagascar does not qualify as a SIDS country due to its large size. SIDS in Latin America and the Caribbean include Antigua and Barbuda, Bahamas, Barbados, Belize, Cuba, Dominica, Dominican Republic, Grenada, Guyana, Haiti, Jamaica, St. Kitts and Nevis, St. Lucia, St. Vincent and the Grenadines, Suriname, Trinidad, and Tobago.

The Poorest Country in Africa: Burundi?

Based on the latest World Bank indicators from July 2006, Burundi is the poorest country, both in Africa and in the world. This classification is based on the criteria of the lowest GNP per capita. However, Haiti, in the Caribbean, also has been established to be the poorest, not only in the Americas, but also in the world. Both countries are indistinguishably poor. Thus, according to the latest statistics, Haiti and Burundi are the poorest nations on Earth.

Burundi's per capital income per year in US dollars is $90. Burundi's low GNP per capita has been caused by:

- The deadly wars and conflicts between the Tutsi tribe (comprising 14 percent of the population) and the Hutu tribe (comprising 85 percent of the Population). The Twa tribe comprises only 1 percent of the population.
- Ethnic conflicts, political rebels, armed gangs, and government forces fighting in the Great Lakes Region, across the borders of neighboring countries into Burundi, and in neighboring DRC, Rwanda, and Uganda.
- Eruption of ethnic hostilities despite the presence of 6,000 UN peacekeeping forces in Burundi since 2004.
- Burundi's trade deficit in 2005 totaled US$150 million. Burundi's exports of coffee cotton, corn, tea, sorghum, sweet potatoes, bananas, manioc (tapioca), beef, milk, and hides, bring in an income of only $52 million per year versus $200 million paid by Burundi for imports (capital goods, petroleum products, foodstuffs, etc.).
- The rapidly growing population of Burundi was estimated at 8,390,505 in 2007 and at 8,691,005 in July 2008.

In like manner, the World Bank estimates reveal that Burundi currently leads the list of 10 poorest countries of Africa and the world.

This is based on GNP per capita, which is calculated by taking the total amount of money a country's consumers spend on all goods and services in a year, and dividing the money by that country's population. The top 10 poorest countries of the world, per capita in U.S. dollars, are as follows:

1. Burundi: $90;
2. Ethiopia: $110;
3. DRC: $110;
4. Liberia: $110;
5. Malawi: $160;
6. Guinea-Bissau: $160;
7. Eritrea: $190;
8. Niger: $210;
9. Sierra Leone: $210;
10. Rwanda: $210;

DEBT AS THE PRIMUS INTER TRES OF AFRICA'S GRAVEST DEVELOPMENT BURDENS

The talk about the debt of African countries is basically about Third World debt that is linked to the poverty syndrome of Third World nations. The developing nations of Africa, Asia, Latin America, and the Caribbean incur "external" or "multilateral debt" when the governments of these nations lack the ability to pay the quantities of their commitments. It becomes "unpayable" external debt when the interest on the debt exceeds what the country's politicians think they can collect from taxpayers based on the nation's gross domestic product (GDP), thereby preventing the debt from ever being repaid. The debt problem is thus both an economic development and political problem, because (external) debt obstructs the development efforts of many developing world nations.

Causes of the Debt Problem

Many of the causes of Third World debt problems have already been mentioned in other contexts, and will be familiar from previous chapters. These reasons include the following:

- Imperialism, colonialism, and colonization of Third World countries by Western powers;
- Colonial policies and practices that created dependency, indebtedness, and cash crop systems in colonies at the expense of subsistence crops;

- Faults of the Bretton Woods institutions and weaknesses of the UN and its system;
- Creditor governments and international financial institutions that tend to shift blame to corrupt governments and leadership; but, in reality, the fault should lie with the creditors for imposing conditions that the debtor cannot meet.
- Banking formulas of World Bank and IMF, including SAPs;
- Creditors that often deliberately push borrowers into heavy borrowing and thereby perpetuate the need for borrowing and paying excessive interest rates (for debtor countries, this is like economic and financial sabotage);
- Creditors that often aim at denationalizing the economies of developing nations to an unacceptable extent;
- Protectionist policies and practices of donor countries that wish to maintain control or influence over getting developing country exports to the markets of developed world nations; and
- Policies or institutions that force developing countries to import more goods and services than they export.

Mexico's Trigger of Third World Debt and Economic Crisis

For all practical purposes, it can be stated that developing country debt as we know it today was triggered by the events that happened in Mexico in August 1982. The history of Mexico's economy shows good performance for many years between the 1930s and 1981. After the Great Depression and after World War I and World War II, Mexico's GDP grew quite well. Between 1978 and 1981, Mexico enjoyed a period of economic boom, with a growth of GDP averaging 8.4 percent. However, problems started to crop up and lead to a decline of economic growth of 0.6 percent in 1982. This deterioration became so grave that the economy suffered a severe breakdown. The following reasons, among others, were responsible for the economic breakdown:

- Development strategy stopped functioning;
- Manufactured imports to exports had a ratio of 4:1;
- Public finances led to a grave financial deficit of 17.7 of GDP in 1982;
- The balance of payment deficits in 1981 amounted to US$12.6 billion;
- Foreign debt grew to more than US$90 billion in 1982, and this raised foreign debt service in 1982 to half the value of total exports so debt could not be serviced;
- A deep financial crisis exploded in August 1982;
- On September 1, 1982, the government took control of the banks;
- By the end of 1982, inflation was very high; and
- A very serious debt crisis spread elsewhere in Latin America and then to other developing countries.

From Mexico, debt became the engine for economic crises in developing areas. In Argentina, for example, the economy suffered a severe crisis in the 1980s. The same fate was suffered by many other Latin American economies where hyperinflation began to reign. A total of US$530 billion in debt was incurred in Latin America, which was 36 percent of the total GNP of Latin America.

Sierra Leone, Burundi, and other countries of Sub-Saharan Africa were the hardest hit of all the countries of the Third World. In view of Africa's high vulnerability to all poverty and developing problems, Africa was vulnerable in every sphere of crisis from energy to agricultural and economic decline, education, increased poverty, and corruption and mismanagement. The 1980s combination of economic and financial crises led to a situation of Afro-pessimism from which Africa has not recovered.

Highly Indebted Poor Countries Initiative

The Highly Indebted Poor Countries (HIPC) Initiative was established by rich nations via the World Bank and IMF in 1996 with a view to ensuring that no poor country faces a debt burden it cannot manage. This initiative calls for the reduction of external debt via write-offs by official donors. It was set up for the poorest of nations that account to World Bank. According to IMF, the HIPC nations' debt was, on average, more than four times their annual export earnings, and 120 percent of GNP.

HIPC is thus a comprehensive approach to external debt reduction for heavily indebted poor countries pursuing IMF- and World Bank–supported adjustment and reform programs' basic criteria for HIPC, as follows:

- Facing insurmountable debt burden beyond traditional debt relief mechanisms,
- Initiation of reforms and policies through IMF- and World Bank–supported programs, and
- Has developed a PRSP via a broad-based participatory process.

Altogether, 40 developing countries have qualified for HIPC status, of which, 33 are African (Benin, Burundi, Burkina Faso, Cameroon, Central African Republic, Chad, Comoros, Eritrea, Congo Democratic Republic, Congo Republic, Cote d'Ivoire, Guinea, Guinea-Bissau, Ethiopia, Gambia, Ghana, Kenya, Liberia, Madagascar, Malawi, Mali, Mauritania, Mozambique, Niger, Rwanda, Sao Tome and Principe, Senegal, Sierra Leone, Somalia, Sudan, Tanzania, Togo, Uganda, and Zambia).

There are three countries with HIPC status in Asia (Yemen Republic, Lao, People's Democratic Republic of Myanmar) and four in Latin America and the Caribbean (Bolivia, Guyana, Honduras, and Nicaragua).

Note that much of the debt burden for low-income countries dates back to the 1970s and '80s. The borrowings by the poor countries were made in order to fund domestic projects on the back of the price boom, but when oil price shocks happened during that time, recessions and high interest rates suffocated the poor countries. The HIPC initiative was thus launched as a multilateral debt reduction effort. A debt sustainability framework was also launched for these developing states.

The HIPC Initiative has been severely criticized for helping the rich nations more than the poor nations. It does not account to its critics and does not provide lasting relief from debt for highly indebted nations of the South. The HIPC Initiative does not per se cancel debts but only ensures their repayment. Thus, the HIPC Initiative per se does not really worry about reducing debt or increasing economic growth. It is designed to manage debt figures down to a level where they would be deemed "sustainable."

IMF's Poverty Reduction Strategy Papers

The Poverty Reduction Strategy Papers (PRSPs) of the IMF were initiated in 1999. They were prepared by member states via the participatory process involving domestic and external participation of stakeholders, including Bretton Woods institutions. PRSPS are updated with annual progress reports once every three years.

PRSPs describe the country's macroeconomic policies to provide growth and reduce poverty, as well as structural and social programs over a three-year or longer horizon. They are prepared by the governments of low income nations, and they have crucial links to MDGs. They provide for concessional lending and debt relief under the HIPC Initiative. At the time of this writing, the IMF and World Bank are said to be working toward a partial reduction or rescheduling of this debt, but they demand obedience to strict economic reforms via SAPs. To qualify for PSRPs requires weak human resources and a low level of economic diversification. Other criteria are based on and include the following:

- Per capita GDP up to US$905 per annum (up from $330),
- Population up to 75 million,
- Education levels,
- Calorie consumption,
- Absolute poverty—low per capita income,
- Growth per capita GNP of less than 3.5 percent per annum,
- Predominance of agriculture and low per capita food and agricultural output,

- Low productivity and loss of terms of trade, and
- High economic vulnerability.

Impacts of Debt Cancellation on Developing Countries

As the saying goes, "misery is the bedfellow of debt," as can be seen from conditions in Africa's poorest countries. Debt cancellation is a complex but extremely useful and pertinent topic, especially now when the global economic and financial crises are bound to hit the developing nations the hardest. Debt becomes a real problem when the debtor is unable to repay and/or service the loan. The effects of the debt on developing nations can be just as devastating as war. But what impacts can, and does, debt cancellation have in these countries? To answer that question requires a discussion of the multilateral debt of the developing regions of the world, as follows in these eight propositions:

1. The focus here on Third World debt does not mean that the wealthiest developed countries, like the United States and the EU nations, have no debt. On the contrary some of their debt is enormous. For example, taking some of the latest data into consideration shows that as of November 19, 2008, the total U.S. public debt, which is normally referred to as the national debt (i.e., the amount of money owed by the federal government to holders of U.S. debt instruments), was US$10.6 trillion (or $37,316 per U.S. resident). In the context of this study, multilateral debt means funds borrowed by a country or international entity from a financial institution like the IMF or World Bank and repaid with interest by a developing country.

2. With debt is the possibility that one or more developing countries will default on their debts. This is a common viewpoint that is, however, questionable in the opinion of this writer. The events that triggered the debt crisis for the developing nations were of various kinds. They included the energy crisis triggered by the OPEC action (oil cartel) in 1973 and the subsequent economic crisis that followed, especially for the oil-importing Third World nations. But the classic case in point was Mexico. The origins of the debt crisis and debt-servicing problems for the developing nations date back to 1982. As outlined previously in this chapter, the Mexican economy stagnated and their GDP declined by 0.6 percent and, in 1983, lost an additional 4.2 percent. The resulting deep financial and economic crisis became unbearable for the government to manage and Mexico declared that she could not readily repay or service its debt. Other Latin American countries started to be affected, and the U.S. neighbor had to stop the crisis that started to have negative impacts in United States as well. This led to a number of actions by the U.S. administrations of the day, starting with the Carter administration and continuing to the Reagan administration.

3. The debt problem arises when high levels of debt repayments—including interest—consume too much of the revenues developing countries need for their development. Most bankers and creditor entities seem to feel and

conclude that the debts of the developing countries are the result of "economic mismanagement" of leaders and governments in the developing world. This writer does not share this view totally because such mismanagement is not the sole cause of the indebtedness of these countries.

4. Debt is obviously connected to the poverty syndrome, therefore, there is a clear link between debt and development, and the main object of reducing, and even trying to forgive, debts is to make efforts to eradicate poverty from the debt-stricken countries of the developing world.

5. The best way to address the debt problems of the developing countries is to put them in the overall context of the origins, causes, and development, as well as the consequences and cures or measures that must be taken to reduce, and eventually eradicate, the debt burdens of the developing nations.

6. Consider the choices offered indebted nations. If you were president of a poor country and the donor community asked you to choose just one option offered to you (with the choices being to cancel your debt, have access to global and developed country markets—no protectionism, or to be given foreign aid) which of these options would you choose and why? One would be better off choosing cancellation of debt because of predictability of income in the absence of debt repayments, whereas with aid and protectinism, there is no assurance that aid will be forthcoming, nor that the protectionist policies will be removed.

7. Protectionism always has strings attached, always;.

8. Development is the overarching issue for the developing countries. In the context of the above analysis, it is instructive to note that development is, sensu largo, a complex and multidimensional process encompassing more than the mere material and financial sides of people's lives and in which the following characteristics prevail:

- Improvements in incomes and outputs, normally measured at national levels in overall and per capita GNP;
- Radical changes in institutions, social and administrative structures, as well as in popular attitudes and even customs, thoughts, and beliefs;
- Reorientation and reorganization of entire economic and social systems;
- Acceleration of economic growth;
- Reduction of absolute poverty; and
- Satisfaction, within an entire social system, of diverse basic needs and desires of individuals and social groups to assure or provide a situation or condition of a better life.

Keeping these facts in mind and realizing that the basic criterion most widely accepted for measuring a country's financial standing is GNP per capita, the remainder of this section focuses on Haiti and Burundi as case studies to further understanding of the impacts of debt cancellation.

Characteristics Shared by Haiti and Burundi

Both countries are Third World nations and former colonies of France (Haiti) and Belgium (Burundi). They are among the poorest countries of the world, and are categorized as LDCs by the UN. Both are the poorest in their respective regions. Based on 2004 per capita in U.S. dollars, Burundi is the poorest nation on earth, with the lowest GNP per capita in Africa and the world. They also have similar populations with Haiti estimated in 2008 at 8,706,497 and Burundi at 8,691,005. One divergent feature is their length of independence—Haiti gained independence in 1804 but Burundi had to wait until 1962.

External Debt

Haiti was the first post-colonial, independent, black-led nation in the Caribbean, and the first independent nation in the Caribbean. It is the only LDC in the Western Hemisphere; the only predominantly Francophone country in the Caribbean—the only French-speaking nation in the Western Hemisphere apart from Canada; and the only nation whose independence was gained as part of a successful slave rebellion.

Halti's debt problem began soon after independence from France in 1804. In 1825, France, with warships at the ready, demanded Haiti compensate France for its loss of a slave colony. In exchange for French recognition of Haiti as an independent republic, France demanded payment of 150 million Francs (current equivalent of $21 billion in U.S. dollars). Impoverishment of Haiti included the looting of the country and theft of the republic's financial resources by two presidents between 1957 and 1986—a father (dictator Papa Doc) and a son (Jean-Claude "Baby Doc" Duvalier). The son stole at least $500 million. His wife spent $20,000 on shopping sprees in New York in the 1980s. External debt at the end of 2008 was about $ 1.4 billion.

Burundi was first known as Ruanda-Urundi, from which two countries emerged: Burundi and Rwanda. Burundi was subjected to colonialism and colonial exploitation that lead to ethnic violence, conflicts, and political rebels, armed gangs, and government forces and regional conflicts involving DRC, Uganda and Rwanda, neighboring states in the Great Lakes Region. Ethnic hostilities erupted despite the presence of 6,000 UN peacekeepers in Burundi since 2004. Its low GNP per capita has been caused by deadly wars and conflicts between the Tutsi (14 percent) and Hutu (85 percent) rivalries. A third tribe, the Twa, are only 1 percent of population. Burundi has a weak economy, 94 percent of which is agricultural farm products (coffee, sugar, tea, cotton, corn, sweet potatoes, animals, manioc [tapioca], and services (4 percent only of the economy). The total deficit in 2005 was US$150 million, with $52 million of Burundi's exports of sugar, coffee, tea, cotton and hides constituting the main exports; $200 million were paid for imports of capital goods foodstuffs, petroleum products, etc. External debt, as of the end of 2008, was about US$1.2 billion.

Consequences of Debt for Third World Countries

There are many and varied consequences of Third World debt. Very severe economic and financial crises of the 1970s and 1980s never really left these countries, and the affects of these crises persist up to today. External shocks, such as when oil prices first shot up in 1973 and later when interest rates soared in the 1980s, also made debts increase dramatically. The negative impacts of these external events on investment and economic growth continue decades later. The continued carry-forward of debt produces high debt-servicing costs as well as unrealistic and inadequate external measures (e.g., in foreign aid). There continues to be a low amount or lack of growth in debt-riddled countries that is worsened by natural disasters such as foods, hurricanes, drought, and other disasters; resource reverse flows to the North from the South; squandering via corrupt practices; and wastage due to technology deficits.

Falling prices for raw materials over a period of years also have resulted in the loss of foreign currency by most of the LDCs, with little or no foreign currency revenues. The low growth was exacerbated by other factors, such as the following:

- Weak institutions;
- Poor governance or a lack of good governance;
- Economic and debt mismanagement;
- Political instability, violent conflicts, and civil and regional wars (e.g., in Burundi, Sierra Leone, DRC, Liberia, and Rwanda between the 1980s and 2000s);
- Huge military expenditures caused by wars and civil strife;
- Failure of the international financial system to draw up successful policies and reach the necessary conclusions; and
- The culture of corruption.

All of these elements resulted in a lack of development and increased debt. In turn, steady growth of new loans lead to more debt. Worsening these countries' abilities to pay back their debt were the following:

- Conditionality of aid (e.g., economic reforms, or other irrelevant demands);
- Protectionism;
- Conditions placed on debts which led to bankruptcy for more than 40 Third World countries;
- High interest rates;
- Odious debt—deliberate, undemocratic, and illegitimate lending of money by creditors to debtors or illegitimate regimes just in order to impoverish them;
- Rising inflation and falling living standards; and

- Increased pressures from climate change and global warming and their effects on vulnerable areas and key sectors of the economy.

Measures for Eradication of the Debt Problem

Economic and financial crises of the 1970s and 1980s led to the creation of the UN's New International Economic Order (NIEO), which was one response to the worsening financial condition of the Third World. Debt reduction measures at national, subregional, interregional, and global (UN) levels include options such as debt rescheduling, postponement, renegotiation, and forgiveness/debt cancellation at national, regional, international, and global levels by governments, international governmental institutions like financial institutions (i.e., the World Bank and IMF), individuals, and other entities. Such previous arrangements include the following examples:

- SAPs of the 1980s, HIPC Initiative (1996), and PRSPs (1996) as previously described;
- G-20 (1999) is a forum of world economic powers from the North and the South that holds meetings at ministerial, central bank governors, and summit levels in order to debate global economic issues and problems, try to resolve them, and promote economic growth and development. The G-20 is comprised of the European Union (represented by presidents of EU Council and EU Central Bank) and 19 countries (Australia, Canada, France, Germany, Japan, Russia, Turkey, Italy, the United Kingdom, the United States, Argentina, Brazil, China, India, Indonesia, Mexico, Saudi Arabia, South Korea, and South Africa).
- The Paris Club (1956), whose original 10 member countries (Belgium, Canada, France, West Germany, Italy, Japan, Netherlands, Sweden, the United Kingdom, the United States) signed the General Agreement to Borrow with Argentina in 1956. Today this is an informal group of financial officials from 19 of the world's richest countries (the original 10 plus Australia, Austria, Finland, Ireland, Norway, Russia, Spain, and Switzerland), which provides financial services such as debt restructuring, debt relief, and debt cancellation to indebted countries and their creditors. Debtors often are recommended by the World Bank or IMF.
- GATT/WTO "Rounds" launched in November 2001;
- The Washington Consensus (1989); and
- Bilateral arrangements over the years.

Other "mixed" measures include and have included dialogues and negotiations at global levels as follows:

- The NIEO global negotiations of the 1970s and 80s energy crisis;
- Creation of categories of states at the UN, including MSAs applying mostly to developing countries like Kenya, which no longer exist. This category of states had temporary problems resulting from the energy crisis of the 1970s;

- Creation of LLDC category of LDCs and holding of three LDC UN conferences to date (Paris, 1981; Paris, 1990; and Brussels, 2001).
- HIPC Initiative (39 countries total, of which 32 are in Africa);
- SIDS (as previously described in this chapter);
- Alliance of Small Island States (AOSIS) 42 states: 36 states + 6 observers)
- International conference system (1960s–present);
- Moral imperative of the haves to help the have-nots of the world;
- Reparations compensation and resource and technology transfers to developing nations;
- Empowerment of the Third World nations and peoples via education and training for development;
- Fair globalization/just and equitable international economic relations;
- Free and unconditional access of Third World countries to global and developed country markets; and
- Realization of ODA flows.

Conceptual Understanding: SAPs

The SAPs were/are economic policies adopted by the World Bank/IMF for the first time in the 1980s with the purpose of addressing the indebtedness of developing countries and thereby reshaping their economies to enable these countries to repay their foreign debt. The developing countries had to follow these policies in order to qualify for IMF and World Bank loans and to help the Third World nations to make debt repayment on the older debts owed to the commercial banks, governments, the World Bank, and IMF. The SAPs introduced a grave situation of conditionality, which served to add to the impoverishment of the poor nations of the developing regions of the world. The requirements and conditionalities of the SAPs include devaluation of currency of the borrower against the U.S. dollar, lifting import and export restrictions, balancing the borrowers' budgets, no overspending, and removing price controls and state subsidies. Common guiding principles and features of SAPs include export-led growth, as well as privatization, liberalization, and efficiency of the free market.

A pattern emerges in which there is heavy borrowing by developing nations. This is followed by an inability of these nations to repay the loans, which forces them to borrow for the second time in order to clear the first loans, and results in a grave situation of indebtedness because these loans have very high interest rates. When the conditionality has been imposed through the SAPs of lending Breton Woods institutions, debtors can borrow, but only if they fulfill the conditions imposed by lending governments and institutions.

The end results are increased impoverishment, especially of the poor nations, in view of such very high interest rates and conditionality.

Creditors often ignore the real needs of the debtors and persist in lending terms that cannot be met without causing harm to the poor debtor nations. To meet the conditions of the loaned funds, poor nations often neglect priority business and trade policies that are most productive for debtor nations. Debtors are forced by lenders to stress the wrong policies/priorities and neglect basic needs and services (e.g., education, health, social care) to balance national budgets, etc. For example, debtor nations will turn to production and export of cash crops (primary commodities) to raise funds instead of subsistence crops to feed the populace.

Debt Cancellations

Benefits or advantages of debt cancellation are many and varied and include the following:

1. Saving and enhancement of the capacity of public services
2. End to hunger and famine and alleviation of debt burdens
3. Prevention of social unrest/instability and increase in investments
4. Increased business opportunities and enterprises
5. Eradication of gender inequality: empowerment of women, youth, girls, and other marginalized strata of society
6. Predictability of income—some funds are better than debt increase
7. Debt cancellation can lead to poverty reduction, increased level of education, and more investment infrastructure, education, and health for sustainable development
8. No debt means increased economic growth, better GNP per annum, and prevention of aggravation of poverty in this global era. Debt cancellation must hence be linked to poverty reduction
9. Political stability and security
10. Self-reliance for development
11. Reduction of impacts of disasters, pandemics—HIV-AIDS and leading to decent living
12. Avoids bankruptcy, protects the environment from degradation, infrastructural development
13. Poverty and famine reduction
14. Improved healthcare
15. Eradication of illiteracy and ignorance via high quality education
16. Political stability and peace
17. Economic development
18. Increased availability of needed resources to the most impoverished countries of the world

19. Debt damages the economy by cutting all disbursements
20. Increases in balance of payments
21. Debt-cancellation contributes to justice
22. Can help raise investments
23. External shocks: the lenders were great causes of external debt crises
24. Increased foreign currency
25. Empowers countries to access their own resources
26. Increased and steady prices for raw materials
27. Helps stimulate the economy and to recognize and promote mutual interdependence of all nations
28. Helps prevent distortion of the economy by reducing loss of lives due to indebtedness
29. Renders opportunity to build successful economies to supply the needs of future generations
30. Can easily halve annual debt servicing payments. The money thus released benefits the people and is invested in infrastructure, education, healthcare, etc.

The following examples of successful debt cancellation are noteworthy:

- In Tanzania, debt cancellation has led to the abolition of primary school fees and an increase of primary enrollment from about 800,000 before cancellation to 1.6 million today.
- In Malawi, the government has used the debt cancellation funds to train new teachers—almost 4,000 per year.
- In Benin, freed funding was used to recruit teachers for vacant posts in rural areas.
- In Mali, debt cancellation funds were used to pay 5,000 community teachers to improve their teaching skills.
- In Bolivia, the freed funds were used to improve healthcare in the past 10 years.

A total of $88 billion of debt cancellation money has been achieved for developing nations. Of the world's poorest nations, Burundi and Haiti have had their debts cancelled. Burundi was one of the 17–18 countries recommended for debt cancellation by the World Bank/IMF. At the July 2008 G-8 Summit in Gleneagles, Scotland, 100 percent of Burundi's debt was cancelled. That act alone enabled the Burundi government to eliminate education fees in 2005 so 300,000 additional children could attend school.

For Haiti, the Inter-American Development Bank started to be involved in the debt cancellation process for Latin America and the Caribbean (LAC) in 2007. By the end of 2008, Haiti, Burundi, Gambia, DRC, Chad, and Guinea had 100 percent of their debts cancelled.

AFRICA AND INTERNATIONAL DEVELOPMENT: RELATIONS WITH THE ASSOCIATION OF SOUTHEAST ASIA NATIONS AND CHINA

As established, Africa is poorer now than she was 25 to 40 years ago. However, 25 years ago most ASEAN countries were as poor as and even poorer than the countries of Africa. Now ASEAN is much richer than Africa. What happened in ASEAN in economic terms to prompt such change? Additionally, China has become an economic and political superpower. Currently, China is developing close cooperation with African countries, especially in the economic field. What are the implications of this new relationship for Africa's development and security?

Divergent Features

The geography, size, and population of Africa, ASEAN, and China are described as follows:

- Africa is a continent with five regions (North, Southern, East, West, and Central). It is the second largest continent after Asia with an area of 11.7 million square miles (30.3 million square kilometers) and population of 952,777,000, as estimated in 2008.
- ASEAN, formed on August 8, 1967, is a geopolitical and economic organization of 10 countries located in Southeast Asia and is a subregion or subcontinent in Asia. It covers an area of 1.7 million square miles (4.5 million square kilometers) and a combined population of 500 million as estimated in 2008.
- China is a superpower in economic and political terms, with the right of veto in the security council of the UN. China claims to be the leader of the Third World. China has an area of 3.7 million square miles (9.6 million square kilometers) and a population of close to 1.4 billion (1,330,044,544) as estimated in July 2008.

China

China has become very economically and politically aggressive on the international stage. In recent years, China has created a special relationship with Africa via the China–Africa Forum and Summit for Cooperation. This is a collaborative partnership with Africa that, in 2006, developed the China–Africa Strategic Partnership Programme that will promote very active political cooperation through high-level meetings and summits between China and Africa, both bilateral and continent-wide in Africa, at presidential and foreign ministerial levels. The issues and dictates of cooperation include trade and investment, energy security (oil and mining) to import from Africa (e.g., Nigeria), and to help develop energy resources and supplies in Africa. China collaborates closely in international fora with

African and other Group of 77 (G-77) developing countries of Asia, Africa, Latin America, and the Caribbean.

The Group of 77 is actually the group of all the developing countries working as a political bloc at the United Nations. This group was created on June 15, 1964, in Geneva by the 77 countries that signed the "Joint Declaration of the G 77 Countries" issued at the end of the first session of the UN Conference on Trade and Development (UNCTAD), established in the UN following the demand of the developing nations of Africa, Asia, Latin America, and the Caribbean for the creation of a body in the UN system that would specifically address the economic development problems and challenges of the newly independent developing member countries of the South; and to start systematically and regularly addressing economic and development issues confronting the countries that joined the UN after years of colonization. Although currently there are 132 members, when the G-77 was created there were only 77 members of the UN, and the name stuck. China joined in recent years and the organization is now known as the G-77 and China. This loose coalition of developing nations at the UN meets once a year at (foreign affairs) ministerial level, usually at the beginning of the regular session of the UN General Assembly in New York in order to adopt a strategy for the group and negotiating positions to be used by the group during the forthcoming UNGA session. However, G-77 meets at ambassadorial level whenever necessary, as convened by its annual chairman, and continues to use the G-27 for formulation of the group's positions on global issues to be articulated by the group as a forum for collective decision-making on economic issues of common interest to the group and to promote collective bargaining to enhance their joint negotiating capacity on major international economic problems, challenges, and issues discussed within the UN system that are of direct concern to the group. The G-77 also enhances South–South cooperation for sustainable development. So far, the G-77 has held two summits only—one at Havana, Cuba, on April 10–14, 2000, and the second summit in Doha, Qatar, on June 12–16, 2005.

In historical perspective China is a world political and economic power. China's significance seems to have been triggered by the decision of the Allied Powers, which, in 1919 following the end of Word War I and the signing of the Treaty of Versailles, gave some Asian territories captured from the "enemy states" to Japan, and not to China. Unhappy with this Western behavior and decision, China decided to ally herself with the Soviet Union and her orbit of socialist states, following the 1917 creation of a Soviet system of government under the leadership of Vladimir Ilyich Lenin, founder of Bolshevik communism in Russia.

In subsequent years, however, differences between Soviet and Chinese doctrines of communism appeared when China's interpretations of communism, and her vast population, prompted a decision to introduce a system of communes in villages. After World War II, when the East–West ideological divide grew between the Soviet orbit of countries and the states of Western Europe plus the dominions of the British Empire (Canada, Australia, and New Zealand), a new world order was born and marked, from 1947, the beginning of Cold War politics in the world.

The differences between China and the Soviet Union deepened when China realized that she could not fit into this kind of politics. Consequently, and especially starting from 1949, a new course was set for China, when Mao Zedong (Mao Tse-tung, 1893–1976), the communist theorist, became the de facto leader of the Communist Party in China—Chairman Mao in the 1950s and 1960s. China embarked on a system of deep revolutions—including the Great Cultural Revolution.

As a nation in existence for almost 3,500 years, China's view and understanding of Africa is much broader than it is perceived, and currently she is developing a new relationship with Africa that has started to concentrate more on economic cooperation and development, rather than on cultural orientation and the traditional political support that she used to offer to Africa and the other countries of the Third World during the Cold War era, against the imperialism and exploitation of Western capitalism, and Eastern Sovietism. The present collaboration between Africa and China is bound to grow even stronger as the new millennium advances.

At the same time, China's economic "aggression" is being felt everywhere in the world. China's trade figures with the United States, for example, reveal a clear trend in China's favor. In 2006 alone, for example, China's exports to the United States were worth US$233 billion, whereas U.S. exports to China were worth only US$55 billion. Thus, China's economic power is not being felt in Africa alone, but it is growing steadily around the globe. This has ushered in a very interesting period to watch. Furthermore, recently it has been reported that the Chinese Parliament passed a law, on March 15, 2007, that will protect private businesses and private ownership of land and other property. This is a major development in China, since it clearly goes against the established doctrine of Chinese communism. In China, the Communist Party has always been the mainstay of policy and governance. The fact that the National Assembly has passed this law, shows how the thinking of the Communist Party has been evolving around social stability in China. This issue of private property ownership in China has been on the agenda for 14 years now, and it is a good sign of great revolution that has, in reality, dominated Chinese political and social thought for 20 years.

The fact that the Communist Party has allowed the adoption of this legislation to legalize private ownership of assets in the country, tells us that globalization, which demands openness and freedom to global markets, is very much at work in China. It also indicates the recognition by the Chinese leadership of the importance and need for free markets for China if her economy is to prosper even more and this, in turn, necessitates domestic reforms for the good of the country. Since it is believed that social stability is the greatest precondition for durable prosperity in China, and the basis for all other dictates and require- ments of peace and stability in the country, efforts must be made first and foremost to attain social stability in the country before addressing the other vital requirements of Chinese society in a multidimensional way: in health, the environment, education, gender equality, etc.

One hopes that Africa can genuinely become a beneficiary of all these initiatives and developments in China.

Independence, Legal Status, Member States, and Membership in International Fora

China gained its independence many years ago. This country is a founding member of the UN and a member of many other interna- tional bodies.

By contrast, Africa is a member of a large organization (OAU/AU) that has a more inward-looking approach than that of ASEAN. Most African countries gained independence after 1960. Within Africa, 54 countries are members of AU, which replaced OAU (created May 25, 1963) in 2002. The OAU/AU seat is in Addis Ababa. The Sahrawi Arab Democratic Republic (SADR) was admitted to the AU in 1982, but Morocco walked out of that summit in protest against the recognition and admission to OAU of what Morocco regarded, and still regards, as part of its territory called Western Sahara. Thus, although recognized within Africa as an independent state, for Morocco, SADR is still Western Sahara and this nation is not recognized internationally (e.g., by the United States or UN). Hence, assistance from the UN goes to Western Sahara for humanitarian and other purposes. Morocco is not a member of the AU. Externally, therefore, there are 53 states in Africa but within Africa, 54 states are counted.

ASEAN was established on August 8, 1967 at a summit held at Bangkok, Thailand, and now has a total of 10 member countries, including 5 original members (Indonesia, Malaysia, Philippines, Singapore, and Thailand). The foreign ministers of these countries at that time were the founding fathers of ASEAN. They were: Foreign Ministers Adam Malik (1917–1984) of Indonesia; Narciso Ramos of the Philippines; Tun Abdul Razak (1922– 1976) of Malaysia; S. Rajaratnam (1915–2006) of Singapore; and Thanat Khoman (1932–) of Thailand. The other members of ASEAN are Brunai Darussalam, Vietnam, Laos, Myanmar, and Cambodia. The ASEAN coun- tries gained independence before the 1960s as follows:

- Indonesia, August 17, 1945 (a founding member of the UN);
- The Philippines, July 4, 1946 (from the United States, but was a founding member of the UN in 1945);

- Vietnam (south), October 26, 1955;
- Laos, October 23, 1953;
- Burma, January 4, 1948; and
- Cambodia, November 9, 1953

Philippines and Indonesia were founding members of the UN and are currently members of many other bodies. The purpose of ASEAN is mainly for economic cooperation. A tight organization with a serious self-interest approach to cooperation in all spheres of development (economic, political, cultural, and social), ASEAN hallmarks are genuine patriotism used to fight against corruption, promotion of competent skills, and self-reliance. Cooperative arrangements for partnerships within the region and with outside regional organizations are maintained. The seat of ASEAN is in Djakarta, Indonesia.

Categorization, Treatment, and Attention by the Outside World

The external world, (i.e., foreign investors and tourists) prefer to go to ASEAN rather than to Africa. It is more convenient that way, and there is also the belief that it is more secure to go to ASEAN than to Africa. Also, the ASEAN nations are more efficient and effective in international negotiations than are African participants, for example, in multinational trade negotiations (MTNS) of the World Trade Organization (WTO). Tourism continues to flow more to ASEAN countries than to Africa, because of the reasons already cited above.

And so, Africa is more neglected, more marginalized, more isolated, and more vulnerable than ever. Increases in investments directed to the ASEAN nations affect the manner of development in Africa and in ASEAN countries differently. The end result is that ASEAN countries emerge as the more favored area in comparison to Africa.

There are many other divergent features of ASEAN and Africa.

Common Characteristics

Among the common characteristics shared by Africa and ASEAN, the following are particularly noteworthy:

- A common colonial past;
- Early participation in international development efforts as part of metropolises;
- Political independence that was not accompanied by economic independence;
- A period of "-zation" including indigenization, which followed soon after political independence, then Africanization, Asianization, Burmanization (Myanmarization), Philippinization, Ghananization, Malaysianzation, Kenyanization, Latin Americanization, Caribbeanization, Nigerianization, etc.

- A few African or ASEAN countries acquired political independence before the 1960s;
- Tourism is an important foreign exchange earner;
- Membership in global and regional organizations (e.g., G-77 and China, NAM) and Third World groupings (LDCs, SIDS, African, Caribbean, and Pacific group (ACP);
- While Africa holds memberships in UMA, SADC, EAC/East African Union (EAU), Common Market for Eastern and Southern Africa (COMESA), ECCAS, IGAD, ECOWAS, NEPAD, OAU/AU, within Asia there is membership in ASEAN, the Colombo Plan (regional intergovernmental organization for socio-economic advancement of its members in South and Southeast Asia, formed on 1 July, 1950, by Australia, New Zealand, Ceylon, India, Pakistan, Canada, and the United Kingdom) and the Asian Pacific Economic Community (APEC—an economic summit that includes developed states Australia, Canada, Japan, the United States, and New Zealand).
- Some African and ASEAN countries changed their names after independence, (e.g., ASEAN's Myanmar previously had been called Burma; Africa's Burkina Faso previously had been called Upper Volta).
- Other common features include the following:
  - Corruption, although resources in ASEAN are used in the countries of the subcontinent, whereas in Africa, the resources are taken out of the countries;
  - Big burden of illiteracy in Africa;
  - Education was not traditionally a priority in Africa where girls were not sent to school, but were to get married, whereas in ASEAN, stress was put on education as an important passport to future good life and enlightenment;
  - Geography and demography, both places shared problems of weather and climatic conditions as well as tropical diseases and population pressures, but these problems were more grave in Africa than in ASEAN;
  - ASEAN's sub-region consisted of smaller areas than those of Africa;
  - Colonial policies and practices, but in Africa, the practices were worse than those applied in ASEAN (e.g., the Portuguese and Belgian policies and practices ignored education, whereas the British system in ASEAN Singapore, encouraged education and training of the colonized populations in all fields);
  - No stress on science and technology, no technical schools;
  - The British settlers in ASEAN brought good schools, tourism and genuine patriotism, whereas in Africa, the small elite was inward-looking and did not stress science and technology in the educational systems that was introduced and applied by the various colonial powers and administrators;
  - Most ex-colonialists continued to stay and work in Africa and greatly frustrated the Africanization policies of the newly independent African nations;
  - Common dependency practices after independence;
  - Frustration/Africanization/Asianization policies of the newly independent countries of Africa and Asia; and

- In ASEAN, self-reliance was promoted already before independence, and stress was put on science and technology; the dependency policies hurt Africa more than ASEAN.

Regional Integration

Regional integration is one area where both ASEAN and Africa have tried hard to attain peace and stability as prerequisites for security and development. It should be noted that although many shortcomings exist, good efforts have been made, and are being made, for the achievement of regional integration for development in Africa. Nonetheless, ASEAN has done much better than Africa in view of the more favorable investment climate, patriotism, and change of attitude in leadership to avoid cultism and parochialism in ASEAN, which is so prevalent in Africa.

In like manner, flexibility and consensus-building for development are more pronounced in ASEAN than they are in Africa. Furthermore, most of the ASEAN states were anti-communist, and had capitalist-oriented economies. They sought to resolve their differences and conflicts via peaceful means, as was the case when Cambodia and Vietnam had rocky relations following the invasion of Cambodia by Vietnam in 1978. Eventually, reconciliation occurred, and Vietnam supported peace.

In Africa, conflicts are usually dealt with through armed conflict and even war, and there is a lot of external interference that divides Africa into the former colonial spheres of influence (Africa's phonist system—Anglophone, Lusophone, Francophone, and Arabphone—is divisive). Moreover, Africa's share in the global economy and trade has dwindled, while foreign direct investment (FDI) in Africa has remained at very low levels. The income gap relative to the advanced nations has widened, so that more than 300 million people south of the Sahara live on less than US$1 a day.

Thus, in order to improve the development situation of Africa, concerted measures must be taken at national, regional, and African continental levels, which should include the following, among many others:

- The African governments must make fundamental reforms in the African economies.
- There must be a clear provision of sufficient funding and technical assistance in support of reform initiatives in Africa.
- Clear goals must be set to transform the African economies in order to attain faster economic growth and development, reduce poverty, and remove the leadership deficiencies in the governance and government of Africa.
- There must be clear commitments of political will and action by African leaders to national development, as opposed to personal self-interest, development, and prosperity.

- There must be fundamental changes in African educational systems to prepare the African countries and peoples for seeking solutions to African problems using African methods (education and training for character formation, leadership qualities, commitment, and sense of duty and belonging to the nation rather than to an ethnicity, improvement in the quality of education from primary to university level for capacity-building, and creation of incentives against "brain-drain" to be replaced by brain trust, etc.).

- There must be sustainability in all spheres of African development and security, in rational use and management of the natural resource base, sustainability science, environment sustainability, and the search for resources to be made available on an assured, predictable, continuous, and adequate basis, in implementation of policy decisions made with full popular participation in empowerment (e.g., of women and the other marginalized groups in African society), and gender equality, as well as disaster reduction, prevention, and management for African development, etc.

- External assistance to Africa should not impoverish the continent further, but rather, it should be genuine and provide and guarantee access of African goods and services to global markets (i.e., against protectionism) and with measures that will reduce the poverty syndrome and burdens of Africa and her countries—forgiveness of African debts and debt servicing, unconditional FDI in Africa, and removal of the burdens of IMF/World Bank Group SAPs from Africa, etc.

These are but some of the main goals and objectives that regional economic groupings in Africa must address in a systematic way. The African groupings include the AU, EAC and EAU, IGAD, ECOWAS, COMESA, UMA, SACU, PTA, Southern African Development Community (SADC), EAC (African Economic Community) CEMAC (Economic and Monetary Community of Central Africa) UEMOA (West Africa Economic and Monetary Union) and UMA (Arab Mghreb Union) and Organisation Commune Africaine et Malgache (OCAM), among others.

Also of particular interest are the efforts of the Great Lakes Region, which, in 2007, established an International Conference of the Great Lakes Region that now assembles in concerted efforts, 10 countries that have started to work collectively on the problems of peace, security, and development of the region. The countries are Angola, the Central African Republic, the DRC, Burundi, Kenya, Rwanda, the Sudan, Tanzania, Uganda, and Zambia.

Secrets of ASEAN Success

The success of ASEAN makes the following points noteworthy:

- The urge to maintain unity in the organization and to settle disputes via negotiations and other peaceful means, and not via fighting—there are no civil or other conflicts or wars because issues are resolved via peaceful means;

- Mainly a consultative body on broad issues;
- Keenness in forging common policies on issues, especially those that might disrupt development efforts, economics, culture, religion, ethnicity, etc.
- A functioning nature of its work vis-à-vis the outside world (e.g., seeking closer relations with the EU and other economic groupings around the globe);
- First-generation leaders of ASEAN were more patriotic and demanded stronger loyalty to the nation than Africa's first-generation leaders who were more inward-looking, ethnically oriented, and tribalistic than those of ASEAN;
- The military in Africa were more interested in politics, security, and shared prosperity than were those in ASEAN;
- Good prioritization of economic development sectors (e.g., creation of incentives in agriculture, tourism, finance/banking, etc.) that has been quite successful because it improves the living conditions of the peoples of the subregion, discourages brain-drain, and encourages brain trust;
- Enjoyment of peace and security leads to political stability and economic development;
- Full commitment of ASEAN members to global negotiations on business/trade and development to intra-ASEAN arrangements for education, commerce, partnership, and economic integration and cooperation;
- Long-term planning and action plans to promote culture and combat corruption, drug abuse, and terrorism;
- Encouragement and existence of a good education system for the subregion, subject, and self-reliance;
- Strong anti-military and anti-corruption sentiments have encouraged resources to remain and be used in the region of ASEAN, instead of over-expatriation of it to foreign banks;
- Strong efforts to attain good governance, competence, tolerance, and determination of competent leadership to accelerate development;
- Determination to prevent cultures and traditions from suffocating development efforts in ASEAN;
- The poorest of ASEAN nations are helped by the richer ones;
- Introduced a good health system that is regularly reviewed and improved;
- No conflicts, civil wars, and strife, thereby assuring stability, peace, trust, collaboration, and development;
- In ASEAN, concerted efforts also are made in such organizations as the Colombo Plan, the Asian Pacific Coconut Community, the Association of Natural Rubber Producing Countries, and APEC (the Asian Pacific Economic Community that is based in Singapore and includes the United States, Mexico, Japan, China, Canada, and other nations of this important regional organization for economic cooperation); and

- As recently as January 2007, ASEAN agreed to establish a free-trade zone by 2015. In a meeting at Cebu, the Philippines, ASEAN nations discussed the goal of economic and political integration; it also agreed to intensify their fight against terrorism, protect ASEAN's migrant workers, and improve their campaign against HIV/AIDS; and they also agreed to draft a new charter with broad enforcement powers.

Africa could learn a lot from the ASEAN experience. Consider the following examples:

- Africa's LDCs, like ASEAN shows, could benefit from the resolve of the entire AU to make Africa self-sufficient.
- African states should, as ASEAN has done, create greater incentives for tourism, investment, security, and shared prosperity, and stop the practice of inward-looking approaches.
- African states should, as ASEAN has done, make a greater investment in agriculture, tourism with increased security, finance/banking, etc., and stop the brain-drain and replace it by brain-trust incentives in Africa.
- African states should make increased efforts to attain peace and stability and resolve differences via peaceful means for the development of Africa and the African peoples.
- Embark upon an African cultural renaissance to give a greater meaning to African cultural values and education and more closely examine the "secrets" that sustain the success of ASEAN, namely in seeking the following:
  - Ways and means of settling disputes through peaceful procedures, maintaining unity in Africa and the AU via negotiations, and avoidance of conflicts and wars in Africa;
  - Consensus in settling problems facing Africa and her countries;
  - Closer relations within Africa and with the outside world for the benefit of Africa and her countries, and not for individual African rulers and their cultism and cronies; and
  - Eagerness to forge common policies on issues and challenges, especially those that may disrupt development, culture, religion, ethnicity, and economics for the prosperity of individual African countries and for the entire African continent.

The Way Forward for Africa

The comparative analysis of ASEAN and Africa raises many questions that need to be addressed and answered as Africa enters the 21st century and faces all of these challenges and issues in African development and security. For example, given that African development and security are the primary responsibility of the African government and their institutions and peoples, what are the conditions for the success of African development initiatives? Is African heritage redeemable in the new millennium and, if so, can African civilization be claimed in the 21st century with appropriate adjustments to meet the dictates of the modern world and attain African solutions to African problems with Africa in her own driver's seat?

Africa and Africans must learn to own Africa and to solve African problems using African ways.

AFRICA AND INTERNATIONAL DEVELOPMENT: AFRICA'S ECONOMY IN HISTORICAL PERSPECTIVE

Africa has a long pre-colonial history of trade and development (e.g. in East and West Africa). There is a long history of merchants, artisans, local markets, regional markets, and ancient trade routes. African markets in pre-colonial Africa served local areas, and Africa's network of markets linked Africa's distant regions together economically.

Over 700 years ago, Africans had already developed a productive and sophisticated economic and trade system. Traders understood the laws of supply and demand, and that for a price, one could supply anything to any one else. Luxurious trade routes were established in ancient times, and kingdoms like, for example, those in East Africa such as Axum, Kush, and Meroe, and at least 35 city-states including those of Malindi, Mombassa, Pemba, Lamu, Zanzibar, Mogadishu, Sofala, and many others in Eastern Africa, as well as Ghana and Mossi in West Africa, and Zimbabwe in Southern Africa. These and other African kingdoms flourished for long periods of time.

Milestones in Africa's business and economic systems and relations include the following:

- African societal and political systems started in small, loose groups of stateless societies already in remotest antiquities of pre-colonial times, when African heritage included trade and business relations among African societies and nations from single units of parents to children and extended families. Extended family codes were instituted; expansionism from family to extended family to village, sub-clan, clan (chieftaincy), sub-tribe, tribe (communities), empire, city-state, and super empire systems were born, with administrative units ranging across sub-locations, divisions, districts, and provinces. These African systems were later corrupted by the European colonial administrators when they arrived in Africa and twisted the African codes to suit foreign colonial policies and practices.

- Early African peoples embarked upon adventures, nomadism, and acquisition of territory from eastern and southern Africa to northern Africa to Egypt and out of Africa and back. Then, expansionism spread within Africa, to the West and Central regions of the continent.

- Stone and Iron Ages: Africans learned how to gather and hunt and make invented tools from stones and iron as weapons for hunting, gathering, and protection from enemies.

- In small groups, Africans learned how to exchange goods and services through barter between and among families, villages, clans, tribes, and groups first as stateless societies until 2,500 years ago—before bureaucracies, state processes, and procedures were introduced in African societies. Then changes were forced upon Africans and their continent by natural order; following the advent of the great Sahara around 5000 BCE when "permanent settlements" had to be introduced in Africa, as the population of the continent had been growing, land was becoming more scarce, natural and human enemies were growing in number and severity, there was need for law and order, and governance and government. Means to forge alliances for business, economic, and diplomatic relations had to be established with neighbors and other African groups for peaceful coexistence; intermarriages; alliances for collaboration and diplomacy; learning how to domesticate animals like sheep, goats, camels, cows, and dogs; learning how to grow crops like cassava, roots, and wheat. Increased value was put on land and agriculture following domestications. Business contacts and trade grew over the years, and trade and economic ties started to play major roles in the earliest societal expansionism of the African social and political systems.

- The institution of slavery and the slave trade in Africa became luxurious businesses within and among the Africans even before the arrival of the Europeans and other foreigners to Africa who made that illegitimate trade a very luxurious global business. The slave trade did not, however, replace the legitimate trade that had also flourished already in pre-colonial times, in primary commodities, minerals, etc.

- The removal of stateless societies and the advent of state societies after the formation of the Great Sahara Desert in Africa increased the value of business relations among African groups and led to the development of the following principles and practices, among many others: increased respect for the African value of extended family, their codes, and the raising of children by the villages; the value of African socialism and governance by consensus; respect of the elderly and use of their wisdom in African governance under hereditary rule principles, business, and management affairs; collective responsibility in business, politics, and society so that the haves are duty-bound to help the have-nots; and stressing duties rather than rewards in the African value system.

- Thus, by the time the first foreigners arrived in North Africa, a distant societal system had been established in Africa many centuries earlier and had stressed the importance of business in African society: the Phoenicians between 1200 and 800 BCE, the first aliens to colonize Africa, came to North Africa along the Mediterranean coastal zones and created fruitful trade links with Carthage and the other business hubs of ancient Africa; the Greeks from 630 BCE; the Romans from 146 BCE; and the Arabs from the 7th century CE.

- A social system in Africa had several million people who had been forced to live in human settlements in sub-Saharan Africa, since the population of Africa had grown and the land had shrunk. There was no more roaming about in small, nomadic groups looking for land, green pastures, etc. Africans faced greater and more fierce natural and human enemies and hence needed better and more assured protection, health services, sanitation, living facilities, water services, skills in dealing with human and natural enemies; better and broader farming implements, skills, and continued domestication of animals to live together to control conflicts or resolve trade and other disputes through a balance of cooperation and opposition; respect for extended family organizations and codes involving kingship behavior; and to maintain law and order, justice, as well as cultural and territorial integrity for the African populations.

- When African societal groups assumed sovereign qualities, state relations emerged. African kingdoms, empires, and city-states flourished enormously, and trade and business relations became inter-city-state (inter-national) relations because the interactions and activities were conducted across borders. Thus, business relations became international business activities.

- The minerals, raw materials, and commodities already "discovered" in earlier times gained greater use and became most valuable. Africa is so rich in natural resources, but very poor in plenty. Commodities (e.g., palm oil, groundnuts, monkey nuts, beans and peas, coffee, cocoa, cotton, sugar, tea, sisal, rubber, pyrethrum) were plentiful. Minerals such as gold, copper, diamonds, zinc, tin, etc., and conventional energy resources of oil, natural gas, and coal were discovered, used, and traded. Renewable energy (e.g., solar, peat, tar sands, ocean energy, biomass, geothermal, charcoal, nuclear, hydropower, wind power, animal draught, etc.) are also plentiful in Africa.

- Africa had other economic wealth in the form of humans (slaves at that time) and many animals.

Trade in pre-colonial Africa consisted of long-distance trade in gold, cowries, copper, ivory, ornaments, barter for cloth, animals, salt, etc. Weapons, monkey nuts, and groundnuts were exchanged for natural resources, manufactured goods, horses, camels, foodstuffs, and the like. Tariffs, customs, and taxes were levied on behalf of emperors, besides fees and hostages for administrative offices.

Thus, prosperity and trade greatly flourished in the ancient African kingdoms, empires, and city-states that arose. Africans learned how to use and share the environment, knowledge, and GPGs—the life support systems of the ecosystem (air, atmosphere, earth, land, etc.). They also learned how to avoid and eradicate GPBs.

In summary, the following principles and practices were maintained, prevailed in Africa over the millennia, and continued to evolve even further:

1. Development and security;
2. Slavery and the slave trade and payments of tributes to paramount chiefs and kings for royal protection and the use of royal assets;
3. Traditional forms of law and order, justice and defense against enemies, African socialism in community values;
4. Democratic governance according to custom and tradition; and
5. Intermarriages for alliances to cement friendships and cooperation among tribal kings, etc.

These principles and practices were changed or destroyed by the colonization and imposition on Africans of alien values and ways of living, especially following the colonization of Africa by the Europeans in the late 19th century.

From colonial times (starting about 1885) to the present, the economic and business relations with, and in, Africa could be summarized as follows:

In colonial times (1885–1960), all of the relations of the African nations were relations between bosses (i.e., the colonial masters and their representatives in the colonies) and subjects (i.e., the colonial peoples and their territories). The colonial economic and trade policies and practices advanced, as explained earlier, into exploitation, transformation, and impoverishment of the colonies and colonial peoples. They were part and parcel of the colonial powers and had to tow the lines and dictates of their masters. Thus, business, economic, and trade relations in colonial Africa benefited European powers much more than their African colonies.

After gaining independence (1960–present), the situation of trade and development, business and economic relations in, and with, Africa in the post-colonial era have been conducted between African nations as sovereign states and their former European colonial masters. These relations have not been limited to contacts with Europe. They have become global, consistent with the purposes and principles of international business and trade laws between and among nations. These relations are explained in subsequent sections of this study.

Fundamental Premises and Proposals

Before further discussion, the following five fundamental premises and proposals are made:

1. What is in this section should be seen as relating to international business in Africa;
2. Concentration is on the history, politics, and economics and/or economy of Africa in the three historical eras of pre-colonial, colonial, and post-colonial periods;
3. Africa has a vast resource base, both human and natural;
4. Africa has a vast potential and opportunities for international business; and
5. The power of African paradoxes and resolution/non-resolution of these ironies is the secret and key to the success or failure of international business in Africa, which lies, and will lie, in finding durable solutions to Africa's paradoxes as analyzed in previous chapters.

Africa in the Global Economy and Markets

Before 1960, a number of African countries gained political independence and participated in multilateral negotiations on trade and development of the UN and GATT systems. By discussing trade issues, the talks touched on business issues. Unfortunately for Africa, she has lacked the capacity and the means to participate effectively and reap the maximum results from these negotiations.

Multilateral/Global Negotiations of the GATT/WTO System

The purpose of international trade negotiations is to discuss issues/differences with a view to finding a common agreement or consensus that can be acceptable to all the parties concerned. Whereas the GATT/WTO negotiations are primarily focused on trade and development, and are global in nature, the negotiations within the UN system are actually a multidimensional conference system of the members of the UN. The purpose of the GATT/WTO negotiations is to reduce trade barriers or tariffs to international trade. GATT was designed to provide an international forum that encouraged (could encourage) free trade between member states, regulating and reducing tariffs on traded goods, and providing a common mechanism for resolving trade disputes. Duties or customs to be paid on imports or exports go to the state on traded goods. GATT was established in Geneva in 1947 at the beginning of the Cold War and held a series of international trade talks known as "the Rounds" on multinational trade negotiations (MTNs). GATT's original members were 23 states, of which 11 were from the Third World. These included African countries that had gained independence before 1960. There were eight rounds before WTO replaced GATT in 1994. The first five rounds dealt with tariffs (line by line) and accessions. The initial rounds were of shorter duration than those in later years and are as follows:

1947: First talks held after the creation of GATT were held in Geneva (First Round).

1949: Second Round was held at Annecy, France.

1951: Torquay (Third) Round was held in Torquay, England.

1955–1956: Fourth Round was held in Geneva.

1961–1962: Dillon (Fifth) Round, held in Geneva, mainly was attended by developed countries and dealt with short-term arrangements covering trade in cotton textiles and clothing. No provisions were made for Third World access to developed markets. Later, long-term arrangements were introduced and remained in force until 1973.

1964–1967: Kennedy (Sixth) Round, added sectoral negotiations and an anti-dumping code.

1973–1979: Tokyo (Seventh) Round, provided across-the-board tariff cuts by one-third, 12 agreements on the Nuclear Test Ban (NTB), and disputes settlement.

1986–1994: Uruguay (Eighth) Round, created the WTO at Marrakesh in Morocco, with its "single undertaking" to reduce world agricultural subsidies, and begin to remove restrictions on cross-boundary trade in services.

The Doha Round Under WTO

The WTO was launched in November 2001 at Doha, Qatar. In 1979 and the decade of the 1980s that followed, a new set of global negotiations was launched within the UN system. Like the GATT/WTO negotiations, those within the UN system dealt with trade and development issues, with special stress on development.

As a global forum and multilateral trading system that aims at promoting international trade for economic development, WTO addresses issues of sustainable development; employment; alleviation of poverty; structural reforms; agriculture; services; intellectual property dealing with trade-related issues; trade facilitation; WTO rules; dispute settlement; trade and the environment; electronic commerce, etc.

In the past seven years, major disagreements have emerged between the North and the South on these issues, and gotten worse, especially on environmental and agricultural fronts, which have led in 2008, to the collapse of the WTO/Doha Round of negotiations. It will take hard decisions and full political commitment to resume the negotiations and reach a fair conclusion of the round.

The UN Conference System

The UN conference system was started with the birth of the UN in 1945. From the 1960s, the UN launched UN Development Decades, better known as the International Development Strategies (IDS), which have continued to aim at helping the developing nations advance on their development paths.

Trade and development issues gained greater prominence from 1960 and later in the 1960s, when the newly independent nations of the Third World joined the UN en masse and demanded organized and systematic approaches to trade and development issues and business, especially for the newly independent, poor members of the UN.

The UN Development Decade system is now in its fifth round (2001–2010). Since the 1970s, the following conferences are among the many that have been organized by the UN to deal with development problems:

- 1972: Stockholm Conference on the Human Environment;
- 1973: OPEC crisis and meetings to address the crisis;
- 1974: 6th Special Session of the UN General Assembly on the New International Economic Order (NIEO);
- 1975: 7th Special Session of UNGA on NIEO;

- 1975: First World Conference on Women, Mexico City, Mexico;
- 1976: UN Habitat I at Vancouver, Canada;
- 1977: UN Conference on Desertification at Nairobi, Kenya;
- 1978: Summit of Third World on ECDC, in Argentina;
- 1979: UN Conference on Science and Technology for Development; Global Negotiations of the UN;
- 1980: 2nd UN Conference on Women, Copenhagen, Denmark;
- 1981: UN Conference on New and Renewable Sources of Energy, Nairobi, Kenya;
- 1985: 3rd UN Conference on Women, in Nairobi, Kenya;
- 1991: International Conference on Water in Dublin, Ireland;
- 1992: UN Conference on Environment and Development, Rio de Janeiro;
- 1994: UN Conference on Natural Disasters at Yokohama, Japan;
- 1995: UN Conference on Women in Beijing, China;
- 1995: UN Summit—Jubilee celebration at UN headquarters in New York;
- 1996: Habitat II, in Istanbul, Turkey;
- 1997: Conference on Climate Change in Kyoto, Japan;
- 2000: The Millennium Summit;
- 2001: LDC Conference in Brussels;
- 2001: Launching of Doha Round at Doha, Qatar;
- 2002: UN Conference on Financing for Development, Monterrey, Mexico;
- 2002: World Summit on Sustainable Development, Johannesburg, South Africa; and
- 2005: Yokohama plus 10 conferences on disasters at Kobe, Japan.

Africa's Participation in Global Negotiations

The following insufficiencies are noted:

- Africa has a very weak impact on global negotiations;
- Lack of capacity; lack of resources to follow-up on the negotiations;
- At time of GATT, most African countries were still European colonies, except Ethiopia, Liberia, South Africa, and Egypt;
- Participation in WTO by Africa is still very weak;
- Minimum benefits from the negotiations and conferences; and
- No real or substantial benefits for Africa from the global negotiations.

History of Development and Business Initiatives in Post-Colonial Africa

At political independence in the 1960s and 1970s, Africa realized that she would have to stand on her own feet. Although Africa's economic performance made gains during the first decade of independence, economic decline and malaise in Africa followed soon thereafter. Many reasons existed for that malaise. Consequently, the African governments, in collaboration with the UN and other parts of the donor community, started to take development initiatives for the economic recovery and development of Africa. Two kinds of development initiatives were taken by the African governments with external support: pre- and post-NEPAD initiatives. NEPAD was a development initiative launched by African leaders with the support of the donor community.

Between 1979 and 2002, the following development initiatives were launched:

- The Monrovia Strategy for the Economic Development of Africa, June 20, 1979;
- The Lagos Plan of Action for the Economic Development of Africa, 1980–2000, and the Final Act;
- Africa's Priority Programmes for Economic Recovery (APPER) 1986–1990 (APPER later became the UN Programme of Action for Africa's Economic Recovery and Development [UN-PAAERD]);
- The African Alternative Framework to Structural Adjustment for Socio-Economic Recovery and Transformation (AAF-SAPM);
- The African Charter for Popular Participations for Development, 1990;
- The UN New Agenda for Development of Africa in the 1990s (UN-NADAF), 1991; and
- The Abuja Treaty Establishing the African Economic Community, Abuja, June 3, 1991 (Treaty for African Economic Cooperation, 1991).

These African development efforts failed for the following reasons, among others:

- Colonial economic policy of dependence in Africa left newly independent nations with undeveloped infrastructure, no educated labor force, and no experienced or trained management force to run the African economies or governments;
- Economic system aimed at supporting only the colonial administrations and producing and exporting primary commodities from Africa to European metropolitans without creating a market for the African continent and countries;
- Development of an economic system that was irrelevant to the needs of society in Africa;
- Sustained neglect of the agricultural sector in Africa's national development plans, and the stress on building industries produced import-substitution strategies to produce previously imported goods to save foreign exchange, which did not happen (import-substitution policy led to losses of earning foreign exchange);

- The stress on industrialization, which did the following:

  - Suffocated economic development in Africa and hurt agricultural sectors;

  - Stimulated rural–urban migrations where jobs were insufficient to absorb arrivals from the countryside;

  - Led to food shortages and insecurity as lands and granaries of food production were abandoned;

  - Reduced investments in the agricultural sector and reduced economic diversification;

  - Reduced revenues from the main African commodities for export—in the agricultural sector this was coffee, cocoa, sugar, timber, sisal, pyrethrum;

  - Encouraged/increased African dependency on former colonial masters; and

  - Increased collaboration of the African elites: political leaders, government officials, military officials, and entrepreneurs with multinational corporations, etc.

The failure of the development initiatives also implied the failure of business efforts in Africa, since no business could thrive in a failed economic initiative.

Post-NEPAD Measures for African Economic Development

The nature and function of NEPAD is an Africa-initiated multidimensional mechanism launched by the African heads of state and government meeting at summit level. As an African summit initiative, NEPAD is comprised of African governments, corporations, and those of the donor community. The partnership was launched in 2002, after extensive negotiations dating back to the time before the Millennium Summit of 2000, which on September 8, 2000, adopted the MDGs and a declaration, in which a special section was included on the "Special Needs of Africa" in the MDGs.

NEPAD[4] is a holistic and integrated sustainable development initiative for the economic and social survival of Africa, involving constructive partnership between Africa and the developed world (donor community). It is a pledge by African leaders that the development of Africa is the primary responsibility of Africa and her own governments, institutions, and peoples. This development initiative stresses overall African development and security in a multidimensional fashion.

The essence of NEPAD lies in its being an Africa-initiated, Africa-developed, Africa-owned, and Africa-managed initiative. Strategic objectives make combined efforts to improve the quality of life of Africa's people as rapidly as possible to eradicate widespread and severe poverty in Africa, reverse or halt Africa's marginalization in the globalization process, promote the role of women in all activities and to empower women by eliminating gender inequality, and to provide an impetus to Africa's development by consolidating and accelerating economic growth and sustainable development in a renewed partnership with the international community.

NEPAD differs from all of the African development initiatives because NEPAD was Africa- conceived, Africa-initiated, Africa-developed, Africa-negotiated, Africa-owned, and is currently Africa-managed, with a review and appraisal mechanism manned/attended by the heads of state and government of Africa as the main actors/decision-makers and directors of the implementation process.

NEPAD has taken initiatives that are being implemented by governments and the NEPAD secretariat based in South Africa. NEPAD's major goals are as follows:

- Recognize and reinforce its primary responsibility for Africa's development;
- Promote self-reliance in Africa and attract external support and resources;
- Encourage and assist Africa to preserve its common heritage and use it to end underdevelopment and marginalization of Africa;
- Help deepen democratic values, practices, and the culture of human rights and tolerance in Africa;
- Provide increased incentives to attract investment in Africa and promote prospects for partnerships;
- Help Africa increase her contributions to science, culture, and technology;
- Strategize for economic growth, business for African development, reduction of poverty and inequality in Africa; integrate Africa economically; and help diversify productive activities in Africa; and
- Systematically address various aspects of Africa's development needs in primary areas, sectors, and issues as outlined in recent African development initiatives.

United States and International Business in Africa

U.S.–Africa relations in historical perspective must acknowledge the three periods of pre-colonial, colonial, and post-colonial African history. Why does Africa matter to America today?

- Africa's gifts to America.
- America's interests in Africa are political, economic, strategic, security-related, and military.

- Business with/in Africa by American private and public sectors is very important to the development of the African countries. Such business benefits both the United States and the African countries concerned. The potential and opportunities for doing business in Africa are great; the untapped recourses are many, and there is plenty of room for development.

New potential and opportunities for American business in Africa include the following areas:

- Banking and investment;
- Small-scale enterprises, microcredit, and microfinance;
- Education and training for capacity-building (knowledge, skills, exchange programs for students and research, schools, centers of excellence, R&D centers, etc.);
- Health (training, pandemic research and avoidance, cures, aid);
- Agriculture (cash crops of cocoa, coffee, tea, cotton, pyrethrum, sisal, rubber) and subsistence farming;
- Industrialization;
- Manufacturing and engineering;
- Legal structures and codes for business enterprises in Africa;
- Disasters, development, and disease;
- Empowerment: women, youth, children, the handicapped, the elderly; girls and the NGO in Africa;
- Natural resources (water, energy, minerals);
- Information revolution (ICTs and energy for sustainable business and development); and
- Mining and minerals for trade.

Actions required to advance opportunities for Africans include the assessment of the potential for increased and more profitable business, evaluation of commodities for commercialized goods and raw materials, identification of countries and institutions in Africa for new business (academic and related partnerships), and discussion among private- and public-sector entities in the United States and Africa.

Dialogues for Exploration of Opportunities

The historical, political, and economic issues mentioned in the previous sections that affect business in Africa have clear implications for the United States. Of the three periods in which Africa's history, politics, and economics are divided, it is only the post-colonial era in which the United States could have major roles to play. There are several reasons for this, but primarily, the policies of the colonial powers in Africa did not allow their colonies to do business with anyone except the mother country. Therefore, the United States could not have had any influence in Africa during Africa's pre-colonial or colonial periods.

However, the United States could, and did, have business dealings with several African countries that either did not fall within the Berlin colonial system established in 1885, or were independent by the time Africa was colonized by Europe. The African countries enjoying "colonial immunity" were Ethiopia, Liberia, South Africa, and Egypt.

Most of Africa's paradoxes do not allow the United States to do good business in Africa. Political insecurity does not attract tourists or investors. Corruption, instability, and bad governance (leadership deficiency) discourages American corporations and the U.S. government from vigorously pursuing business interests in Africa. In cases where mineral resources are exported, like oil in Nigeria, Angola, Gabon, Libya, Algeria, Equatorial Guinea, Egypt, the Sudan, and other African oil-producing countries, as well as gold, diamonds, platinum, and uranium in South Africa, the U.S. government and companies do show interest and a desire to explore the potential opportunities for American companies to do business in Africa.

The best way to do business is to start doing business!

The Way Forward for Africa

The problems and challenges mentioned above, and others facing Africa in the new millennium, will still be haunting the African nations and peoples in the coming decade and beyond. In particular, the following challenges are among the most obvious:

- Africa's major enemies of development, i.e., poverty, ignorance (illiteracy) and disease;
- Debt and debt servicing;
- Africa's paradoxes and their implications for African development and security;
- Problems of African leadership, ethnocentrism *versus* patriotism; democracy and democratization;
- Environmental sustainability: climate change, disasters, and global warming;
- Sustainability science;
- Agriculture, industrialization;
- Education and empowerment of women and the generally marginalized strata of the African society (girls, the youth, elderly, handicapped);
- Development ownership of Africa by Africans;
- Humanitarianism: refugees, displaced persons, conflicts;
- Human security;

- The economy: trade, business (liberalization), energy for development; and
- Mismanagement, corruption, etc.

IMPACT OF AGENDA 21 ON THE AFRICAN DEVELOPMENT PROCESS

Agenda 21 was the outcome of the UN Conference on Environment and Development (UNCED) held at Rio de Janeiro, Brazil, on June 5–8, 1992. Agenda 21 had three constituent elements for sustainable development: economic growth/development; social development or equity, and protection of the environment. The stories of development and international cooperation as initiated in the post–energy crisis era of 1973 were vividly revived by the Rio process. For the first time in several decades, African development "from within" and "from without" Africa assumed a new face in international development as a process undertaken by countries, especially developing nations and international organizations, with assistance from other nations, especially the developed countries and their governments, as well UN system institutions like the IMF and the World Bank, WMO, and civil society organizations (CSOs), including NGOs. Agenda 21 was thus one of the outcomes on environment development from UNCED. UNCED adopted more decisions than Agenda 21, which included nine major groups for government, environment, civil society partnerships; three conventions on climate change, biodiversity, and one to combat desertification. It also initiated the Kyoto process on climate change, global warming, and ozone layer depletion, and reinforced the convention and IPCC, which is a WMO/United Nations Environment Programme (UNEP) Joint Responsibility with WMO hosting the secretariat, which are vital Rio process measures. The process is a success story—perhaps one of the very few really successful stories and outcomes of the UN Conference System. Africa participates in these processes and is helped in diverse ways to combat many of Africa's poverty problems.

The Rio process major groups are an important part of the Agenda 21 UN System development agenda. These groups advance cooperation and partnerships for sustainable development in the identified nine areas or major groups:

1. Farmers/agriculture;
2. Labor movement;
3. Scientific, technical, and technological communities;
4. Youth;
5. Women/girls;
6. Industry;
7. Indigenous population (people);

8. NGOs; and

9. Trade unions.

International development as advanced by the Rio process of sustainable development did make important breakthroughs in the debt alleviation and reduction in Africa, especially with intensive involvement of the major groups as multidisciplinary agents of human development for the advancement of livelihoods and greater and better quality of life for Africans and other humans.

Of particular significance in this politico-development process has been the stress of the major groups and the donor community on issues of international development encompassing the following:

1. Good governance;

2. Healthcare;

3. Education;

4. Gender equality;

5. Disaster preparedness, prevention, mitigation, and management;

6. Infrastructure improvement and development;

7. Economics;

8. Climate change and global warming;

9. Human rights (protection and observance), accountability, and transparency; and

10. Environment (protection) and issues related to democracy and the above dictates.

Where these dictates exist in Africa, there is bound to be poverty alleviation and even reduction and, hence, durable development.

The Rio Summit of 1992's Agenda 21 had three constituent elements which had actually, to a certain extent, been promoted or initiated in 1947 by the Marshall Plan for Europe that produced the World Bank and IMF assistance system first for Europe and currently for the developing world. At the time, U.S. Secretary of State George Catlett Marshall (1880–1959) introduced the concept of international development for the common good of all in his statement of June 5, 1947, to the graduating class at Harvard University, in which he laid the foundation in the aftermath of World War II for a U.S. program of aid to the European nations whose economies had been devastated and cities flattened during the war. In 1948, the U.S. Congress approved the Marshall Proposal, and by 1952 the United States had channeled US$13.3 billion in economic aid to 16 European countries, namely: Germany, France, the United Kingdom, Italy, Netherlands, Greece, Austria, Belgium, Luxembourg, Denmark, Norway, Turkey, Ireland, Sweden, Portugal, and Iceland. What an example of political commitment and delivery!

CAN THE MDG PROCESS MEET AFRICA'S DEVELOPMENT GOALS?

The idea of convening a special session (at the summit level) of the UNGA to discuss the subject of MDGs was implemented in the year 2000, when the special session was held at UN headquarters in New York from September 6–8. At least 146 heads of states or governments, kings, and crown princes attended that UN Summit. However, the origins of the conference can be traced back to September 1995, when, also at UN head-quarters, many heads of state or government, and other leaders attended the opening of the regular session of the UNGA, but preceded it with a special session of the assembly that marked the golden jubilee (50th anniversary) of the founding of the UN in San Francisco, California, United States, in October 1945. There was a lot of debate at the Millennium Summit of 2000, which adopted a Millennium Declaration on September 8 of that year.

At the UN Summit of 1995, in floating the idea of a special session to discuss development goals of the world community for the new millennium (21st century), the world leaders looked ahead to a new millennium that would commence from January 1, 2001, and hence they decided that at the session called "the Millennium Summit," the goals and objectives that that session would adopt for the development of nations in the new century should be called "the millennium development goals," nowadays better known as the MDGs.

Africa as the Least "Developed" and Most Vulnerable Continent

Obviously, as host to 34 of the 50 least LDCs in the world, Africa deserved, and still deserves, special attention. The declaration that was adopted at the Millennium Summit contained a separate chapter on "the special needs of Africa." This author followed quite closely and actively participated in the discussions of the MDG issues and was fully convinced that the target year of 2015, when the MDGs should be attained, was too unrealistic and overambitious.

So the question is: Can the MDG process deliver its promises to Africa? Look to the year 2015 as the timeframe for realization of the MDGs, but in this author's conviction, the response to this question must be given in the negative.

Can the MDG Process Bring Tangible Benefits to Africa?

It should be noted at the outset that the MDGs are an essential process of the international development practicum. Among the positive aspects of this process should be included the following:

- Raising public awareness on the need to tackle development issues addressed under the MDG banner: the eight goals, the targets, and the indicators. That awareness prompts government, other institutions and policymakers, and relevant non-governmental entities including national and international development NGOs, to plan and try to assess MDG situations in various countries of the developing world, as well as the needs for meeting the goals.

- Making appeals for tackling the MDG challenge in order to promote development in development-deficient countries.

- Recognizing that MDGs have contributed, and will continue to contribute, to the on-going constructive global debate about how to make (foreign) aid more effective in aid-receiving developing countries.

In like manner, it should be stressed that progress and, in some cases even considerable progress, will be possible toward the attainment of the MDGs by the timeframe of 2015. Having said the above, however there are two fundamental questions that must be asked and answered, with regard to the MDGs. How will the MDGs help the poor nations of Africa and others be more competitive and self-reliant? Will the pursuit of the MDGs help or hurt development, especially of Africa? Convincing responses to these questions are still lacking.

For the MDGs to be achieved by the year 2015, certain conditions must be met, and they include the following:

- The economy must grow by 7 percent per annum. There is no way that in Africa there can be an economic growth of 7 percent per annum by 2015. And for sure, no economic growth equals no self-reliance and no attainment of MDGs in Africa—or elsewhere, for that matter. Thus, there is no way severe poverty can/ will be halved in Africa, especially in southern Saharan Africa by 2015.

- MDGs will not, in this way, develop Africa, because they do not focus on growth and productivity.

- Africa's fiscal standing is not going to change substantially by 2015. The ODA formula of 1970 is still far from being achieved by most of the major, developed, donor countries. A lot of development aid to Africa does not really help Africa, but helps developed country-contacts; aid is wasted in elephant projects and has too many strings attached to it; SAPs impoverish the developing nations of Africa (and others in the Third World) even more; aid is very badly mismanaged or goes to ill-advised policy implementation. And since African nations lack the resources to support efforts to improve the lives of their citizens, African countries will not have the required economic growth and other basic development necessities by 2015.

- Numerical goals as in the MDG document create an unintended behavioral consequence. Thus, in asking governments to measure their success based on reducing the visible signs of poverty—hunger, low incomes, diseases, etc.—MDGs actually focus on symptoms rather than causes. As repeatedly argued, it is essential to diagnose the disease before prescribing medication to cure the illness.

- MDGs oversimplify (e.g., sending female children to primary school neither guarantees gender equality nor empowerment of women in Africa). In like manner, universal primary education does not mean, or lead to, development.
- There is no indication that African goods and services, industries, etc., will be allowed and guaranteed freedom of access to the world market.
- It seems evident that the kind of dialogue essential for African development, in which the people become the primary actors in decision-making on issues affecting their daily lives, is not to be guaranteed by the MDGs, which means that the MDGs will not bring about empowerment of the African people. Only through dialogue, will effective government be attained in Africa.
- Political commitments on paper alone, and development strategies, vision, resolutions, optimism, and the like, are good and necessary. Unless they are translated into concrete and practical actions, however, the MDGs cannot be attained by 2015. Hence, the significance of follow-up to, and implementation of, the decisions, pledges, and promises that are made by nations and the international community.
- Finally, the MDGs cannot deliver any long-term promises to Africa as long as Africa lacks (and continues to lack) major industries that would help end poverty in Africa.

DEFINING GLOBALIZATION

Globalization is a multidimensional process of universalization. It has two aspects: ancient universalism, and modern universalism. Ancient universalism's constituent elements include civilization, empire (imperialism and colonization), commerce, religion, etc. Ancient universalism was practiced by the Phoenicians, Greeks and Romans in North Africa.

Modern universalism refers to trade and the global economy. This is economic/trade/business globalization. This is the sense in which the expression is used.

Premises of Modern Globalization in the African Context

Premise 1 is that the forces of economic and trade universalism aim at reducing or eliminating borders between states and creating borderless sovereign statehood for free movements of goods and services, messages, ideas, people, investments, etc.

Premise 2 is that globalization has not, to date, been really beneficial to Africa and most of the Third World nations.

Premise 3 is that Africa is not benefiting from globalization. Why? Because Africa still lacks the capacity to compete competently, adequately, and equitably in global markets, as well as to face, and resist, the pressures to accept the consequences of the following:

- Internationalization (i.e., increased free movements of people, messages, ideas, etc., between borderless sovereign entities for historic and colonial heritage reasons);

- "Supraterritoriality," (i.e., reduction or elimination of sovereign statehood);

- "Globalism" (i.e., militarization and global dominance of the rich North, which imposes its might on the poor nations of Africa, and the other countries of the South, and drains the poor countries of their resources), better known as reverse resource flows from Africa to the North; and

- Destruction of self-reliance and self-ownership of Africa, which are crucial for sustainable African development by Africa for economic liberalization and effective productive entrepreneurship;

- Africa still suffers from Afro-pessimism (i.e., from all sorts of crises and conflicts: population crisis, ecological/environmental degradation, and other crises including in education, leadership, the economy, finance, dependency, health, infrastructural development, etc.);

- The grave poverty syndrome in which Africa is still the poorest continent on Earth—poorer now than she was 25 to 50 years ago.

- The paradox of poverty in plenty, in which Africa still hosts 34 of the 50 poorest countries of the world (with the graduation of Cape Verde from the LDC category as approved in 2007, the new figures will be 33 in Africa and 49 globally). And yet Africa is so rich in natural and human resources;

- The high indebtedness, with shrinking ODA flows, very few debt cancellations, growing protectionism, and the ever-worsening global economic and financial crisis; and

- The historical injustices of deprivations, exploitation, plundering, and impoverishment of Africa by European imperialism, colonization, slavery and slave trade, and their consequences in Africa, as well as the corruption, mismanagement, irrational use of resources, and deficiencies in the leadership of Africa in colonial and post-colonial eras of Africa.

Premise 4 is that globalization is a double-edged sword. Why? Because globalization, which is controlled by rich countries, preaches economic liberalization, international trade, investment, finance, and liberation of global markets, etc., but does practically nothing to help Africa access these markets in an equitable manner. So the beneficiary of the globalization process is not Africa, but the rich North. The developed nations also preach pluralism but do practically nothing to help Africa sustain her efforts for

- Poverty eradication;
- Increased ODA flows to Africa;
- Increased technology transfers to Africa; and
- Ending the reverse resource transfers from Africa to the North, etc.

Likewise, the developed nations preach free and unlimited access to global markets, as well as to African markets, and also to other southern markets, but apply protectionism and protectionist policies and subsidies for the farmers of the North, and deny Africa and the other southern countries free and unlimited access to the markets of the North, and of the rest of the world.

GLOBAL NEGOTIATIONS: ISSUES, CHALLENGES, AND OPPORTUNITIES FOR BUSINESS AND DEVELOPMENT IN AFRICA

Africa as a Global Marketplace

Africa offers a huge marketplace for international business, and this has great potential for the following:

- Improving African and global economies;
- Harnessing vast natural and human resources and raw materials;
- Providing an enabling environment for multinationals to conduct trade and make profit for themselves, and thereby create an environment for African development and security;
- Eradicating poverty and improving living standards of the people, via investment; African tourism; the prevention of brain-drain and creation of brain-trust in Africa; creation and promotion of information and knowledge, incentives, inspiration, imagination, investment, inputs, income, interest, invention, innovation, (popular) involvement, inclusion, and critical analysis of economic indicators and indices; and
- Promulgating new paradigms, ideas, etc., on globalism, globalization, global capitalism, multilateralism, international trade, sustainable development, and security in Africa.

Africa as Participant/Shareholder in Global Economy/Trade and Actor in Global Negotiations

In order to participate in global trade, Africa had to decolonize. After 1960, independence was granted to the remaining African countries that had not yet gained independence. The era of complete decolonization of Africa was from 1960 to 1977. In 1977, the last country to gain independence in Africa was Djibouti.

Decolonization Doctrines

Decolonization doctrines had their origins in the Back to Africa Movement of the 1800s in the United States. From Pan-Africanism originating in the United States in 1776 to 1964, the following doctrines were prominent:

- Political independence: unity;
- Uti possidetis juris;
- Irredentism;
- Colonial heritage: legacies and remnants;
- Economic challenges: from Afro-optimism to Afro-pessimism;
- Acquisition of sovereignty and international legal personality: sovereign equality and international recognition as part of the global system (Africa as a subsystem of the international/global system);
- Voluntary membership and of commitment and participation;
- Need for territory and territorial integrity, borders, population (voluntary affiliation) and government;
- Ability and capacity to negotiate and participate in global negotiations and in a just global economic system consisting of:

  - Free trade in goods and services;
  - Unrestricted capital flows with reduced national restrictions;
  - Stress on endogenous, rather than exogenous, abilities;
  - Interconnection and expansion of economies beyond national borders; and
  - Deep involvement of national and transnational corporations in business transactions and in the globalization of markets, finance, communications, and labor force.

Africa in International Trade and Development

International trade and business as instruments of development and security in Africa developed as a multidimensional process. International trade is a cornerstone of sustainability for economic, social, and environmental progress and is critical to the alleviation and eradication of poverty and its syndrome in Africa. Improvements in the living conditions of the African people are tied to trade. Africa's participation in business and development efforts are tied to the welfare of the African people. However, there are many challenges and barriers to the level of trade and development required to improve the African Condition.

First Decade in Post-Colonial Africa: Sound Economic Performance, 1960–1970

Initially, post-colonial Africa made economic progress and showed developmental gains. Reasons for these advances included the availability of economic, political, educational, and other systems and institutions that were already in place and still in operation at the time of independence and were based on those of former colonial mother countries. Also, African political leaders of the independence decade were civilians and staunch nationalists/Pan-Africanists—they were imbued with nationalism and patriotism, and interested in the welfare and stability of their countries and continent, rather than in ethnocentrism, personal glory, greed, or personal enrichment. Africanization policies and programs were still strong during the first 10 years of African independence, and this also supported post-colonial Africa. Not to be overlooked is that Africa was a huge marketplace for the external world, for business and trade with everybody on equal terms, rather than on terms set by the former colonial powers in their "spheres of influence" in Africa, as had been the case during the colonial era.

Later, changes at the end of the first decade of Africa's independence led to weakened economies and economic malaise, as well as to politico-social decline. Reasons for this included the following:

- Lack of adequate preparation of Africans for self-government and governance;
- Frustration of the Africanization policies and programs of independent Africa by the colonial policies and practices of the outgoing colonial administrators;
- Leadership deficiencies including military and other coups, corruption, etc.;
- Other forces both endogenous and exogenous, such as the energy crises of the 1970s and 1980s, SAPs, protectionism, debt, and more debt-servicing, monopolies of transnational corporations, decline and degradation in quality of education, the environment, etc.;
- Growth in the poverty syndrome, which was fueled by disasters;
- Legacies and remnants of colonial heritage such as dependency, conditionalities, impoverishment, reverse transfer of resources, brain-drain; and
- Lack of prioritization of economic sectors: agriculture; human resource development and capacity-building; infrastructural development; industrialization, energy sector development; healthcare (disease, poverty, and illiteracy), etc.

African Development Efforts in Post-Colonial Historical Perspective

Initiatives for African development started in the late 1970s and were not effective. There were two levels of initiatives: endogenous (i.e., intra-African) and exogenous (i.e., external), especially initiated and managed by the UN. These failed initiatives stretched from 1979 to 2002. Endogenous efforts initiated in Africa but with no significant African inputs included the following:

- 1979: Monroe Strategy for African Economic Development;
- 1980: Lagos Plan of Action for African Development;

- 1985: APPER;
- 1989: African Alternative Framework to Structural Adjustment Programs for Socio-Economic Recovery and Transformation;
- 1991: Treaty Establishing the African Economic Community (AEC: the Abuja Treaty);
- 1995: Cairo Agenda for African Development;
- 2001: Millennium Africa Programme (MAP);
- 2001: OMEGA, Senegal;
- 2001: Merger of MAP and OMEGA creates the New African Initiative (NAI); and
- 2002: NEPAD, a by-product of NAI.

Exogenous efforts initiated with the full support of external groups and institutions mainly included the following UN system-supported development efforts:

- 1989: World Bank's Long-Term Perspective Study on Africa;
- 1986–1990: UN-PAAERD;
- 1991: UN-NADAF;
- 1994: Cairo Conference on Population and Development;
- 1994: UN Conference on SIDS-Barbados in April and May; and
- 1996: The UN-Special Initiative on Africa (UN-SIA), which was reviewed in 2002 and absorbed into NEPAD.

Main reasons for failure of the initiatives included remnants of colonial influences and policies. There was a lack of financial resources for project and initiative implementation. The initiatives were not Africa-initiated, Africa-developed, Africa-run, Africa-managed, and Africa-owned proposals. Africa's increased and perpetual poverty (Afro-pessimism) fed a continuation of colonial economic policies of dependence and dependency in post-colonial Africa. Inadequately addressed were the development of infrastructure and education of labor force (no trained cadre to run African economy, etc.).

Some of these failed African development initiatives were unsuccessful because they established economic systems that supported colonial administrations and produced and exported primary commodities to Europe instead of creating markets for them in Africa. Others failed because they developed education systems that were based on those of the former colonial powers, and these systems were not relevant to the needs of the African society. Still others failed because they sustained the neglect of the agricultural sector in African national development plans, or neglected to develop building industries and introduce import substitution, which drained the African countries' foreign exchange earnings. Excessive stress on industrialization for economic development in Africa was still another reason for failure.

NEPAD

NEPAD grew from the general failure of development initiatives taken in post-colonial Africa (as previously mentioned in this chapter) and the general shortcomings of other African regional economic institutions like the Intergovernmental Authority on Drought and Development (IGADD), IGAD, ECOWAS, SADC, etc. Also contributing to the creation of NEPAD was the failure of development initiatives taken from outside of Africa (e.g., by the UN). The pre-NEPAD development efforts for Africa failed to attain the set goals and objectives of development and had a very small positive impact on the critical economic and social situations in Africa, which were aggravated by the global economic crises of the 1970s and 1980s. Additionally, they lacked "Africanness" and African ownership in them, as well as commitments in terms of investment and ODA flows to Africa by most of the richest countries of the world.

The cause of failure of some initiatives was a lack of the political will of developed countries and their failure to meet the ODA targets of 0.7 percent of their GNP for ODA resource flows to developing nations,[5] and of 0.15–0.20 percent of ODA to LDCs per the LDC Conference Action Plan of 1990 in Paris. Inadequate FDI flows to Africa and the other Third World nations for at least four decades (since independence), and the constant interference of external interests in African affairs during the Cold War era also were contributing factors.

The Cold War era produced a lack of accountability for project implementation because there was no way of monitoring initiatives. Also produced was a lack of popular participation in development projects and a lack of good governance, peace, and stability in African, and other, developing nations.

African Peer Review Mechanism

Another way of African involvement in African development efforts at the summit (heads of state and government) level, the African Peer Review Mechanism (APRM) is a novel method that, if applied carefully and systematically in Africa, could make a difference since the negotiators and decision makers in the talks are the heads of state and government (summit talks and decision making). APRM provides an ever-growing mechanism for African development and security.

Regional Integration in Africa

Five economic zones exist in Africa, each having regional arrangements for economic and related development: UMA for North Africa; ECOWAS for West Africa; SADC for Southern Africa; EAC for East Africa; ECCAS for Central Africa, and other similar machinery.

- These constitute the best success stories of African development efforts;
- They deal with other issues (e.g., conflict resolution by ECOWAS in Liberia, and SADC in Zimbabwe); and
- Experience many challenges and need broader involvement in regional affairs.

Africa in Global Negotiations

The United Nations is both a system and an organization. As a system, the UN comprises many organs, organizations and bodies. As an organization, the UN is a political institution that has organs such as the General Assembly and the Security Council and bodies such as the UN Development Programme (UNDP) and the UN Environment Programme (UNEP).

As mentioned previously, the UN as a political organization has a dual purpose. It is charged with being both the keeper of international peace and promoter of welfare. In its welfare promotion role, the UN focuses on the socioeconomic development of the world, especially of the developing nations born after World War II, subsequent to the decolonization process in Africa. The birth of new nations necessitated the creation of institutions and the making of arrangements to advance and support globally the development efforts of the newly independent countries in developing areas of the world from a global perspective via GATT/WTO.

The UN system addresses development and related issues such as economic, social, women, refugees, climate change and the environment, natural resources, energy issues, SAPs, debt, poverty eradication, disease (pandemics like HIV/AIDS), ODA, finance, and industrialization.

At the Paris Conference of 1990 on LDCs, the action plan also agreed that the developed countries, in addition to the 0.7 percent of GNP, would commit themselves to provide to LDCs from 0.15–0.20 percent of their GNP. These targets have not been met up to today (as of the time of writing these notes, i.e., October 18, 2008).

Creation of UNCTAD (UN Conference on Trade and Development), 1964

UNCTAD was established on June 15, 1964, in Geneva, on the request of the newly independent countries of Africa, Asia, Latin America, and the Caribbean. These countries had recently gained political independence from their former colonial (European) masters, and were now demanding assistance from these ex-colonial bosses, most of whom continued to carry the "big stick" toward their former colonies in the developing regions of the world. The new nations had just joined the United Nations (in the 1960s) and were asking not only for compensation from their former colonial masters, but especially for help in capacity-building and aid in their business and other development needs, to enable them to act effectively on the international stage as sovereign entities, stressing the importance of development in their regions and for their respective peoples and institutions.

At that time (1964), there were only 77 developing countries from the developing world which had joined the UN. The young nations created a bloc within the UN to serve as their development forum, and they called it the "Group of 77" Developing Countries. This group is still referred to as the Group of 77 (G-77) even though there are now more than 130 developing countries members of the UN. A few years ago, China decided to join, and so the group is now known as the Group of 77 and China.

Africa's Participation in Global Negotiations: Potential and Handicaps

Africa has great potential. Africa is a huge marketplace for international trade/business with a vast natural resource base and raw materials, but to be successful Africa needs effective participation in global negotiations of the UN system/GATT/WTO in order to benefit from international business and the global economy. There are plenty of opportunities but too many handicaps, such as a lack of trained negotiators and lack funds for attending international conferences.

Africa and the UN Conference System

The UN, UN organizations (UNOs), and UN systems have different mandates and participation dictates. Nonetheless, these organizations serve the same governments/countries. WTO (Trade) and International Atomic Energy Agency (IAEA) have specialized membership mandates and association with the United Nations. Additionally, there are specialized agencies such as FAO, International Fund for Agricultural Development (IFAD), ICAO, IMO, ITU, ILO, UPU, United Nations Educational, Scientific and Cultural Organization (UNESCO), United Nations Industrialization Development Organization (UNIDO), WHO, WMO, WTO (Tourism), World Intellectual Property Organization (WIPO), World Bank, and IMF.

Although there is active African participation in many of these groups, there are limited results in terms of benefits.

Africa and the Lomé Convention

The Lomé Convention was a trade system process agreement signed in 1975 between the then European Economic Community (EEC, now known as the European Union [EU]), and its former colonies in Africa, the Caribbean (Latin America and the Caribbean), and the Pacific (Asia). It was a collective group partnership for mutual aid in trade and development, where the ACP (African, Caribbean, and Pacific) was the clientele. The First Lomé Convention (1975) dealt with trade, aid, investment, industry, and stabilization of ACP (export) earnings (STABEX).

Most of the ACP countries were LDCs (i.e., the world's poorest countries) as categorized by the UN. Currently, Africa is host to 33 of the 49 LDCs in the world. Africa is the poorest continent on Earth, which is a huge paradox since Africa has vast natural and human resources.

Goals of the Lomé Convention (better known as the ACP/EEC/EU) included the following:

- Assisting ACP states in their efforts for development;
- Promoting relations of ACP with EEC/EU countries through privileged access—especially, free access to 15 EU markets with guaranteed quotas for some major ACP products;
- Promoting export compensation within the STABEX fund guaranteeing agricultural earnings and the SYSMIN fund underwriting earnings from mineral exports of ACP countries; and
- Financial aid to ACP countries.

There have been four Lomé Conventions; all were signed in the Togolese Capital of Lomé as follows:

- Lomé I signed in 1975,
- Lomé II, signed in 1980,
- Lomé III, signed in 1985, and
- Lomé IV, signed in 1990 for 10 years and represents the most extensive and expansive development cooperation in agriculture between the northern and the southern countries.

The scope of the Lomé Convention was aid and trade. ACP offers potential markets for the EU. The commodities/exports of the ACP were cash crops for foreign exchange earnings (e.g., coffee, cotton, cocoa, bananas, tea, pineapples, etc.) These crops had traditionally been denied access to global markets. So the Lomé Convention was a special instrument/arrangement between the former colonial masters and their ex-colonies for trade. In 1994, there was a mid-term review of Lomé IV, and the Lomé Convention system expired in 2000, following the adoption at the UN of the MDGs.

While active, the Lomé Convention required the following:

- For the ACP/EU to seek and honor/apply preferential treatment (trade preferences) toward ACP states;
- Areas of cooperation including trade, industrial cooperation, and financial and technical cooperation/funding flows to ACP;
- Consultation;
- Stabilization of commodity prices (STABEX) in the Common Fund for Commodities and UNCTAD;
- Transfer of technology to ACP;
- Linkage of ACP/EEC/EU process with UN IDS; and
- Many other issues (e.g., education, energy, disaster reduction and prevention, the global environment, poverty eradication, leadership efficiency, and actions against international terrorism.

When the ACP/EU expired in 2000, it was believed to have succeeded in its original objective of reducing dependency of the ACP countries on the industrialized world. It was most effective in the area of agriculture, especially for the export commodities mentioned above.

Africa and the Lomé Convention Negotiations: Success Stories

Africa's participation in the Lomé Convention negotiations was one of the best success stories for Africa. Based in Brussels, African and other missions were effective in the promotion and defense of African and national interests of the individual African country members of ACP.

As a long-term participant in those negotiations, this writer can testify to the success of the Lomé Convention system for Africa. In like manner, Africa's participation in the regional integration negotiations for African development has been, and continues to be, effective and valuable, despite the many handicaps that are encountered in those regional conferences, which, although basically of an economic development nature, do nonetheless address other development issues and challenges facing Africa in a multidimensional fashion.

Africa and the Global Negotiations of the GATT/WTO System

Africa experiences serious weaknesses that impede its ability to utilize this system. Africa's participation in these negotiations has been limited and less than successful because of the specialized nature of the talks. Other reasons include:

- The poverty syndrome and impoverishment of Africa as initiated and perpetuated by the slave trade, colonization, and the colonial policies and practices of isolation, humiliation, acculturation, fragmentation, the divide et impera colonial doctrine, and the many other paradoxes that confront post-colonial Africa;

- Lack of skills and capacity to negotiate;
- Lack of incentives and knowledge and improvements in performance.
- Lack of financial resources—these are very expensive negotiations without adequate representations in African diplomatic missions abroad;
- Lack of technological and technical know-how in global negotiations;
- Most of the African countries were still colonies when the GATT system was created in 1947;
- Problems of blank positions on global issues and often assuming the stands of the Group of 77 and Third World countries without refined African country individual stands in many cases.
- Misplaced and ill-advised policies, and the problems of dependency, dependence, and incompetence;
- Inefficient/ineffective participation in international discussions due to many reasons, including the lack of clear or timely instructions to be used in global negotiations;
- Fear among representatives to take stands on certain issues (limited liberty and skills incapacitating negotiators without authority, and often without express support from headquarters);
- Often no attractive terms of service, which leads to lack of self-confidence and inaction in certain cases;
- Insufficient patriotism and nationalism due to the poverty syndrome;
- Ethnocentrism, nepotism, corruption, cronyism, etc. which must be eradicated from officials who serve their countries both at home and in the field;
- Inadequate preparation to effectively tackle the problems encountered in global negotiations;
- Globalization, unfair competition, and no trade liberalization such as unfair trade and protectionism, conditionalities; no just export earnings for African commodities and other raw materials (exploitation), and no free access or easy access to global markets and to markets of the North; subsidies in developed countries,
- Colonial heritage, legacies, and remnants; climate change and global warming; disasters and environmental degradation; SAPs;
- Diminishing or no adequate funding for African development;
- Lack of ODA transfers;
- Increased reverse transfer of resource flows from Africa to the North;
- Lack of clean drinking water supplies in most of Africa;
- Many external shocks (e.g., the financial and oil/energy crises, excessive food prices, problems of insecurity and political instability due to conflicts and internal wars);
- Increased diseases/pandemics such as HIV/AIDS;
- Inadequacy of multidimensional development of Africa and the South in general;

- Too many refugees and displaced persons, especially in the Sudan, Somalia, Zimbabwe, Sierra Leone, Guinea, and other "hot spots of Africa"; and
- Lack of competitiveness and export diversification because of a limited number of export commodities.

CLIMATE CHANGE AND AFRICAN POLITICS

The issue of climate change is, for Africa, multidimensional: it is scientific, economic, political, social, and environmental. It is a huge agenda for Africa both at home and abroad. Everybody now knows what climate change and global warming mean as general problems, but if asked to explain precisely what these expressions mean, very few people understand their impacts on humans around the globe. Some governments even still believe, surprisingly, that these phenomena do not pose any threats to humankind. This view is very false, for indeed climate change and global warming are real dangers to humanity, and Africa is probably the most vulnerable continent to climate change as it is the most vulnerable to natural disasters.

In this chapter, there is no endeavor to discuss the scientific aspects of climate change and global warming, but of vital interest to Africa in this area are the political and economic issues arising from global warming and climate change. Politically, these issues are quite divisive in their discussions. For example, in the climate/global warming forum of the IPCC, the developing countries including African countries argue that problems of climate change and global warming are caused by the consumption and production patterns of industrialized countries such as the United States. On their part, the United States and other industrialized nations hold some developing countries like China and India responsible for some of the problems that cause climate change, such as greenhouse gas emissions.

Major Economic Sectors Affected by Climate Change in Africa

For Africa, the major economic sectors affected by climate change and global warming include agriculture and human settlements—especially those in arid and semi-arid lands (ASALs) where the lack of arable and fertile land triggers and intensifies the crowding of populations in small areas. This results in population explosion, degradation of the environment and the life support systems, etc.

When climate change results in floods or drought, water resources get depleted, resulting in deforestation, desertification, and the need for irrigation schemes that are too expensive to be afforded by most Africans and their governments. In like manner, crop failures due to lack of water or excessive water may result in famine and increased infestations of insects that cause diseases like malaria.

Africa in the Global Climate Environment[6-10]

Of instructive importance was the outcome of the IPCC meeting held at Nairobi, as reported in the media on April 10, 2009. Highlighting the risks of Africa from climate change and global warming, the *IPCC Report on Africa* published by the International Panel on Climate Change (IPCC) stressed a number of problems including the following.

Africa is headed for environmental and climatic disasters and other natural phenomena that pose enormous problems to Africa. The gravity of Africa's vulnerability to climate change and global warming is notable. Particularly vulnerable are the economic sectors of agriculture, infrastructure, wildlife (species), and coastal zones; other issues to be addressed include fisheries. Rises and falls in temperatures have impacts in various places in Africa (coastal sea-level rise); energy and industrial development; drought and desertification, especially in Africa's ASALs (where water scarcity for drinking and irrigation pose grave problems); and natural phenomena; human behavior (production and consumption patterns in Africa, but especially in the industrialized nations of the North); lack of capacity in Africa to deal with these natural hazards of climate change and global warming.

The poverty syndrome is multidimensional in Africa and is the factory of many of her development problems (e.g., it is estimated that a rise in temperatures by 3 degrees C [5 degrees F] can, and will put at least 1.8 billion people in Africa at the grave risk of water stress in the new millennium). Since Africa's population is bound to grow during this very period, the poverty syndrome would be dramatically increased unless the population is prevented from exploding, through planning, education, and information. In like manner, some species of wildlife and crops/plants might be wiped out—some have already been wiped out in Africa due to the excessive use of chemicals as fertilizers (e.g., in the Kenyan zones where the cultivation of sugar cane has steadily increased from around 1968 onward). The damage to wildlife and to agriculture has been dramatic, with some plants like wheat, millet, and some medicinal herbs disappearing, and perhaps disappearing altogether, in a relatively short period of time, due to global warming and climate change, especially in sub-Saharan Africa.

In Eastern Africa—in Eritrea, Ethiopia, Sudan, Tanzania, and Kenya, as well as in West Africa—in Benin, Guinea, Ghana, Côte d'Ivoire—and elsewhere in Africa, menaces of sea-level rise are already overwhelming. Coastal zonal crops such as coconuts, palm oil, and mango trees are not only being affected negatively, they may start to diminish in appearance. Some island nations like the Maldives might disappear as well. With such threats to food security, coastal survival, etc., there is an urgent need for measures to be taken to contain and stabilize the climatic change and global warming challenges facing Africa in the 21st century.

Africans participate actively in the international politics of climate survival; in the efforts to implement the stipulations of the Kyoto Protocol that will be expiring in 2012; in demands for the industrialized nations of the North to initiate and sustain deep cuts in emissions of greenhouse gases and their negative impacts on/in Africa in the new millennium; in global collaboration to assure food security and implementation of the MDGs in Africa; in global efforts for disaster management to prevent flooding, drought, and desertification and thereby prevent the skyrocketing costs of food and other necessities that would dramatize and accelerate bills in GDP; in setting targets to help reduce greenhouse gas emissions; in increasing investments and setting aside a reasonable percentage of GDP per year for the purpose of reducing greenhouse gas emissions in every country, in ensuring that effective adaptation to climate change in Africa is reached for the purpose of improving Africa's production and consumption patterns; reducing population pressures in Africa; and making hard decisions to promote awareness of the gravity of climate change and global warming as parts of the fight against these threats to humanity.

All in all, Africa must take charge of the fight against climate change and global warming. Then, the external world will have to step in to assist Africa in this fight, especially by helping in empowerment and capacity-building for climate and weather-related capacities against global warming and climate change menaces, which is a fight for the cause of humanity!

When wildlife and domesticated animals begin to perish because of drought and desertification, African nations begin to lack foreign exchange earnings, since tourism does not flourish where there are not enough varieties of animal species. Combinations of food insecurity, lack of foreign currency, poor sanitary and health conditions, and failures of both staple crops like maize and cassava and cash crops like cocoa, sugar, tea, and coffee cause hardships on Africans, and these demands translate into political problems because governments have the duty to provide the necessaries of life to their citizens.

The services rendered by having developed infrastructures and efficient communication and transport facilities are vital to development, and where there is development, there is no poverty, and where there is no poverty, there has to be peace and stability. Any good domestic politics of peace and stability are good for international politics.

In cases where global warming and climate change pose problems (i.e., in the natural resources of African nations), businesses and trade do not flourish, and since international and national business and trade are good for the development of Africa, it is essential that the problems of climate change be addressed because natural disasters negatively impact business and trade. In like manner, the social services are impacted negatively by climate change due to destabilizing of trade and degrading of infrastructure. Therefore, public information and education programs at all levels should be initiated and sustained that can and will assist the youth and other vulnerable strata of society—especially women and girls in Africa who play major roles in African families—to be familiar with the ways of tackling these problems.

It is clear that the hardest hit continent is Africa and the least prepared people for climate change are Africans. Capacity-building, research and development, and incentives need, therefore, to be undertaken in and out of Africa to promote the politics of sound planning for climate change and global warming. These issues should be elevated in African national funding as priority development issues. International aid to Africa should always target the African environmental and climate change fields for resolution.

African policies should accord priority to climate change issues in the IPCC, WMO, and other international fora where these issues are discussed. In the UN-Habitat, WHO, UNESCO, United Nations Development Programme (UNDP), IMO, UNEP, FAO, WTO, UNCTAD, and other relevant international fora (the AU, EU, EAC, SADC, ECOWAS, etc.), as well as in UN Economic Commissions for the World Regions, issues of climate change and of implementation of the Agenda 21 outcomes, conventions on climate change, biodiversity, and the convention to combat diversification, the Kyoto Protocol of 1997 (which is now operational), and the Convention on Ozone Layer Depletion—all of these should be examined in the African context by African governments and institutions. Leaders should pay particular attention to the African problems (e.g., precipitation and droughts, of wildlife habitats, of sea-level rise for the small island states of Africa in the Indian and Atlantic Oceans and other SIDS) as well as to the policy-making mechanisms to produce sound policies and budgets to combat climate change and weather-related issues.

All the above problems, if resolved, will help reduce the poverty and other diverse socioeconomic impacts on Africa and her people.

Africa should play major roles in international conferences convened to discuss climate change issues such as the one held October 12–14, 2009 in Copenhagen, Denmark. It is the African ministers of the environment who bear the responsibility for such international efforts. International climate change and global warming will continue to feature prominently in the new millennium. Africa should, therefore, call for increased actions of the world community to intensify its funding and resolution on greenhouse gas effects. The causes and consequences of climate change and global warming in Africa require increased efforts, as well as funding for economic growth and sustainable development necessary for poverty reduction and eradication in Africa. African schools, colleges, and universities should teach these issues through a well-prepared curriculum for all levels of education. This also applies to issues and problems of natural disasters and the environment.[11]

Summary

Africa has three overarching challenges: poverty, disease, and ignorance or illiteracy. Poverty is the primus inter tres (the first among the three) because poverty results from many wrongs, shortcomings, and problems. Poverty eradication can happen only if root causes are diagnosed, consequences systematically tackled, and cures planned and executed with the fullest involvement of Africans and their institutions.

There must be constructive bilateralism, multilateralism, empowerment of Africans—especially women and the other neglected strata of the African society—and ownership of the African development destiny by Africa. Capacity-building is a strong tool for poverty alleviation and eradication. Debt relief and debt cancellation are more important and effective debt relief mechanisms than foreign aid or access to foreign markets because debt cancellation releases predictable income that can be used for development purposes.

Problems of African leadership and democracy, an effective education system and delivery for the good of every African country, as well as effective participation of Africa in the UN system, in global negotiations of the WTO system, and of other global debates, can, if used competently, reduce the poverty syndrome.

The future of African efforts to eradicate poverty will depend on the kinds of measures, investment, and involvement that Africa develops in the coming years. Africans and their nations must learn from past failures in order to avoid them in the future. African development and security is the primary responsibility of the African governments and their institutions. This overall responsibility should never be ignored nor taken lightly in Africa.

NOTES

1. S.D. Kertesz, *The Quest for Peace Through Diplomacy*, (Englewood Cliffs, NJ: Prentice Hall, 1967).

2. McGeorge Bundy, Henry Kissinger, W.W. Rostow, James R. Killian Jr, Adolf A. Berle, Livingston Merchant *The Dimensions of Diplomacy*, E.A.J. Johnson, ed (Baltimore: Johns Hopkins Press, 1967).

3. See the relevant UN system web sites, charters of the UN system organizations, handbooks and outcomes reports of conferences and related meetings of these organizations, like those of the WTO, UNCTAD, FAO, WMO, WHO, WIPO and the UNO.

4. For information on the origins and development of NEPAD, consult the following UN documents: A/58/15, part IV; A/58/254; A/58/178; and A/58/16, or see www.nepad.org and www.un.org/esa/africa.

5. UNGA Resolution 2626, XXV, paragraph 43, October 24, 1970.

6. International Panel on Climate Change. *IPCC Report on Africa* (IPCC, April 2009).

7. Peter G. Jones and Philip K. Thornton, "The Potential Impacts of Climate Change on Maize Production in Africa and Latin America in 2015," *Global Environmental Change 13*, No.1, 51–59.

8. M. Hulme, R.M. Doherty, T. Ngara, M.G. New, and D. Lister, "African Climate: 1900–2100," *Climate Research 17*, No. 2: 145–168.

9. David Henderson and Richard Grove, *Conservation in Africa: Peoples, Policies and Practices* (Cambridge, England: Cambridge University Press Publication, 1987).

10. Peter Obunde et al., *Policy Dimensions in Human–Wildlife Conflicts in Kenya: Evidence from Laikipia and Nyandarua Districts* (Nairobi: Institute of Policy Analysis and Research, 2005).

11. For more comprehensive information on the vulnerability of Africa to climate change and global warming, see relevant reports of the IPCC on African conditions, *Report of the African Conservation Foundation on Climate Change and Global Warming*, reports of WMO on these issues, and those of other groups such as the Climate Institute.

CHAPTER 20

African Poverty and Attempts to Overcome the Poverty Syndrome in Contemporary Africa

AFRICA IN THE GLOBAL ECONOMY

The best way to understand the gravity of Africa's poverty syndrome and forge out measures to alleviate poverty in Africa is to analyze the African poverty situation in the context of Africa's presence in the global economy.

International Aid to Africa

On the question of foreign aid to Africa, it should be noted at the outset that the countries of North Africa have not required as much financial aid as have those south of the Sahara where all of Africa's LDCs (at least 34 of them as of 2007) are situated. The talk then about foreign aid to Africa is basically about international aid to sub-Saharan Africa and from the donor community consisting of bilateral aid donors such as the United States Agency for International Development (USAID), Canadian International Development Agency (CIDA), Swedish International Development Agency (SIDA), Finnish International Development Agency (FINNIDA) and Norwegian Agency for Development (NORAD), and multilateral (e.g., from the EU, G7, and others) donors.

Additionally, foreign aid to Africa has broadened its scope, ranging from the ODA commitments of 1970 for 0.7% of GNP of the donor countries, which has not been met with the exception of only four countries (Denmark, Sweden, Norway, and the Netherlands), to various kinds of foreign aid promised through the UN and other international conferences such as the LDC conferences of 1990 and 2001, the Monterey Platform of 2002, the

World Summit on Sustainable Development (WSSD) held in South Africa in 2002, and the Millennium Summit and its MDGs of 2000, whose Millennium Summit Declaration granted a special needs position for Africa in all these and other global development measures. It is clear that no realization of the promises of the summit goals will be met even by 2015. There is no way foreign aid to Africa will or can effectively meet the development challenges that were supposed to be met with the implementation of the MDGs and of the goals of climate change as outlined by the Intergovernmental Panel on Climate Change (IPCC). The World Bank and the IMF have promised more aid than delivered to Africa. The promises of G-8 under the constant urges of British Premier Tony Blair seemed very promising, especially at the 2006 Gleneagles G-8 Summit, which promised enough aid to Africa. But no delivery has happened so far. In like manner, poverty reduction in Africa requires increased aid by the donor community, including the WTO, but no delivery has happened so far. There are a number of reasons why foreign aid to Africa has been a disaster, but it is important to see why aid is not working and determine if there is another way for Africa to get aid.

Any aid based on charity has never worked because it is fraught with conditionalities that prevent such aid from being beneficial to Africa. The best way to get good, productive development aid is to secure that which is earned by Africa (e.g., via investment, trade, micro-finance, micro-credit, and government-to-government aid given on the basis of equal treatment). Another way of providing useful aid is to give in ways that do not exploit the aid recipient. Thus, capacity-building through education and training would be more beneficial to Africans than giving conditional aid. The main purpose of aid is to help the country. Development is a multidimensional process, and of the various kinds of aid, the financial, technical, and bilateral types are the most common.

When elevated to the global scene, the system of economic activity in an African country or region becomes a global economy. The talk about "global capitalism," "globalism," and "globalization" is basically one of an economic or trade nature, at least in the context of this study. The global economy is actually an international economy among nations, which comprises a number of constituent elements, such as the following:

- Free trade in goods and services,
- Unrestricted capital flows even if with reduced or weakened national restrictions,
- Stress on exogenous rather than endogenous forces or factors of international trade,
- Interconnection of the economies of the world, and
- Expansion of economics beyond national borders, especially expansion of production by trans-national corporations to many countries around the world.

Impact of Foreign Ideologies on African Development: From Global Capitalism and Globalism to Globalization

Imperialism was a 19th century ideology and policy in Western Europe that aimed at creating and maintaining empires in which states and populations were spread over wide geographical areas and controlled by dominant states. This ideology/policy impoverished Africa when she was colonized beginning from the late 19th century. Global capitalism is, on the other hand, a Western policy that has had a great influence on African leaders because of their leanings to the one or other ideology in the East–West confrontation for "survival." Thus, foreign ideology and policy in Africa produced a second "Scramble for Africa" in the period of the Cold War (1947–1990). There was a very negative influence on the African political system. As seen earlier in this study, the East–West ideological divide produced three systems of political doctrines in post-colonial Africa. One of them was African capitalism or Afro-capitalism by which the African leaders were forced to abandon the genuine traditional political systems of African socialism and Pan-Africanism, which had been embedded in the African spirit that was destroyed when European colonization transformed Africa and deprived her on her Africanness in development pursuits.

African socialism demanded the assumption of primary responsibility by Africans for African development as follows:

- Poverty eradication;
- Empowerment of women, girls, and youth to participate in development initiatives and efforts;
- Changes in mental attitudes of African leaders;
- Eradication of cultism and corruption from African leadership;
- Genuine patriotism in Africa;
- Improvement in the African education system for capacity-building, knowledge, skills, and contributions; and
- Africa's specialization and application of the new development paradigm.

All these ideals could not survive in the midst of "global capitalism" and foreign aid that did more harm than good to the African economies. International aid to Africa has never been without strings attached. Thus, foreign aid helps the donor community more than the recipient African state. Global capitalism can never support African development because such capitalism is always exploitative and aims at enriching the capitalist state and impoverishing the African state. Global capitalism can never promote African development security (which can be described as the freedom from want, hunger, violence and persecution, and death caused by murders and killings) because of the strings that capitalism attaches.

It was in the interest of European capitalism that trade in captured Africans flourished for four centuries in the triangular passage of Africa, Europe, and the Americas. Those African captives became the property of Europeans and Americans. When Europeans shipped Africans to European buyers in the Americas they did so in promotion of global capitalism and in impoverishment of Africa when her sons and daughters were reduced to objects and commodities for trade through a process of capturing innocent Africans through kidnapping, banditry, trickery, and warfare.

Thus, global capitalism, globalism, and globalization refer to the global economy of goods and services and capital, and of being interconnected, with many networks of connections across continents and global trade.

The main actors in the global economy include governments; multilateral organizations, transnational corporations (TNCs), multinationals (MTNs), multilateral corporations, businesses, and even individuals; and other international legal persons (e.g., UN system, WTO). This results in the shrinking of the world into a "global village" by the information revolution, and promotes/prompts interconnectedness in global economic relations.

Global Capitalism

Global capitalism should not be equated with Nazism or fascism. There should be no unfair international trade and finance, no reverse resource flows from Africa (for example to the North), and no exploitation of the South by the North.

Global capitalism is a system of production for profit that elevates capitalism to a global scale. Global capitalism promotes trans-nationalism, trans-border companies' business, global strategic alliances, and trans-world business association. Global capitalism causes and promotes globalization. But it further disrupts whole societies and often promotes inequalities and injustices in societies. It also promotes monopolistic tendencies and practices of multinational corporations (MNTCS).

Market liberalization by itself does not, and cannot, lift all boats. In some cases, it has caused severe damage to poor nations. Multinationals have contributed to labor, environmental, and human rights problems as they pursue profit around the globe. Reckless investment has done harm. Globalism disrupts whole societies of the developing world. Global capitalism promotes "transformationalism."

Consequences of Global Capitalism

Consequences of global capitalism include the following:

- Globalization;
- Reduction of sovereign statehood;

- A rise of supra-territorial constituencies;
- A potential decline in interstate warfare;
- Increased constraints on state provision of social security;
- Impracticability via the state alone;
- Growth of multilateralism;
- Growth of trans-boundary relations among nations in international business (global markets);
- Global production, which reduces costs of production;
- Global commodities represent a shift from "merchandise" (i.e., traditional trade and industry via global finance, global communication, global organization, global labor, taxation, and legal costs) to intangibles such as finance, information, and communications which, because of globalization surplus, is also accumulated through electronic financial transactions, production of data, and flows of images and sounds—thus, there are no complete dealings with tangible commodities, and thanks to globalization, international business is, and can now be, transacted via "communication" to new kinds of items (articles).
- Formation of global business organizations and rise in trans-boudary company discussions by MTNs (Multinational or Transformational Corporations are the same as trans-boundary business enterprises—strategic alliances between business enterprises); and
- Global money and finance are detaching money from the territorial space of coinage, paper bills, etc., with a clear national identity by globalization—now, banking computers, ATMs, online and electronic transfers have replaced the material forms of money and transfers by land and sea.

For Africa, global capitalism has to be seen in terms in terms of global negations. These do not help Africa much as Africa does not really benefit from global capitalism and globalism.

Globalism and Globalization Compared

Globalism is an expression used to mean different things. For example, globalism refers to the economic aspects and describes the reality of being interconnected. Globalism also describes and explains a world that is characterized by networks of connections. This is a network dating back to ancient times, and it can bring increased interdependence.

Globalism has four distinct dimensions: (1) global economy—long distance flows of goods, services and capital, information, and perceptions accompanying market exchange, (2) environmental globalism refers to long-distance transport of materials in the atmosphere or oceans, or of biological substances such as pathogens or genetic materials affecting human health and well-being, (3) military globalism refers to long-distance networks in which force and the menace or promise of force are deployed (e.g., "balance of terror" between USA and USSR during Cold War era), and (4) social and cultural globalism involves movements of ideas, information, images, and people who carry ideas and information with them (e.g., movement of religions, diffusion of scientific knowledge). Economic globalism rose between 1850 and 1914 and fell between 1914 and 1945. Globalism, like globalization, is often defined strictly in economic terms. It does not imply universality.

The poverty syndrome in Africa denies her the ability to reap maximum benefits at the national and international levels. The reasons for Africa's extreme poverty include the slavery and slave trade that rocked Africa for so many centuries; impoverishment of Africa by the European colonial policies and practices including taxation (even on mud huts) and a trade system that favored exports of cash crops from Africa to Europe; protectionism practiced by major Western economic powers against African goods and services (i.e., export commodities); and the SAPs of the Bretton Woods institutions, World Bank, and IMF. Africa's poverty also is caused by global and external forces. These include dependency and neo-colonialism of the former colonial masters of Africa (e.g., the phonist system and other colonial legacy remnants). Africa's poverty also has been deepened by natural and man-made causes such as the following:

- Floods, drought, and desertification;
- Locusts;
- Cronyism, corruption, conflicts, coups, civil strife, and wars;
- Irredentism;
- The AU/OAU African doctrine of uti possedetis juris;
- Ethnicity, tribalism, and related corrupt practices;
- Nepotism;
- Ignorance, especially a lack of good education and illiteracy among girls, youth, and women in Africa;
- Diseases including incurable and other pandemics like HIV/AIDS, Yellow Fever;
- Ill-advised policies, mismanagement, or irrational use of natural resources;
- Bad governance: lack of justice, transparency, accountability, human rights observance, etc.;
- Lack of right to development as a human right;
- Lack of the right mental attitude/change among most African leaders;
- Lack of democratization;
- Rapid population growth and pressures;
- Poor economic performance, and falling prices of Africa's primary export commodities; and
- Lack of self-reliance in the daily lives of the African populations.

For a historical perspective of Africa's poverty syndrome, and additional information on the causes and perpetuation of impoverishment in Africa, see Chapter 13 of this volume.

PAX AFRICANA AS THE LAST RESORT TO AFRICA'S OWNERSHIP OF AFRICA

Throughout this study, emphasis has evolved around the fact that nothing is given to Africa for free. Nothing. Everything received from the donor community always has strings attached. This is why the Chinese saying continues to be famous: "Teach me how to fish rather than giving me fish just to eat!" For Africa, this means that ways and means must be found by Africans—their leaders, governments, and institutions—to solve African problems using African methods and means. Foreign aid is helpful, but it should only be supplementary to African self-help and self-reliance. This requires Africa to be in the driver's seat and drive herself to her destiny. This also means that the primary responsibility for the multidimensional development of Africa not only rests with Africans and their institutions, but all development initiatives for African development, including in particular, changing mental attitudes of Africans and their leaders, must be Africa-initiated, Africa-developed, Africa-owned, Africa-run, and Africa-managed. There can be no shortcut to this requirement. This is the sine qua non condition for the durable survival of Africa as a subsystem of the global system.

An earlier stage of this study showed that there existed similarities and divergences in the search for unionism in the United States, and for unity in Africa. Also shown were that sharp differences occurred among the founding fathers of the United States and of Africa, which led to the emergence of three different schools of thought both in America and in Africa. Compromises were worked out that saved both the federation in the United States and African unity in Africa. Also noted was that in the United States, the architect of the compromise was the respected Roger Sherman from Massachusetts, whereas in Africa, it was the young and brilliant foreign minister from Ethiopia, Ketema Yufru, who was instrumental in getting the differing political camps to agree to an African summit under the chairmanship of the revered Emperor Haille Sellassie of Ethiopia.

Compromise in Africa

The three schools of thought in the search for African unity, as expressed at their first Conference of Independent African States hosted by Kwame Nkrumah in April 1958, were a testimony to the fact that deep disagreements had arisen at that Accra Conference. The contention centered around the kind of political system that should be put in place and followed in post-independence Africa: to adopt a United States of Africa approach, or to have a continent of independent African states? Prior to that conference, earlier in 1958, a four-day mini-summit—the First African Integration Conference of the Leaders of Ghana, Guinea, and Liberia (Nkrumah, Sékou-Touré, and Tubman, respectively)—was held at Sanikoli, a village in Liberia. Here, integration issues for independence and solidarity, including the "Founding Acts" of African unity, and the general future of African unity were discussed. In addition to the nine independent African countries at that time—Ethiopia, Liberia, Libya, Tunisia, Morocco, Egypt (United Arab Republic, which was a federation formed between Egypt and Syria), Sudan, Ghana, and Guinea, some observers from a number of African colonies, writers, political activists, academicians, and others also attended the conference. South Africa was independent but not included because of the government's Apartheid policies.

The observers who attended the conference came from the colonial countries of Algeria (Ben Bella); Tanganyika (Nyerere); Kenya (Tom Mboya, whom Nkrumah asked to chair an important committee of the conference even though Mboya was only 27 years old); the Union of Cameroonian Peoples; Nigeria (Azikiwe); and other leaders and representatives (e.g. from Dahomey). This was a historic conference—the first Pan-African conference held on African soil. It represented the collective expression of the African people's disgust with the system of colonialism and imperialism. So Africa was, at long last, ready to start a process of applying pressures to lead to total African political liberation, free from the colonial burdens that had incurred so much suffering of the African people. The conference clearly defined Pan-Africanism and the need for total unification under scientific socialism and political independence. This goal was stressed in the Addis Ababa OAU Conference, which adopted the OAU charter on May 25, 1963. The charter was a compromise document in which the African founding fathers agreed to establish a loose association of sovereign African states based on the principles of public international law and the UN charter.

RECLAIMING AFRICA'S CIVILIZATIONS IN THE NEW MILLENNIUM

One of the gravest howlers that some European powers ever committed in global politics was their efforts to make Europeans out of Africans, or to believe that Africans were not capable of self-rule. In South Africa, for example, Hendrik Verwoerd (1901–1966), the Boor prime minister and Apartheid architect in South Africa, and his cronies who supported and imposed Apartheid policies on South Africans from 1949 to 1994, and even earlier, and Ian Smith head of the racist minority regime in the 1960s in Southern Rhodesia, which is present-day Zimbabwe, declared that Africans were not capable of ruling themselves until perhaps after 1,000 years of European preparation. And when slavery and the slave trade in captured Africans became perhaps the most lucrative business of all time, many were convinced that the African was less human than Europeans. Alas, even some Roman Catholic clergy, including popes and other clerical leaders, supported slavery and slave trade perhaps because they believed that Africans had no souls, or that they would and could be better "civilized" if they remained in the hands and care of Europeans! So slavery and the slave trade in Africans were supposed to be good practices for Africans.

As it turned out, the colonial expansion and subjugation of Africa lasted for far less time than the predicted 1,000 years—even less than 100 years! But within this very short period of time, historically speaking, the Europeans succeeded in transforming Africa and Africans perhaps forever, and making Africans the mere by-products of Western civilization. The European colonial policies and practices succeeded in destroying and eradicating most of the values, customs, traditions, cultures, and civilizations of Africa. The question then, that one can rightly and properly ask, is whether the transformation of Africa and Africans is permanent, or if there is room for Africa and the African people to reclaim their civilizations and even redeem them in the new millennium? Have African civilizations been lost forever?

It has to be in the above context that Pax Africana should be analyzed and evaluated. The present writer is convinced that the fundamental test and challenge confronting contemporary Africa is whether the spirit, identity and soul of Africa that existed before the Europeanization of Africa, can be reclaimed and redeemed in the 21st century. This then must be a century for Africa's examination of Africa! The following analysis endeavors to provide possible responses to these challenges of Africanness.

For Anima Africana to be regained, Vox Populi, Vox Africae must become the managing director of Pax Africana. In the first instance, we need to define the meaning of "Pax Africana," "Anima Africana," and "Vox Africana." Thereafter, it becomes necessary to explain how Pax Africana is, and should be, the instrumentality through which Africanness, civilization, and soul shall be regained, recognized, and reasserted for the common good of Africa and the African people. Then ultimately, we need to see how Pax Africana is, and should be, the foundation par excellence of African foreign policy, African diplomacy, and African international relations.

DEFINING PAX AFRICANA

For all practical purposes, "Pax Africana" is a system of norms governing international conduct in Africa. These norms address weaknesses and vulnerabilities, which will however, be there irrespective of the changes and dictates that may shape Africa in the future. The norms also aim at helping to address and attain Africa's international basic needs.

"Pax Africana" is a Pan-African doctrine rooted in the African values of Amana and Ubuntu that produced Pan-Africanism. Amana is a Hausa (Nigerian) concept encompassing faith, trust, and honesty. Amana is applied widely in northern Nigeria's traditional life. Trust and honesty are essential for socioeconomic transactions and for contacts between the state and society. Inter-human relations cannot exist and prosper without Amana. It is believed that without the spirit of Amana, projects and programs such as NEPAD cannot, and shall not, succeed in Africa.

Ubuntu on the other hand, is an expression in the Bantu languages of Southern Africa, meaning interconnectedness, intertwining of peoples, and the affirmation of human interdependence—the forging of a true community, society, and the world—a common humanity belonging to the society where one lives with duties, responsibilities, and rights. Communal happiness, individual identity, dignity, and respect are among the human values that characterize Ubuntu. It also includes African socialism, Harambee (Swahili for "let us pull together"), and the like.

PAX AFRICANA CONCEPTS OF AFRICAN UNITY AND POLITICAL INDEPENDENCE

At an earlier stage of this study, while comparing American and African concepts of political union and unity, we touched on the doctrines that prevailed in America during her founding years. In Africa, many political philosophies also arose, dictated both by African customs and traditions—African heritage—and by alien types of heritage, including the European colonial heritage. The following are among the well-known and applied doctrines on the African scene of Pax Africana.

Empirical Tradition

Empirical tradition in Africa comprises complete existential attitudes, beliefs, conventions, and institutions rooted in the experience of the past, exerting and orienting a normative influence on the present, and with the ability to reclaim and redeem Africanness and civilizations of the past. In this regard, Pax Africana is a "rediscovery" of Africa by Africa, and, hence, the fight for decolonization of Africa and the search for African foreign policy, diplomacy, and international relations dating back to the 1800s in the United States and the West Indies, where Pan-Africanism actually started as was determined earlier in this study. Also previously discussed were the roles that the Pan-African congresses of the 1900s played in this decolonization process, the important date of 1776 when the seeds of Pan-Africanism were planted in America; the shaping of the independence movements for Africa; the Pan-African efforts of the late 1950s and 1960s; Point No. 5 of Woodrow Wilson's 14 points to LON on self-rule; the schools of thought that emerged in the early years of Africa's political independence, starting at the first conference in Accra, Ghana, in 1958, of all the independent black African countries, through the periods of the African conferences and summits held between 1958 and 1963 for the political unity of post-colonial Africa; the roles of the decolonization process including the UN's historic resolution and declaration of the General Assembly No. 1514 dated December 14,1960 on the Granting of Independence to Colonial Countries and Territories; and even the Resolutions of the Monrovia Group of Independent African States that sought a Pax Africana that would be moderate to accommodate past, present, and future policies and diplomacy of African states as members of the international system and that rejected the minimalist approach of the Brazzaville Group and the radical approach of the Casablanca Group of African states. All these were historic additions to the nature and function of Pax Africana that culminated in the May 25, 1963 adoption of a Charter of the Organization of Africa Unity (OAU) at an African summit held at Addis Ababa in Ethiopia.

Pan-Africanism thus matured as a political doctrine when it assumed a sovereign voice on the international scene, at the independence of the African states that sought and received international recognition as sovereignly equal political entities on the global scene. At that stage, African foreign policy, diplomacy, and IR had to be reshaped to fit into the new international order of the 1960s and beyond in which Africa found herself, at Addis Ababa, Ethiopia, and thereafter.

Nationalism

Nationalism was, and is still, the self-conscious desire, aspiration, will, or assertion of a group of people to form an autonomous political community. African nationalism is the doctrine that promotes devotion to the interests and culture of an African nation or continent, and aspires for national independence. African nationalism is also opposed to divisive tribalism, nepotism, cronyism, and corrupt practices that breed obstructive chieftainships, and stagnating customs and traditions; promote colonialism and neo-colonialism; and promote futurism. It is the opposite of European and Western nationalism, which stresses individualism, among other things.

African nationalism thus ultimately aims at welding peoples of diverse languages, traditional cultures, and customs, etc., into one nation. This does not tally too much with European nationalism, which, especially in the 19th century, aimed at fitting people sharing the same culture, and the same language, into one nation-state.

Pax Africana is thus a huge factory for African international relations, African foreign policy, and African diplomacy. These were derived from the Pan-African spirit of the early 20th century, up to 1945 when Pax Africana was groomed to oppose slavery and the slave trade in captured Africans, oppose imperialism and colonialism, and differentiated itself from Pax Europaea, Pax Americana, Pax Britannica, and even the earlier Pax Graeca and Pax Romana of ancient times, which had all, in one form or another, sought conquest through military and other might. Pax Africana, on then other hand, grew out of African integration, unity, cooperation, and interdependence based upon the African traditional values, which must cement the concept of African union or unity and aim at retaining, or reclaiming and redeeming where necessary and possible, the African spirit and identity that were destroyed by the European colonization of Africa.

As a vital and central ideology of Africa then, Pax Africana promoted political aspects via the long decolonization process, running through the following:

• The Pan-African Congress of 1945 at Manchester, England;
• The First Conference of Independent African States of 1958 at Accra, Ghana;
• The doctrines of the three schools of thought born at Accra in 1958;
• The adoption of the OAU charter in 1963;
• The doctrine of uti possidetis juris of 1964, which rejected the doctrine of irredentism and reaffirmed the inviolability of the borders as fixed in Africa by the General Act of Berlin of 1885—this is a controversial issue that will have to be revisited often, with a view to finding just and lasting solutions to African conflicts emanating from border disputes;
• The adoption of diplomacy as an instrument for resolving differences and conflicts in Africa and elsewhere;
• Human rights, regional integration, and women's rights as vital tenets of Ubuntu, Amana, Ujamaa, Harambee, African socialism, etc.;
• International law and peace, territorial integrity, and sovereignty;
• The role of intra-African and international trade and development, business and negotiations for the common good of Africa;
• Aiming at rejecting Western values if they collide with the right and just dictates of Africanness and African development and security: self-reliance,

democracy the African way, peaceful coexistence, education, equity and equality of opportunity, etc.;

- Observance of the UN Charter Principles and Provisions; and

- To ensure the maintenance of growth of the real determinants of Pax Africana, inter alia: Pan-Africanism, nationalism, and patriotism; decolonization against dependence and dependency; loyal police and armed forces in Africa; democratization of Africa the African way; stability, national unity, anti-tribalism, and anti-fragmentation; avoidance of divisive politics often induced by external forces; and Africanness; and

- An African doctrine of "Hands off Africa."

AFRICA–U.S. RELATIONS IN THE NEW MILLENNIUM

The special historical relationship that has existed between Africa and the United States is bound to be revived in the new millennium, given the fact that for the first time, an African American of Kenyan extraction has been elected to the U.S. presidency: Barack Obama. This development, with other dictates of the new millennium requiring Africa and the United States to collaborate more closely, would require that a deeper and closer examination be made of the Africa–U.S. relationship, and this is something that the current writer believes will be most worthwhile to do. This is going to be a fascinating period to watch in the Africa–U.S. relationship.

U.S. Policy toward Africa

For all practical purposes, U.S. policy toward Africa can be clustered into three eras: the era before 1960; the 1960–1990 era of Cold War politics; and the post–Cold War Era from 1991 to the present, better described as the era of Cold Peace.

As indicated above, a number of issues characterized U.S.–Africa relations before 1960. The colonial times did not offer much to the African–U.S. relationship, because the African colonies were parts of the colonial metropolis. Hence, foreign policy applicable in the African colonies was basically that of the European mother country. Before the colonization of Africa, not much had developed either, between the United States and Africa, with a few exceptions (e.g., when the young United States entered into a special relationship with Morocco, when the two nations signed a Treaty of Friendship in 1786 and Morocco was the first country in the world to recognize U.S. independence). During the kingdom, empire, and city-state eras in Africa, practically nothing special existed between the United States and Africa because the United States traces its origins only to the 17th century.

In the 20th century and the post-colonial era, between 1960 and 1991, the world had experienced two world wars, and the number two continued to dominate international politics and IR because there were then two superpowers, two Europes (East and West); two military alliances (NATO and the Warsaw Pact); two ideologies (communism and capitalism); and two world orders. In Africa, that was a period of gaining political independence, and hence Africa was a victim of the East–West ideological divide. "Where two elephants fight," as the Swahili proverb says, "the grass suffers the most!" But for Africa, given the extent of destruction and exploitation that was done, it was better that the giant elephants had been fighting. If they had been making love, which is a slower and longer process, the African grass would have suffered even more because Africa's wealth was overwhelming, and making love over it would have impoverished the continent even more.

The United States was thus involved in the second "Scramble for Africa," in the form of an ideological war, and continued to demand that multipartyism be reinstalled in Africa. As long as there was the East–West divide, however, it was better for Africa, since the continued scramble for Africa by the West and the East tolerated an overlooking or letting pass, of some political and other errors that had been going on in Africa for fear that strong actions against the offending African regimes might have prompted the latter to move toward the one or the other superpower of the two ideological camps. This is a huge paradox in itself. For this reason, African regimes like those of Mobutu Sese Seko in Zaire were able to get away with so many injustices to the African people. In the post–Cold War Era, however, things are different, and worse, for African regimes, since the absence of an ideological struggle and competition in global politics ignores the existence of Africa somewhat. No one to defend African regimes on an ideological front means a kind of neglect of African regimes as orphans with nobody to take too much care of them. The result of all this has been American neglect of Africa in favor of the ASEAN nations in terms of investment, trade, and other kinds of bilateral, regional, and multilateral arrangements.

The Cold Peace politics are thus an era of a new world order with one superpower, the United States. There is continued demand for multipartyism in Africa, and an end to corruption, human rights violations, and a need for accountability and good governance. But what do all these mean? What is often forgotten is that democracy as conceived and practiced in African contexts means completely different things for Africa and Africans than for Americans. The confusion of Westernization and modernization in Africa collides with African values. African democracy the African way and U.S. democracy the American way are a good example of this.

Many issues of political, economic, business, military, strategic, environmental, humanitarian, moral and other imperatives and dictates dominate Africa–U.S. relations in the contemporary world. The forging of coalitions with Africa at the UN and in other fora, and support for African causes, are bound to grow during this century. But the burden is on Africa, as any improvement of U.S.–Africa relations will have to be initiated by Africa if that relationship will benefit Africa.

African Foreign Policies toward the United States

As in the case of U.S. relations toward Africa, one cannot talk of African policy toward the United States; or U.S. policy toward Africa. They must be described in the plural, as determined in an earlier phase of this study. African policies toward the United States used to be dominated by the fear of the West and the fear of the East because of the East–West ideological divide. This is no longer the case following the collapse of the communist ideology that started to crumble with the tearing down of the Berlin Wall on November 9, 1989.

The 21st century offers an opportunity for improving Africa–U.S. relations, partly because of the changed times, witnessing an African American in the White House, and partly because the times are ripe for more fruitful and non-ideological considerations in U.S.–Africa relations. This is an important period to watch.

Today, African policies toward the United States are basically of two types: those that are initiated by the African countries, whether individually or collectively, and all are mainly of an economic nature. There are moves for tourism, business, like under the AGOA (the African Growth and Opportunity Act of May18, 2000); access of African goods and services to the U.S. market, and U.S. facilitation of such access to global, industrialized markets; increased ODA flows from the United States and the North to Africa; removal of protectionism; encouragement of U.S. public and private investments in Africa; education: scholarships and training for capacity-building in Africa; infrastructural development; debt and debt servicing, debt relief and cancellation, etc. Then there are the politically triggered African policies toward the United States (e.g., nonaggression, security, disease issues, etc.).

The second category of issues in Africa–U.S. relations are those that are patterned or initiated on the basis of U.S. policies toward Africa. For example: the fight against international terrorism; strategic, oil, and military interests; the Horn of Africa route to the Middle East; human rights, and governance issues, democratization and globalization issues; globalism; disarmament and denuclearization of the Indian Ocean; development issues such as those initiated by UN strategies and action plans like the MDGs; climate change, ozone layer, biodiversity, desertification, and global warming conventions; and other issues as tackled by the UN system such as food through the Food and Agriculture Organization (FAO) and World Food Programme (WFP); weather and climate (WMO); health (WHO); intellectual property (WIPO); information technologies (ICTs, ITU); trade and development (UNCTAD); education, culture, and science (UNESCO); business and trade negotiations (WTO); poverty and natural disasters (HIPC, SIDS, LDCs, LLDCs); war, peace, human rights, and social agenda issues, etc.

As time passes and new and emerging issues grow, like HIV/AIDS, Ebola, and globalization and new development paradigms start to grow, the relationship between Africa and the United States is bound to change. Global change will demand increased capacities for self-reliance and the full implementation of the now established evidence that the primary responsibility for the development of Africa lies with African governments and their institutions and people. As the world has shrunk because of the information revolution, technology, the Internet, etc., interdependence has become a reality, and the stress of this is likely to be directed toward utilizing the GPGs for the common good of the people. Interdependence, mutuality of interests, and vulnerability of Africa and the United States will require closer cooperation between the United States and Africa. The Obama administration will be required to take some concrete measures to promote U.S.–Africa relations. He and his successors will be dealing with an Africa that is more integrated into global politics. The United States will thus, as the single superpower of the world, be expected to play a key role in the process. We shall watch and see what will happen.

IN SUMMARY: PAX AFRICANA, VOX POPULI AFRICANI

Pax Africana should be promoted because it is regarded as the ethic for rebuilding Africa and reclaiming African civilizations.

Every effort must be made to promote Pax Africana because, as a philosophy, Pax Africana is regarded as a socio-spiritual ethic for rebuilding Africa and reclaiming African civilizations that will harvest from Africa's fertile cultural acreage to create a Pan-African philosophy of development. No Afro-pessimism, but reidentifying Africa's ideals, like Africa's founding fathers did, as being fundamental to Africa's progress or development.

Aims of Pax Africana

The aims of Pax Africana include the following:

1. Recover Africa's traditional values that have been distorted or destroyed over the centuries by alien colonial European rule;

2. Reject or readjust Western democracy imposed upon Africa by colonial policies and practices—the greatest of the Europeans' unrealistic and overambitious philosophies and policies of the 19th and 20th centuries was, in this writer's view, their efforts at installing, having, and promoting an education system in Africa that aimed at turning Africans into Europeans by all standards; and

3. Attain a genuine homegrown philosophy in African societies that aims at ascertaining popular representation—democratization; decision-making by consensus; extended family codes; African sociocultural values that are decent, humane, and just; and societal integration leading to regional and African continental integration. This, in turn, leads to larger markets, economic unity, and benefits, as well as a larger and richer pool of human and intellectual capital, and trade relations that existed before colonialism and colonization were imposed on Africa and the Africans.

Dictates and Pillars of Pax Africana

Ubuntu, Ujamaa, Amana, African socialism, and Harambee are among the fundamental pillars of Pax Africana. Included among others are the need for Africa to use her GPGs for the eradication of the GPBs. Among the GPGs must be included: sustainable development; a sound global environment; international financial stability and market efficiency; natural resource protection and utilization for national prosperity; appropriate use of the ecosystem, life-support systems; health; knowledge; peace, security, and stability; and human rights and humanitarian rights.

These GPGs are non-excludable. Each produces benefits that are impossible to prevent everyone from enjoying. They also are anti-rivalry—meaning, their consumption by one person does not detract from another's consumption. For example, when we use clean air, no one is made to have less or more—there is no rivalry.

CHAPTER 21

African Geopolitics in the 21st Century

CAN AFRICA'S PAST MEET THE PRESENT IN THE NEW MILLENNIUM?

To better understand African geopolitics in the 21st century one has to relate Africa's past to the present, with a view to mapping out a strategy that will make corrections in order to learn from past mistakes and avoid past failures in the new millennium. In this regard, issues in African international relations need to be clustered into appropriate eras, tracing their origins and development from remotest antiquity to the present.

This chapter addresses African international politics as the area of African international relations in which power coercion and bargaining happen in order to determine how Africa's participation in global politics and the acquisition of global resources and favors has to be divided. African international relations can be divided into three periods in which Africa has experienced three kinds of African international relations and heritage. Each era or period has been marked by issues and challenges falling within a number of periods and subperiods which we have explained before but whose outline at this stage of the study will help explain from how far Africa has come to the present era—the contemporary period in African history and global geopolitics.

In the so-called African heritage of international relations, influences were either not known at all, or they did not have any historical significance. The period spanned from prehistoric times to the ancient world (i.e., more than 10–15 million years ago to 500 BCE). During this period in the ancient world, we can trace the origins and development of African relations and relationships starting in remotest antiquity from family and extended family to community, village, and sub-clan alliances to clan and tribe to city-state, nation-state, tribal kingdoms, empires, super empires and super states. Nomadic expansionism continued into the African ancient era, which was in ancient times (sometimes this period of ancient Africa in the ancient world is given as having lasted from 50,000 BCE to 500 BCE and from 6200 BCE to 400 CE). Ancient times are considered to be from 500 BCE to 500 CE. The accurate timeframe for this period also known as the historic period in ancient times lasted from 500 BCE to 476 CE. The latter year marked the end, or fall, of the Roman Empire in the West, however, the year 500 CE has been chosen here for the purpose of convenience. Ancient Africa was fixed as the period 500–1415 CE and was noteworthy in African relations with the external world as the fall of the Roman Empire in 476 CE marked the end of the ancient world during which Africa north of the Sahara had been colonized three times (once each by the Phoenicians, Greeks, and Romans). In 1415, the first European contacts with "modern" Africa happened and marked the beginning of a new relationship between Africa and Europe that eventually led to the Europeanization of Africa into a by-product of Western civilization. The last leg of the pre-colonial Africa period happened between 1415 to 1883 CE. This latter date is the eve of the beginning of the colonization of Africa. The years 1885–1960 were the colonial period of Africa following the holding of the Berlin Conference of 1884–1885. Thus, sensu largo, Africa has witnessed three broad eras and the past colonial era. Within the same timeframes, African international relations have been clustered with the African heritage and the postcolonial or "mixed" heritage. Obviously, there have also been other kinds of heritage in Africa, like religious heritage of Christianity and Islam, which were globalized and brought to Africa in the 1st and 7th centuries CE, respectively. Of the "minor" periods of Africa's historical development, the following are noteworthy:

- Period 1. More than 2 million–500 BCE;
- Period 2. 800 BCE–1415 CE;
- Period 3. 1415–476 CE;
- Period 4. 476–1453 (fall of Constantinople in the eastern part of the Roman Empire);
- Period 5. 1453–1807 CE;
- Period 6. 1808–1885 CE;
- Period 7. 1885–1960 CE; and
- Period 8. 1960 CE to the present.

Generally speaking however, the historical period of "modern Africa" started from around 1800 to the present, although it has also been variably argued that modern Africa started from 1919 to the present. Other dates have also been suggested.

Thus, in trying to analyze the events and dictates of today's geopolitics involving Africa, it should be remembered that the present heritage and remnants of the past in African international relations have negative and positive implications for Africa in her geopolitical standing both at home and abroad. Thus, Africa's two types of African international relations—endogenous and exogenous (i.e., intra-African and extra-African) have been divided into three clusters in order to facilitate the understandings of the African condition in pre-colonial times, when no states existed in Africa but small groups came together for survival, trade, conquest, diplomacy, and security via alliances and other actions, proactions, interactions, and contacts. Those were not international relations but tribal and inter-tribal groupings, and inter-kingdom relations. Expansionism started at subregional and regional levels of the same ethnic groups, language, and "neighborhood." These were followed by inter-regional trade and other contacts including trans-Saharan contacts and commerce into north and eastern Africa. This activity was carried out by people who traded with each other and perfected their skills in science, technology, and medicine (e.g., caesarean section, hieroglyphics writing in Egypt, about 4,000 years ago), inventions, stone cities, and tools and construction in Zimbabwe, where a great civilization grew up and flourished. Astronomy flourished before the Common Era in Egypt and Kenya. In the latter for example, the Namoratunga or "the stone people" in Turkana who lived on the edge of Lake Turkana displayed great prehistoric cultural development, especially in sub-Saharan Africa. The Africans were great astronomers, navigators, and mathematicians and, in Egypt, architects who built the pyramids, like the Shona pyramid in Zimbabwe. They did long-distance communications and traveled long distances across Africa building coalitions, discovering new areas and green pastures, and perfecting agriculture, especially along the banks of the Nile where huge fluvial sediments attracted extensive settlements after the occurrence of the Sahara Desert. Gathering and hunting were replaced by farming, and herbs and plants were discovered as medicine and food. Writing spread to Nubia and, with the spread of conquest and territorial acquisitions in Africa, relations eventually developed into inter-African nation-state relations since they became interactions and dealings across national borders of what had become super states and were actually conducted by state-based actors, although not of the Western type. The African heritage was thus a very long geopolitical happening in the pre-colonial period stretching from ancient times up to the year 1885, which serves as the milestone marking the end of the pre-colonial phase of the African geopolitical condition. By then, Islam had invaded Africa in an extensive way via trans-Saharan commerce (e.g., in Ghana and West Africa where economic and business relations created between Arabia and West Africa spread elsewhere in Africa and established the roots of the geopolitical situation that still exists in parts of Africa today). That marked the formal ending of the purely African heritage period. Then, the colonial period of the African geopolitical condition was launched by the advent of colonial rule. The colonial times heritage stretching from the late 19th century to 1960 introduced a new kind of geopolitical condition in Africa in that there was no equality of partners but relationships between bosses (the colonists) and subjects (the African peoples and their territories). Although not unique to Africa, colonial relations introduced new international relation (IR) concepts, conforming basically to Western values. Thus, even though many of the issues, challenges, priorities, and needs in Africa could not be confined to pre-colonial times and this specific phase, it was the masters—the colonial powers and their agents in Africa—who were the actors of colonial geopolitics. Those times pushed Africa's roots of antiquity even further away from the later African heritage. Then there followed decolonization with its new phase of African international relations and geopolitics.

ISSUES IN AFRICAN INTERNATIONAL RELATIONS AND GEOPOLITICS

Major issues in African pre-colonial times included the following, among others:

- Replacement of African nomadism by permanent settlements and development of authority patterns;
- Formation, development, and survival of human groupings and leaderships into patterns of rule and governance into the city-state systems in Africa;
- The development of international relations (IR) from city-states to empires and to super-empires and super-state relationships;
- Containment and incorporation of invading alien cultures, religions, languages, and customs into the African cultural settings; and
- The maturity and maturation of African international relations and African geopolitical policy (AGP) from within Africa as well as from without Africa.

This last condition created two kinds of African international relations and AGP: intra-African (i.e., endogenous) and extra-or international (i.e., exogenous) aspects of African international relations and AGP. Thus, there is a progression from Diasporanism of the 1800s and 1900s to maturation of African international relations and African foreign policy. Pan-Africanism movements also housed the origins of modern African international relations and African foreign policy. Trade, diplomacy, alliances, governance, government, advanced social and political groupings and systems, despotic, democratic, monarchial, dictatorship, socialism, theocracy, plutocracy and communalism (Ubuntu, Ujamaa) likewise had influences.

The main political systems in Africa consisted of at least the following six categories:

1. Rule by custom and tradition—which flourished especially in pre-colonial times where African socialism required decision-making by consensus and by counsel of the councils of elders/advisors;

2. Various forms of democracy—autocracy/despotism/dictatorship;

3. Republicanism, communism;

4. Socialism (Soviet and/or Chinese style);

5. Rule by inheritance (learned from the Greeks and Romans via Western civilization); and

6. Afro-capitalism (patterned on Western capitalism).

BUSINESS AND TRADE PRACTICES IN PRE-COLONIAL AFRICA

The maturation of African international relations and the African geopolitical condition also appeared in the field of business and trade practices in the early periods of African international relations. The contradictions in this field happened when, for example, these practices of pre-colonial times were rejected in the colonial era, which ignored the following pre-colonial practices:

- The long tradition and history of merchants, artisans, and local or regional markets for goods and services from within Africa;

- The development and use of African trade routes in ancient times, which promoted inter-relationships between and among African tribal kingdoms, empires, city-states, and the super empires of Aksum, Mali, Ghana, Congo, Dahomey, Mossi, Nigeria, and 35 or so autonomous city-states of East Africa (Mombasa, Lamu, Sofala, Mogadishu, Buganda, Wanga, etc.);

- The above political units of Africa, and others, promoted African markets that served local areas and market networks that linked together many and varied markets of those flourishing African tribal kingdoms, empires, and city-states. The African geopolitics of those centuries were improved in the post-colonial era of Africa in which business activities are conducted at bilateral and multilateral levels, as well as at national, subregional, regional, and African continental levels—at the AU level.

- Multilateral exogenous entities, groups, and international companies and concerns do engage themselves in the geopolitics and business actives of, and in, Africa. Already in the eras of the city-states and super empires, trade relations with far away countries and kingdoms—as far away as China and Arabia—were maintained using monsoon trade winds.

ISSUES IN AFRICAN INTERNATIONAL RELATIONS AND AFRICAN GEOPOLITICAL POLICY DURING THE FIRST 20 POST-COLONIAL YEARS

Most of the issues and challenges outlined and analyzed above still face Africa in the new millennium. Trade and business relations are still sought and maintained from within and from without Africa. These issues have grown in number, complexity, and gravity as the years passed, as explained elsewhere in this study. The fundamental issues and challenges confronting Africa in the 21st century include the following:

- Poverty, disease, ignorance (illiteracy), and other weapons of mass destruction obstructing development in Africa;
- The environment, climate change, and the global warming;
- Globalization, conflicts, and their consequences;
- Global development and Africa's involvement in the development paradigm of the 21st century;
- Problems of regional integration, "Afro-pessimism," security, sustainability, and problems of statehood in Africa;
- Education, empowerment, and equality of gender for women and girls;
- Democratization;
- Capacity building and ownership of the African development destiny by Africa;
- State survival against subalternism in the "power balance" theory of African international relations and AGP;
- Multilateralism and bilateralism in development assistance for poverty reduction and eradication, cultural development, African civilization "recovery" in modern times, and access to international trade and markets;
- Funding for African development;
- Infrastructural development;
- Technology and science for development: ICTs, Internet, and other information revolution necessary for Africa;
- Reductions in Africa's paradoxes, especially those relating to impoverishment, economic underdevelopment, poverty and acculturation, leadership deficiency, and education for sustainable African development;
- Africa's vulnerabilities to global capitalism, exploitation, dependency, and dependence, for example, limited commodity exploits cash crops such as coffee, cotton, or cocoa and tea in exchange for manufactured goods—price fluctuations and problems of greed, corruption, governance, and human rights observance.
- Resource nationalism for African sustainable development to be controlled and owned by Africa for the benefit of African natural resources, and human development for the common good of Africa; and
- Colonial remnants in Africa as an issue in the 21st century.

Colonial Remnants in Africa

Colonial remnants in Africa include the following:

- The artificial borders—geographical lines drawn on the African map as borders that have either divided nations or amalgamated, conglomerated different nations into large political units experiencing internal and continental conflicts, civil strife, and wars;
- The dependency syndrome;
- Loss of African identity—cultural clashes, etc.;
- Corruption, tribalism, communalism from colonial policies and practices;
- Racial stratification of Africa societies along racial lines;
- Continued frustrations of Africanization policies—exploitation, social injustice, gender inequality;
- Cultism, dictatorship, autocracy versus democratization;
- Reverse resource transfers from Africa to the Western world;
- Alien, European systems of government that replaced African systems originally based (rooted in) customs, traditions, heredity;
- European education system, European economic system, Africa as a by-product of Western civilization;
- Effective participation of Africa in the international/global system, including criteria challenges of the international relations of the UN system;
- Language and modernization in Africa that are challenges of the new millennium; and
- Many other issues falling within the endogenous and exogenous agendas of Africa as a subsystem of the global system.

Thus, at inter-continental levels, practically all the above enumerated issues can, and will, be tackled from within Africa under at least five agendas as follows:

- The Social Agenda, to address issues such as pandemics like HIV/AIDS, empowerment of women, girls and youth, gender inequality, human rights and governance issues, as well as poverty and illiteracy in Africa.
- The Political Agenda, which comprises leadership and cultism in Africa, corruption, competent governance, subalternism, and other African political doctrines like irredentism "uti possidetis juris," democracy and democratization, conflicts and conflict resolution, peacekeeping and peacemaking. Transfer of power to the younger generation of leaders from the first generation (1945–1990) and second generation (starting from 1991) are difficult to determine because they have been overlapping since the attainment of independence of the African states. Some of the "younger generation" leaders of the second stage would include President Museveni of Uganda; Prime Minister Meles Zenawi of Ethiopia, Preidents Issayas Afferworki of Eritrea, Paul Kagame of

Rwanda, and Jerry Rawlings of Ghana. But for these to hand over power to the younger generation they themselves might no longer qualify for their description as "younger generation" leaders!

- The Environmental Agenda is a difficult agenda for Africa, given Africa's vulnerability to the global environment, climate, and lack of capacity to handle issues of the environment and natural phenomena such as global warming and climate change, support of the ecosystems, disasters and development, natural disaster, and environmental impacts of African business, as well as sustainability in science, the environment, and other sustainability disciplines.

- The Development Agenda has been broadly explained earlier in this study with proposals for tackling Africa's development problems on a systematic basis; the MDGs, Agenda 21, GPGs versus GPBs; multilateralism; Afro-pessimism and the poverty syndrome; multidimensionalism in African development and security and many other related issues, such as oil and other natural resources, renewable energies, and resource nationalism revisited.

- The Economic Agenda deals with the African economies which are based on agriculture. The African economies do well or badly depending on many factors, including the weather, natural disasters, political leadership in the country concerned, the global economic and financial situation, and other factors. In most cases, economic crises lead to "Afro-pessimism"

Thus, Africa's overall agenda for intra-African geopolitics includes practically all of the issues that are tackled at global levels, and they all remain as valid in the 21st century as they were in the 20th century.

EXTRA-CONTINENTAL GEOPOLITICS OF AFRICA

In Chapter 5 of this study, discussion was advanced on African foreign policy and diplomacy as conceived and practiced from ancient to medieval times. It was established that African foreign policy, diplomacy, and foreign relations have had roots, determinants, and foundations dating back to remotest antiquity in many of the sources of these three constituent elements of the African Condition in global geopolitics, which are the very foundations of Africa's existence as a continent and first habitat to the human race. Also shown was that issues of sovereignty, statehood, national interest, security, and international law, among others, play vital roles in Africa's foreign policy, diplomacy, and international relations. It was further determined that the foreign service of each African state plays major roles in implementing the foreign policy decisions of its nation as managed by diplomacy.

In this chapter, no effort will be made to define the understandings of these expressions. Nonetheless, it is essential to recall that the roots and foundations of African foreign policy, African diplomacy, and African international relations are basically similar, if not the same issues, dictates, and requirements of the national interests of Africa as they were in medieval times, and even before.

Thus, custom and tradition, languages, African values, assets, and other endowments that require national protection, promotion, promulgation, preservation, and defense are as valuable and vital to African nations as they always have been. They should all therefore be borne in mind even when dealing with case studies as contained later in this chapter.

FOREIGN POLICY AND DIPLOMACY OF AFRICAN STATES IN THE FUTURE

Good leadership is, and will be, one of the fundamental requirements for the success of African foreign policy and diplomacy in the new millennium. Leadership qualities must include the following:

- Possession of Africanness, being/having loyalty to nation before tribe or self and other individuals;
- Prioritization of issues versus ill-advised policies and decisions involving social, environmental, economical, development, security, unity issues;
- Full grasp of nation's needs and national interests;
- Good judgment;
- Humanity;
- Patience and calmness;
- Values;
- Readiness to lead promptly and effectively but impartially;
- Ability of leaders to surround themselves with good and competent people: no nepotism, and no cronyism; and
- Readiness to be commander-in-chief.

Defining Foreign Policy

Foreign policy is the totality of actions and non-actions, reactions and proactions, interactions, and contacts taken by a sovereign state toward another sovereign entity or entities, or conducted between one sovereign state and another or others. Foreign policy is thus the elevation of domestic policies to the international level or scene.

Foreign policies aim at protection, promotion, and preservation of national interests and promote the image of a nation. Protection means nation first, and national interests means the population/people. A nation's other assets are security, welfare, the economy, preservation and conservation of national values such as human rights, dignity, freedom, independence, and security.

Africa's foreign policy is based on the system of the ex-colonial powers' foreign policy, which became the main source of Africa's post-independence foreign policy, in partnership with diluted Pan-Africanism that led to the birth of African unity and self-determination. Thus,

African nationalism, identity, unity, political doctrine/philosophy, and foreign policy, all trace their origins to Pan-Africanism, which, in turn, originated from the African Diaspora that was born out of the slavery and slave trade by Europeans and Arabs who sold African captives from Africa to five continents and subcontinents (Europe; North Africa/Middle East/Arabia; the Western Hemisphere, which includes North America, the Caribbean and Latin/Central/South America; Asia; and Australia).

The African Value System as Factory for African Foreign Policy, Diplomacy, and International Relations

Culture and civilization, Negritude and Pan-Africanism, African socialism, Ubuntu, Ujamaa, etc. are vital root sources of African foreign policy, African diplomacy, and African international relations.

Thus, in the African context, foreign policy is, and can be derived from, various sources and roots. The African value system, for example, based upon custom and tradition, is one of the fundamental determinants of African foreign policy and diplomacy. Whereas the terms "culture" and "civilization" stem from Latin, "policy" and "diplomacy" are derived from Greek. As shown, however, both these groups of expressions share the same nature of pluralitantism. Thus, "foreign policy," "diplomacy," "culture," and "civilization," although usually used in the singular, nonetheless have plural meanings. Consequently, "African foreign policy" and "U.S. foreign policy" actually mean "African foreign policies" and "U.S. foreign policies."

In like manner, as important parts of the African culture and value system, and civilization of Africa—like African ideology, Negritude, Pan-Africanism, African socialism, phonism, cultism, and the like—do have important impacts on the making and even implementation of African foreign policy and diplomacy in the context of Africa's relations at home and abroad. These relations are shaped by African values. These values include Negritude, for example, which is an ideology that was advanced by Aimé Cesairé, the French-speaking West Indian-Haitian whose philosophy of pride and beauty in African "blackness," became quite popular in subsequent years, for example, when S. Senghor of Senegal adopted this doctrine and advanced it in his writing. Negritude was a doctrine parallel to Pan-Africanism. Both African ideologies carried the same message, namely, that the black man need not be an inferior replica of the white man; that the black man or woman had and has his/her own distinctive culture and history behind him or her, about which they should be very proud. Also promoted was the idea that if only the peoples of African descent could unite, absorb what they needed from white culture, and not let it absorb them, then the African nation would be reborn and could equal, or even surpass, anything the whites could do.

Phonism in Africa and its Impacts on African Foreign Policy, African Diplomacy, and African International Relations

In like manner, phonism, although a language system and by-product of European colonization of Africa, is nonetheless an important determinant of African foreign policy. Phonism emerged strong following the decolonization of Africa and the remnants of Europeanism in independent Africa. Thus, the African subsystem in the global system recognizes the phonist system, which originated in the Berlin Conference of 1884–1885 on the partition of Africa into European "spheres of influence," with Great Britain (Anglophone), France (Francophone), and Portugal (Lusophone) as the main providers of the phonist system in Africa. However, the Islamization of Africa also produced an important Arabphone in Africa. After all, Arabs arrived in Africa much earlier than the Europeans, following the birth of Islam around 600 CE. The dictates of leisure/vacations, trade, culture, settlements, and religious globalization of Islam led to the invasion of Arabism in Africa.

Thus, even though phonism has messed up Africa and done Africa more harm than good, it is believed, nonetheless, with some justification, that phonism has brought some advantages to Africa, including coordination and cultural preservation; trade and mutual assistance, especially in Arabphone Africa; special relationships of culture, education, commerce, and religion, as well as social and humanitarian ties; mutual support in domestic, intra-African, and external relations; and the forging of more effective and better structured and productive contacts, especially in times of "common" enemies or threats like in Middle Eastern politics, or in economic needs, as was the case during the oil crisis of the 1970s.

Ironically, Germany, which was the architect and host to the Berlin Conference of 1884–1885 at the urging of Portugal, never produced Germanphonism in Africa. A similar situation occurred with Italy and Spain, both of which also attended the Berlin Conference. Spain had her hands full with expansionism in Latin America, and Italy, even though it held colonial possessions, never played a major role as a colonial power. The United States likewise had no phonism in Africa—most probably as a result of the spirit of the American Revolution of 1776 and of the Monroe Doctrine of 1823, which focused on keeping Europe out of the Western Hemisphere, and could not, hence, entertain any double-standard of producing a U.S. phonism in Africa.

DIPLOMACY AND FOREIGN SERVICE IN AFRICAN INTERNATIONAL RELATIONS

Conceptual Definitions

Diplomacy is an art, a way of doing things. It is the management or adjustment of international affairs or relations by envoys/ambassadors, by or through negotiation or persuasion of diplomats, who aim at promoting and cementing relations of all kinds—diplomatic, economic, business, military, strategic, etc. These representatives are supposed to take maximum advantage for their country or agency, and ensure a minimum disadvantage to their country or agency. In this regard, diplomacy in practical terms entails trustful reliance and expectations of help from comrades, allies, and social friends, and aims at facilitating communication between and among nations and sovereigns through means other than the use of force in order to resolve differences that may exist between or among nations (the diplomat's state/agency, and the host country/agency).

One can also say that diplomacy is the conduct or management of inter-state relations. Diplomacy is the art of adjusting the varying and often clashing/conflicting interests of states *to the advantage* of the state that the diplomat represents, but also in order to preserve friendly and amicable relations with other states where possible.

Thus, diplomacy as an art and a duty is applied or used in order to serve various purposes, including the following, among many others: representation; negotiation; promotion and preservation of international peace and security; administration of law and justice; advocacy for peaceful coexistence and for decent rules of international behavior; promotion of regional integration and collaboration; mobilization of international resources (e.g., for development); promotion of multidimensional international cooperation via the UN system and other organizations; and reconciliation of different national interests and seeking common-ground agreements, solutions to problems, and the promotion of peaceful coexistence.

Foreign Service

The foreign service (F.S.) of a country is its professional staff through which the head of state or government (foreign minister) and other relevant organs manage the foreign relations of that country. Thus, Foreign Service aims at promoting, projecting, promulgating, propagating, protecting, and defending the image and interests of the nation via envoys, ambassadors, and others representing the country through the F.S.

Thus, African foreign policy, African diplomacy, and African foreign service are vital managers of African international relations. It is noteworthy that international relations is, sensu largo, an arena for sovereign states to pursue their national interests that, sensu stricto, can, and do, include considerations other than strict national interests (e.g. ideological, moral, and emotional considerations and criteria). In this overall structure of international relations must be stated that the primary national interest of any state or nation is its citizens and population. When, therefore, political leaders are chosen to serve the country, their primary target should be the people—citizens who elect the politicians;

and hence the need for engaging in the activities of the state that defend and protect the wishes and desires of the electorate. The structure of African international relations thus must include statehood, sovereignty, territorial integrity, and international law and rules to govern the state's relations with other sovereign entities—via international law, conventions, principles, custom and tradition, and general practice accepted as norms of behavior.

African diplomacy therefore refers to the management of African affairs in which skills are employed with a view to resolving, through means other than war or coercion, differences and disputes that may arise between and among an African state and another non-African sovereign state of legal person such as the UN organization. African diplomacy also means promotion of peaceful coexistence between and among nations for the purpose of the ultimate achievement of collaboration, consultation, and coordination of international efforts for development in its multidimensional form.

In contemporary international relations, diplomacy and foreign policy have become crucial managers of relations among sovereign nations and whose emphasis has been shifting from the basic goal of maintaining international peace and security to diplomacy for development in all its forms. This is particularly important for Africa as a developing region that requires durable development and security in the 21st century. In this regard, a quick historical perspective on African foreign policy, African international relations, and African international diplomacy follows.

Historical Perspective

Just like African international relations, African foreign policy and African diplomacy can be clustered in periods, the first of which lasted from remote ancient times to 500 CE. This period lacked any real African international relations, African foreign policy, and African diplomacy as they became known and as will be seen herein below from the definitions of diplomacy, international relations (IR), and foreign policy. Some prototypes of these disciplines did exist as far back as then, even in the absence of state sovereignty as established by the peace treaty of 1648 (Westphalia).

By 500–1415 CE, some forms of IR, foreign policy, and diplomacy had occurred under the city-state of the times. The European contacts with Africa did trigger some alien interest that later had impacts on those three African disciplines.

From 1415 to 1884 was still a pre-colonial period of Africa. During this period, many historical events happened. For example, Africans were taken into slavery and the slave trade, and Europeans came to Africa as missionaries, adventurers, explorers, journalists, and geographers and "discovered" some parts of Africa.

From 1885–1960 CE was the colonial period of Africa.

The post-colonial era from 1960 to the present is actually the period of sovereign actors of Africa as full members of the international system. A brief explanation of each period of African diplomacy follows.

Foundations of African Diplomacy

Historical Perspective from Ancient Times to 1883–1884

This period is known for the following:

- Customs and tradition;
- Development and refinement of language and linguistic skills as valuable tools for communication;
- The African value system, moral imperatives, and cultural values of settling disputes, discords, and differences by means other than use of force or armed conflict;
- African socialism and "vox populi vox dei" and "vox societatics," process, procedures, mutual oral agreements;
- The wisdom of old age;
- The value of negotiation, compensation, and exchanges of prisoners, goods (e.g., cattle versus cattle rustling, land), arbitration, etc.;
- Recognition of territorial borders, boundaries as demarcated by nature, rivers, mountains, forest ranges, etc.;
- Importance of extended family and business codes, barter and trade relations, peaceful coexistence, expansionism;
- Continuation of mere traditional diplomacy ways from earliest tribal groupings and societies through the eras of permanent settlements, governments, and governance to city-state and super empire relations that actually were interactions across state borders and, hence, international relations;
- Importance of language orientations and diplomacy skills for dowry and intermarriages for cementing friendships; negotiations, fixing of borders, demands for recognition, and territorial integrity; needs for collaboration against human and natural enemies; and for forging durable friendships, camaraderie, alliances, common sharing, and peaceful coexistence, etc.; and
- Early external influence on African diplomacy (e.g., early contacts of foreigners with North Africa for commercial/trade and colonial purposes) with the Phoenicians from 800 BCE, with the Greeks from 631 BCE, with the Romans from 146 BCE.

Lessons: conquest, negotiations, territorial expansionism (aggrandizement), domination of foreign lands and peoples, treatment of enemies, compensation for losses of property, territory, power, and revenues, etc.

Historical Perspective from 1884 to 1960

Impact of European imperialism transforms Africa to Western values. African diplomacy would henceforth have to conform to Westernism. Africa became a by-product of Western values and civilization.

Struggles of Africanism versus Westernism apparent in diplomatic doctrine. No distinct African diplomacy practice but "boss-subject" relations replaced the subject-to-subject diplomatic dealings and contacts of pre-colonial Africa.

Difference between African diplomacy based on African traditions and African diplomacy based on Western traditions has prevailed into post-colonial period.

Historical Perspective from 1415 to Present

Post-colonial diplomacy and diplomatic practice is a mix of pre-colonial, colonial, and post-colonial practices. They are based on European (Western) and American diplomatic practices as used at the UN in global diplomacy. The European era of adventures beginning in the 15th century CE led to European expansionism outside of Europe, and Africa became one of the obvious destinations for various European adventures and interests. Africa was ignored for a long time and was described as a "Dark Continent" in the 19th century.

New and Emerging Foundations, Issues, and Dictates in African Diplomacy

Internal forces include the following:

Phonism;

Poverty, disease, ignorance;

Colonial heritage, legacy/remnants, practices, processes, and procedures of ex-colonial masters;

Diplomatic styles and traditions;

Diplomatic processes and procedures;

Diversity of issues and cultures as great determinants of modern African diplomacy (e.g. trade, disease/pandemics, development, disasters, global warming, and climate change);

Peace versus conflicts, peace pacts, agreements;

Judicial versus imperial statehood;

Global negotiations on business and development and investment;

Debt and debt servicing;

External forces include the following:

International policies;

International economics;

Development initiatives and strategies for Africa;

Other priorities in diplomatic dealings (agriculture, education, infrastructure, industrialization, energy, tourism, climate, environment);

Political issues (governance and government, democracy and democratization, human rights and social justice/equality, refugees, immigrants, and displaced persons, conflicts, border disputes); and

Leaderships: foreign and many others.

In short

- African diplomacy today covers a much wider area of operation than in pre-colonial, colonial, and early post-colonial times.
- African diplomacy now has to manage African international relations and implement African foreign policy on a daily basis.
- F.S. and diplomacy in Africa have become vital tools for improving Africa's image, African international relations, and foreign policy in global politics. Therefore, improvements must be made to enhance the roles of F.S. and diplomacy in African foreign policy and in African international relations.

Foundations of African Foreign Policy

Historical Perspective from Ancient Times to 500 CE

First alien contacts with Africa (Phoenicians), followed by alien colonization in Africa in 800 BCE (also Phoenicians), 334 BCE (Greeks), and 146 BCE (Romans).

Historical Perspective from 500 and 1515 CE

Reasons for success of European expansionism and domination of Western European civilization and values included the following:

- Curiosity;
- Territorial aggrandizements; imperialism;
- Discovery, exploration into African interior, nature, geography, demography (African colonization and transformation);
- Sui generis case of Boer settlement and colonization of African interior; and
- Implications of African diplomacy and foreign policy.

Historical Perspective from 1415 to 1883–1884

This period is marked by legitimate and illegitimate trade (slave trade) with Africa as well as the origins and development of the triangular trade in captured Africans.

Religious globalization and globalization of Christianity reaches North Africa; globalization of Islam and legitimate trade relations forged with North and Southern Africa (in north and trans-Saharan Africa contacts).

The first European/Portuguese contacts with Africa in post-ancient times occur in 1415 CE.

European Renaissance and Global Capitalism

Religious globalization continued European expansionism following the Renaissance, a time of rebirth or renewal. This period is marked by multidimensionality in Europe (the Florentine Renaissance and the Dark and Middle Ages).

Rationale for European globalism of post-Renaissance era focused on the following three goals:

The three Gs—glory, gold, gospel and

The three Cs—civilization, commerce, Christianity.

CASE STUDIES

The United States

From the beginning of the new millennium, the United States entered a fascinating period in her relations with Africa. This is partly because the 44th U.S. president, Barack Obama, has his roots in Africa—in Kenya. The historical significance of this development in U.S.–African relations deserves a separate analysis at another time. For now, it is worthwhile to examine U.S.–African relations in historical perspective, in the comprehensive analysis that follows.

U.S.–African Relations in Historical Perspective

As a starting point, one must look at African and American value systems. A value is a thing of worth (e.g., life is worth living and has valuable things to offer). There are two kinds of value: material and intangible things of worth, and supernatural things.

African values include truth, goodness, beauty, family, children, dowry-bride wealth, dance, music, celebration, worship, religion, Christianity, Islam, animism, hospitality, African socialism, Ubuntu, love for community, ancestor worship in African culture, human life, love for/ practice of extended family, respect for elderly people, customs, traditions, cultures and civilization, the aged, parents, superiors like teachers, elders, grandparents, rulers, inheritance, supernatural worship, ancestor worship, events and practices, nationalism, Pan-Africanism and its political systems, Negritude, consensus in traditional decision making, village as the home of humanity and of extended families, loyalty to ethnicity, parochialism, regionalism, majimboism, ethnocentrism, and diversity of cultures. New and emerging African values including religion (the supernatural, Christianity, Islam), and values in urban area.

Western values include money and other economic imperatives, education, home and self sufficiency, modernization and divestment of colonial legacies and remnants, humanism and values of Africanism and cultures, no exploitation, no slavery, no racism or discrimination.

American values include Western values, money, education, constitutionality, Bill of Rights, constitutions and declarations on human rights, liberty, freedoms of expression, equality, democracy and democratization, competence versus nepotism, capitalism, equality of opportunity, rights of the individual, superiority of race, ownership of property, different political doctrines and cultures, equality of sexes—women and men—protection of rights, protection of law, rule of law and basic freedom.

Divergent Cultures

African culture stresses collectivism, extended family codes, village parenthood, African socialism, but African culture was transformed by European colonial policies, which rejected African values in favor of Western values.

Transformation of Africa in colonial times means the tying of Africa on Western civilization that originated form the advent of imperialism/colonialism/colonization of Africa, which not only acculturated Africa by destroying the African spirit, identity, and Africanness, but also transformed Africa's ways of living and communicating, and destroyed African cultures, traditions, languages, customs, and civilizations. Western civilization downgraded African values and civilizations to nothing, or to inferior and primitive values, were in need of being replaced by Western (American/European) values.

Clashes of cultures and civilizations of Africa and the United States are seen in the following:

- Diverse cultures, civilizations, individuality;
- Diverse heritage: Africa has customs and traditions; America has democracy, rule of law, legal inheritance;

- Roots: Africans have home, village, heritage, education, agriculture, farming, land cultivation, rural life as main concentration, African socialism (which was for welfare of relatives); Americans have urbanism, industrialism, urban life, and amenities; and
- Family values: Africans had extended family codes, large families, and children; stress on customs, traditions, marriage and big families, not education; barter economy, African socialism. There were rituals (i.e., traditional worship and ancestors). Americans had small families, Western education, money, economy, equality of opportunity, and individualism.

Common heritage between Africa and America is as follows:

- Common colonial past: Africa has a colonial legacy and European nations' colonial remnants; the United States has the United Kingdom as a former colonial master, although the populace is different, mainly European, extraction;
- String colonial dominance;
- Common Europeanism and value system;
- Problems of "roots";
- Political culture is based upon European culture;
- Paradoxes;
- Schools of thought;
- Acknowledgement of good and bad policies and practices and their consequences; and
- Africans and African-Americans.

Divergent Features

Paradoxes in Africa include vast wealth of natural resources in vast poverty. In the United States there is poverty in vast wealth.

An examination of the schools of thought, independence, national unity, and doctrines of the founding fathers of Africa and the United States reveals that Africa had the following three schools of thought:

(1) Casablanca, which was radical and subscribed by Kwame Nkrumah of Ghana, Ahmed Sékou-Touré of Mali, Modibo Geita of Mali, Gamal Abdel Nasser of Egypt, Jomo Kenyatta of Kenya, Ahmed Ben Bella of Algeria;

(2) Brazzaville, which was minimalist and was subscribed by the leaders of ex-French colonies like S. Senghor, Ahmadou Ahidjo of Cameroon, and Félix Houphouët-Boigny; and

(3) Monrovia, which was lead by moderates who included William Tubman, Namdi Azikiwe, Ethiopian emperor Haile Selassie, Ketema Yifru MFA, and Sir Alhaji Abubaker Tafawa Balewa.

America's founding fathers included radicals such as Samuel Adams, George Mason, Thomas Jefferson, John Hancock, Thomas Paine, James Madison, George Washington, and Abraham Lincoln. Radicals were the founding fathers of America who were against the U.S. Constitution as drafted because they said it would open way to tyranny by central government. So they drafted a declaration (the Bill of Rights) and annexed it to the constitution to guarantee individual human rights and individual immunities. The rest included John Adams, Andrew Jackson, and Alexander Hamilton, among others.

The U.S. Declaration of Independence was made on July 4, 1776 and the U.S. Constitution was enacted in 1787. African declarations of the bills of rights are annexed to constitutions but not completely honored.

Note that the United States is a country, not a continent. Africa is a continent, not a country.

Success Measurement

The United States: money and education are key passports to success.

Africa: many handicaps to success, which are passports to misery like poverty, contradictions, de-Africanization, dependency (i.e., neo-colonialism), etc. as passports to misery.

The United States: conditionality and arrogance of power are guiding tenets in foreign policy. American conditionality and exploitation are facts in African international relations. Colonial legacy and remnants are important determinants of Africa foreign policy.

Africa: many handicaps to success. Humiliation and exploitation are facts in African international relations. Colonial legacy and remnants are important determinants of African foreign policy, dignity, and Africanism as a philosophy against poverty in plenty.

Independence and Leadership

The United States: Revolution against Great Britain, a violent reaction against the alleged tyrannies of the British Government.

The American Revolutionary war lasted from 1775 to 1783. The Americans fought versus Britain, and versus British colonial tyranny. The Declaration of Independence was signed on July 4, 1776. Signatories to the Declaration were 54 delegates including: George Washington, Thomas Jefferson, James Madison, Benjamin Franklin, Andrew Jackson, Benjamin Harrison, Alexander Hamilton, John Adams, Roger Sherman, Samuel Adams, Thomas Payne, and John Hancock. The constitutionalists who believed that the central government must be strong included, Alexander Hamilton and John Adams. The U.S. radicals included Abraham Lincoln, George Mason, Thomas Jefferson, Thomas Payne, Samuel Adams, and John Hancock. They held the view that central government must be weak and concede power to states.

Africa: Decolonization process from 1865 to 1977 included struggles for independence in the following three ways:

• Fighting/gaining independence from colonial powers,
• Surrender by colonial powers,

- Negotiations from World War I, LON 1939 mandates, and UN treatment of World War II trust territories.

Culture Shocks

Clashes of cultures and value systems include the following: traditional tribal life and ways of doing things (e.g., customs, traditions, behavior, languages); extended family codes: it takes a village to educate a child, village parenthood; inheritance of land—restrictions; rule by consensus; cultivation of individuality and national prosperity; and worship and sacrifices to ancestors and dates.

Political Heritage

Africans have a strong cultism of political leaders, ethnocentrism versus patriotism and nationalism, coups, corruption, conflicts, wars (civil and inter-African), national wealth, opportunism, and nepotism.

Americans have democracy and political maturity, patriotism, nationalism, resources, and global capitalism spent in the United States, a different type of corruption.

Africans have juridical statehood, problems of irredentism, seclusion, separation, and amalgamation.

Americans have empirical statehood and unionism.

There are the following four questions to be asked and answered in dealing with the common and diverse cultures, customs, and traditions of Africa and the United States:

- Question one: Is it mine or ours, yours or theirs that I have borrowed?
- Question two: Decision about nation or individual decision?
- Question three: Role of education—does it help or hinder in diverse cultural relations? (Result: superiority complex or inferiority complex.)
- Question four: What best describes national identity? Is it ethnocentrism (Africa), national unity (identity), and patriotism? Is it us first, or me and mine first?

Eras of U.S.–Africa Relations

There have been three eras of U.S.–Africa relations in Africa's pre-colonial period, colonial period, and post-colonial period.

Pre-Colonial Era

Africa's presence in the Americas dates back to ancient times—prior to Columbus's "discovery" of America. In 3000 BCE, according to archeological evidence, Africans were living in Panama and other parts of the Americas. The pyramids in Mexico indicate a clear connection with the pyramids of

Egypt. Visits and possible immigrations of Africans to the Americas seem to have happened long before the arrival of Europeans in the Western Hemisphere.

Thus Africa's gifts to the Americas date back to earlier than the era of slavery and slave trade. Similarly, no special relationship between Africa and the Americas/United States is recorded in the period of 1620–1776 when the United States was a territory of mostly European immigrants that became a British colony.

There was not much, if any, trade except later in the slave era and trade in captured Africans for 400 years. There were benefits to Europe and the United States. With the emergence of slavery and the slave trade, commercial activities were conducted on a triangular basis. First, involving legitimate trade in gold and other minerals from Africa, and salt, cowries, and agricultural goods like coffee and cocoa, rubber, sisal, and cotton. They traded in the 1440s and later traded in slaves and Africans captured and sold to the Americas, Europe, Middle East and the Far East. However, the United States was not really involved in other relations with Africa except for the slavery and slave trade as initiated by some European nations including Great Britain, Denmark, Netherlands, Spain, Portugal, France, and other European powers. The goods, natural resources, and slaves were taken to the Americas.

The slave trade and ensuing birth of the African Diaspora in the Americas linked Africa to the United States.

Colonial Era: 1885–1960

By 1795, the interior of Africa had been colonized by the Dutch starting with the Cape of South Africa in 1652. Thereafter, other European interests in Africa grew—astronomy, geography, exploration, and discoveries of nature (e.g., rivers, mountains, etc.), which led to Europe's three goals in Africa (the three Gs and three Cs): glory, gold, gospel, civilization, commerce, and Christianity.

Grave impoverishment of Africa occurred because of colonial interests, policies and practices, exploration and colonization, cash crops, minerals, wealth sent to the North, direct business with the Americas was almost nonexistent since as colonies, African nations/nation-states, etc., were European colonial possessions following the Berlin Conference of 1884–1885. Therefore, American commercial contacts with Africans and Africa had to be "sanctioned"—allowed by the European colonial power under whose influence the business would be conducted. Callings in African ports by passing American trading ships was possible, especially with African territories claiming sovereignty, as was the case between the young American republic and the Kingdom of Morocco—agreement versus piracy against American ships in the North Atlantic.

U.S.–Moroccan Treaty of Friendship is the oldest U.S. treaty. It was signed by John Adams and Thomas Jefferson in 1786 with Sultan Sidi Mohamed of Morocco. A letter from President George Washington was sent to the sultan after adoption of the U.S. Constitution in 1787. The United States' first diplomatic property was the Tangiers Consulate.

This vested interest of Europe in Africa grew and led to the "scramble" for Africa in the late 19th century. In 1884–1885, the emperor, Kaiser Otto von Bismarck, convened a European conference on the partition of Africa (Berlin Conference of November 15, 1884 to February 26, 1885). That conference partitioned Africa into European spheres of influence, and was attended by 14 states, including France, Germany, Denmark, Sweden, Russia, the United States, Belgium, Italy, Spain, Portugal, Norway, and Luxembourg. The outcome of the conference was the partitioning of Africa into European influence spheres for African administration. The United States had no share in the African cake. So no special U.S.–African relations could be advanced directly. Thus, there was little or no direct U.S. influence in Africa for commerce of business.

Actors were of four kinds

- Government to government leaders of Africa (i.e., presidents, first- and second-generation leaders) and the United States; attitudes on politics, economics, development;
- Government to governmental institutions (e.g., parastatals); representatives; trade negotiations, investment, tourism;
- Corporate to corporate; and
- Individual entrepreneurs.

Post-Colonial Era 1960–1994

Periods of African decolonization were 1945–1960, 1960–1970, etc. Although, South Africa gained independence in 1910, majority African rule was not gained until 1994. Prior to this, Zimbabwe had gained independence in 1980, and Eritrea separated from Ethiopia through a plebiscite in 1993. The last African country to be granted political independence from the status of a colony was Djibouti, and that was in 1977 when the country became an independent state from France.

It was in Africa's post-colonial era that the United States started to have direct contacts—business, political, and otherwise—with Africa. The Kennedy administration took increased interest in the granting of independence to African countries in an era that saw more intensified Cold War politics, as Africa became an obvious political battleground, especially for the two "elephants"—the superpowers, the United States and the Soviet Union. As the Swahili proverb goes, "Where two elephants fight, it is the grass that suffers most." Africa thus became a victim of Cold War politics and rivalry, and had to live with the situation of the collapse of the Soviet

Table 21.1
U.S. Presidents and Secretaries of State: 1960–2009

President	Secretary of State
John F. Kennedy (1961–1963) assassinated	David Dean Rusk (1961–1963)
Lyndon B. Johnson (1963–1969)	David Dean Rusk (1963–1969)
Richard M. Nixon (1969–1974)	William Pierce Rogers (1969–1973)
Gerald R. Ford (1974–1977)	Henry A. Kissinger (1973–1977)
James Carter (1977–1980)	Cyrus Roberts Vance (1977–1980)
	Edmond Sixtus Muskie (1980–1981)
Ronald Reagan (1981–1988)	Alexander Meigs Haig (1981–1982)
	George Pratt Shultz (1982–1989)
George H. W. Bush (1989–1992)	James Addison Baker (1989–1992)
	Lawrence Sidney Eagleburger (1992–1993)
William J. Clinton (1993–1997) (1997–2001)	Warren Minor Christopher (1993–1997)
	Madeline Korbel Albright (1997–2001)
George W. Bush (2001–2008)	Colin Luther Powel (2001–2005)
	Condoleezza Rice (2005–2008)
Barack Obama (2009–)	Hillary Rodham Clinton (2009–)

empire in 1989/1990. Apart from Cold War interests in Africa, the United States also showed keen interest in the education of Africans in the post-colonial era. It was also during the Kennedy administration that many African students went to study in the United States, and one of them was the father of the current U.S. president Barack Obama, whose father obtained a scholarship to study in the United States from Kenya.

Why Africa Matters to the United States

Issues in U.S.–African relations/foreign policy and diplomacy are many and varied. They are, for example, as follows:

- Political;
- Economic/business in oil, minerals, trade;
- Socioeducation;
- Environmental;
- Global;
- Strategic for peace, security; and
- Include diplomatic and foreign policy dictates, foreign policy, democracy, good governance, human rights, trade, IR, development, and business.

Actors include governments: the three branches of government, governmental institutions, private sector, entities, individuals, international institutions.

Africa's gifts to America included:

- The descendants of slaves from Africa;
- Slaves and free/very cheap slave labor;
- African Diaspora; and
- Services of Africans—in the military, congress, academia, science, etc. from beginning of Africans in the United States (e.g., during the American Civil War of the 1860s).

Africa offers potential as a global market and natural and human resource base.

American interests in Africa include political, foreign policy, and economic (oil, commodities), strategic, military, security, and others.

U.S.– Africa Business Potential and Opportunities

What is possible? What capacities exist? What resources are there for doing business? What organs of enterprise exist?

Assessments of private and public sectors show the new potential and opportunities for American business in Africa include the following:

- Banking and investment, micro–credit/micro–finance for women, small-scale enterprises (projects);
- Education and training for human development, capacity-building skills, and know-how (knowledge);
- Exchange programs for students, study tours abroad, research and development, schools, centers;
- Health care training, cures, aid;
- Disaster and disease development;
- Agriculture, commodities;
- Industrialization;
- Manufacturing, investment;
- Engineers;
- Legal structures and business codes for international business in Africa;
- Housing/construction industry;
- Empowerment of women, girls, youth, the elderly, handicapped;
- Energy for business and development—four sources of energy are oil, coal, and new and renewable sources of energy (NRSE);
- Information revolution: technology and communications, e-mail, Internet, ICTs, satellite for education, resource location in oceans, rivers, etc.;
- Service industry;

- Mining of minerals;
- Military bases;
- Business climate environment;
- Potential minerals;
- Commodities, agricultural goods, and services;
- Postal services;
- Airways, harbors;
- Sports games and tourism;
- Business groups, research groups, academic exchanges;
- Insurance companies; and
- Security, food, travel versus famine.

Africa and Decolonization: Categories and African Foreign Policy Foundations

Ethiopia (Abyssinia) was not colonized but gained its independence in 982 BCE. The first emperor of Ethiopia, Menelik I was the son of King Solomon of Israel and Queen Sheba of Ethiopia. He began his rule of Ethiopia in 982 BCE. Liberia began as an African American settlement of freed slaves who bought territory in West Africa with the support of the U.S. administration of President James Monroe in 1823. Liberia was not colonized.

Colonial immunity (which means that a country could be colonized for a short time [e.g., Ethiopia by Italy/Eritrea in 1936] or a long time [e.g., Morocco by France], but their colonization was not under the Berlin conference system started in 1885) and European decolonization is as follows:

- Ethiopia, 982 BCE (illegitimate emperor Menelik I, son of Queen Sheba and King Solomon started to reign in 982 BCE);
- Liberia, 1847;
- South Africa, 1910;
- Egypt, 1922;
- Libya, 1951;
- Morocco, 1956;
- Tunisia, 1956 (ex-French);
- Sudan, 1956 (ex-English–Egyptian);
- Ghana, 1951 (ex- English, first to gain independence);
- Guinea, 1958;
- Dahomey, 1959.

Origins of Pan-Africanism are from 1880 to 1885. Independence by African Americans 1800–1963 to present. Independence by African nationalists occurred in 1900s–1963 and 1960–2008, and by UN pressures 1945; 1960–1977.

Historical Perspectives: 1800–1885

From Pan-Africanism to African unity, 1800–1963, conferences, congresses, and meetings by Pan-Africanists were needed.

The beginning was Colonization I—Phoenicians form 800 BCE; Greeks from 630 BCE, Romans from 146 BCE. Then came Colonization II: European powers after/by Berlin Conference (1884–1885). The last Portuguese African colonies to get independence were Cape Verde, São Tomé and Príncipe, Guinea Bissau, Angola, and Mozambique.

The apartheid was opposed by the front-line states (FLS) Angola, Botswana, Mozambique, Tanzania, Zambia, and Zimbabwe. These were South Africa's neighboring countries. They joined forces to oppose the apartheid of South Africa and its impacts on its neighbors.

U.S.-Africa Foreign Policy Relations

There are two kinds of foreign policy. There is that of Africa toward the United States and of the United States toward Africa. African policies are of two types: those initiated by African states and those initiated by the U.S. government.

These policies impact:

- Goods and services between the United States and Africa;
- U.S.–Africa trade and business relations;
- African Diaspora;
- Government-to-government trade relations;
- Executive: USAID, industry, projects;
- Congress: Congressional Black House Subcommittee on Africa Relations;
- Senate: Subcommittee on Africa Relations; and
- Private partnerships between individuals.

Specific issues, for example, include business and trade and the development agenda (defining sustainability development, energy, women and business, development, agriculture, commodities, subsistence and cash crops, raw materials, minerals, as well as integration of development and business-related institutions). Partnerships for business and development in Africa faced problems of investment, incentives, prioritization, capacity-building, governance, oil, and strategic and military bases (e.g., in Kenya, Ghana, Liberia, Gabon, and Namibia).

External factors include national interests, democracy, democratization, diplomacy, investment, dictates of global markets, risks of disasters, climate change and global warming, international terrorism, international security, oil and oil companies, and renewable energy sources.

ASIA

A comparative analysis of China and Africa and ASEAN was given in Chapter 19 of this volume. Apart from ASEAN states, Japan is another Asian nation with which Africa maintains sound bilateral and multilateral economic and diplomatic relations. The Tokyo International Conference on African Development (TICAD) system has been operational for a number of years, and good projects are being funded by Japan.

Asia is self-reliant from the Indian Ocean to Japan. India has a close eye to China; the two fought a border war in 1962. In the Cold War, there was less worry by India about China because India was close to the Soviet Union. Now, with only one superpower, which is the United States, India feuds to be closer to the United States because of China's threat to India. China and Japan are the economic superpowers of Asia now. Before there were South Korea, Taiwan, and Hong Kong. All together, big regional powers are aggressive to Africa and later America, especially now China. Africa, China, and Latin America have become close allies in various fields, including the economic field and in global markets, Asia is bound to decline. The United States will remain a power to reckon with, but she will not dominate as hitherto.

U.S. interests in the Middle East and in Afghanistan and Pakistan will remain for a long time. India may be close to the United States because of China, but not as close as U.S.–Europe or U.S.–U.K. relations. Poverty in India is grave, but India remains a great asset in democratic values given its vast population and economic power. The next decade will be very interesting, specifically in terms of watching China and Africa.

Africa needs resources. Darfur is in global relationships with regimes. China is a big shareholder in Africa's trade—up to 25–40 percent of the share benefits. Competition is growing. China has no coherent foreign policy toward Africa or any other country. Trade relations of China and Africa are growing with the Sudan and Angola (oil), Zambia, the DRC, and other African states. One wonders what China's relations with Africa ultimately will mean. It is just a guess for many observers in Africa and elsewhere in the world. No doubt China has become a world economic power that now competes with the United States, EU, Japan, and India.

America needs capital to sell bonds so these are sold to China. China has her own money and has not been borrowing from lenders. This situation may end soon because of recession and the 2009 economic and financial crisis.

There is a recession in the United States but inflation in China. Chinese relations with the West, as with Africa, are still to evolve more clearly. Competition is bound to escalate, and this might lead to a decline in China–West relations. The Chinese could get richer and get out of abject poverty. But so far, China has a serious inflation problem. In 2009, inflation and the environment were big problems to India, China, and Japan. These countries have been expending foreign aid and receiving aid in order to get resources from Africa as a reward. China also tries to get involved in other countries of the world, investing to build roads, just like the Japanese have been doing around the globe.

In the 1980s, Japan changed her policies for commercial interests. Since then, Japan's economy has been declining. Japan faces problems of aging and population rigidity in Japanese society, but her economy, banking system, and finances have been doing well.

Japan also faces environmental challenges, as does China. India has a higher poverty rate than China. India's global economic influence is greater, but it was slower to liberalize than China, until five years ago. How President Obama will be viewed in Asia and Africa symbolizes a revival of the United States after eight years of problems in Iraq. There is need for change everywhere in America. Everybody is watching and wants to know what will happen with Obama in the United States. Under the Obama administration, some foreign and trade policies will have to be made toward Africa, China, India, Japan, and the rest of Asia and Europe. This is because of the great expectations that the first African American president has raised in African and other Third World peoples.

AFRICA AND THE ISLAMIC WORLD

Islam in Africa was introduced in the 7th century CE following the globalization of the region to North Africa and the spread of the Islamic culture across Africa. Conversion to Islam in Africa also introduced increased relationships within the African continent in the fields of commerce (OPEC oil, banks such as the Gulf Bank, imports of cars, clothing, manufactured goods, and real estate business, etc.). Conversion to Islam was, and still is, a passport to preferential treatment by fellow Muslims or the Islamic world in all kinds of dealings, such as business transactions.

In the political field, the African countries with heavy influences of Islam have traditionally collaborated with the Muslim world in special relationships on international issues of interest to the Arab cause (e.g., the Palestinian question on which the countries of North Africa and other heavily Islamic nations have always voted, for example, at the UN for support of the Palestinian cause).

In the field of education and culture, many schools and mosques are built and sponsored in many African countries. Young boys and girls are sponsored by Islamic countries like Saudi Arabia. The end result is conversion of many African youth and even adults to Islam. In this way, the Arab and Islamic culture is easily spread across Africa, and this helps cement special relationships between Africa and the Islamic world.

If we take Kenya as a case study, then we find that the Somali Muslims are gradually controlling many sectors of the Kenyan economy and politics, especially in the fields of real estate, leadership in some government sectors such as the police force, electoral commission, defense, the offices of some key government officials, and the like. Questions have been raised as to how so many finances find their way into the country without the knowledge of the central bank. This big question mark is triggered by the glaring silence of the authorities. The amazing fact is that the transactions are done using tremendous amounts of cash. Given the fact that money is the backbone of the economies of the countries of Africa, the above information helps to explain the growing influence that Islam and its culture is imposing on the economies of the African countries.

Furthermore, since in Africa the cultism personality and character of an African leader play major roles in the choice and implementation of foreign and domestic policies, Islam's influence shall grow in Africa in greater extent in those African countries where political and other leadership shall be exercised by a Muslim. This is because leadership in Africa is an institution. Thus, the future of the relationship between Africa and the Muslim world is going to be a fascinating period to watch.

FORMER COLONIALIST EUROPEANS

Phonism comes from the colonial legacies of the post-colonial era in Africa in the countries that, at independence, forged special relationships with their colonial masters in practically all spheres of life, diplomatic, political, economic, financial, and military fields. This special relationship seems to serve the African nations well with their former colonial powers—Belgium, Italy, Spain, Portugal, France, the United Kingdom, and Germany. Special agreements and MOUs with the former colonial powers gave the ex-African colonies special access to resources and the protection of their former colonial powers. This happens in bilateral and multilateral relations, and the course will most certainly be stayed during the 21st century.

THE WEST EUROPEAN AND OTHERS GROUP

The West European and Others Group (WEOG) is one of the influential groupings in the UN bloc politics. The UN divides member states into African, Asian, Latin American, and Caribbean Groups, as well as WEOG, which consists of the United States, Canada, New Zealand, and the European Union UN member states. Africa maintains good relations with most of these countries, but with the collapse of the Soviet Bloc and the forming of its members into NATO, some realignment will have to be made in the coming decade and beyond, but it is evident that Africa and WEOG will maintain close economic, commercial, diplomatic, and other relations in view of UN affiliations, such as the British Commonwealth (United Kingdom, Australia, New Zealand, and Canada), the Francophone, and the nonaligned countries of which Africa is a vital part.

SUMMARY ON THE MAKING AND EXECUTION OF AFRICAN FOREIGN POLICY AND DIPLOMACY

From the analysis in this chapter, it can be safely stated that African foreign policies and diplomacy, although complex and even confusing, are nonetheless fascinating areas of the study of African international relations. They involve issues and challenges; sources and determinants; formulation, implementation, monitoring, and review and appraisal; theories and realities of subalternism, alternative statehood, African doctrinal inheritance, and practices; common and divergent characteristics often determined by phonism and inherited from the past colonial policies and practices of Europe; religious inheritance, including Christianity and Islam; and Pan-Africanism and its related doctrines of African socialism, Ubuntu, Ujamaa, and the like.

Then there is the conceptual definition of African policy and diplomacy, which like the other pluralitantum expressions of these disciplines (national interest, international relations theory, politics, economics, etc.), have, in effect, a plural meaning. Thus, the foreign policy of an African state is the totality of the actions, reactions, proactions, interactions, contacts, and non-actions that the African country, as a sovereign state or entity, decides to take, or not to take, in pursuit or fulfillment of the dictates (goals and objectives, demands, situations, requirements, etc.) of safeguarding the African country's national interests, in both domestic (i.e., national/endogenous), and external (i.e., foreign/exogenous/global) environments, in which the African state, through, or by means of, its state-government-based actors, has to operate or perform cross-national/border activities in its relationships with other actors, particularly other sovereign states, as a member of the African subsystem, and of the international system. In this latter system, states participate on the basis of sovereign equality, and of the other principles of the natural law and power theories of international relations. The overall essence of such a definition of foreign policy is that it touches on the domestic and external determinants and aspects of Africa's condition as a subsystem of the global system—it is an all-embracing definition. It establishes endogeneity and exogeneity of a nation's character in its international relations, and as springing right from the prototype of nationhood, and not from the mere moments of political independence, nor of European colonization of Africa, as some writers have erroneously tended to define it.

Thus, foreign policy, diplomacy, and international relations of the African nations should not be traced to the colonial or even post-colonial era of Africa's history. They must be traced to moments in remote antiquity, enriched and cemented in subsequent years, on the domestic front by Pan-Africanism, Negritude, and the related African ideological orientations of nationalism, unity, socialism, Ujamaa, African continental socialism, national identity; supranationalism, national interests, and security, as well as in issues of African leadership, borders, public opinion, and the makers and executors of foreign policy and diplomacy (the elites and the political operatives) who all are responsible for the making and implementation of African foreign policy and diplomacy.

As can be seen, the determinants of African foreign policy and international relations are of diverse types at the national level, as well as at the global levels. The external level thus merely elevates the domestic level interests and policies for the external and internal good of the country. African foreign policies are the products and by-products of the transformed nature of Africa as a continent formerly sandwiched between the two opposed ideologies of the East–West divide as expounded by the Cold War politics of "capitalist exploitation" and "communist protection" of Africa in the East–West ideological divide.

In this sense, African foreign policy and diplomacy had to be nurtured and developed on the basis of the international power theory of the two ideological camps of the Cold War Era. On the other hand, and in the sense of survival of Africa in the global power struggle, Africa had been a victim of subalternism, baby of the colonial era, and a by-product of the colonization and transformation of Africa by European colonial rule.

Thus, the power of nonalignment to which Africa would automatically resort to has been challenged by the dictates of state survival within the global ideological divide between the East and West—Cold War politics and influence; the Cold Peace condition after 1990; the marginalization of Africa in economic and business/international trade regimes, as well as of her values and vital issues in the post-Cold War Era; the neo-colonial interests of the powers—the United States, United Kingdom, Germany, France, Italy, USSR/Russia, Portugal, Belgium, Japan, and Spain—as the participants in the Berlin Conference of 1884–1885 on the parceling of Africa among the European powers. Other dictates also must be considered and enumerated, as playing major roles in the making and execution of African foreign policy and diplomacy. These would include the cultism, personal bonds, marriages, neighborhoods, ethnicity; the impacts of the international community like the UN and its reforms, human rights, NEPAD, IDOs, IGOs, NGOs; economic and gender issues; democracy and democratization; pressures of debt and debt servicing; poverty reduction; new and emerging issues; pandemics like HIV/AIDS, etc.; friendships and family relationships of African leaders in their external dealings. Of the African leaders who are either well known nationalists, or suffered a lot from cultism or were staunch nationalists should be included the following which had to deal with issues in Africa–U.S. relations from the 1960s to the present: Lumumba of DRC; Mobutu of Zaire; Senghor of Senegal; Tubman of Liberia; Taylor of Liberia; Sékou-Touré of Guinea; Nkrumah of Ghana; Nasser of Egypt; Bourguiba of Tunisia; Azikiwe and Balewa of Nigeria; Kenyatta of Kenya; Nyerere and Mkapa of Tanzania; Obote and Museveni of Uganda; Mandela of South Africa; Banda of Malawi; Kaunda of Zambia; Moi of Kenya; Chissano of Mozambique; and many others. All these with such leadership problems as well as the new and emerging issues of law and justice; finance and development; home affairs; energy and industry; and other issues handled at presidential, premier, and other governmental levels.

All the above issues, including those regulating the Africa–U.S. relationship, deserve a separate treatment, and this needs to be done, given the new relationships that exist now between Africa and the United States in a new study.

CHAPTER 22

Conclusion: Greatness or More Dashed Expectations?

From the foregoing analysis of Africa's international relations, foreign policy, and diplomacy from remotest antiquity to the 21st century, it is evident that this mighty continent of Africa has come a very long way. It is like the whole continent was innocent, wealthy, beautiful, and vast, but condemned to fail in many respects, not so much because of its own making, but by history—as if Africa was condemned to be a burden bearer for Europe, condemned to enslavement and exploitation, to impoverishment and paradoxes. But is Africa really doomed to remain poor forever? Will Africa ever claim her gorgeous and glorious civilizations and values? Will anybody pay compensation to Africa for the wrongs, deprivations, and impoverishment that were imposed on her? Will Africa's endogenous problems be resolved on a permanent basis by Africans using African ways and means to solve their own problems? Will the rich North continue to receive Africa's resources unfairly through inter alia reverse resource flows and brain-drain? Will sustainable development be attained by Africa, with the full primary responsibility for development of Africa being borne by African governments and institutions and populations? Will the international community as represented by their UN membership, become more potent, effective, and efficient in executing the purpose, principles, decisions, and commitments that they voluntarily make as political entities enjoying sovereign equality under international law? Will the gravest enemies of Africa—poverty, disease, and ignorance—ever be solved equitably for, and in, Africa for the common benefit of all Africans? Will fair and just international economic and business relations be put in place for fair competition and just and free access to global markets? Will the MDGs ever meet the promises that they promised to Africa in 2000?

All of the above questions present outcries to every member of the global system and to all of the friends of Africa.

WHO MAKES AFRICAN FOREIGN POLICY?

African foreign policy, to be effective, will have to be revamped with a view to making it more systematic and efficient. As it is made, its efficiency and effectiveness depends on the character, cultism, personality, and lifestyle of the African leaders—heads of state or government. Thus, if you have a president or premier interested in foreign affairs, then you have a foreign policy that is sound, effective, and respected. But if the heads of states or government do not care too much about foreign affairs, then the end result is a foreign policy that is haphazard, bureaucratic, and negligible. The foreign policy of an African state can be, and is, made in various ways, as described in the remainder of this section.

Through Ad Hocism

When a foreign policymaker makes impromptu utterances calling for implementation such statements, through written or oral instructions, telexes, faxes, and even via e-mails, this is ad hoc policy-making. Often, political statements and utterances are issued by the foreign minister or permanent secretary (director-general) without any planning or discussion.

Through the "Think Tank" Method

Policy decisions are made via planning, research, debate, and ultimate decision. In such cases, the policymaker is given options from which to select that which is deemed appropriate for the issue or problem concerned. The policy-planning machinery may be at the presidential or premiere levels, or even be handled through the minister of foreign affairs.

Through the Influence of Public Opinion

In some cases, public opinion is aired via the mass media—external and domestic press from headquarters or elsewhere. This is a democratic way of having a situation of "vox dei, vox populi" (the people's voice is God's voice) via referenda, press conferences, etc. The dictates of foreign policy making can be many and varied, and may include invasions, partnerships and cooperation, persuasion, diplomatic initiatives, and the like.

THE ACTORS IN FOREIGN POLICY

Apart from the head of state or government, prime minister, and the minister for foreign affairs, the other players in foreign policy and diplomacy situations and arena include the ministries of home affairs and international security (and immigration), finance, planning and development, tourism and wildlife, defense, environment and natural resources, trade and development, and others.

In foreign policy, formulations and execution have tended to shift from the traditional peace and security issues to development, environment (climate change), and related issues. However, this shift has not affected the traditional essence and purposes of African foreign policy and diplomacy. Historical perspectives of diplomacy cluster it into the "old" and "new" diplomacy, both of which basically aim at resolving disputes and differences between and among states and other political entities via negotiation and management—through peaceful means like diplomacy, foreign policy and political science. These are arts, not sciences, unless by "science" one means "a study area." The issues and challenges of contemporary diplomacy and foreign policy remain basically the same as they evolve around the national interest of the member states. Obviously, African foreign policies and diplomacy have failed in some cases but succeeded in others. Whatever the outcomes, conditions for the success of African international relations, foreign policy, and diplomacy depend on many factors.

Common Characteristics of African Foreign Policies and International Relations

Africa's foreign policies and international relations have more in common than in divergence. There are four kinds of heritage that are discernible: the African heritage, the religious heritage, the colonial heritage, and the post-colonial or independence heritage that, in effect, is a "mixed bag" heritage.

In African heritage, the African values dominated the processes and procedures that were governed by custom and tradition: ways of life and living of the African peoples as reflected in their customs, traditions, cultures, and civilizations. The roots of African heritage include land, farmlands, reserves and their usage; agriculture, which is at the core of the African culture of producing and consuming goods and services; peasants, homesteads, and family labor for subsistence; African traditionalism as advanced in pre-colonial practices; kingdoms and local communities; family and tribal alliances, co-existence, and sharing of natural resources (African Socialism); environmental influences and protection; and empowerment of women and recognition of their vital contributions and roles in African society. The religious heritage consists of Christianity and Islam. The colonial heritage emerged as the most influential, even in the post-colonial era. The colonization, political dependence, and domination that the European colonial powers had designed to last for at least one thousand years lasted for less than one hundred years. But within this relatively short period of time, European colonialism and colonization transformed Africa, perhaps forever. This transformation of Africa has resulted in Afro-pessimism, paradoxes, poverty, exploitation, and impoverishment, as well as environmental imperialism, socioeconomic decline and malaise, and dependency. These challenges continue to confront Africa and the Africans whose continued use of forms of European institutions, structures, and values presents serious a challenge to African identity.

From the colonial heritage, there are numerous remnants of colonial policies and practices that dominated the conduct of behavior in Africa. The stage was set by the Berlin Conference of 1884–1885, where geographical lines were drawn on the African map by a group of Europeans who suffered from African ignorance and yet did not include African presence in those fateful decisions that they made on the future of Africa. The consequences of colonial heritage continue to haunt Africa today. The loss of a common African identity has triggered other problems of moral and cultural values; imperatives and clashes; impoverishment and enslavement of Africans; imposition of Western European values of education, government and governance, civilization; downgrading the position of women in Africa, and other African values in society; corruption, alien governance, tribalism, and communalism (via "divide and conquer" tactics) resulting from European colonial policies and practices; racial stratification giving prominence to class in society according to the color of one's skin (the whites at the top and blacks at the bottom of the societal ladder); conflicts causing crises and brewing tribalism, besides ethnic and racial tensions; superiority complexes resulting in frustrations of the Africanization policies of independent Africa; and the reproduction of European systems of government, institutions and practices of culture, language, and administration; domination over, and subordination of, African values, and promotion of unequal relationships in all spheres of life as inherited and promulgated by the new African leadership practices—leaders who themselves were/are by-products of Western civilization par excellence, having been educated in the Western tradition, and trained by the colonial masters and in principles and practices of the colonial mother countries. The African leadership has been challenged for failure to forge new thinking and governance processes and procedures that would be Africa-conceived, Africa-initiated, Africa-developed, Africa-owned, Africa-run, and Africa-managed. This would be the only way of reclaiming the original African civilizations to be adapted to the dictates and demands of modernism and modernization, and to find solutions to African problems employing African methods and know-how.

Other colonial heritage remnants in Africa include the phonist system of Commonwealth Anglophone, Lusophone, Francophone, and even Arabphone; dependency or neocolonialism as perpetuated by the former colonial powers for control and exploitation, as well as coordination of domination, and continued impoverishment of the African continent inter alia via protectionism, conditionalities, SAPs of the Western-dominated international financial institutions, etc.

Thus, African foreign policy is based on the system of ex-colonial powers' foreign policies, which became the main sources of Africa's post-independence foreign policy, in partnership with diluted Pan-Africanism that led to the birth of African unity in 1963. The schools of thought that emerged at the decolonization stage in Africa were patterned on the ideologies of the former colonial powers, and, hence, the differences that led to the birth of subalternism of contemporary African continental politics. In like manner, this common colonial past of African foreign policy, as greatly influenced by the colonial policies and practices, has produced unipartyism and multipartyism, with all their clashes of ideology and political orientations of alliances, coexistence within national borders; irredentism; and other post-independence doctrines of uti possidetis juris, secession, Majimboism, and the like. After all, the Charter of African Unity made it clear that it was not going to be a supra-governmental organization, nor a federation, but rather a mere association of sovereign African states that would never be subjected to one another. This helps explain the difficulties of forging a United States of Africa doctrine as initiated by Kwame Nkrumah of Ghana and pursued so vigorously nowadays by Muammar Qaddafi of Libya.

Other common features of African foreign policies and international relations evolve around a new identity in IR; strong pressures for liberalization, multipartyism, and democratization against every tendency toward unipartyist dictatorship, bad governance, and gross violations of human rights. Then there is a common fear in Africa of domination by the West, especially in this post–Cold War Era where the conscious capitalist exploitation of the developing world is no longer challenged by the unconscious communism, as was the case before in the East–West ideological confrontation. Moreover, all of the African states are faced with domestic and African regional and continental conflicts, civil strife, and suffering at home, whether because of politics, tribalism and ethnicity, insecurity, or political instability, or due to disease, poverty, and illiteracy (better known as ignorance). Similarly, all of Africa is united against racial discrimination of the Apartheid type, and suffers from ineffectiveness and lack of adequate competence and an authoritative, effective voice in international fora and negotiations, and world politics and economics.

Africa still has to forge a strong presence in multilateralism as opposed to the domination of unilateralism in African international relations at domestic and external levels. This, in effect, means that African foreign policy and diplomacy shall continue to be based on the tenets of Pan-Africanism and continental African unity; fight against racism, exploitation, Euro-neo-colonialism and neo-imperialism; and avoid racial stratification in African society. In like manner, non-alignment will continue to be important in African foreign policy and diplomacy, just as cultism and the personality and character of African leaders and actors in foreign policy and diplomacy shall continue to exert maximum influence on African foreign policy-making until new generations of leaders will emerge to be groomed to succeed the first, second, and even third generation of leaders in Africa.

Of particular significance would be reviewing African foreign policies, taking into account the first decade of stability in post-colonial Africa (1960–1970), when peaceful democratic elections were held, and economic development was sound at least for the period 1950–1962. But the advent of military and civilian rule as "mixed bag" governance practices, especially after 1965, led to new challenges in African international relations, and in African Foreign Policy and African Diplomacy practices of interchangeability in the post-colonial era. The challenges of the new millennium might even be harder to resolve!

THE FUTURE OF AFRICAN INTERNATIONAL RELATIONS, AFRICAN FOREIGN POLICY, AND AFRICAN DIPLOMACY

In looking at the future of Africa international foreign policy and diplomacy the following issues automatically come to mind:

- Determinants;
- Issues and challenges in general and in the next decade and beyond; priority challenges; and
- Measures.

From within Africa

Mobilize appropriate machinery at national, subregional, regional, and African continental levels to discuss in the following two major categories to:

1. Identify and outline the root causes of Afro-pessimism and the poverty syndrome.
2. Suggest measures in concrete and practical terms, that must be taken from within Africa and from outside Africa to address the future of African international relations, African foreign policy, African foreign service, and diplomacy.

From Outside Africa

Mobilize the international community at bilateral, multilateral, and global levels to discuss and recommend ways and means of assisting

Africa in her efforts to map out and implement strategies that will help improve and make more effective, productive, and beneficial to Africa international relations, diplomacy, negotiations, and development aid, which will address Africa's multidimensionalism for durable development of Africa in the coming decade and beyond.

Determinants

Africa's international relations, foreign policy, foreign service, and diplomacy will be shaped by, among many other events and determinants, the consequences of the end of the Cold War and the emergence of Cold Peace; issues of the new world order; competition arising among the great powers in post–Cold War politics, etc.; democratization and leadership in Africa; the era of multipartyism to struggle against reinstitution of unipartyism, dictatorship, and control of African politics by the ruling elites; and the dictates of decolonization versus dependency—neocolonialism and neoimperialism, which will probably experience the following forces:

- Increased ability of new-generation African leaders to assume greater management and control of African international relations, foreign policy, and diplomacy in their own flavor and, hence, their future desire to stop controlling political and other developments in Africa and increasing pressures and demands among Africans in Africa to benefit Africa more in the future;
- Increased roles of women and empowerment in African governance and government;
- Increased control of Africa foreign policy and diplomatic processes by Africans in the era of Cold Peace, even though Africa often feels like an "orphan" abandoned in the global politics, deprived of Cold War protection and favors;
- Increased democratization process that will result in diverse kinds of reforms in law and development approaches in diplomatic and foreign service prioritization, land reforms, business practices, and all types of "vox populi, vox dei" initiatives requiring command of African development destiny by Africans and their relevant institutions;
- The assertiveness of the people's regional powers in African society is bound to produce African leadership that will not be ethnocentrist nor Majimboistic but will stress the oneness and patriotic spirit of Africa versus tribalistic tendencies and practices;
- Increased Africanization of African institutions in Africa triggered by regional integration efforts in Africa and many other determinants of the African spirit for the future of African international relations, African foreign policy, and African diplomacy;
- Increased targeting of Pax Africana politics in African peace and development efforts, which will aim at tackling differences, conflicts, and wars in Africa via diplomatic and negotiated methods. There must be found and devised new ways and means of conflict containment, reduction, mitigation,

preparedness, prevention, and durable management for the common benefit of Africa. Thus, the rights of the underprivileged—women, refugees, displaced persons, etc., will be protected and helped;

- Resource mobilization for human development and institutional improvements;
- Systematic tackling of the weapons of mass destruction in Africa such as poverty, disease, and illiteracy; brain-drain; natural and human disasters; environmental degradation, climate change, and global warming, etc.;
- Prevention of international terror for African development;
- Use of the ICTs for sustainable African development;
- Debt cancellation and relief and an end to the problems of debt servicing via SAPs, aidism, etc.;
- Encouragement of South/South cooperation for poverty alleviation and eradication;
- The need to end corruption, SAPs in Africa, protectionism against Africa, capitalist exploitation, and improvement by external designs and practices.

Main Issues and Challenges Facing Africa from the 1990s into the 21st Century

These challenges have included the following:

- High energy cost (crisis),
- High food crisis—food imports are insufficient,
- Low/no economic growth,
- Unproductive business efforts,
- Aidism and aid fatigue—no foreign aid for African development,
- No debt relief/cancellation/forgiveness for Africa,
- Increased protectionism and subsidies by major donor-developed states—especially Europe and the United States,
- No ODA target advancement—increase, and
- Challenges from the 1980s and 1990s, including the following examples:
  - Increased dependency/neocolonialism;
  - Dictatorships, leadership deficiencies;
  - Dividing forces of Cold War; and
  - Unjust international relations.

Recommendations for Measures and Conditions for Success

Included are the following:

- Patriotism versus ethnocentrism;
- Corruption;

- Subalternism (i.e., state weakness and collapse);
- Management of resources, resource nationalism, and global capitalism in favor of Africa;
- Economic development agenda;
- Environmental issues—climate change, global warming;
- Social agenda—pandemics, etc.;
- Education efficiency;
- Leadership efficiency and democracy;
- Democratization;
- Reclaiming African civilizations;
- Development ownership—owning, controlling, and being master over development destiny;
- Global financing for development; partnerships for development;
- Rational use of value versus squandering, irrational use, and mismanagement;
- Change of mental attitudes;
- Africa and the global economy, free trade in goods and services, unrestricted capital flows, competitiveness, strategies for good performance, and free access to global markets;
- The political agenda—conflicts and conflict management and resolution, conditions of subalternism and of failed or weak states (e.g., Somalia, Darfur in Sudan). All doctrines on African unity should be kept on the AU agenda as a "standing order" or item, Cold Peace issues among/between Europe, the United States, and China in Africa; Islamic fundamentalism, terrorism, oil as a weapon for conflict, democratization, and good global governance against political mismanagement and deficiencies;
- Environmental protection, security, and governance; and
- Civil society organizations and NGOs in African development and security.

Issues and Challenges of Disasters

Matters related to natural and other disaster situations in Africa include the following: recurrent drought, irrational use of natural resources, pestilence, floods, wars, civil strife, landslides and mudslides, volcanic eruption, and tsunamis.

Strategies and measures

Strategies and measures facing Africa are as follows:

- Empowerment of women and other marginalized strata of society;
- Training and education;
- Disaster awareness;
- Leadership;

- Good governance;
- Popular participation in rescue, recovery, rehabilitation, development;
- Partnerships;
- Mechanism coordination;
- Funding; resource mobilization; and
- Actions by Africans in Africa.

Challenges Confronting Africa

Global issues in the next decade and beyond include the following:

- Poverty versus sustainable development;
- Diseases, pandemics (e.g., HIV/AIDS);
- Debt and debt servicing;
- Environmental sustainability and sustainability science, natural disasters, environmental degradation, climate change, global warming;
- Industrialization, private investments;
- Agriculture and food security;
- Development ownership, capacity-building;
- Humanitarianism—refugees, displaced peoples, conflicts, insecurity;
- Empowerment of women, girls, and children;
- Human security and development, human resource development;
- The economy—trade, business/liberalization, energy crisis;
- Mismanagement;
- Globalization; and
- Phonism.

Impacts of Phonism

The "phone-system" in Africa is a product of European colonization of Africa from the late 19th century. Here, "phone" means language system in Africa.

The Berlin Conference of 1884 to 1885 partitioned Africa into European "spheres of interest" with the following languages as the predominant colonial languages: French (Francophone), English (Anglophone), Portuguese (Lusophone), and Arabic (Arabphone, although Arabs had no political colonization of Africa). Arabphone spread in Africa—especially in North Africa—with its cultural, economical, political, and linguistic affinities to the Middle East. North Africa is closer to the Middle East than to sub-Saharan Africa. Another reason was religion (i.e., Islam). African unity and other political setups unite North Africa to sub-Saharan Africa.

A challenge to Africa is how to turn the phonist situation into a united system stressing Africa and her development.

Impacts of phonism in Africa, and the special phonist relationship perpetuated between ex-colony and ex-colonial power include the following:

- Perpetuates close polity, education, economic, social, legal, diplomatic, and business ties with former colonial masters, ex-colonial influences;
- Promotes subalternism in Africa because of dependency/neocolonialism, education system, government system, institutional systems, and structures;
- Weakens Africans' nationalism and patriotism;
- Reduces African nationalist approaches through continued dependency;
- Promotes special relationships between former bosses and their ex-colonies, perpetuates more effective diplomatic, economic, military, strategic, and other relations with former colonial masters;
- Perpetuates membership of ex-colonial states in clubs/associations of former colonial masters;
- Often "encourages" and results in rifts/divisions within Africa; and
- Maintains strong loyalty to former colonial master.

Priorities in African Development

Priority areas for African development are as follows:

- Water and related issues;
- Environment;
- Food security;
- Poverty/hunger/alienation eradication;
- Health and disease eradication (Ebola, AIDS, etc.);
- Urbanism/urbanization;
- Natural disasters and other disaster situations;
- Information Revolution/ICTs and science and technology for development;
- Population expansion and gender issues, empowerment;
- The right to development;
- Trade access and trade opportunities;
- Climate and weather-related issues;
- Regionalism, regional cooperation, and integration;
- Security and conflict resolution/management;
- Increased resource flows and mobilization;

- Promotion of self-reliance, capacity-building, human and institutional resource development;
- Industrialization;
- Agriculture; and
- GPGs and GPBs.

At independence, African states, especially in sub-Saharan Africa, inherited those things that the colonial powers left behind. Many, as follows, were still in relatively good order at independence and included:

- Education system;
- Administration;
- Infrastructure;
- Agriculture and rural development;
- Health and pandemics;
- Industrialization; and
- Housing and settlements.

In the 1960s and 1970s there were good economic systems. The following Africanization programs launched later were to be problems:

- Debt and debt servicing;
- Disasters;
- Global SAPs;
- Political, economic, climate, and environment mismanagement;
- Insecurity;
- Aidism;
- Food insecurity;
- Ideological inventions/invasions;
- Social agenda—inequality, empowerment; and
- Colonial legacy and heritage/remnants.

CONFLICTS IN AFRICA: CONCEPTS, CAUSES, CONSEQUENCES, AND CURES

Causes, Concepts, Consequences, and Cures include the following:

- Colonial remnants and grouping in African political units according to arbitrary borders, irredentism, secession, separatism, Majimboism;
- Leadership elites;
- Poverty, population explosion, exploitation;

- Territorial disputes;
- Territorial occupation;
- Ethnic, racial, tribal, ideological/political differences;
- Corruption, greed, exploitation, injustices; conflict countries (hot spots) since 1990s, especially Algeria, Angola, DRC (Zaire), Sierra Leone, Liberia, Sudan, Rwanda, Burundi, Somalia, Ethiopia, Eritrea, Libya, West Sahara, Côte d'Ivoire, Guinea Bissau, and Chad in the late 1990s and early 2000s;
- State collapse—causes are exploitation, corruption, inequality, subalternism, state weakness, artificial boarders, failed states;
- Armament and proliferation of arms (i.e., small arms);
- Natural resources and environment, minerals, oil, water, disasters, land degradation;
- Uneven development in the country (i.e., unfair distribution of wealth and power);
- Gangsterism (e.g., cattle rustling, raiding, killings); and
- Racial causes—Apartheid, xenophobia, Nazism, and concept of the "pure Caucasian race."

Cures, for example, include the following:

1) Meditation—leaders, UN, NGOs, etc.;
2) Dialogue—fairness, change of attitude, peacekeeping, justice, equality;
3) Wealth and power distribution, constitutional bonds;
4) Regional integration; and
5) Constant conflict management.

Conflict and conflict management should become a "standing order" or item on the agenda of AU. Policy reviews and reforms could help resolve differences through diplomatic means.

OWNERSHIP OF AFRICA BY AFRICA: THE ROLE OF AFRICAN SOCIALISM

African socialism and Pan-Africanism exist in the African spirit, which was destroyed when European colonization was imposed on Africans. Colonization also transformed and deprived Africans of development pursuits. African socialism demanded assumptions of primary responsibility by Africans for African development; poverty eradication; popular (women and youth) participation in development efforts. Needed are a change of attitudes, eradication of cultism and corruption from African leadership, genuine patriotism, protection, improvement in the education system for capacity-building, knowledge, skills and contribution to society. Also needed are sustainability science (i.e., cohabitation of man and nature, man and life support systems), sustainability, and sustainable development.

Africa in the Middle Ages

At that time some African societies equaled or even surpassed European nations in culture, education, and wealth. Looking at who's who in medieval history, some remarkable individuals lived in Africa and were important in history.

Medieval Catalan maps of Africa show some of the most fascinating civilizations flourishing in Africa from the 14th century. They show animated contacts between and among African, European, and Asian cultures. The topics that interested them included the great trans-Saharan trade and the trade routes of Ghana, Mali, and Songhai.

As a historical period, the Middle Ages included European history for a thousand years from the fall of the Western Roman Empire in 476 CE to the beginning of the early modern period (ca. 1453 CE). The 16th century was marked by division of Western Christianity during the Reformation, the rise of humanism, and the Renaissance. The Middle Ages thus stretched from antiquity to the Renaissance, from 400–476 CE (sacking of Rome by the Visigoths and the disposing of Romulus Augustus) to 1453–1517 CE (the fall of Constantinople).

There were the following three stages of medieval times:

1) Classical civilization of antiquity,
2) The Middle Ages, and
3) The modern period.

Reasons for Africa's Extreme Poverty

Africa is poorer now than she was 25 years ago, and even poorer than at independence almost 50 years ago. This has been caused by set of diverse reasons that include the following:

- Slavery and the slave trade;
- Impoverishment by colonial policies and practices;
- Protectionism;
- SAPs;
- Global/extreme forces;
- Dependency/neocolonialism and exploitation;
- The paradoxes of Africa—acculturation, conflicts and coups, ethnicity, tribalism and cronyism, nepotism, and ethnocentrism;

- Diseases;
- Ignorance;
- Natural disasters and man-made hazards;
- Ill-advised policies and practices (e.g., bad governance, incompetence);
- Lack of democratization;
- Lack of changes in mental attitudes;
- Poor economic performance;
- Afro-pessimism and incorrect ideological orientation and practices, falling prices of Africa's primary exports of commodities;
- Debt and debt servicing; and
- Lack of self-reliance and capacities to deal with issues in daily life.

Global Negotiations: Africa's Weaknesses

Africa's weaknesses include the following:

1) Very weak negotiating capacity in terms of human and material inadequacies;
2) Lack of competence—no special capacity to negotiate;
3) Lack of funding—resources are very expensive;
4) Lack of technological and technical skills;
5) Inadequate instruction—in most cases, no clear or dynamic/progressive instructions from capitals, tendency to repeat same stands for years, or to "drift along" with rest of Africa and Third World, G-77 nations;
6) Insufficient effectiveness, insufficient knowledge on issues due to a lack of specialization;
7) Lack of (enough) incentives and liberty to negotiate with authority and fullest support of headquarters/superiors—no attractive terms;
8) Insufficient patriotic nationalism due to poverty syndrome, ethnocentrism versus nationalism—some African elites live abroad for long periods of time to save to buy cars/houses and school their children; and
9) Misplaced or ill-advised priorities.

On Good Governance In Africa

In this context, "good governance" means the method of rule whereby rulers exercise authority and power to realize democratic principles of governance, which consist of the following constituent elements:

1) A clear dimension of democratic functions between the legislature or parliament, the executive government, and the judiciary (law and justice) branch in a system of checks and balances;

2) Involvement of the people (popular participation) in decision-making processes on issues affecting the people's daily lives, the hoi polloi, civil society, NGOs;

3) Accountability so those who rule must consider and fulfill the wishes of the people and report in a transparent way, especially on how funds are spent; thus, accountability, transparency, and consideration of popular wishes are essential to check on corrupt and ill-advised policies and ways of governing;

4) A parliament—a representative body to effectively monitor the executive body and formulate national policies via legislation based on peoples' wishes and aspirations—a system of checks and balances is essential;

5) An independent judicial system for fairness, justice, law, and order in society;

6) Democratization and decentralization of the executive branch of the government to counter the authoritarian legacies of colonization (i.e., divide and rule policies and practices as inherited and continued in Africa by rulers/leaders);

7) Berlin Conference of 1885 partitioning of Africa into geographical lines called borders which failed to conform to African realities of consolidated nationalism

8) Government of the Western style introduced in Africa which ignores African realities as the governance; Western style is highly personalized and ignores concepts of African socialism.

9) Tendency to resort to military rather than political and diplomatic responses to conflicts/problems in Africa. There is need to recognize a) the value of democracy; b) pursuit of legitimate interests; c) the value of dissent and political opposition that is non-violent.

10) Lack of respect (gross violations of) for: human rights; good governance; rule of law; democratization; transparency; accountability.

11) Stagnation and lack of requires reforms.

Governance in Africa: Further Requirements

Civil society involvement at national level must be strong to protect, fight for, and defend the public. The mass media should speak up in favor of popular participation in political, economic, social, and other processes. Democratic decentralization of government should be promoted to reduce the monopoly and centralization of power and decision-making in local governments. Decentralization should lead to empowerment of local authorities to interact directly with the masses.

Through all of this process is a need to educate and mobilize the masses—the population—to demand their rights and democratization for popular bottom-up governance implementation.

Conditions for the Success of Africa's Economic Power

Ending Afro-pessimism in Africa will not happen unless and until the African people themselves take actions to improve the performance of their economies. This is because the primary responsibility for the development of Africa lies with the African governments and institutions.

Economic power in Africa cannot and shall not succeed unless it is people-based: there must be a bottom-up approach whereby the African people are engaged and involved in all the stages of their development and are empowered to participate sufficiently and appropriately in the decision-making processes and procedures on issues affecting their daily lives.

Conditions for economic power in Africa thus include the following, among many others:

- Brain power development and sustenance through education and training for capacity-building and the development of skills;
- Improved education system, quality of education, and university education all working to raise the educational level and enable disciplined intellectual pursuits rather than having greedy leaders;
- National pride and discipline versus individualism and self-elevation of parochialism;
- Change of attitudes to industrious spirit of progress in society;
- No greed and no irresponsibility; sense of accountability, honesty, decency, and other human values;
- High standards of political leadership and statesmanship—accountability, competence, commitment, efficiency and sense of fairness in society and leadership; the need for understanding the country and not being parochial or tribalistic, and not having minimalistic postures and composure;
- Discipline and the promotion of Afro-progressive values such as African Socialism, Ubuntu, Harambeeism, and Ujamaa;
- Emulation of ASEAN: studying how the Asian countries of the Association of Southeast Asian Nations have progressed from their early stages of poverty to their current level of "Asian Tigers"; and
- Acceptance by Africans of their primary responsibilities. This Africans must do inter alia by working on ownership of Africa by Africa—doing their utmost to ensure that they make maximum contributions toward the development of Africa, end nepotism and corruption, and use Africa's human and natural resource bases for the common good of Africa.

Required Actions versus Constants and Challenges

Taking the above-mentioned measures into consideration, the following are further requirements which should be met inter alia in order to attain self-sufficiency and sustainable development in Africa:

- Resources;
- ODA—predictable, adequate, and assured, as stipulated in the decisions of the United Nations dating back to 1970, when the international community agreed to the call for Official Development Assistance from the richest countries of the North to the poor nations of the South;

- Resource mobilization both by the North and South countries and the international development community, including the UN system and the European Union;
- Accountability;
- Decency of government and government leadership;
- Efficiency/competence in African development;
- Governance and government;
- Opposition to protectionism; equity/justice;
- Opposition to conditionality in economic relations; and
- Opposition to corruption and reverse resource transfers; and
- Vox populi vox pacis et progressus in Africa: empower the people with clear rules to shape African leadership to "behave" and make government for, with, and by the people.

THE FUTURE OF AFRICAN INTERNATIONAL RELATIONS, FOREIGN POLICY, AND DIPLOMACY

The second transformation of African international relations was triggered by the end of the Cold War (1989–1990), which gave birth to Cold Peace and a new world order. This has prompted the following:

- Democratization of Africa and its foreign policies—multipartyism must be reintroduced and cemented wherever it does not exist;
- Further marginalization of Africa in absence of rivalry over mastery of Africa;
- Need for vigorous and aggressive defensive strategies by Africans—rising competition among world powers over Africa will require increased African unity and solidarity versus foreign powers; rising assertiveness of African regional, economic, cultural, political, and military powers;
- Opportunity for new generation of African leaders (e.g., Menes Zenawi [1955–] of Ethiopia, Aferwerki Eferwora [1946–] of Eritrea, Paul Kagame of Rwanda [1957–], and Benjamin Mkapa [1938–] former president of Tanzania) to shape and take charge of their own nations and international relations;
- End continued exploitation and interventions in Africa by UN and developed states/powers and financial institutions versus conditionality, protectionism, excessive dependency of African market and currency;
- End dependency syndrome via regional integration in Africa; and
- Create African regional mechanisms to advance and promote democratization, democracy, and regional security.

Future of African International Relations and Measures/Recommendations

Africa must look at ways and means of making African international relations, foreign policies, and diplomacy more effective and relevant to Africa's needs and defense of African national interests. For example, can the AU doctrine of inviolable borders (uti possidetis juris) be discussed for possible amendment? Can the AU discuss the question of enforcement of unity, peace, and security in Africa in accordance with the UN Charter's Chapter VII? Can a lasting solution be found to irredentism?

Africa must look at African international relations prior to colonization and explore ways of rehabilitating and adapting these methods. Stop isolation and marginalization of Africa and launch a vigorous campaign for discussion of Africa in academic and scientific visits, etc. Regularly explore millennium development challenges and issues facing Africa in international relations and prioritize new development paradigms on the basis of MDGs and building on NEPAD structure.

Additionally, Africa should concentrate on the following actions:

- Assure effective participation of Africa in the international development practicum and increase scope and magnitude of Africa-initiated, developed, owned, and run/managed initiatives like NEPAD;
- Address African paradoxes and determine how to implement measures to change them—especially Africa's paradoxes of economic retardation, marginalization, humiliation, isolation/acculturation—using an aggressive African information network run by committed Africans;
- Explore status of women and gender issues in Africa, and transform/empower women in politics, development, society, and the environment;
- Work toward sustainable development in Africa; and
- Address the question, "What would have happened to Africa if Africa had been allowed to develop without alien rule and influences?"

Other conditions for the success of African intra/extra relations should be met as follows:

- Adequate representation in the UN and other international organizations to hone competence and skills in representation;
- Reform of African diplomatic and foreign services, as well as foreign policy establishments;
- Elimination of the dependency syndrome;
- Change of attitudes in African's minds for a new approach to African issues and challenges; and
- Creation of a fund for Pax Africana to be mobilized and replenished only by Africans and their governments.

Furthermore, the following measures need to be taken:

- Create common education standards, use common language, experiment with different ways to achieve communication across Africa;

- Develop and use an aggressive information/advocacy system networking for Africa and run by Africans;
- Elect and install African leaders with the right psychology for African socioeconomic and political progress and environmental soundness and protection—disallow military civilian dictatorship;
- Devise ways of funding African solutions to African problems—Africanization of thinking in Africans to promote loyalty to African nations and continent, change in mental attitudes, reclamation and redemption of Africa's glorious civilizations in the new millennium;
- Use African foreign policies and diplomacy to promote, defend, protect, project, propagate, and defend not parochial sectional or ethnic preferences, but African national and continental interests;
- Create an African market and reliable external markets for Africa;
- Create an African currency to be pegged to major international currencies (e.g., the U.S. dollar, French franc, Euro), but allow for the existence of currencies in respective African nations;
- Refine African cultures, customs, and traditions to eradicate negative customs and practices and reclaim the glory of African civilizations;
- Create an African Esperanto in Africa, and enhance Esperanto vernacular in all schools in every African country to amalgamate these languages and major African languages like Swahili, Lingala, Hausa, Zulu, Shona, Matebele, Kikuyu, Luhya, Luo, and others;
- Devise ways of making African international relations more effective and relevant to Africa's needs and defense of African national interests;
- Provide real empowerment as a mechanism for peace and security in Africa;
- Eradicate gender inequality in Africa via constitutional transformation and empowerment of women in preventive diplomacy, development, democracy, and women's rights (as well as all human rights);
- Shape sustainable development in Africa to deal with Africa's crisis;
- Enhance Africa's presence in the international community;
- Try a "Marshall Plan" for Africa;
- Institute a mobile ambulance service in Africa for dealing with HIV/AIDS and other pandemics;
- Address Afro-pessimism crises systematically; and
- Perform a five-year experiment in which African leaders and people, after thorough assessment of top requirements for the continent's peace, stability, and development, pledge and raise funds for mobile hospitals, banks, African university with branches in various parts of Africa, etc., so Africans invest in Africa.

Specific measures on Africa and the global economy and globalization should include the following:

- Aim at removing the negative impacts of Africa's paradoxes;
- Address the challenges of SAPs;

- Ensure education, leadership efficiency, ownership of African development to solve African problems, etc.;
- Empower Africans to deal with disasters through preparedness, awareness, prevention, and disaster management;
- Enforce democratization the African way with African values of justice, socialism, consensus, Ubuntu, Harambee, etc. in human rights, empowerment of women/girls and other marginalized social strata, etc.;
- Find durable cures to causes of conflicts and their consequences;
- Encourace huge humanitarianism for all;
- Foster bottom-up development and empowerment of the people;
- Enact laws to liberate and attract foreign private capital into Africa;
- Encourage and develop business enterprises, tourism, etc. in Africa;
- Support debt cancellation for LDCs, HIPCs, LLDCs, SIDs, and other indebted developing countries;
- Hold special programs for development, protection, and stability of UN-based categories of nations (LDCs, DCs, HIPCs, SIDs, etc.);
- Involve Africa in implementation of obligations arising from international agreements on development, finance, capacity-building, education of women, etc.;
- Involve Africa more strongly in multilateral and global negations of the UN conference system and WTO, GATT/WTO Rounds, UN system conference negotiations on technology and science, sustainability science, environmental sustainability, business development and promotion, etc.;
- Work toward a cure, awareness, training, and education on pandemics;
- Industrialize Africa by privatizing industries, cutting corporate taxes, and Africanizing industries;
- Undertake economic reforms in Africa; support private sector development; create incentives for investment and popular enterprises on joint basis; remove restrictions to foreign investment;
- Expedite the process of economic democratization for Africa—increasingly engage Africa in global economic exchanges, and improve African legal regulatory environment necessary for domestic entrepreneurship and productivity;
- Invest heavily in education at all levels, research and development, capacity building, leadership skills, agriculture, ICTs, and Internet infrastructure;
- Empower poor people to be more productive;
- Attain universal access in Africa to basic services of health, education, water, sanitation; and
- Take measures to reduce the negative impacts of Africa's paradoxes.

AFRICA MUST OWN AFRICA

In order to move forward, Africa must own Africa. This can be brought about by challenging Africa's ways of living and doing things, having

Africa take primary responsibility for her development, building capacity via education and training—in other words, Africa needs to learn how to fish and replace ways of being fed with conditionalities. African values (e.g., village parenthood, African socialism, Ubuntu, pride, Negritude) should be used to reinforce and strengthen society. Development initiatives must be Africa-initiated, Africa-developed, Africa-run and Africa-managed.

For Africa to own Africa, Africa's civilizations should be reclaimed and adapted to modernity. Modern ways of living must be introduced. In addition, the following "new ways" must replace bad habits and remnants of colonization:

- Patriotism and loyalty to state/country versus ethnocentrism;
- Nationalism versus tribalism or regionalism; and
- Resource nationalism, investment in Africa, commerce, and rational use versus corruption.

From the foregoing it is evident that the future of African international relations, foreign policy, and diplomacy in the new millennium face grave challenges. Many conditions will have to be met before success can be derived in these disciplines for Africa in the future. At the moment, reasons for more dashed expectations are overwhelming, but we all have to wait and watch to see what will happen. This is going to be an important period to watch in African international relations.

Appendix

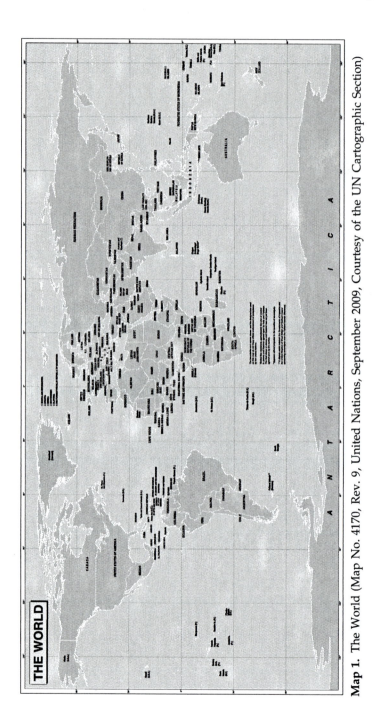

Map 1. The World (Map No. 4170, Rev. 9, United Nations, September 2009, Courtesy of the UN Cartographic Section)

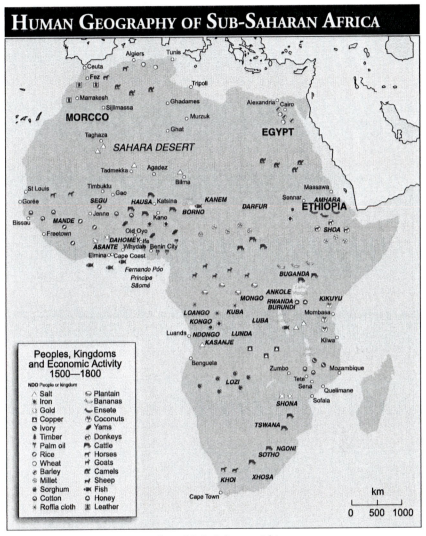

Map 2. The Human Geography of Sub-Saharan Africa

Map 3. Africa, 1914

Map 4. African Independence, 1910–1975

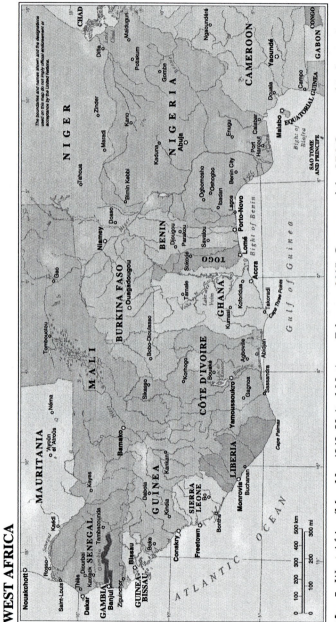

Map 5. West Africa (Map No. 4242, United Nations, February 2005, Courtesy of the UN Cartographic Section)

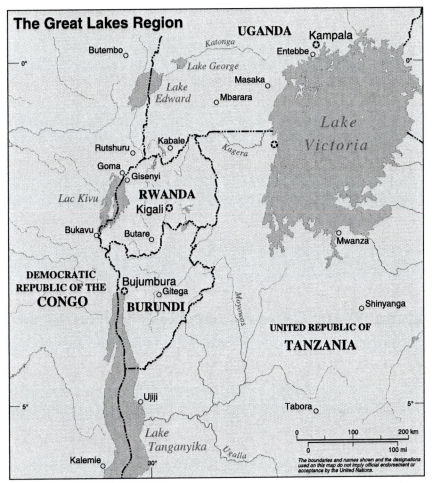

Map 6. The Great Lakes Region (Map No. 3921, Rev. 2, United Nations, January 2004, Courtesy of the UN Cartographic Section)

EAST AFRICA

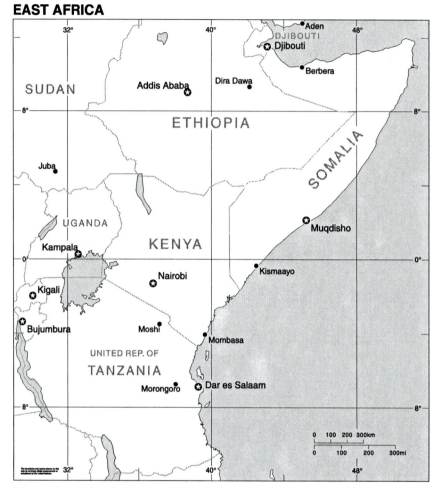

Map 7. East Africa (Map No. 3857, United Nations, November 1994, Courtesy of the UN Cartographic Section)

Map 8. Horn of Africa (Map No. 4188, Rev. 2, United Nations, May 2007, Courtesy of the UN Cartographic Section)

SOUTH EAST AFRICA DRAINAGE MAP

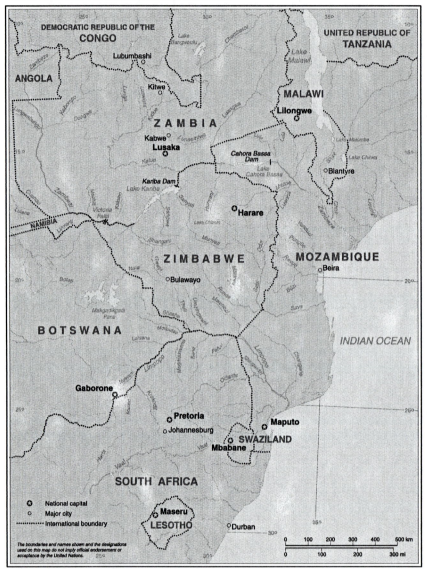

Map 9. Southeast Africa (Map No. 4070, Rev. 2, United Nations, January 2004, Courtesy of the UN Cartographic Section)

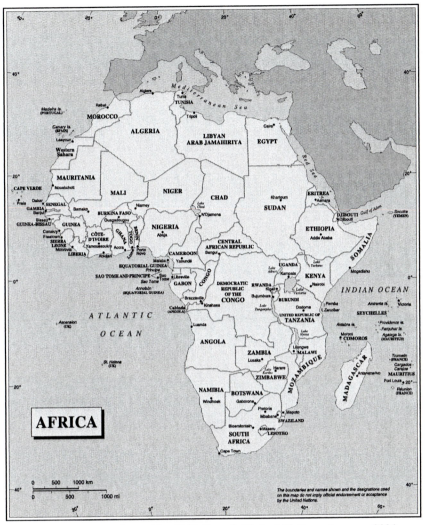

Map 10. Africa, 2004 (Map No. 4045, Rev. 4, United Nations, January 2004, Courtesy of the UN Cartographic Section)

Abbreviations

AAD	Cairo Agenda for African Development, 1994
AAF-SAPM	African Alternative Framework to Structural Adjustment for Socio-Economic Recovery and Transformation
ACP	African, Caribbean, and Pacific
ACP/EEC	African, Caribbean, and Pacific/European Economic Community
ACP/EU	African, Caribbean and Pacific/European Union
ACS	American Colonization Society
AEC	Africa Economic Community
AFP	African Foreign Policy
AGP	African Geopolitical Policy
AIDS	Acquired Immunodeficiency Syndrome
AIR	African International Relations
ANC	African National Congress
AOSIS	Alliance of Small Island States
APPER	Africa's Priority Programmes for Economic Recovery
APRM	African Peer Review Mechanism
ASALs	Arid and Semi-Arid Lands
ASEAN	Association of Southeast Asia Nations
AU	African Union
B.G.	Brazzaville Group
BWI	Bretton Woods Institutions
CAF	Central African Federation
CARICOM	Caribbean Community
CEMAC	Economic and Monetary Community of Central Africa
C.G.	Casablanca Group
CIDA	Canadian International Development Agency

COMESA	Common Market for Eastern and Southern Africa
CSOs	Civil Society Organizations
DAC	Development Assistance Committee of the Organization for Economic Cooperation and Development (OECD)
DANIDA	Danish Agency for International Development
DIEC	Development and International Economic Cooperation
DRC	Democratic Republic of the Congo
EAC	East African Community
EACU	East African Customs Union
ECA	Economic Commission for Africa (UN)
ECCAS	Economic Community of the Central African States
ECDC	Economic Cooperation among the Developing Countries
ECE	Economic Commission for Europe (UN)
ECLAC	Economic Commission for Latin America and the Caribbean (UN)
ECOSOC	Economic and Social Council (UN)
ECOWAS	Economic Community of the West African States
ECSWA	Economic and Social Commission for West Asia (UN)
EEC	European Economic Community
ESCAP	Economic and Social Commission for Asia and the Pacific (UN)
EU	European Union
FAO	Food and Agriculture Organization
FDI	Foreign Direct Investment
FINNIDA	Finnish International Development Agency
FNLA	Front for the National Liberation of Angola
FRELIMO	Front for the Liberation of Mozambique
FS	Foreign Service
G-2	refers to the United States and China
G-7	Meetings of finance ministers and governors of the Central Banks of seven countries of the North: Canada, France, Germany, Italy, Japan, United Kingdom, and United States
G-20	A forum of the economic powers of the world from the North and the South. Comprises the European Union and 19 countries: Australia, Canada, France, Germany, Japan, Russia, Turkey, Italy, United Kingdom, United States, Argentina, Brazil, China, India, Indonesia, Mexico, Saudi Arabia, South Korea, and South Africa, and EU represented by Presidents of EU Council and EU Central Bank.
G-27	The "cabinet" of the Group of 77
G-77	The "Group of 77"; the group of all the developing countries working as a political bloc at the UN
GA	General Assembly (UN)
GATT	General Agreement on Tariffs and Trade
GBP	Geosphere-Biosphere Programme
GCA	Global Coalition for Africa
GDP	Gross Domestic Product

GE	Global Economy
GNI	Gross National Index
GNP	Gross National Product
GPBs	Global Public Bads
GPGs	Global Public Goods
GT	Global Trade
HDP	International Human Dimensions Programme on Global Environmental Change
HIPC	Highly Indebted Poor Countries
HIV	Human Immunodeficiency Virus/Acquired Immunodeficiency Syndrome
IAEA	International Atomic Energy Agency
IBRD	International Bank for Reconstruction and Development
ICAO	International Civil Aviation Organization
ICJ	International Court of Justice
ICSID	International Centre for Settlement of International Disputes
ICSU	International Council for Science
ICTs	Information and Communication Technologies
IDA	International Development Association
IDNDR	International Decade for Natural Disaster Reduction
IDOs	International Development Organizations
IDS	International Development Strategy (UN)
IFAD	International Fund for Agricultural Development
IFC	International Finance Corporation
IGAD	Intergovernmental Authority on Development
IGADD	Intergovernmental Authority on Drought and Development
IGO	Intergovernmental Organization
ILO	International Labour Organization
IMF	International Monetary Fund
IMO	International Maritime Organization
IMO	International Migration Organization
IPCC	Intergovernmental Panel on Climate Change
IR	International Relations
ISDR	International Strategy for Disaster Reduction
ITU	International Telecommunications Union (UN)
JICA	Japan International Cooperation Agency
KADU	Kenya African Democratic Union
KANU	Kenya African National Union
LDCs	Least Developed Countries
LLDCs	Land-locked Developing Countries
MAP	Millennium African Programme
MDGs	Millennium development goals (UN)
MG	Monrovia Group
MIGA	Multilateral Investment Guarantee Agency
MNTCs	Multinational Corporations
MOU	Memorandum of Understanding
MSA	Most Seriously Affected State

MTN	Multinational Trade Negotiations
MTNs	Multinationals
NAI	New African Initiative
NAM	Non-Aligned Movement
NATO	North Atlantic Treaty Organization
NGO	Non-Governmental Organization
NGO	New Girl Order in Africa
NEPAD	New Partnership for African Development
NIEO	New International Economic Order (UN)
NORAD	Norwegian Agency for Development
NPA	Nairobi Plan of Action on New and Renewable Sources of Energy (UN), 1981
NRSE	New and Renewable Sources of Energy
NTB	Nuclear Test Ban
OAU	Organization of African Unity, 1963
ODA	Official Development Assistance (UN), 1970
OECD	Organisation for Economic Cooperation and Development
OPEC	Organization of Petroleum Exporting Countries
PAC	Pan-African Congress (South Africa)
PRSPs	Poverty Reduction Strategy Papers (IMF)
PTA	Preferential Trade Area of Eastern and Southern Africa
RENAMO	National Resistance Movement of Mozambique
SADC	Southern African Development Community
SADR	Sahrawi Arab Democratic Republic
SAPs	Structural Adjustment Programmes
SC	Security Council (UN)
SG	Secretary-General (UN)
SIDA	Swedish International Development Agency
SIDS	Small Island Developing States
SSA	Sub-Saharan Africa
TB	Tuberculosis
TCDC	Technical Cooperation among Developing Countries
TICAD	Tokyo International Conference on African Development
TNCs	Transnational Corporations
UAM	Africa and Malagasy Union
UEMOA	West Africa Economic and Monetary Union
UMA	Union of Maghreb Arabs, North Africa (Union du Maghreb [Maghrib] Africaine); Union of Madagascar (Malagasy) and Africa
UN	United Nations
UNA	United Nations Association
UN-NADAF	United Nations New Agenda for the Development of Africa in the 1990s
UN-PAAERD	United Nations Programme of Action for Africa's Economic Recovery and Development
UN-SIA	United Nations Special Initiative on Africa

UNCED	United Nations Conference on the Environment and Development
UNCTAD	United Nations Conference on Trade and Development
UNDD	United Nations Development Decade
UNDP	United Nations Development Programme
UNDS	United Nations Development Strategies
UNEP	United Nations Environment Programme
UNESCO	United Nations Educational, Scientific and Cultural Organization
UNFPA	United Nations Fund for Population Activities
UNGA	United Nations General Assembly
UN-HABITAT	United Nations Human Settlements Programme
UNICEF	United Nations Children's Fund
UNIDO	United Nations Industrialization Development Organization
UNITA	National Union for the Total Independence of Angola
UNO	United Nations Organization
UNSG	United Nations Secretary-General
UN System	United Nations System
UPU	Universal Postal Union
USAID	United States Agency for International Development
USSR	Union of Soviet Socialist Republics
WEOG	Western European and Others Group
WFC	World Food Council (UN)
WFP	World Food Programme (UN)
WHO	World Health Organization
WIPO	World Intellectual Property Organization
WMO	World Meteorological Organization
WRCP	World Climate Research Programme
WS	World Summit (UN Jubilee, 1995)
WSB	World Summit on Women (Beijing, 1995)
WSSD	World Summit on Social Development (Copenhagen, March 1995)
WSSD	World Summit on Sustainable Development (Johannesburg, 2002)
WT	World Trade
WTO	World Trade Organization, World Tourism Organization

Index

About the Author

DANIEL DON NANJIRA has been teaching as a professor since 2005. He has taught in New York at Hunter College; at Columbia University's School of Public and International Affairs (SIPA), and at Manhattanville College, and Iona College. He teaches African and comparative studies, including African Internatinal Relations, Foreign Policy and Diplomacy; African Development and Security, alias Africa and the International Development Practicum; Swahili Language and Culture; Development and International Economic Cooperation; and Africa in World Politics, as well as International Business in Africa, and Public International Organization and Administration of the UN system. His research interests include the roles of African Women Leaders from Antiquity to the 21st Century; New and Renewable Sources of Energy (NRSE); Disasters, Climate Change and African Development; and the Challenge of Ownership of Africa by Africa.

From 1970 to 2004, he was a career diplomat in the Kenya Foregn Service and within the UN system. Between 1987 and 1992, he served as Ambassador of Kenya to Italy, Greece and Poland, with residence in Rome, and as Kenya's Permanent Representative to UN system Agencies based in Rome (FAO, IFAD, WFP and WFC). He was also responsible for Kenya's relations with Turkey, Cyprus and Malta. From 1992 to 1995, he was Kenya's Ambassador/Permanent Representative to UN sytem Organizations based in Geneva, and in Switzerland, as well as to the International Atomic Energy Agency (IAEA) and the UN Industrialization Organization (UNIDO) based in Vienna, Austria, with residence in Geneva. Between 1995 and 2004, he served at director level as Special Advisor to the WHO Director-General on Policies for Africa (1995–97) based in Geneva, and as Representative at UN Headquarters of WHO and WMO (1997–1998). From 1998–2004, he served as WMO Representative to the UN and Other UN system Organizations in North America, with residence in New York.